The IDG Books *Creating Cool*™ Series Advantage

We at IDG Books Worldwide created *Creating Cool Interactive Web Sites* to meet your growing need for quick access to the most complete and accurate computer information available. Our books work the way you do: They focus on accomplishing specific tasks — not learning random functions. Our books are not long-winded manuals or dry reference tomes. In each book, expert authors tell you exactly what you can do and how to do it. Easy to follow, step-by-step instructions; comprehensive coverage; and convenient access in language and design — it's all here.

The authors of IDG books are uniquely qualified to give you expert advice as well as to provide insightful tips and techniques not found anywhere else. Our authors maintain close contact with end users through feedback from articles, training sessions, e-mail exchanges, user group participation, and consulting work. Because our authors know the realities of daily computer use and are directly linked to the reader, our books have a strategic advantage.

Our authors have the experience to approach a topic in the most efficient manner, and we know that you, the reader, will benefit from a "one-on-one" relationship with the author. Our research shows that readers make computer book purchases because they want expert advice. Because readers want to benefit from the author's experience, the author's voice is always present in an IDG book.

In addition, the author is free to include or recommend useful software in an IDG book. The software that accompanies each book is not intended to be casual filler but is linked to the content, theme, or procedures of the book. We know that you will benefit from the included software.

You will find what you need in this book whether you read it from cover to cover, section by section, or simply one topic at a time. As a computer user, you want a comprehensive resource. We at IDG Books Worldwide are proud to deliver that resource with *Creating Cool Interactive Web Sites.*

Brenda McLaughlin
Senior Vice President and Group Publisher

Internet: YouTellUs@idgbooks.com

CREATING COOL™ INTERACTIVE WEB SITES

Paul M. Summitt
Mary J. Summitt

CREATING COOL™ INTERACTIVE WEB SITES

Paul M. Summitt
Mary J. Summitt

IDG Books Worldwide, Inc.
An International Data Group Company

Foster City, CA ♦ Chicago, IL ♦ Indianapolis, IN ♦ Braintree, MA ♦ Southlake, TX

Creating Cool™ Interactive Web Sites

Published by
IDG Books Worldwide, Inc.
An International Data Group Company
919 E. Hillsdale Blvd.
Suite 400
Foster City, CA 94404

Library of Congress Catalog Card No.: 96-76245

ISBN: 1-56884-842-0

Printed in the United States of America

10 9 8 7 6 5 4 3 2 1

1A/SU/QV/ZW/IN

Distributed in the United States by IDG Books Worldwide, Inc.

Distributed by Macmillan Canada for Canada; by Computer and Technical Books for the Caribbean Basin; by Contemporanea de Ediciones for Venezuela; by Distribuidora Cuspide for Argentina; by CITEC for Brazil; by Ediciones ZETA S.C.R. Ltda. for Peru; by Editorial Limusa SA for Mexico; by Transworld Publishers Limited in the United Kingdom and Europe; by Al-Maiman Publishers & Distributors for Saudi Arabia; by Simron Pty. Ltd. for South Africa; by IDG Communications (HK) Ltd. for Hong Kong; by Toppan Company Ltd. for Japan; by Addison Wesley Publishing Company for Korea; by Longman Singapore Publishers Ltd. for Singapore, Malaysia, Thailand, and Indonesia; by Unalis Corporation for Taiwan; by WS Computer Publishing Company, Inc. for the Philippines; by WoodsLane Pty. Ltd. for Australia; by WoodsLane Enterprises Ltd. for New Zealand.

For general information on IDG Books Worldwide's books in the U.S., please call our Consumer Customer Service department at 800-762-2974. For reseller information, including discounts and premium sales, please call our Reseller Customer Service department at 800-434-3422.

For information on where to purchase IDG Books Worldwide's books outside the U.S., contact IDG Books Worldwide at 415-655-3021 or fax 415-655-3295.

For information on translations, contact Marc Jeffrey Mikulich, Director, Foreign & Subsidiary Rights, at IDG Books Worldwide, 415-655-3018 or fax 415-655-3295.

For sales inquiries and special prices for bulk quantities, write to the address above or call IDG Books Worldwide at 415-655-3200.

For information on using IDG Books Worldwide's books in the classroom, or ordering examination copies, contact the Education Office at 800-434-2086 or fax 817-251-8174.

For authorization to photocopy items for corporate, personal, or educational use, please contact Copyright Clearance Center, 222 Rosewood Drive, Danvers, MA 01923, or fax 508-750-4470.

About the Authors

Paul M. Summitt taught broadcasting at the college and university level for ten years. He has worked with TV and film since 1970 and with computers since 1972. Paul enjoys researching his family genealogy, watching movies, and discussing quantum realities.

Mary J. Summitt is the owner of a research and publishing company. She enjoys reading, researching various topics, watching movies, and discussing quantum realities.

Mary and Paul are both interested in cyberspace and virtual reality. They hope to one day buy a sailboat and sail off to their own quantum reality.

Welcome to the world of IDG Books Worldwide.

IDG Books Worldwide, Inc., is a subsidiary of International Data Group, the world's largest publisher of computer-related information and the leading global provider of information services on information technology. IDG was founded more than 25 years ago and now employs more than 7,700 people worldwide. IDG publishes more than 250 computer publications in 67 countries (see listing below). More than 70 million people read one or more IDG publications each month.

Launched in 1990, IDG Books Worldwide is today the #1 publisher of best-selling computer books in the United States. We are proud to have received 8 awards from the Computer Press Association in recognition of editorial excellence and three from Computer Currents' First Annual Readers' Choice Awards, and our best-selling *...For Dummies®* series has more than 19 million copies in print with translations in 28 languages. IDG Books Worldwide, through a joint venture with IDG's Hi-Tech Beijing, became the first U.S. publisher to publish a computer book in the People's Republic of China. In record time, IDG Books Worldwide has become the first choice for millions of readers around the world who want to learn how to better manage their businesses.

Our mission is simple: Every one of our books is designed to bring extra value and skill-building instructions to the reader. Our books are written by experts who understand and care about our readers. The knowledge base of our editorial staff comes from years of experience in publishing, education, and journalism — experience which we use to produce books for the '90s. In short, we care about books, so we attract the best people. We devote special attention to details such as audience, interior design, use of icons, and illustrations. And because we use an efficient process of authoring, editing, and desktop publishing our books electronically, we can spend more time ensuring superior content and spend less time on the technicalities of making books.

You can count on our commitment to deliver high-quality books at competitive prices on topics you want to read about. At IDG Books Worldwide, we continue in the IDG tradition of delivering quality for more than 25 years. You'll find no better book on a subject than one from IDG Books Worldwide.

John Kilcullen
President and CEO
IDG Books Worldwide, Inc.

IDG Books Worldwide, Inc., is a subsidiary of International Data Group, the world's largest publisher of computer-related information and the leading global provider of information services on information technology. International Data Group publishes over 250 computer publications in 67 countries. Seventy million people read one or more International Data Group publications each month. International Data Group's publications include: **ARGENTINA:** Computerworld Argentina, GamePro, Infoworld, PC World Argentina; **AUSTRALIA:** Australian Macworld, Client/Server Journal, Computer Living, Computerworld, Digital News, Network World, PC World, Publishing Essentials, Reseller; **AUSTRIA:** Computerwelt, PC TEST; **BELARUS:** PC World Belarus; **BELGIUM:** Data News; **BRAZIL:** Annuário de Informática, Computerworld Brazil, Connections, Super Game Power, Macworld, PC World Brazil, Publish Brazil, SUPERGAME; **BULGARIA:** Computerworld Bulgaria, Networkworld/Bulgaria, PC & MacWorld Bulgaria; **CANADA:** CIO Canada, ComputerWorld Canada, InfoCanada, Network World Canada, Reseller World; **CHILE:** Computerworld Chile, GamePro, PC World Chile; **COLUMBIA:** Computerworld Colombia, GamePro, PC World Colombia; **COSTA RICA:** PC World Costa Rica/Nicaragua; **THE CZECH AND SLOVAK REPUBLICS:** Computerworld Czechoslovakia, Elektronika Czechoslovakia, PC World Czechoslovakia; **DENMARK:** Communications World, Computerworld Danmark, Macworld Danmark, PC World Danmark, PC World Danmark Supplements, TECH World; **DOMINICAN REPUBLIC:** PC World Republica Dominicana; **ECUADOR:** PC World Ecuador, GamePro; **EGYPT:** Computerworld Middle East, PC World Middle East; **EL SALVADOR:** PC World Centro America; **FINLAND:** MikroPC, Tietoverkko, Tietoviikko; **FRANCE:** Distributique, Golden, Info PC, Le Guide du Monde Informatique, Le Monde Informatique, Reseaux & Telecoms; **GERMANY:** Computer Business, Computerwoche, Computerwoche Extra, Computerwoche Focus, Electronic Entertainment, GamePro, I/M Information Management, Macwelt, PC Welt; **GREECE:** GamePro, Macworld & Publish; **GUATEMALA:** PC World Centro America; **HONDURAS:** PC World Centro America; **HONG KONG:** Computerworld Hong Kong, PCWorld Hong Kong, Publish in Asia; **HUNGARY:** ABCD CD-ROM, Computerworld Szamitastechnika, PC & Mac World Hungary, PC-X Magazine; **INDIA:** Computerworld India, PC World India, Publish in Asia; **INDONESIA:** InfoKomputer PC World, Komputek Computerworld, Publish in Asia; **IRELAND:** ComputerScope, PC Live!; **ISRAEL:** PC World 32 BIT, People & Computers; **ITALY:** Computerworld Italia, Computerworld Italia Special Editions, Lotus Italia, Macworld Italia, Networking Italia, PC Shopping, PC World Italia, PC World/Walt Disney; **JAPAN:** Macworld Japan, Nikkei Personal Computing, SunWorld Japan, Windows World Japan; **KENYA:** East African Computer News; **KOREA:** Hi-Tech Information/Computerworld, Macworld Korea, PC World Korea; **MACEDONIA:** PC World Macedonia; **MALAYSIA:** Computerworld Malaysia, PC World Malaysia, Publish in Asia; **MEXICO:** Computerworld Mexico, GamePro, Macworld, PC World Mexico; **MYANMAR:** PC World Myanmar; **NETHERLANDS:** Computable, Computer! Totaal, LAN Magazine, Macworld, Net Magazine; **NEW ZEALAND:** Computer Buyer, Computerworld New Zealand, MTB, Network World, PC World New Zealand; **NICARAGUA:** PC World Costa Rica/Nicaragua; **NIGERIA:** PC World Africa; **NORWAY:** Computerworld Norge, Computerworld Privat, CW Rapport Klient/Tjener, CW Rapport Nettverk & Telecom, CW Rapport Offentlig Sektor, IDG's KURSGUIDE, Macworld Norge, Multimedia World, PC World Ekspress, PC World Nettverk, PC World Norge, PC World's Produktguide, Windows Spesial; **PAKISTAN:** Computerworld Pakistan, PC World Pakistan; **PANAMA:** GamePro, PC World Panama; **PARAGUAY:** PC World Paraguay; **P. R. OF CHINA:** China Computerworld, China Infoworld, Computer & Communication, Electronic Product World, Electronics Today, Game Camp, PC World China, Popular Computer Week, Software World, Telecom Product World; **PERU:** Computerworld Peru, GamePro, PC World Profesional Peru, PC World Peru; **POLAND:** Computerworld Poland, Computerworld Special Report, Macworld, Networld, PC World Komputer; **PHILIPPINES:** Computerworld Philippines, PC Digest, Publish in Asia; **PORTUGAL:** Cerebro/PC World, Correio Informático/Computerworld, Mac•In/PC•In Portugal; **PUERTO RICO:** PC World Puerto Rico; **ROMANIA:** Computerworld Romania, PC World Romania, Telecom Romania; **RUSSIA:** Computerworld Rossiya, Network World Russia, PC World Russia; **SINGAPORE:** Computerworld Singapore, PC World Singapore, Publish in Asia; **SLOVENIA:** MONITOR; **SOUTH AFRICA:** Computing S.A., Network World S.A., Software World; **SPAIN:** Computerworld España, COMUNICACIONES WORLD, Dealer World, Macworld España, PC World España; **SWEDEN:** CAP&Design, Computer Sweden, Corporate Computing, MacWorld, Maxi Data, MikroDatorn, Nätverk & Kommunikation, PC/Aktiv, PC World, Windows World; **SWITZERLAND:** Computerworld Schweiz, Macworld Schweiz, PCtip; **TAIWAN:** Computerworld Taiwan, Macworld Taiwan, PC World Taiwan, Publish Taiwan, Windows World; **THAILAND:** Thai Computerworld, Publish in Asia; **TURKEY:** Computerworld Monitör, MACWORLD Turkiye, PC WORLD Turkiye; **UKRAINE:** Computerworld Kiev, Computers & Software Magazine, PC World Ukraine; **UNITED KINGDOM:** Acorn User, Amiga Action, Amiga Computing, Amiga, Appletalk, CD Powerplay, CD-ROM Now, Computing, Connexion, GamePro, Lotus Magazine, Macaction, Macworld, Open Computing, Parents and Computers, PC Home, PC Works, The WEB; **UNITED STATES:** Cable in the Classroom, CD Review, CIO Magazine, Computerworld, Computerworld Client/Server Journal, Digital Video Magazine, DOS World, Electronic, InfoWorld, I-Way, Macworld, Maximize, MULTIMEDIA WORLD, Network World, PC World, PUBLISH, SWATPro Magazine, Video Event, WebMaster; **URUGUAY:** PC World Uruguay; **VENEZUELA:** Computerworld Venezuela, GamePro, PC World Venezuela; and **VIETNAM:** PC World Vietnam 10/17/95a

Dedication

To our children and grandchildren. May you never close your eyes to the wonders of exploring the unknown.

Credits

Senior Vice President & Group Publisher
Brenda McLaughlin

Acquisitions Manager
Gregory S. Croy

Acquisitions Editor
Ellen L. Camm

Software Acquisitions Editor
Tracy Lehman Cramer

Marketing Manager
Melisa M. Duffy

Managing Editor
Andy Cummings

Administrative Assistant
Laura J. Moss

Editorial Assistant
Timothy J. Borek

Production Director
Beth Jenkins

Production Assistant
Jacalyn L. Pennywell

Supervisor of Project Coordination
Cindy L. Phipps

Supervisor of Page Layout
Kathie S. Schnorr

Supervisor of Graphics and Design
Shelley Lea

Reprint Coordination
Tony Augsburger
Theresa Sánchez-Baker
Todd Klemme

Blueline Coordinator
Patricia R. Reynolds

Project Editor
Pat Seiler

Development Editor
Susan Pines

Technical Reviewer
David Elderbrock

Associate Project Coordinator
Debbie Sharpe

Graphics Coordination
Gina Scott
Angela F. Hunckler
Brent Savage

Media/Archive Coordination
Leslie Popplewell
Melissa Stauffer
Jason Marcuson

Production Page Layout
Brett Black
Drew R. Moore
E. Shawn Aylsworth
J. Tyler Connor
Maridee V. Ennis
Mark Owens
M. Anne Sipahimalani
Michael Sullivan

Proofreaders
Michael Hall
Christine Meloy Beck
Nancy Price
Dwight Ramsey
Carl Saff
Robert Springer
Karen York

Indexer
Steve Rath

Book Design
Theresa Sánchez-Baker

Acknowledgments

This is our second book with IDG, and the people are still fantastic. Special thanks again to **Ellen Camm** for continuing to believe in us, to **Sue Pines** for her continuous support, to **Tracy Cramer** for her invaluable assistance with the CD-ROM, to **David Elderbrock** for his efforts on the technical edit, and, of course, to **Pat Seiler** for her, as always, skillful and insightful editing. Thanks also to IDG Books staffers **Laura Moss** and **Debbie Sharpe**. To the others at IDG Books, from the lady's voice on the answering machine to **Patrick J. McGovern**, thank you for all of your efforts.

A special thanks to **Victor Hirst** of Pittsburg Online who provided access for VREvolution's Web site, to the people at EarthLink for access and service, and to all of the service providers, such as America Online, CompuServe, NETCOM, and PSI. We appreciate the efforts of companies such as Borland, Caligari, Catalyst, Chaco, Dart, Distinct, Frontier, IDS, InterVista, Microsoft, Netscape, Portable Graphics, Q&D Software, Quarterdeck, RealAudio, Softquad, Sun, Symantec, Virtus, and WebMaster, who kept us supplied with information and, when possible, products that made our site and this book possible.

A very special thanks to **Mark Owen** and the staff at WebMaster for their efforts on the CGI applications.

To our friends on CyberForum, again, thanks for listening.

To our brothers **Randy** and **Bruce**, keep hacking. That's where the true beauty and the joy in computers lie.

To **Catherine**, how's it feel to be retired?

John Gwinner, "you are, and always will be, [our] friend."

(The publisher would like to give special thanks to ***Patrick J. McGovern****, without whom this book would not have been possible.)*

Contents
at a
Glance

Table
of
Contents

xix

Introduction

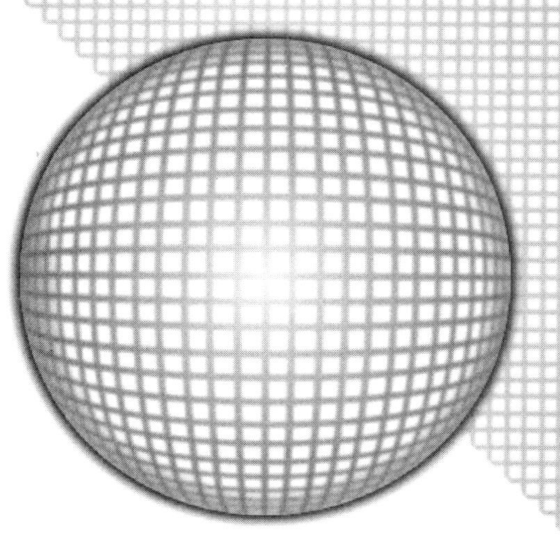

Probably the most explosive growth on the Internet today lies in the development of the World Wide Web. The interest of millions of people has been sparked by the possibilities of the Web. William Gibson's vision of the matrix in *Neuromancer, Burning Chrome, Count Zero,* and *Mona Lisa Overdrive* and Neil Stephenson's vision of the metaverse in *SnowCrash* seem to be coming into the realm of the possible as companies and individuals begin to homestead their own parcels of cyberspace.

You're thinking about homesteading cyberspace or you wouldn't be thumbing through the pages of this book. Unfortunately, few road maps are available to guide you and other potential settlers through this wilderness of the virtual. Yes, you can gather dozens of books and magazine articles that may lead you down part of the trail, but nowhere does a map exist leading to your individual vision of a personal virtual El Dorado.

This book is just such a guide. It provides you with the information and tools necessary to begin homesteading cyberspace for a reasonable cost in time and money. Each chapter is a listing of the choices available and the options that we chose in setting up our first Web site. Each chapter concludes with a look at our decisions about the software and hardware that we chose.

As more and more people take up virtual residence in cyberspace, this book will help you become a neighbor in the virtual community. The next few pages show you what to expect.

Who This Book Is For

If you are somewhat familiar with the Web and want to create and establish your own Web site, then this book is for you. You don't have to know programming (although it does help) in order to operate a Web server. If you already know how to program using Visual Basic 4.0, then you're one step ahead (source code for Visual C/C++ 4.0 users is available on the *Creating Cool Interactive Web Sites CD-ROM*).

In this book, we show beginners through intermediate users of Windows 3.1, Windows NT, and Windows 95 what the least expensive and least time-consuming methods are of operating a Web site. Even expert users can find some tips on how to improve their Web sites.

What This Book Is About

Creating Cool Interactive Web Sites is intended to be the North Star for today's Leif Erikssons and Amerigo Vespuccis of cyberspace as they set sail into the virtual seas of the unknown. Are you one of those explorers? Are you a person of vision?

We think so, or you wouldn't have this book in your hands right now. You are one of the explorers and settlers of the cyberfrontier. The path is before you. You and a few others, among all the masses, have the determination to help create the many new worlds that are coming in the future. You have made a decision to be part of these brave new worlds.

That decision behind you, you are about to be faced with many other choices and options. To help you with this task, we've included sections discussing our experiences in setting up VREvolution's Web site. VREvolution is our company, which is dedicated to educating and informing people about the possibilities and uses of virtual reality. You'll find our experiences under the VREvolution Site Diary icon.

We need to define something right away. In this book, when we speak of a Web *site,* we are discussing much more than just the HTML pages. A cool interactive Web site includes many pages that use HTML, Java, VRML, CGI, and other applications. It also may include server software. If you have a Web page somewhere, you have a Web site. Therefore, this book has to look briefly at a lot of things.

We also need to consider the question of interactivity. Just what does it mean to have an interactive Web site? In this book we show you a wide range of elements that you can add to your Web site to make it more interactive. These elements range from adding forms to your pages, to creating animations, to exploring VRML worlds. Your site will display movement and seem to respond to your visitors as you add some of these interactive elements.

Part I of this book begins by presenting you with an explanation of what choices and options you have for the set up of your Web site.

Part I: Choices and Decisions

Although you have made the decision to establish a Web site, many decisions still face you. A cool interactive Web site costs both money and time. It is best if you're aware of just how much it may cost of both before you begin to homestead cyberspace.

Chapter 1: Deciding to Homestead

This chapter introduces you to the various possibilities and uses of a Web site. You visit and explore several different types of Web sites, and Webmasters from some of these sites comment on why they decided to create their sites.

The first matter you face concerns the decision to create a full-time Web site. You look at the pros and cons in terms of the time and money involved.

This chapter concludes, as will all the rest, with an excerpt from the VREvolution Site Diary.

Chapter 2: Go It Alone or Join a Colony

The next decision you face centers on whether to set up your own Web server or to lease space on an existing Web server. You examine each of these alternatives and weigh the advantages and disadvantages of each option in terms of time and money.

The section of the chapter that deals with setting up your own Web server examines such issues as choosing a service provider, determining your leased line speed, choosing your server hardware, and choosing your server software.

Chapter 3: Building Your Virtual Home in the Wilderness of Cyberspace

If you've decided to lease space on an existing server, you can skip to Part III of this book. Otherwise, we assume that you've decided to set up your own server or you haven't made up your mind yet. In that case, you should go ahead and read the rest of Part I and Part II.

Chapter 3 deals with choosing the platform on which your Web site will operate. Choosing the hardware and software for your Web site is a very important decision. We look at three basic alternatives for your server platform: Windows 3.1, Windows 95, and Windows NT. This chapter is divided into five sections dealing with the hardware and software costs involved with selecting any one of these options. Time factors are also considered. Software, some of which is included on the CD-ROM, is discussed for each platform.

Part II: Protecting Your Virtual Home in Cyberspace

Although both fun and exciting, operating your own Web server demands time and resources that you must be aware of. This portion of the book discusses some of those issues and provides guidance in avoiding some of the obstacles and pitfalls that await the unprepared.

Chapter 4: Virtual Bandits on the Frontier

Chapter 4 deals with a potential danger of the cyberspace frontier: People who want to enter your server to disrupt and pillage your cyberhome. Security for your Web site is discussed in general terms.

Chapter 5: Managing Your Real and Virtual Resources

Setting up the server requires planning the server's physical network parameters, designing the server's directory structure, using and configuring the server-generated directory indexes, configuring the MIME types necessary for launching viewers, and implementing password security and access control for the server. Each server configuration command is explained, and the plain text configuration files are discussed in a step-by-step manner.

Part III: Furnishing Your Virtual Home in Cyberspace

You can spruce up your cyberhome with many furnishings — HTML, VRML, Java, and audio and video clips, just to name a few. The chapters in this part discuss how you can use these tools to make your cyberhome more enjoyable for yourself and your visitors.

Chapter 6: HTML

The heart of every Web page is the Hypertext Markup Language that makes it all possible. This chapter covers the basics of HTML and tells you how to create the documents that explain to cybertravelers what your Web site is all about.

Applications and utilities on the CD-ROM that enable you to create and edit HTML documents are examined and discussed. Sample HTML documents are created to demonstrate a variety of the possibilities that HTML offers.

Chapter 7: VRML

One of the most exciting new technologies available on the Web is VRML (Virtual Reality Modeling Language). This chapter provides examples of using VRML on your Web site.

VRML viewers are discussed and examined in terms of what potential visitors may have available to use. World creators offer recommendations about how to best use VRML to communicate with your visitors.

Applications and utilities on the CD-ROM that enable you to create VRML files for your page are examined and discussed; example worlds are constructed and explained.

Chapter 8: Java

Using Java can transform your static Web pages into living and interactive applications. Chapter 8 provides examples of how you can use Java to create these exciting Web applications. Java creators provide insights into using Java to your advantage, and using Java to develop more intricate and complicated applications and applets for your Web site is also discussed.

Chapter 9: Audio and Video Clips

HTML enables you to include audio and video segments in your Web pages. This chapter discusses how to best make these files available.

Part IV: Managing Your Corner of Cyberspace

Each Web site has a purpose, even if that purpose is just to show off your résumé. Part IV discusses several methods for managing your site so that you can achieve the purpose for which you created it.

Chapter 10: The Common Gateway Interface (CGI)

The Common Gateway Interface (CGI) is the heart of providing interactive capabilities for your Web site. You can use QuickBasic, Visual Basic, and Visual C/C++ to write CGI scripts.

We show you how to use Visual Basic 4.0 to write CGI scripts. The example script files are on the *Creating Cool Interactive Web Sites CD-ROM.*

Chapter 11: Databases, Search Engines, E-Mail, and Image Maps

Chapter 11 covers the creation and use of image maps on your Web site. You also look at the use of search engines and databases with your Web site. Finally, you look into how to use e-mail to create two-way communication and interaction on your Web site. Examples are examined and discussed.

Chapter 12: Web Site Usage Statistics

Creating and using applications that provide information about visitors to your Web site can make maintaining your site more manageable. This chapter discusses and explores some of these applications.

Chapter 13: Promoting and Advertising Your Web Site

Chapter 13 deals with getting the word out about your Web site. Reasons for not advertising your site are also discussed. Examples of these advertisements are examined and discussed.

Depending on which service provider, server hardware, and server software you choose, the costs of creating a cool Web site can be high. You may be able to recoup some, if not all, of these expenses from the operation of your site. This chapter covers some possibilities that exist for making money on the Web.

Part V: Appendix: The Accompanying CD-ROM

The appendix includes installation instructions for the software provided on the CD-ROM.

Icons Used in This Book

Icons are pictures that are designed to draw your attention to specific kinds of information. Here's what the icons used in this book mean:

Make sure that you pay attention to this icon. Failure to do so can lead to considerable costs in time and money.

You'll see this icon any time we discuss the software that's provided on the *Creating Cool Interactive Web Sites CD-ROM* or give information on installing the software.

This icon tells you where to look for more information on a topic.

Although, in most cases, we'll refer to the server in software terms, a Web server is also hardware oriented. You'll see this icon when we deal with specifics concerning what hardware must be used with your server as well as when we deal with other hardware issues.

This icon lets you know that there is something you'd best remember because it will come up again.

You'll see this icon where we discuss the VREvolution Web site and the decisions made concerning its operation and setup.

This icon signifies information that can save you time and money (or at the very least considerable frustration) in the operation of your Web site.

Why a Book on Setting Up Your Own Web Site?

Operating a Web site is not an easy task. Neither is it inexpensive in terms of either time or money. Depending on what type of platform you choose, the amount of time you spend setting up and maintaining your site can range from reasonable to exorbitant. The hardware and software costs also can vary considerably depending on your choice of platform.

This book is intended to be a real world, easy-to-understand explanation of how you, Joe or Josephine Average Citizen, can build and operate your own World Wide Web site as inexpensively as possible. In other words, this book is *not* written in Nerdite Computerese.

No, we're not down on those who speak Nerdite Computerese. They are an invaluable asset to the cyberspace community and frontier (and besides, it's getting to be politically correct to accept these types at all social gatherings). This book, however, is aimed at the rest of us: those who barely understand a DOS prompt and could really care less about Mozilla extensions. (Just in case you do care, and are therefore bordering on learning to speak Nerdite Computerese, Mozilla was Netscape Navigator's code name for a period of time. The name was based on the cartoon character that graced Netscape's home page and Web site.)

How to Use This Book

We believe that the best way for a group of people to reach the same location in the quickest amount of time is to take the same path. Going by different routes leads to different arrival times.

At the same time, sometimes the greatest discoveries are made by those who leave the beaten path. There are few beaten paths in cyberspace today. You'll only be able to follow a few of them before you'll be forced to strike out on your own.

This book is filled with information. Some of this information can be best understood only by first understanding the material that comes before it.

Yes, you could skip around in the book, reading first this and then that, but that method might lead you down a path that leads to a dead end. We recommend that you begin at the beginning and read through each chapter till you find yourself forced to be a trailblazer.

Conventions Used in This Book

Some text in this book looks different from the rest of the text or is on a line by itself. This section explains some of the conventions we've used to make things clearer for you.

Things that you should type appear in bold, like this: Type **INDEX.HTM** for the filename.

When you should press an arrow key, the following symbols are used: (↑) for the up-arrow key, (↓) for the down-arrow key, (→) for the right-arrow key, and (←) for the left-arrow key.

Internet addresses appear in computer font, like this: `vrevolution.pitton.com`.

Listings of computer code and other things that appear onscreen look like the following line. Notice that things that can change (variables) appear in italic.

```
<A HREF="URL">variable</A>
```

Occasionally, this book's pages are not wide enough to accommodate the number of characters that need to be on a given line of code. To solve this problem, we have used the ⮐ symbol to denote that the line continues with the characters that follow this symbol.

The Creating Cool Interactive Web Sites CD-ROM

We won't go into a great deal of detail here but the CD-ROM that comes with this book includes what we believe to be some of the most useful products available for creating cool interactive Web sites. Keep in mind that the software provided is demos and Beta releases that are subject to the limitations and restrictions that are normal for these types of applications.

Web Addresses

We've tried to provide the most up-to-the-minute Web addresses for the people and companies we discuss in this book. Keep in mind that the Web is growing and changing every minute. These URLs may change.

Where to Go from Here

You are now an explorer, discovering and civilizing new sections of the cyberfrontier. As you work through the following pages, keep that in mind. We begin the next chapter with the second choice you have to make. You've already made the first decision. You can now consider yourself a pioneer on the cyberfrontier.

Turn the page and move into cyberspace.

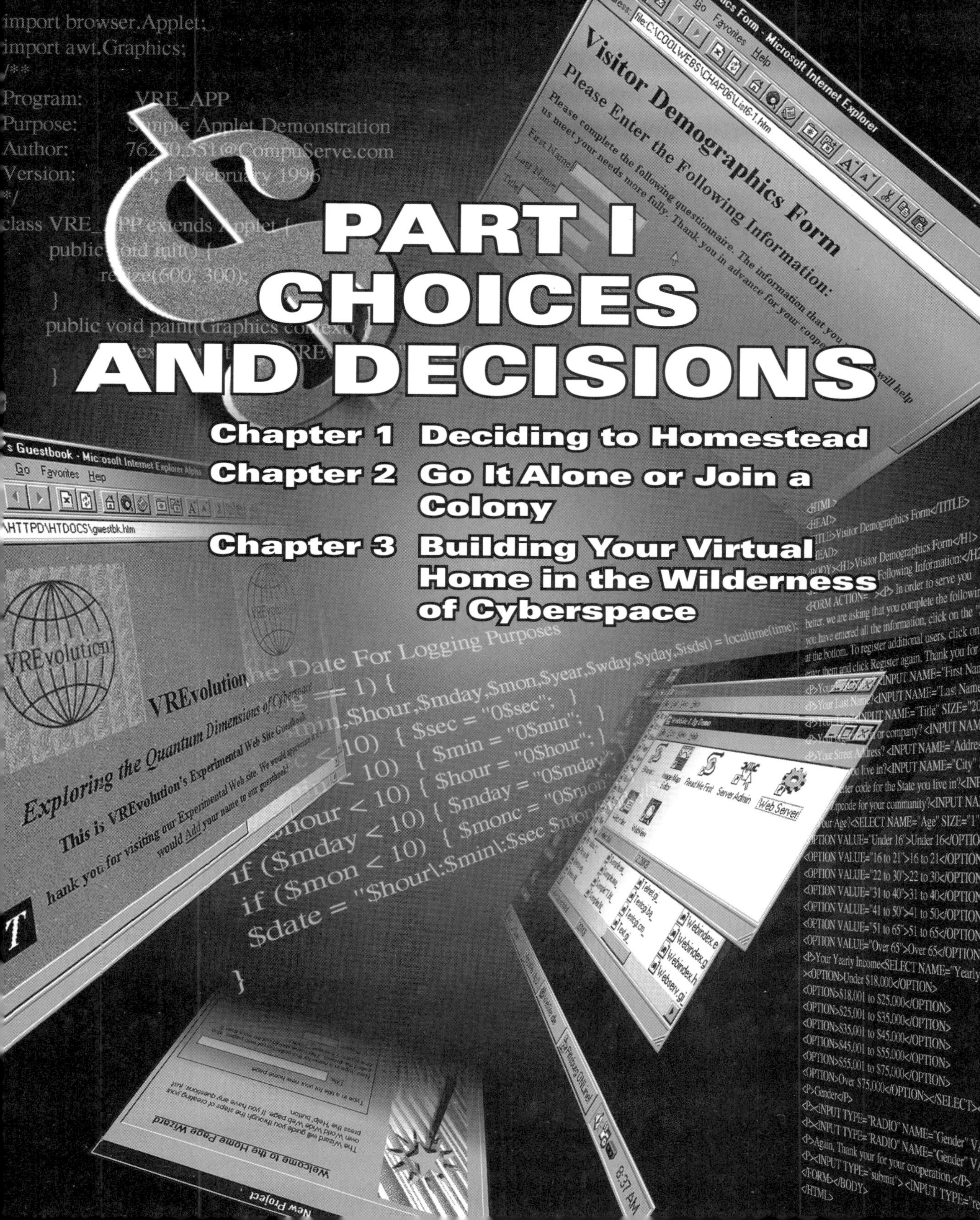

PART I CHOICES AND DECISIONS

For the next several pages, some of you may think that we're trying to talk you out of creating your own cool interactive Web site. The reason that you may get this idea is that the first part of this book is about the choices that you will face if you decide to create your own cool interactive Web site.

A Web site costs both money and time. A cool interactive Web site costs more money and more time. It's best to be aware of just how much it may cost before you begin to homestead cyberspace.

Deciding to Homestead

In This Chapter

Exploring Web sites

Choosing a method of accessing the Web

Choosing a Web browser

Deciding whether to have a part-time site or a full-time site

Considering alternatives for setting up a site

Seeing how VREvolution's sites were set up

This book is about choices. Some of you may have already made some of the choices that we look at in this chapter and can, therefore, skip this material. This chapter is about choosing your Internet Service Provider and your Web browser. If you've already made these decisions, you can skip ahead to Chapter 2.

A Web Site Is Full of Possibilities

In this chapter, you find out about some of the various possibilities and uses for a Web site. When we say "possibilities," we're not just talking about the technical capabilities of the equipment. We're also looking at the quantum realities that are possible for your Web site. These possibilities range from business and capitalistic opportunities to an educational and informational Nirvana.

You'll look at three different types of Web sites and explore them to see how they are used by their Webmasters. We talk with one of these Webmasters, and you learn some reasons for creating your own individual Web site.

Finally, you'll look at the reasons behind VREvolution's decisions concerning its Web site.

Exploration tools

The first step in colonization and homesteading is to explore new territory. Because exploration is quite different from colonization and homesteading, the tools that you need for exploration are different too. At the exploration stage, you need, in order of priority, a computer, an Internet connection, and a Web browser.

Your computer

Although any computer, no matter how old, can be useful for a variety of purposes, in order to explore the Web you need a computer that meets the minimum hardware requirements described in this section.

Note that the hardware requirements for running a Web site, which we discuss in Chapters 2 and 3, are much higher.

The CPU

For full graphical access to the World Wide Web, most browsers that are currently available require at least a 386SX computer with a speed of at least 20 MHz. We began exploring the Web with such a machine. If your computer is this slow, be prepared to wait a long time for the Web site graphics to load.

You'll be much better off with at least a 486 with a speed of 33 MHz. Speed is important, in some respects, so the faster your CPU, the better off you'll be. Rather than completely getting rid of our 386SX, we took the route of upgrading it by adding a 486 upgrade chip that sits on the motherboard directly on top of the 386SX CPU. Although this chip does not make our computer a full 32-bit machine, it increases the machine's speed to about 50 MHz and enables it to read the 486 command set.

Memory

The more memory your computer has, the better off you'll be. Our 386SX had 6MB of RAM, and although the machine was slow, we were able to use it to get our first exposure to the Web.

Some browsers will work with as little as 4MB of RAM, but for exploration purposes, 8 Megs is more than adequate for most applications. We run a minimum of 8 Megs on each of our machines and try to run 16 Megs whenever possible. The memory requirements for the Web site machine are similar.

Modem

Speed is an important factor with many applications that are run on Web sites. For exploration purposes, some people have used a minimum of 9600 baud, but we don't recommend it. Some Internet providers require you to connect to their systems with a 14.4K baud modem or better.

You need at least a 14.4K baud modem or higher. Otherwise, you'll be sitting around waiting for what seems like forever to see even a simple Web page. We recommend that if you're serious about exploring and colonizing cyberspace, you use a minimum 28.8K baud modem.

Platform

The platform that you use for exploration is a matter of choice. This book covers the use of the various Windows platforms (including Windows 3.1 and 3.11, Windows for Workgroups 3.11, Windows 95, and Windows NT), with particular emphasis on using the Windows 95 platform. The software applications discussed in this book require at least the Windows 3.1 platform.

Storage

You probably need a minimum of 120MB storage capacity on your hard drive just to hold the operating system and the access software. However, to be completely comfortable with your ability to download some of the tools you'll find at various sites, you probably should have a minimum of a 420MB hard drive.

Internet access

You can use a variety of relatively inexpensive methods to access the World Wide Web. In fact, there are far too many service providers to cover here. For exploration purposes, any of the following Internet access providers furnish acceptable passage. Look for the CD-ROM icon in this book for a description of the browsers and other software that are on the *Creating Cool Interactive Web Sites CD-ROM.*

In the following sections, we discuss the three major online services (America Online, CompuServe, and Prodigy), but you can connect to the Internet without going through them. You can find many other routes onto the information superhighway in the Providers of Commercial Internet Access (POCIA) Directory and The InterNIC Internet Service Providers List, whose FTP addresses follow. You also can use one of the special introductory deals offered by service providers, including software on the *Creating Cool Interactive Web Sites*

CD-ROM. Many of these providers include FTP software in their packages.

The POCIA directory is available by FTP at

```
ftp.teleport.com/vendors/cci/pocia/pocia.txt
```

The InterNIC Internet Service Providers List is available by FTP at

```
ftp://is.internic.net/infoguide/getting-connected/united-states/⮐
internic-us-provider-all
```

Some of the following software can be found on the *Creating Cool Interactive Web Sites CD-ROM*. Installation instructions for these applications are in the appendix.

America Online

Version 2.5 of America Online's (AOL) software for Windows is for the Windows 3.1 platform. This software includes a Web browser, as shown in Figure 1-1. In fact, AOL and Microsoft recently announced that Microsoft Internet Explorer would be the browser for America Online's 5 million subscribers.

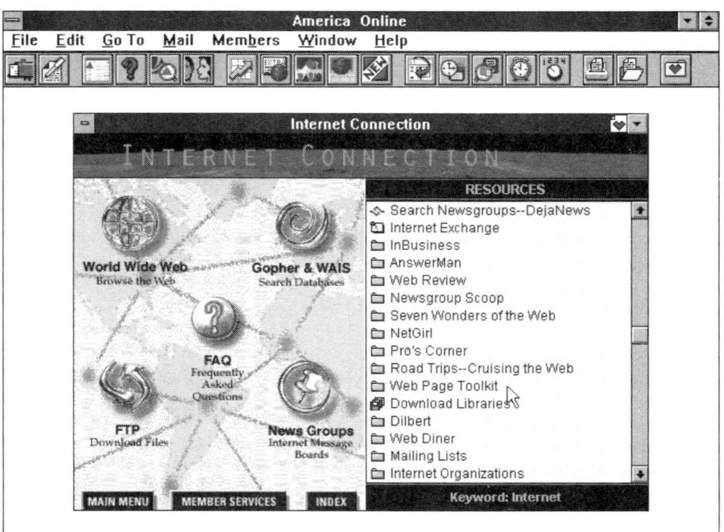

Figure 1-1: Internet exploration is easy with AOL's Internet access software.

One positive aspect of AOL's service is that AOL has an 800 number that you can call for access. If you are anywhere in the United States where AOL doesn't have a local access number, you can use the 800 number for a minimal charge to your account.

CompuServe

CompuServe's WinCIM, Version 2.0.1, is on the *Creating Cool Interactive Web Sites CD-ROM*. Version 2.0.1 comes with an integrated version of SPRY Air Mosaic and runs under Windows 3.1 and 3.11, Windows for Workgroups 3.11, and Windows 95. Installation instructions are in the appendix. One trick you may want to remember with Windows 95 is to copy CompuServe's Winsock into every CompuServe subdirectory. Then Windows 95 can replace the CompuServe Winsock in the Windows subdirectory (which it will do anyway) and prevent CompuServe's software from looking outside its own subdirectories for the Winsock it needs.

Figure 1-2 illustrates the use of WinCIM on a system that is running Windows 95.

Figure 1-2: CompuServe's service software and the SPRY Air Mosaic browser software work together online.

The introductory CompuServe package on the *Creating Cool Interactive Web Sites CD-ROM* gives you your first month's membership and ten hours of access free. You need to use these hours during the first 30 days after you sign up. You must notify CompuServe during that first 30 days if you decide that you don't want to continue the service. Otherwise, you will be charged.

As with AOL, a positive aspect of CompuServe's service is that CompuServe has an 800 number that you can call for access. If you are anywhere in the United States where CompuServe doesn't have a local access number, you can use the 800 number for a minimal charge to your account.

EarthLink Network, Inc.

The EarthLink Network software (see Figure 1-3) comes complete with TotalAccess Internet Dialer, Netscape Navigator, and Eudora e-mail software.

Figure 1-3: EarthLink is another complete Internet access package.

As with CompuServe and AOL, EarthLink provides an 800 number for access from areas of the country that do not have local access numbers.

NETCOM

The *Creating Cool Interactive Web Sites CD-ROM* includes NETCOM's software, NetCruiser Version 2.0 for Windows. Figure 1-4 provides an example of what signing on to the Web using NetCruiser looks like.

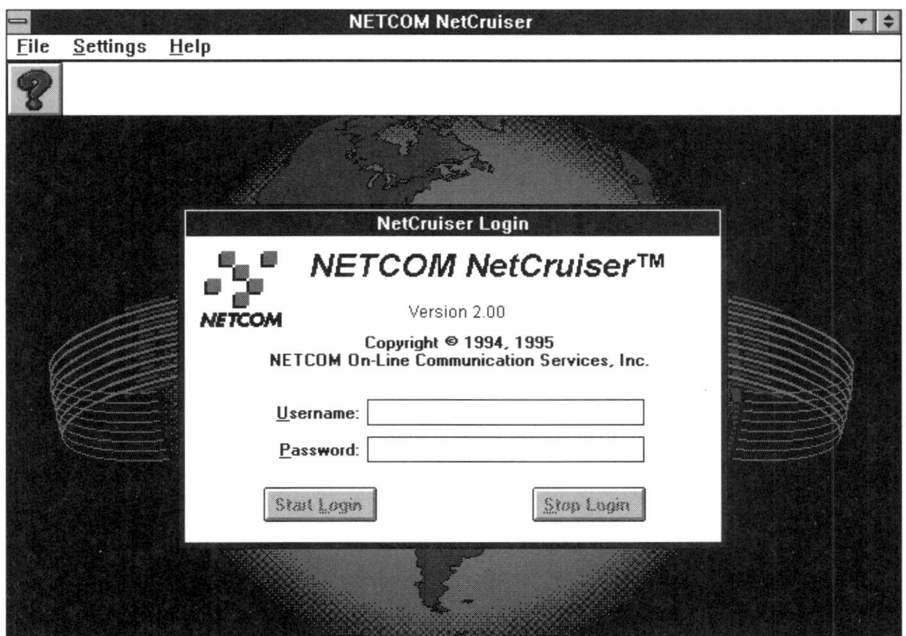

Figure 1-4: NetCruiser is NETCOM's Web access software.

NETCOM does not have an 800 access number, so if you are in one of the cities where NETCOM does not have a local access number, you have to pay long-distance charges to use this provider. A list of cities and local access numbers appears onscreen during the installation of the software.

Pipeline USA

PSI's Pipeline USA software, Version 3.3 for Windows (see Figure 1-5), is on the *Creating Cool Interactive Web Sites CD-ROM.*

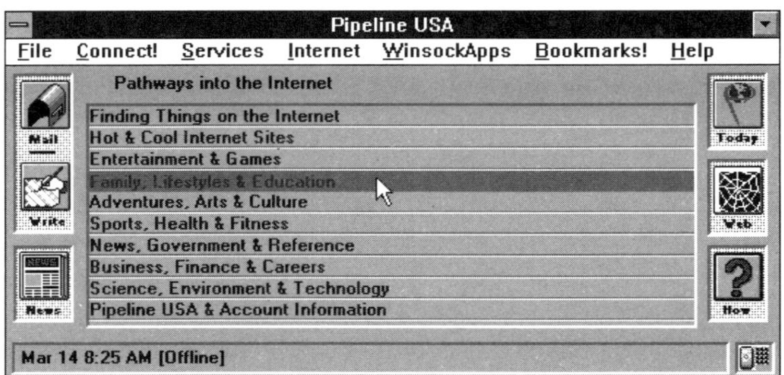

Figure 1-5: Pipeline USA's software provides easy access from many locations in the United States.

Pipeline USA is one of the service providers whose services are not available in every location in the U.S. When you install the software according to the installation instructions provided in the appendix, you see a list of access numbers during registration. If you do not live in one of the locations that has a local access number, you incur long-distance charges if you use Pipeline USA to access the Internet.

Prodigy

Prodigy's Windows service software can be used to provide access to the Internet. Prodigy does not have an 800 number. As a result, you will incur a long-distance charge if you use Prodigy from any area that does not have a local access number.

PSINet Internet Valet

PSINet's Internet Valet software is for Windows, Windows NT, and Windows 95. During installation, you see a list of phone numbers from which to access PSINet. If you do not see a local number, using this service provider will add the expense of long-distance charges.

Your choice of a Web browser

For a long time, the two dominant Web browsers were Netscape Navigator and the various forms of NCSA Mosaic. That situation is changing as Microsoft Internet Explorer moves quickly onto the World Wide Web. If you choose one of the big three online services or one of the major Internet access providers discussed in the preceding sections, you receive a Web browser as part of your sign-up package. The following sections provide a brief introduction to those browsers. Where we know of more detailed user information, we've noted it.

Microsoft Internet Explorer

Within the past couple of years, Microsoft has discovered the Internet. As a result, a number of new software applications have been made available — some of them for free. Internet Explorer falls into this category.

Internet Explorer 2.0 is available on the CD-ROM and for download from

```
http://www.microsoft.com/windows/ie/ie.htm
```

As we mentioned earlier, America Online and Microsoft announced in March 1996 that Internet Explorer would be the Web browser of choice for AOL. A considerable amount of free information concerning the use of this software is available at Microsoft's download site.

NCSA Mosaic

One of the first graphical Web browsers available came from the National Center for Supercomputer Applications (NCSA). Mosaic is available for personal use at no charge and can be downloaded by anonymous FTP from `ftp.ncsa.uiuc.edu`. At the same location, you can also get information about obtaining the source code for the Mosaic software.

Netscape Navigator

Netscape Navigator is a product of Netscape Communication. The browser is mostly referred to as *Netscape* (and sometimes referred to as *Mozilla,* after Netscape's mascot, the cartoon dragon that appeared on Netscape's Web pages).

You can get a copy of Netscape via anonymous FTP at `ftp*.mcom.com`. Replace the * with a number between 1 and 12 to access one of Netscape's many FTP sites. The number replaced by the * keeps rising as Netscape keeps adding FTP sites.

This unsupported version of Netscape is free for personal use. A version of Netscape is available for almost every computer platform in regular use (but unfortunately not for our poor little 8-bit Atari 800XL).

Also, you get Netscape when you install the EarthLink software, which we described previously. No matter where you get it, it is extremely easy to use. Moving around the Web is as simple as moving your mouse cursor over one of the hyperlinks and clicking on it with the left mouse button.

Here's a shameless plug for another book published by IDG Books Worldwide, Inc. Paul Hoffman's *Netscape and the World Wide Web For Dummies,* 2nd Edition, provides an excellent introduction and guide for using Netscape on the Web. This book is an excellent resource for learning how to get around the Web with Netscape.

Quarterdeck Mosaic

A full version of Quarterdeck Mosaic is available in encrypted form on the *Creating Cool Interactive Web Sites CD-ROM.* This browser is one of many browsers that are based on the original NCSA Mosaic. When you double-click on SETUP.EXE in the QDECK program folder, you will be led through a series of screens about paying for and registering Quarterdeck WebServer and Quarterdeck Mosaic. You may wish to check Quarterdeck's Web page at `www.quarterdeck.com` to see if a trialware version of Mosaic is available for downloading.

SPRY Air Mosaic

If you choose CompuServe as your Internet service provider, you get SPRY Air Mosaic as a Web browser. This browser also is based on the original NCSA Mosaic.

Initial explorations

After you obtain and configure your exploration tools, you can begin reaching out into the darkness of the unknown. Your first step is to access your service provider.

Make sure that all of your tools are properly configured. Because different readers will choose different tools (hardware, software, and access provider), we can't provide step-by-step instructions about configuration. The information in the README and documentation files that accompany the various applications is sufficient in most cases.

In this section, you explore three kinds of Web sites: a personal home page, the home page for an educational institution, and a commercial home page. Keep in mind that in addition to HTML, tools such as CGI (Common Gateway Interface), VRML (Virtual Reality Modeling Language), and Java may also have been used in the creation of these pages.

Chapter 6 covers the use of HTML to create Web pages. We discuss VRML in Chapter 7 and Java in Chapter 8.

Here's another shameless plug for several books from IDG Books Worldwide, Inc. Dave Taylor's *Creating Cool Web Pages with HTML,* 2nd Edition is an excellent introduction and guide for using HTML to create Web pages. *HTML For Dummies,* 2nd Edition, by Ed Tittel and Steve James, is also a great help for learning the ins and outs of HTML. Our own *Creating Cool 3D Web Worlds with VRML* is an excellent resource for creating VRML applications for the Web.

Introduction to Web browsing

As we stated earlier in the chapter, because we have no idea which browser and service provider you have chosen, providing you with step-by-step instructions for accessing the Web is extremely difficult. We will, however, attempt to provide you with a brief introductory lesson in using a Web browser for getting around on the Web. Follow these instructions, using the service provider and browser of your choice:

1. **Access your service provider.**
2. **Start your browser software.**

   Your browser automatically opens the Web page that is declared as the default page for your browser. You can change this default, but the method for doing so differs from browser to browser.

   No matter which browser you have chosen, you should see the word or words *Location, Address,* or *Web Page* in the upper-left area of the screen.
3. **Click in the text box (the white area) to the right of this word.**

   The URL listed in this text box should be highlighted in blue.
4. **Type the following address:** `http://www.w3.org`.

   The highlighted material should disappear when you type the first letter.
5. **Press Enter.**

   You see the home page of the World Wide Web Consortium. Explore a little bit. Scroll down the page. Click on the blue highlighted and underlined words and groups of words. See where they take you.

Remember that you can use this method to go anywhere you want to go. Experiment. Play around. You learn by doing. Don't worry; you really can't hurt anything.

Next, you explore and examine three specific types of Web pages.

Exploring a personal home page

You begin with a quick tour of a personal home page that resides on the server of the University of Missouri at Columbia. This page belongs to John C. Dailey, who is a doctoral candidate in the Communication Department. His personal home page, as shown in Figure 1-6, is at `http://www.missouri.edu/~c611954`.

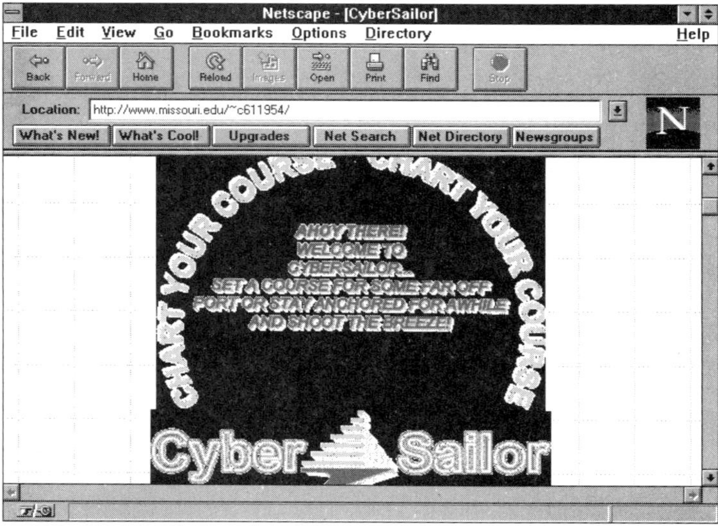

Figure 1-6: *John Dailey's personal Web page makes use of the surf-and-sail motif to represent the Internet.*

Dailey's home page, as shown in Figure 1-7, has a hyperlink to an area concerning human-computer interaction research. Take the time to explore Dailey's page.

Exploring the home page of an educational institution

Next, you explore the home page of an educational institution — the home page for the Communication Department at the University of Missouri at Columbia. This page, shown in Figure 1-8, is at `http://www.missouri.edu/~commwww`.

Figure 1-7: John Dailey's home page has a hyperlink to a research area concerning human-computer interaction.

Figure 1-8: The Communication Department at the University of Missouri at Columbia provides examples of course syllabi on its Web page.

In addition to links to the semester schedule and course syllabi, this page also provides hyperlinks to communication research areas and to Web pages for some of the faculty of the department. As with John Dailey's page, take the time to explore some of these pages. You'll find some interesting people here with interesting ideas.

Exploring a commercial home page

Finally, you look at a home page for a commercial enterprise, WebMaster, Inc. The page shown in Figure 1-9 is at `http://www.Webmaster.com`. This page is linked to many pages at WebMaster's site. Take the time to check out several of these pages. You'll find a discussion of the company and its purpose, pages discussing the various products offered by WebMaster, links to the pages of the people who work there, and many other topics.

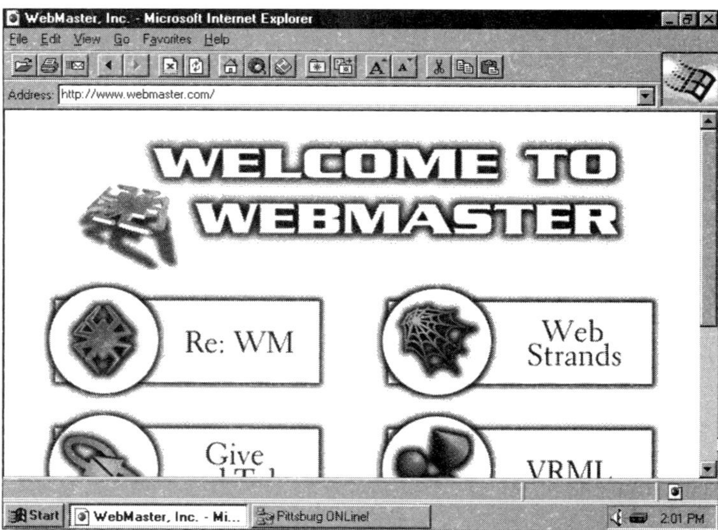

Figure 1-9: WebMaster, Inc., is a commercial enterprise that helps others use the Internet and the Web.

As you examine the pages at WebMaster, you'll find one area of interest that we look at more closely in Chapter 7. That area is VRML. We also examine WebMaster's VRServer, which can turn your Web site into a 3-D delight.

Different yet the same

All right. You've looked at what we have called three different types of Web pages. The first was a personal page. Its purpose is to enable the individual to express his views on a variety of communication topics. The second was an institutional page. Its purpose is to provide information concerning courses offered at a university. Finally, the third was a commercial page. The purpose of this site is to sell products and services. In ways, they were all different.

Yet, in other ways, they were all the same. They were promotional pages. They promoted the individual, the institution, or the commercial organization. At this point in time, the Web is one large public relations press release.

We're not getting down on the Web. On the contrary, promotion and communication is what you want to use the Web for. It is why you picked up this book.

Just keep in mind as you view the pages on the Web, that they are not necessarily what you might consider to be the truth. A perfect example of this was brought to our attention by our editor as we were finishing this book. If you aim your Web browser at `http://www.whitehouse.gov`, you will find the Web page for the White House. If, however, you type `http://www.whitehouse.net`, you will find a parody of that page. This parody has links to the actual White House site, so if you aren't paying careful attention, you could be getting false information.

But, not to pick specifically on the White House, who is to say that the information provided at the actual site is true information? What happens when someone creates parodies of your Web page and a potential customer accesses the parody instead of your actual site?

How Much Do You Want to Do Yourself?

Now that you've had a look at some pages and ways that pages are used on the Web, you need to start making a few decisions about your Web site. Here are two things that you need to keep in mind when you are examining the choices that you have:

- The World Wide Web is up and running 24 hours a day. It's always eight in the morning somewhere. Running a part-time Web site is not a practical alternative; the site must be up when people try to access it.
- Installing an Internet connection and setting up a Web server require a big investment in time and money.

Two options are available for you to consider if you aren't interested in making the kind of time and resource commitment that is required to set up and maintain a full-time server. In the next few sections, we discuss those two options and the alternative. We begin with the options that require the least effort and move on to the one that requires the most effort.

Alternative #1: Use a service provider's space but create the Web page yourself

One option is to use space provided by an online service provider, and perhaps software that the service provider makes available for creating a Web page. Some of the service providers whose software is available on the *Creating Cool Interactive Web Sites CD-ROM* offer both Web publishing software and space for your page.

You can use the following software to create your Web pages. The *Creating Cool Interactive Web Sites CD-ROM* includes all of the software except for America Online's Web Page ToolKit. Installation instructions for the provided software are in the appendix, and Chapters 2 and 6 include short tutorials on using the software.

- America Online's Web Page ToolKit
- CompuServe's Home Page Wizard and Publishing Wizard
- HoTMetaL
- Microsoft's Internet Assistant for Word software add-on

America Online's Web Page ToolKit is accessible online for AOL subscribers. AOL provides space for your pages as part of your monthly subscription fees.

CompuServe's Home Page Wizard and Publishing Wizard are available on the *Creating Cool Interactive Web Sites CD-ROM.* Installation instructions are in the appendix, and a short tutorial on the use of this software is in Chapter 2. CompuServe provides space for Web pages for its subscribers as part of the monthly fees.

HoTMetaL is available on the *Creating Cool Interactive Web Sites CD-ROM.* Installation instructions are in the appendix, and a short tutorial on the use of this software is in Chapter 6.

Microsoft's Internet Assistant for Word software add-on is available on the *Creating Cool Interactive Web Sites CD-ROM.* Installation instructions are in the appendix, and a short tutorial on the use of this software is in Chapter 6.

Alternative #2: Hire a Web consultant

Three of the most useful sites on the Web are

- http://www.yahoo.com
- http://www.lycos.com
- http://www.wwww.com

At these sites are three of the search engines that you'll come to use more and more as you explore the Web. We discuss applications that use these search engines, as well as creating your own search engine, in Chapter 11.

For now, though, you can use these search engines to find consultants who can set up and maintain your Web site for you if you don't want to do it yourself. Although all of these search engines work similarly, we use the Yahoo search engine as an example.

Follow these simple instructions to access the Yahoo search engine.

1. **Load your browser and aim it at** `http://www.yahoo.com`**.**

   See Figure 1-10 to find out how the Yahoo site looks if you access it by using Microsoft Internet Explorer.

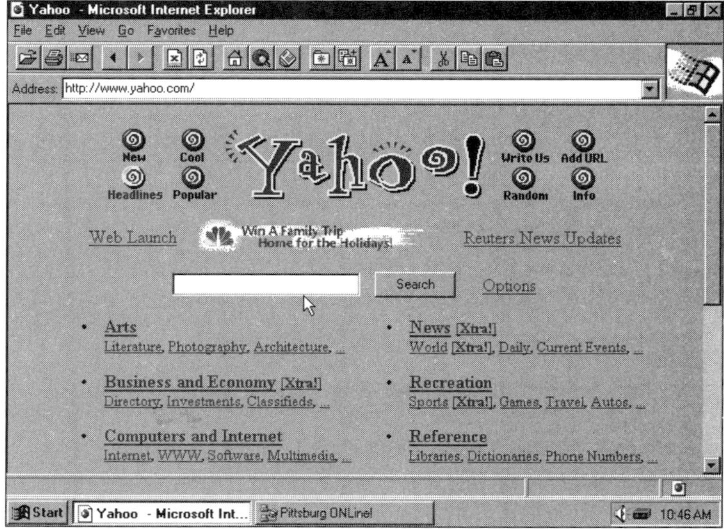

Figure 1-10: Using Microsoft Internet Explorer to access the Yahoo site.

2. **Type** web, consultants **into the search text box, as in Figure 1-11.**

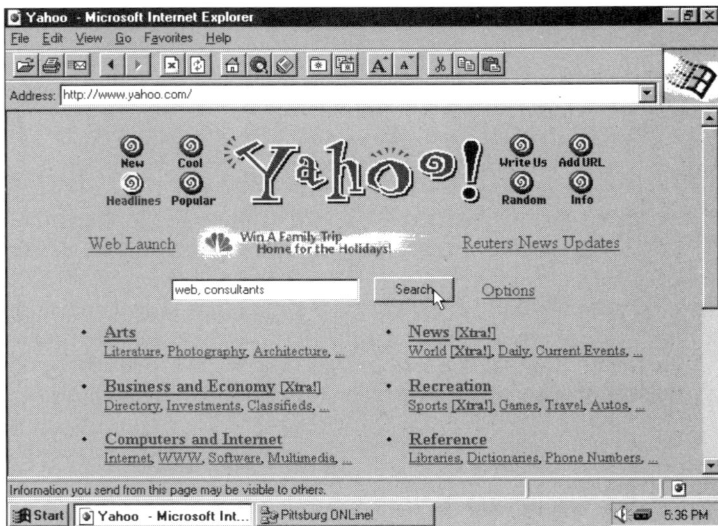

Figure 1-11: To find the names of some Web consultants, use the search string `web, consultants` in the Yahoo search engine.

3. **Click on Search to see a list of matches (see Figure 1-12).**

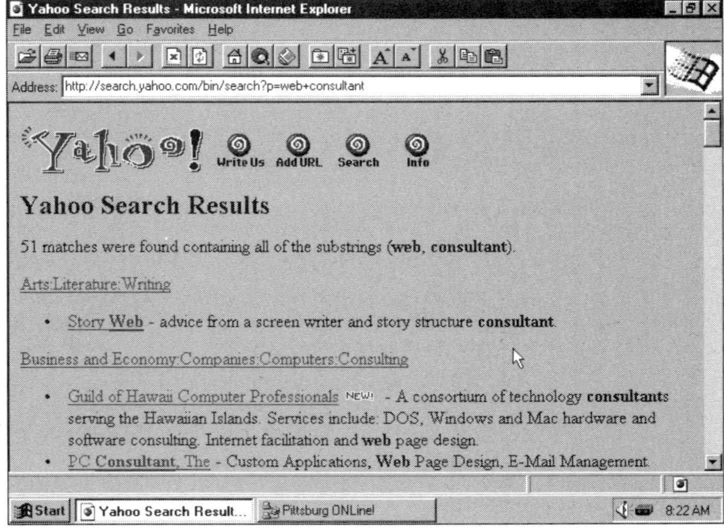

Figure 1-12: The Yahoo search engine turned up 51 matches on this particular search.

This search turns up consultants whom you can contact about creating and maintaining your Web site for you. Fees for their services can range from about $25 per month to well over $100, and the storage spaces available vary from 1MB to 2MB for this range of fees.

The number of consultants that the search will yield varies from one search to the next, partly because of additions to and subtractions from Yahoo's lists.

If you would like the names of more consultants, access the other search engines to find out whether they can provide new matches for your search. Gathering information should be one of your first efforts in building your site.

Alternative #3: Building your own server

This alternative is the central idea behind this book. Although building your own server requires more time and financial resources than the preceding alternatives, it also can provide the most rewarding experience of any of the three.

Chapter 3 discusses servers that will run on Windows NT, Windows 95, or Windows 3.1 machines. Installation instructions and operating and setup tutorials are provided.

VREvolution Site Diary: Installment 1

This is the first installment of the Site Diaries that appear at the end of each chapter. One thing a teacher learns right off is that if you want to learn something well, you should volunteer to teach it. The installments at the end of each chapter discuss the experiences of Mary's VREvolution as we set up and run a Web server for writing this book.

The basic purpose behind VREvolution has always been to inform and educate the masses about the communicative possibilities of virtual reality. The Web, with all its public relations capabilities, was a logical direction for VREvolution to take. We quickly decided that the VREvolution Web site would be a virtual reality site that is capable of providing VRML worlds to our Web visitors.

We began by building a Web presence for ourselves on one of the various service provider systems that were available to us. Those first pages are at

```
http://ourworld.compuserve.com/homepages/PSummitt/
```

We created those pages with CompuServe's Home Page Wizard and Home Page Publisher software. We also experimented with pages at AOL and EarthLink. Further exploration and study resulted in our using Microsoft Internet Assistant for Word to create new pages. These pages were submitted to Mark Owen of WebMaster, Inc. Owen modified some of the links and changed some of the backgrounds. The pages were then placed at

```
http://www.Webmaster.com/VREvolution/
```

These examples represent our experiences with the first two alternatives: using leased space and doing it yourself, and hiring an outside consulting organization. The final alternative, that of setting up our own server, began with our contacting Victor Hirst of Pittsburg OnLine! We discuss the choices that we made next in more detail in the next few chapters.

Why are you creating your Web site?

In our earlier exploration of Web sites, you visited WebMaster, Inc. According to press releases, WebMaster is a company that is committed to making the Web intuitive, accessible, and productive by using the possibilities presented by 3-D graphics on the Internet. WebMaster is located in Santa Clara, California. The company is an engineering, technical marketing, and publishing company with a unique emphasis on providing software and services for Internet-oriented virtual reality and 3-D. Its innovative team of engineers, marketing and public relations specialists, graphic artists, and programmers includes some of the postproduction animators who created some of the Emmy award-winning visuals for the *Babylon 5* TV show. WebMaster has been active in the VRML community since the beginning of the format's development and has worked closely with both Mark Pesce and Tony Parisi, the cocreators of VRML.

During an online e-mail discussion about creating a Web site, we asked Mark Owen, vice president for marketing for WebMaster, Inc., what some of the questions are that he asks potential clients concerning their reasons for building a Web presence. Here's what he said:

First, I think that one of the most important questions is, What does the client want out of the Web site? This is a pretty large question; it's actually several questions in one. Many times, customers have no idea what they want out of a site. A typical reaction might be more of, "Well everyone is doing it," or "I have to have one because my competition has one."

These generally aren't good responses. The first step should be to have a business plan for the Web. You shouldn't just create a site for its own sake. Ask yourself questions such as the following:

- What is the site's purpose (business, information, customer support, and so on)?
- What are the demographics of your customers (age, income, geographic location, and so on)?
- Do you plan to conduct sales over the Net?

The answers to these questions give us tips not only on the goals but also on the design for the site. If the site is for customer support, we probably want to go "graphics lite." If it's for information, we want to gear the site toward the demographics of the recipient. Different demographics require different types of sites. If the site is only corporate, we can design "graphics heavy," because the target market will probably have faster modems or a T1. Look at Sun's or SGI's site — both of those companies have corporations as target audiences, and both sites are graphics intensive.

Our press person is providing information, so he has a site with few graphics. He would rather get the information to his audience quickly and with little hassle.

The games companies are geared toward an audience that has slower access but expects cool graphics.

Another question is, Do you plan on conducting commerce over the Net? The answer to this question tells us how technical a site they need and what kind of server package is required.

The next questions are then pointed to what type of site they want. Some obvious questions are

- How much do you want to spend?
- How fast do you need the site up?
- Do you have the source documentation (product information, press releases, support notes, and so on)?

Summary

In this chapter your first step was to look at the tools that are necessary for the exploration phase of your journey. These tools include your computer, your Internet connection, and your Web browser software.

You then explored a personal home page, the home page of an educational institution, and a commercial Web page to see some of the ways that such pages can be developed.

You found out why you should establish a full-time Web site and then examined three alternatives for operating a full-time Web presence.

Finally, you took your first look at the VREvolution Web Site Diary. Here we explained some of the decisions that we made and steps that we took in constructing our Web presence.

With this preparation, you can now consider the next choice that you have to make: to go it alone or to join a colony.

Go It Alone or Join a Colony

In This Chapter

- Looking at where you'll put your Web site
- Putting your Web page on someone else's server
- Setting up your own server
- Deciding how to get your page on the Internet
- Looking at VREvolution's decision

When it comes down to it, you have only two choices for establishing a Web site: You can rent space (or use free space on someone else's server), or you can go it alone and build your own server. This chapter is about choosing between those two options.

In the next several pages, you find out more about some of the online services and other companies that provide space, services, or products that can make your colonization of cyberspace easier and, perhaps, more profitable.

Joining a Colony

When we discuss joining a colony, what we are proposing is that, as a relative beginner in cyberspace, it might be easier for you to learn by using the Web page creation software that the service providers have developed and made available. For example, in this section of the chapter, we show how a home page can be created and installed in a variety of locations. These locations include America Online (AOL), CompuServe, EarthLink, and Prodigy. These locations are sometimes referred to as *free Web space* because the regular monthly fee that you pay for access to your service provider also covers the use of a specific amount of space where you can store your Web pages and other users can access them.

We don't walk through the entire process of creating a Web page here or anywhere else in this book. Plenty of other books can show you how to create a Web page, but this book is about creating an interactive Web site. If you're looking for a book about creating Web pages, we suggest *Creating Cool Web Pages with HTML,* 2nd Edition, by Dave Taylor, and *HTML For Dummies,* 2nd Edition, by Ed Tittel and Steve James (IDG Books Worldwide, Inc.). Interactive Web sites require more than just using HTML.

In this chapter, you find out about some of the options that are available for creating your own Web site. These options may or may not allow for more than the inclusion of materials other than HTML.

America Online

America Online is one service that enables its members to create a personal Web page online. America Online wants to help members become their own publishers, on both AOL and the Internet. AOL's Personal Publisher is one of the first steps toward AOL's goal of personal empowerment for its members. Without paying additional charges, members can use tools that were designed especially for them.

The limitations of AOL's free Web space

One of the first observations that we can make about using AOL's software and its Web services is that the software, although extremely easy for beginners to use, is also extremely limiting. AOL does, however, enable you to create Web pages with other software and then upload the files to the AOL Web site. This option enables you to use software that better suits your needs.

Another problem is the limited amount of space available. Because you get only 2MB of storage for material, you need to do some careful planning if you want to use many graphics.

A good rule of thumb when using graphics is to try to keep each graphic to under 35K in size and keep the number low. This will speed up the presentation of your page.

Final comments about AOL's Web space

If you are planning more than a few simple HTML pages, AOL's Web site is not going to suffice. Although AOL's beginner software is extremely limiting, you can use other software to create your AOL Web page and thus take advantage of the many capabilities that AOL's server offers and other service providers do not. Also, AOL provides only a limited amount of interactivity on pages located on its Web server.

CompuServe

CompuServe provides two software programs, Home Page Wizard and Publishing Wizard, for creating and updating your Web site on CompuServe's server. Both of these programs and their installation programs, as well as CompuServe's WinCIM Version 2.0, are on the *Creating Cool Interactive Web Sites CD-ROM.* Installation instructions for these three programs are in the appendix.

The Home Page Wizard is an authoring tool that makes it easy to create a home page on the World Wide Web through CompuServe's Personal Home Page Service. Home Page Wizard offers drag-and-drop editing, templates, tips, and context-sensitive help to assist in creating a home page. The program also has a Test button that displays your page in your Web browser before you place it on the Web.

The only online charges that CompuServe members pay are the standard connect time charges, plus any supplemental network surcharges while they are placing their pages on the server.

You also can update your pages as often as you want. The only charges for changes or updates are the standard connect time charges and any supplemental network surcharges that apply while you're placing the changes on the server.

CompuServe gives members a maximum of 1MB of storage space for Web page materials.

Establishing a Web site on CompuServe

Establishing a Web presence using CompuServe's software is relatively easy. After installing the software according to the instructions in the appendix, follow these simple steps:

1. **Double-click on the Home Page Wizard icon in the CompuServe Program Group window.**

   The first time you start the program, you see a New Project window that looks similar to Figure 2-1.

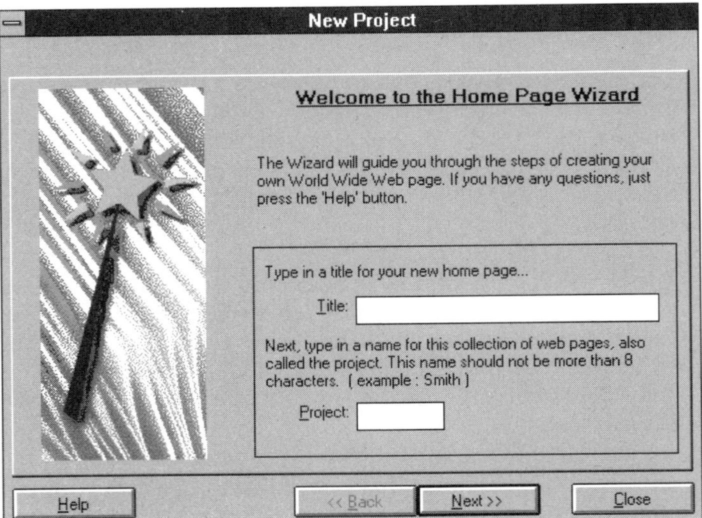

Figure 2-1: The New Project page in CompuServe's Home Page Wizard.

2. **Type a home page title and a name for the home page project.**

   Project names help Home Page Wizard keep the information and materials for this particular group separate from any other group that you are working on. You can have any number of projects going at the same time, but you can have only one project group at a time published on the Web.

3. **Click on Next.**

   When you are creating a new project in Home Page Wizard, you can use some aids to help you get started. The first such aid, shown in Figure 2-2, gathers your personal information so it can be used by the available templates.

4. **Type the personal information and click on Next.**

   The next step is to choose a template, as in Figure 2-3. Home Page Wizard gives you three choices: Career, Fun, and Nature.

New Project

Personal Information

First Name: Paul MI: M.
Last Name: Summitt
City: Pittsburg
State: KS Country: USA
Occupation: Author/Consultant
Hobbies: Video/Music/Geneology
Email address: 76270.551@Compuserve.com
☒ Use Personal Information in Home Page

Help | << Back | Next >> | Close

Figure 2-2: In order for the templates to automatically include personal information about you, the Wizard must know this information.

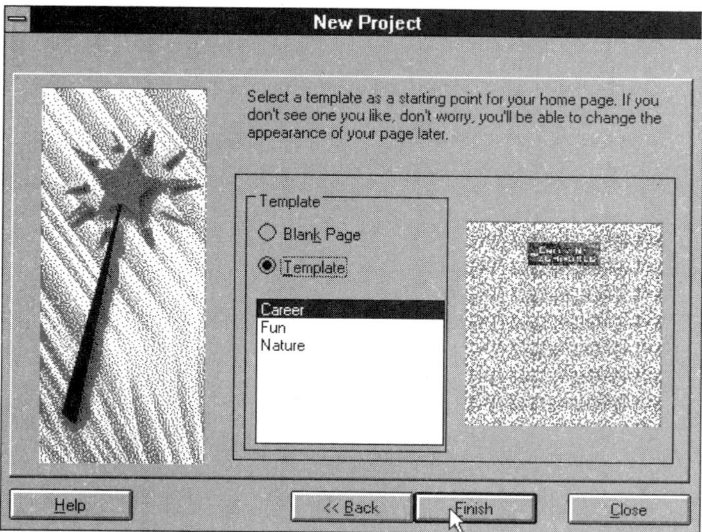

Figure 2-3: Choose from the list of optional templates.

5. **Choose a template and click on Next.**
6. **Fill in each of the fields in the template.**

   Keep in mind that you can make any changes you like; the templates are only starting points. Or, if you prefer to use your own style, you can begin with a blank template and build your page from scratch.

   After you've finished with the template, you're ready to move on to the main Home Page Wizard window, as shown in Figure 2-4.

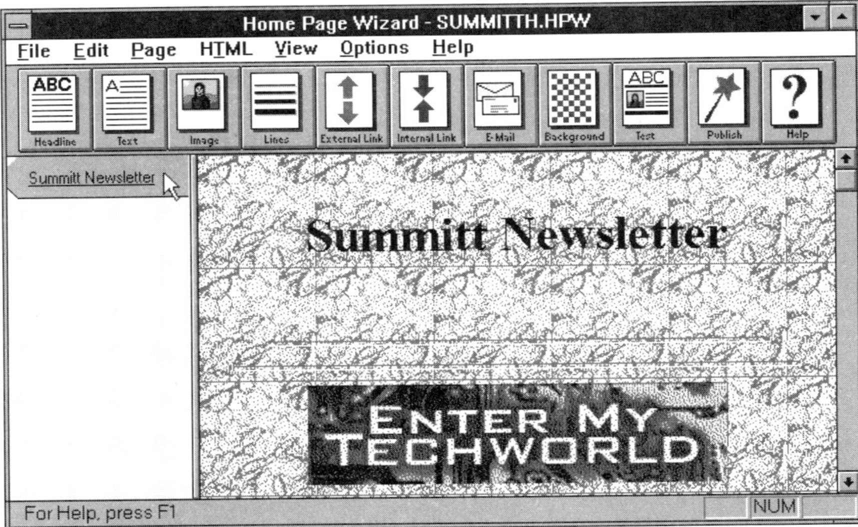

Figure 2-4: The main Home Page Wizard window provides a workplace where you can modify your new home page.

Working with Home Page Wizard

Along the top of the Home Page Wizard window is the Home Page Wizard toolbar. The icons on this toolbar enable you to format and compose your pages. You can use two methods with these icons:

- Drag the icon to wherever you want to insert something. When you drop the icon, a window opens where you can compose text, select a picture, or do whatever else you want to do.
- Double-click on the icon that you want to use. A window opens where you can create an item. After you complete the item and exit the window, you drag and drop the newly created item to the location where you want to place it.

In the next few paragraphs, we describe the icons in the Home Page Wizard toolbar. We begin at the left of the toolbar and work our way to the right.

You choose the Headline icon when you want to create a section title or emphasize something. Six headline sizes are available, and you can center the headlines on the page.

The Text icon enables you to create basic text blocks. You can center the text on the page, place a bullet in front of the text, or set it as preformatted to include line breaks and columns.

You use the Image icon when you want to place pictures and graphics on your page. You can use either .GIF or .JPG images, and you can center, expand, or shrink them, maintaining their height and width ratio, or stretch or squeeze them, changing the image's original height and width ratio.

Click on the Lines icon when you want to create horizontal lines to partition your pages or add lines as simple decorations. You can set the lines to thin or wide, and they can cross all or just part of the page.

The External Link icon enables you to create a link to a Web page that is separate from your own. You need to supply Home Page Wizard with the other page's Internet address (URL).

Just a reminder, before creating a hyperlink to another Web page, it's only polite to ask permission from the owner of the other page. Also, you should check the other Web page frequently. Its content could change, or the page could disappear completely. If your external links are bad, visitors to your page may start blaming you for the bad hyperlinks and not come back to your pages.

Click on the Internal Link icon to create an internal hyperlink that connects your home page to other pages within your project.

Use the E-Mail icon to create a hyperlink to your Internet e-mail address and take advantage of the only form of interactivity that's possible using Home Page Wizard. This feature enables visitors to your page to communicate with you via e-mail.

The Background icon enables you to change the background of your Web page. You can select a color, or you can place a graphics image as the wallpaper for your Web page.

By clicking on the Test icon, you can check how your pages will look before you place them on the Web. You first see which files are being used to create your Web pages, and then the home page is loaded into the browser that you have specified. If you want to view any other pages that are part of the project, you simply click on their internal links.

When you are ready to place your pages on the Web, you simply click on the Publish icon. This action starts the Publishing Wizard part of this software combination. Within minutes after you provide the information that the Publishing Wizard requests, your pages will be up on the Web for millions to read.

Home Page Wizard provides standard Windows-style Help files that you can call up at any time by clicking on this Help icon.

Changing items before you publish

At any time, you can change the various parts of your project by clicking on the item that you want to modify and then clicking on a toolbar icon. You also can simply double-click on the item that you want to edit to have Home Page Wizard open a window containing the information you want to modify.

Updating your pages

After you've published your pages, you can always improve them or make changes to them. You can either delete all the information contained on your CompuServe Web site or replace portions of the information.

Checking out our examples

You can see an example of what can be done with CompuServe's Web sites at `http://ourworld.compuserve.com/homepages/PSummitt/summitth.htm` (see Figure 2-5). This is one of the Internet sites for the Summitt Quarterly Newsletter, a family history journal dedicated to the history of the Summitt family.

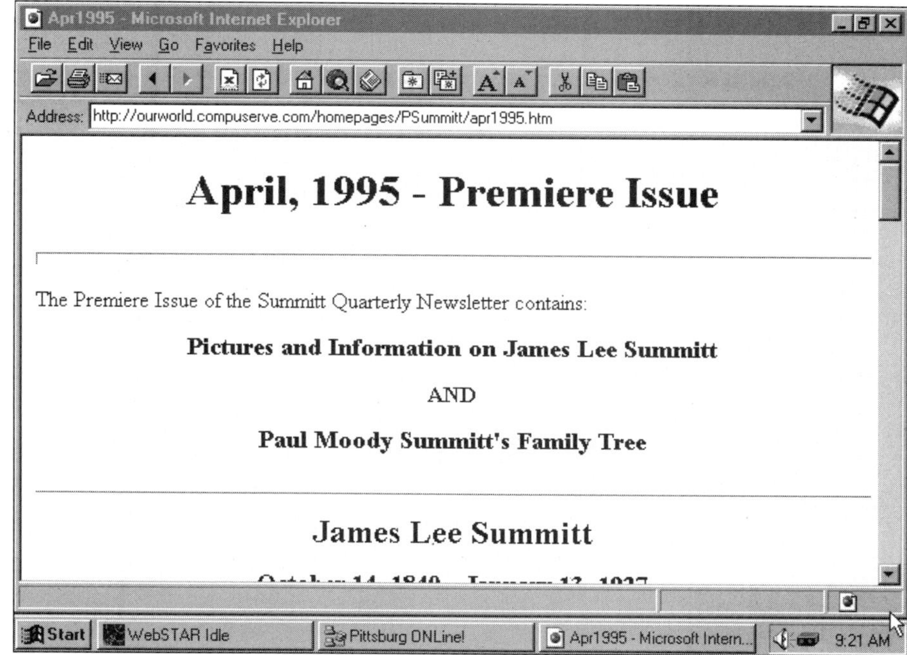

Figure 2-5: Paul and Mary's home page is the Web home of the Summitt Quarterly Newsletter.

Make sure that you examine the pages at this site carefully. We used most, if not all, of the current capabilities of Home Page Wizard in creating these pages.

The limitations of CompuServe's free Web space

One of the first observations we can make about using CompuServe's software and Web site is that interaction between the creator of the page and the visitors to the page is limited. Other than e-mail, no interaction is possible; you can't even use interactive forms.

Another problem is the space limitation. Having only 1MB available requires you to do some careful planning if you want to use many graphics.

Final comments about CompuServe's Web space

If you are planning more than a few simple HTML pages, CompuServe's Web pages are not going to suffice. For example, Home Page Wizard does not allow for the inclusion of a hyperlink to a VRML world, nor to an image map.

Although the price is nice, the limits on what you can do make CompuServe's free Web space an option for use only for providing information.

EarthLink

EarthLink doesn't provide any specific software for you to use in creating your Web site, so you can use just about whatever Web page authoring and creation software you like. We discuss the Web page authoring and creation software on the *Creating Cool Interactive Web Sites CD-ROM* in Chapter 6. Right now, we want to discuss the options that are available if you choose to place your pages on EarthLink's server.

Establishing a Web site on EarthLink

EarthLink Network, Inc., is a full-service Internet access company that specializes in providing Internet services to individuals and businesses across the U.S. You have two choices for accessing the service: Use a local number if one is available or use EarthLink's 1-800 number.

Netscape is the Web browser that EarthLink subscribers use. After you load EarthLink's home page, one of the hyperlinks available is information about EarthLink's free Web space (see Figure 2-6).

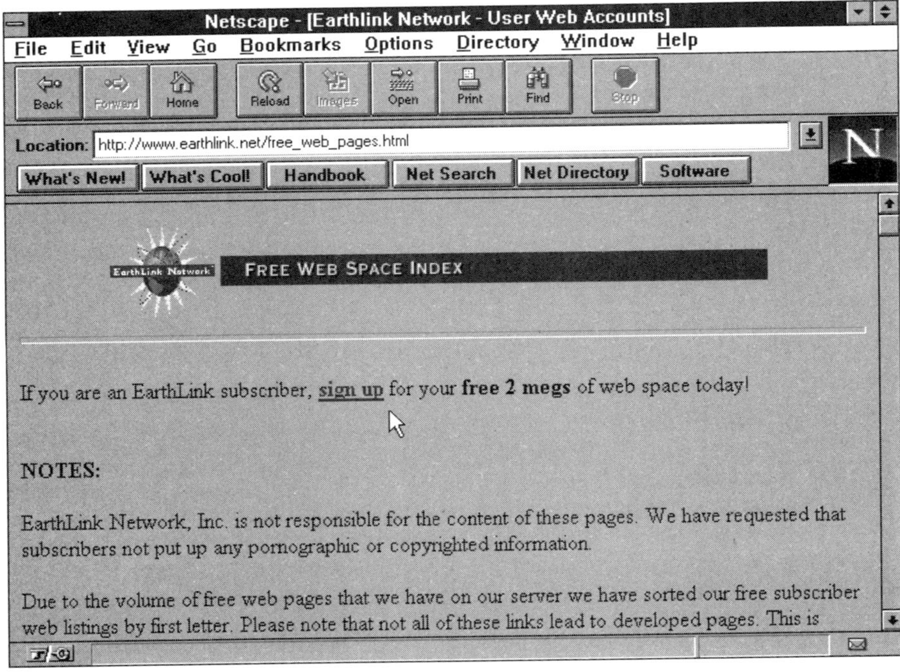

Figure 2-6: EarthLink offers up to 2MB of free Web space to its subscribers.

You can load up to 2MB of material on the EarthLink server. To sign up for your free Web space, you complete a form that asks a few simple questions about your account and then submit the form. In a few minutes, you receive an automatic e-mail response about how to use your free Web space. You should print this e-mail message immediately. It informs you that you now have an account on EarthLink's Web server and that a directory has been set up with your username. In our case, this directory is at `http://www.earthlink.net/~psummitt/`. This message also provides your username and the password that you need to use when you upload your Web pages via FTP to EarthLink's server.

EarthLink provides a number of hyperlinks to useful online Web page authoring guides on its Web pages, as shown in Figure 2-7. These hyperlinks include Creating Web Pages, Internet & Web FAQs, and Internet Tutor, just to name a few. Read these guides; they provide free information about how you can put your Web pages together. Some of these guides also give information on HTML, image maps, Common Gateway Interface (CGI) scripts, and PERL. You may not know what these things are yet, but don't worry. By the time you finish this book, you will.

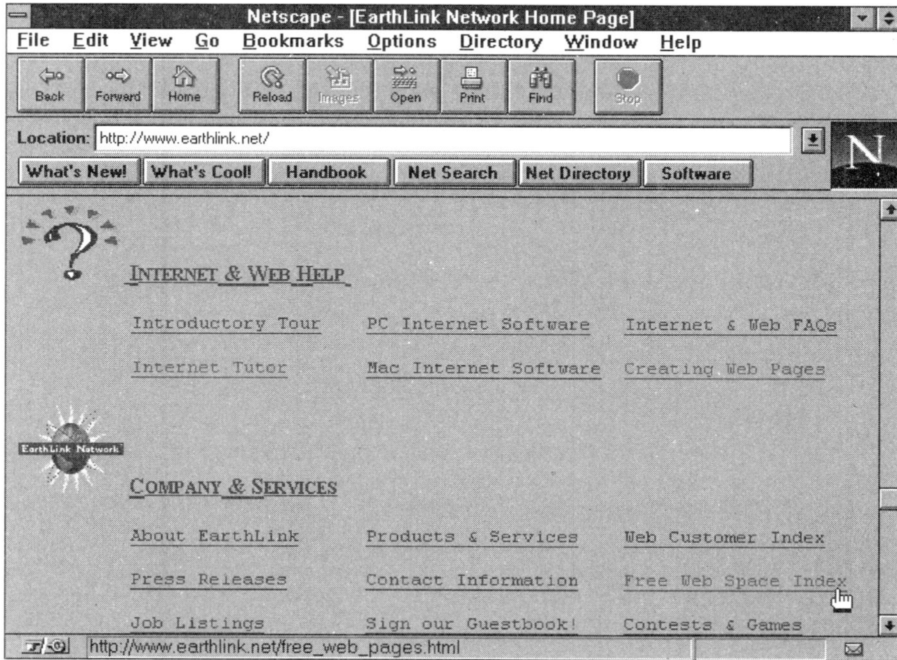

Figure 2-7: EarthLink provides several hyperlinks to Web authoring guides.

Notice in Figure 2-7 that the cursor (represented by a hand) is pointing to the hyperlink Free Web Space Index. This page, which is the same one that you saw in Figure 2-6, is where you sign up for your free 2MB of Web space.

Only commercial subscribers can implement CGI scripts on EarthLink's server, but the information on CGI scripts is useful if you plan to become a commercial subscriber or to set up a Web site somewhere else where you'll be able to implement CGI scripts. The CGI scripts on EarthLink's server must be written in either PERL or a shell program. In Chapter 10, we discuss CGI and describe how to use Visual Basic and C/C++ for creating CGI scripts.

One of the most important things that you need to remember about EarthLink's free Web space is that your main home page must be named index.html. If you're using Windows 3.1 software, you need to change the name of the file after you upload it because Windows 3.1 is not capable of four-character extensions. If you're using Windows 95, just name the file index.html while you are creating it.

Also remember that EarthLink's UNIX server, like all UNIX servers, is case sensitive. Make sure that you name your home page index.html and not INDEX.HTML or Index.html. The server will never be able to find your file if you use the wrong case.

We next discuss uploading your files to EarthLink's server.

Uploading your Web page files to EarthLink

So, we assume that you've created your Web page. The next step is to upload your files to the space EarthLink has made available to you on its server. In order to upload your files, you need to use an FTP program.

The process of placing files from your machine on EarthLink's server is called *uploading*. The process of getting files from another machine and placing them on your machine is called *downloading*.

An *FTP*, or *File Transfer Protocol*, program is what you use to transfer files from your machine to your Web site on EarthLink's server. The EarthLink software package includes an FTP program.

You'll find a variety of demo FTP programs in the various TCP/IP packages on the CD-ROM.

FTP programs have different procedures for you to follow in uploading and downloading files. We recommend that you find the Help files for the particular program that you are using and check to see how the set up and operation of the program are handled. For most programs, you access the Help files by clicking on the Help option in your program's menu bar.

No matter which FTP program you use, you'll probably need to make sure that you've selected Binary when you're uploading data files, such as image, executable CGI, or sound files, and ASCII when you're uploading text files, such as HTML, map, and most shell CGI files.

The limitations of EarthLink's free Web space

Unless you are willing to pay for a commercial site with EarthLink, the amount of interaction between you and your page's visitors is rather limited. E-mail is one of the few forms of interaction possible. EarthLink provides little support for users of its free Web space.

The 2MB space limitation is not as restricting as others we've discussed, but again, you need to do some careful planning if you're going to use many graphics.

Final comments about EarthLink's Web space

If you are planning more than a few simple HTML pages, EarthLink's Web space may not be enough to fill your needs. Limited interaction is allowed but, as mentioned earlier in the discussion of EarthLink, unless you're willing to pay for a commercial site, CGI is not supported.

Again, the price is nice, but the limits on what you can do make this an option to use only to provide information.

Making Your Decision

It all comes down to this: It's your decision. Should you set up your own server, or should you use space on someone else's server?

Although setting up your own server gives you much more freedom in publishing your documents on the Web, it also makes you much more responsible financially and timewise. Here is where you may want to consider contracting an outside service that provides development, hosting, and maintenance of the pages themselves and allows you to focus on your business plan. The choice also has to do with your needs regarding access versus costs as a Web publisher.

Access

Access is probably the most difficult issue confronting you as you make your decision. Most of the advanced techniques that we discuss as we progress through this book, techniques that make your site a cool interactive Web site, require that you, as the Web publisher, have read/write access to the lower-level directories of the server that you are publishing on.

If you're using only standard HTML functions (such as text, limited graphics, and limited multimedia), as provided for in the free Web spaces offered by the commercial service providers we discuss earlier in this chapter, then you don't need access to anything but the directory on which you'll be placing your Web documents.

If, however, you're planning to use forms, image maps, or gateways to programs such as Archie or finger, then, at the very least, you need access to the \cgi-bin\ subdirectory on the server you're using. Some system administrators may be reluctant to give you this type of access, and setting up and using your own server may be your only option.

The costs of renting Web space

Although the free Web pages we discussed previously have their limitations, they also have one big advantage: They are relatively free. If you rent commercial Web page space, most service providers charge, in addition to setup fees and a monthly account fee, a per-megabyte transfer fee for Web access. What this means is that the more people access your site, the more it's going to cost you.

Most service providers charge between $50 and $150 a month for a commercial account with Web pages available. They also charge from $.02 to $.10 per megabyte of data transfer per month. Although these amounts sound relatively small, ten users a day at 2MB per visit make your charges between $12 and $60 per month. Add this to the $50 to $150 monthly charge, and you're running from $62 to $210 per month for your Web service.

We next look at three of the companies that offer commercial Web space. Keep in mind that this information was obtained in late 1995 and early 1996 and may change before you read this. Also keep in mind that this information is for just three of the companies that offer these kinds of services. For a more complete list of Web consultants and service providers, use a Web search engine such as Yahoo and search on Web consultant.

NaviSoft

The first company we look at is NaviSoft. For a price, NaviSoft will host your site 24 hours a day, seven days a week. You'll receive NaviService software to help you create and manage your Web site. NaviSoft offers four levels of service, so you can upgrade your service as your needs change.

- The first level of service includes up to 20MB of disk space and up to 500MB of data transfer a month. NaviSoft considers this level ideal for a personal home page, a few family pages, or a startup business that wants to exhibit product information or recruit potential customers. Password protection and full editing privileges on your Web pages are included. This service level has a $99 startup fee and a $19.95 monthly fee.
- The second level of service raises the amount of disk space to 50MB and allows up to 1,500MB of data transfer per month. NaviSoft considers this level suitable for established small businesses and agencies that want a unique domain name and a distinctive URL on the World Wide Web. This level requires a startup fee of $199, a $100 two-year InterNIC Domain registration fee, and a monthly fee of $99.
- NaviSoft recommends the third level of service for busy, small- to medium-sized businesses and interdepartmental Web sites. This level extends the service to 100MB of disk space and up to 3,000MB of data transfer per month. This level also includes full administration access, database access, and scripting facilities. Enhanced server permissions include full WWW page read/write authority, a dynamic table and forms builder, and a site activity query facility for reports. This level requires a $249 startup fee, $100 for a two-year InterNIC Domain registration fee, and a $199 monthly fee.
- Finally, NaviSoft's fourth level of service offers full system access, CGI and TCL (Tool Command Language) programming extensions, and a choice of hardware and software configurations. This service includes facilities for secure financial transactions and provides up to 1GB of storage space with 15,000MB of data transfer per month. Maintenance service options are available. NaviSoft recommends this level of service for more complex businesses that can use information management and design tools for creating custom Web applications, such as modules, scripts, or database applications. This service has a $499 startup fee, a $100 fee for a two-year InterNIC Domain registration, and a $1,499 minimum monthly fee.

Keep in mind that all NaviSoft prices and programs are subject to change and that these services require full Internet access through SLIP, PPP, or equivalent accounts, or through GNN or AOL accounts (for Windows users only).

You can get more information about NaviSoft from the Internet Services area on America Online.

Home Pages, Inc.

The second company that provides commercial sites that we'll examine is Home Pages, Inc. Home Pages offers a wide range of services for individuals and businesses that want to create an Internet presence. Its site development services and its pages on home page authoring tools are of considerable interest.

Home Pages has a list of ideas about what you might want to put online. This list includes your corporate vision, jobs that might be open within your company, maps of where you are, your company's performance on the stock market, new product or service alerts; informational and educational materials about your area of specialty, customer surveys, tours of your company's facilities, and your company archives.

You can obtain more information about Home Pages, its services, and its prices by contacting Home Pages at `info@homepages.com`.

WebMaster, Inc.

The last company we look at that provides commercial sites is WebMaster, Inc.

WebMaster provides software and services that emphasize Internet-oriented virtual reality and 3-D.

WebMaster specializes in communications products and services for the World Wide Web. As a result, it has arranged to be the exclusive distributor for a variety of communications products. Available products include

- VRServer, an HTTP server that enables you to create a VR, VRML-compliant, 3-D representation of your server for use on the Web from Tenet Networks, Inc.
- WorldView, a 3-D VRML Web browser from InterVista, Inc.

Services include graphical design and layout using HTML and VRML, artwork creation, and the creation of special effects. WebMaster will also operate and maintain your Web site on its dedicated servers and provide you with access information, statistics, and maintenance.

You can obtain more information about the products and services available from WebMaster at the WebMaster Web site (`http://www.webmaster.com`) or by sending a message to `info@webmaster.com`.

Now that we've examined some of the options available by using other companies' servers, we need to look at the requirements and costs of setting up your own server.

Going It Alone

The flip side of all of this is the amount that it would cost you to set up your own server.

The costs of setting up your own server

Your first step is to figure out what expenses you're going to have in regard to hardware, software, and personnel.

- You need a computer. We recommend that you use a Pentium operating at a minimum speed of 90 MHz, with a minimum of 16MB RAM and a 1.2GB hard drive, running Windows 95, and having a minimum 28.8 Kbps modem. These computers now sell at local department stores for less than $3,000. With amortization over 12 months, we can assign a monthly cost to the server of about $263.
- You need a dedicated phone line for your 28.8 Kbps modem. Depending on your phone company, this cost can vary from $16 to $36 per month.
- You need a service provider that will dedicate a 28.8 Kbps line to your server. This cost can range from $50 to $150 per month, depending on the provider and the region of the country.
- Finally, so you can really get an idea of the cost of the services you get with rented space compared with the cost of running your own server, you need to include paying yourself as system administrator. Figure one-fourth time at $30,000 a year, for a total of $600 a month.

Your final total for running your own server is between $929 and $1,049 per month.

As costs come down for reasonably high-performance computers that are running Windows 95, the cost of running your own server will probably become less and less. Keep in mind that when you hire a Web consultant, you are paying for equipment, communication facilities, and time.

Notice that we've included 10 hours per week or about 43 hours per month for maintenance of your server. Someone has to maintain it, and if you set up your own server, that someone may or may not be you. Your time, or the time of an employee, is not free. Also, if you or your employee earn more than $30,000 per year, the cost for the system administrator is higher. You can lower the costs by applying your own pay scale for your time, but don't completely forget it. Not unless your time and work are not worth anything.

Depending on what your Web page needs are, if using a consultant and renting space on a server is going to cost more than $700 per month, we recommend that you seriously consider setting up your own Web server.

Which platform?

For all practical purposes, most any computing platform made in the past eight years is capable of operating as a server for at least light traffic loads. By *light traffic loads,* we are referring to as many as eight to ten simultaneous users.

Because this book is for PC users, we don't discuss anything other than the various DOS and Windows platforms.

Choosing hardware

Whatever platform you choose, you are better off using at least a 486 with VESA, EISA, or PCI capabilities. ISA is slow, and you'll be much better off with the faster adapters.

Choosing a software environment

Windows 3.1*x*

We begin by looking at Windows 3.1*x*, a single-user operating system. Many Web consultants and experts don't believe that single-user operating systems are a good choice for permanent information servers on the Internet. The reason is that one General Protection Fault (GPF) under this platform takes the server down for ten minutes or more.

If you must use Windows 3.1*x* as a server environment, don't use your machine for anything else. Windows 3.1 was not designed for network server activity. Don't put any other software on it, and don't use it even momentarily for anything else.

Several Web server packages are available for Windows 3.1*x*, including NCSA's HTTPD for Windows, SerWeb, and Web4Ham. One of the biggest advantages of using NCSA's HTTPD for Windows is that it relies on Microsoft Visual Basic 3.0 for scripting.

LINUX

Popular and widely supported, LINUX is a public domain UNIX for PCs. Many people on the Internet use LINUX, and posting a question to a LINUX Usenet newsgroup should get you quick and supportive assistance.

Windows NT

Windows NT comes supported directly by its own native server. HTTPS is a full-fledged Web server for Windows NT. The features of HTTPS match those of current UNIX servers.

VRServer, which we discuss earlier in the chapter, and NTWEBSRV are also Windows NT servers.

OS2

OS2 is also directly supported by a native server and operates well using Web2.

Windows 95

Relatively young as an environment, Windows 95 already has a couple of native servers, and some Windows NT servers will also run under Windows 95.

VREvolution Site Diary: Installment 2

As we continued to explore the possibilities of Web publishing, we quickly discovered that although most free Web space and many of the lower-cost commercial sites are suitable for limited informational purposes, they do not provide the access, space, and functionality that VREvolution requires. The storage requirements of photographs, sound files, movie files, and VRML files generally far exceed the 1MB and 2MB limitations of many free Web space locations. Accessibility for the use of CGI is also lacking in many of these locations. After carefully examining the platform and server alternatives, we decided to choose the Windows 95 environment and use Quarterdeck WebServer as the server application software.

Our reasons for choosing Windows 95 were as much a mixture of what we didn't want as of what we did want. We didn't want to use Windows 3.1*x* because of the relative instability of the environment when used in a multiuser system, but we did want to use the familiar user interface that Windows provides. We didn't want to use Windows NT because of hardware incompatibilities, but we did want to use a 32-bit platform. We didn't want to use any of the various PC UNIX operating systems because they would require us to learn UNIX, but we did want to have the ability to work with CGI scripts.

We decided to use Windows 95 because it provides a familiar user interface and at the same time a more stable multiuser platform than Windows 3.1*x*. Windows 95 also provides a 32-bit platform while avoiding many of the hardware incompatibility problems that currently exist with Windows NT. Finally, Windows 95 and the new Visual Basic 4.0 provide us with an excellent scripting language.

Summary

In this chapter, you looked at the two choices you have for setting up a Web site: renting space on an existing server (joining a colony), or building your own server (going it alone).

You examined some of the options, products, and services that are available if you decide to use the free Web space that is available from a variety of sources.

You found out about some of the commercial Web space that exists and the services and products that are available from these sources.

You examined the costs involved in setting up your own server.

You saw some of the server software that's available for the various PC-based software platforms.

You found out why we decided to use Windows 95 and WebServer to build VREvolution's server.

In the next chapter, we revisit the various platforms and server software packages as we show you how to set them up and discuss what hardware they require.

Building Your Virtual Home in the Wilderness of Cyberspace

In This Chapter

Setting up server software for Windows 3.1*x*

Setting up server software for Windows 95 and Windows NT

Looking at the VREvolution Site Diary

Before you get very far into this chapter, the first thing you need to know is that if you are sure that you do not want to set up and run your own server, you can skip this chapter and move on to Part II. If, however, you've decided to set up your own server or you haven't made up your mind yet, you need to read this chapter carefully.

A server is a combination of hardware and software that allows client software, such as a Web browser, to access files on your computer via the Internet or another type of network. There are a number of different types of servers: FTP servers, Gopher servers, and, of course, Web servers. These applications *serve* documents, files, or whatever is requested by the client that the client has been granted access to. We discuss access as we examine the various server applications.

This chapter deals with choosing which platform you're going to run your Web site on. The site is the combination of the server, HTML, and other applications that make up what you want to present to the world via the Web. We cover choosing both hardware and software. Software platform choices include Windows 3.1*x*, Windows 95, or Windows NT. We discuss Windows 95 and Windows NT together.

Choosing between a 16-Bit Platform and a 32-Bit Platform

Using either the 16-bit version of Windows (Windows 3.1*x*) or one of the 32-bit versions of Windows (Windows 95 or Windows NT) has both advantages and disadvantages. In this chapter, we look first at the platforms, with their advantages and disadvantages, and then at some of the software for use on the platforms.

Examining the 16-bit platforms

We discuss Windows 3.1, 3.11, and Windows for Workgroups 3.11 all together under this 16-bit platform label. In general, if a server will run on one of these platforms, it will run, with minor modifications, on the others.

Advantages

One of the first and most apparent advantages of using a 16-bit Windows platform is its low cost. Until late 1995, 16-bit Windows platforms came preinstalled on almost every computer sold. You probably already have a copy of this operating system, so, for all practical concerns, it's free.

Another practical advantage is familiarity. You've probably used Windows for some time and have grown relatively accustomed to its operation.

Finally, the Windows 16-bit operating systems operate on hardware that is, for the most part, considerably less expensive than most other operating systems. The price difference between the hardware required for Windows 3.11 and Windows 95 is not great, but there are some cost differences. These differences will probably disappear as Windows 95 becomes more dominant and Windows 3.1 begins to fade out of use.

Disadvantages

One of the most apparent problems with using a 16-bit operating system is that, in long-term use, single-user operating systems such as Windows 3.1 and 3.11 are generally not suitable for permanent installation as information servers. These systems are rather fragile, and one GPF (General Protection Fault) can bring down the entire server for ten minutes or more.

The 16-bit operating systems also lack sufficiently powerful multitasking capabilities. Simple searches and other applications that run in the background can bog down a PC that is running Windows.

Finally, keep in mind that Windows operating systems are graphical systems (see Figure 3-1) and therefore eat up a considerable amount of system resources and memory just for the graphical interface. Unless you have plenty of RAM, a 16-bit server that is running Windows will probably not do very well at all.

Figure 3-1: *The 16-bit Windows 3.1x operating systems make use of resource-hungry graphical interfaces.*

Keep in mind that although modifications have been made to allow multiuser capabilities for Windows for Workgroups 3.11, it is still a 16-bit environment.

Final words on 16-bit platforms

If you decide to use one of the 16-bit environments, you should follow these guidelines:

- Don't use the machine for any purpose other than being a server. Don't install any other software on this machine and don't allow anyone else to use it for any reason, even for a few minutes.
- Install as much memory on the machine as you can afford.
- Refrain from using anything more than standard HTML documents on this server.

If you follow these guidelines, most of the 16-bit server software packages that we discuss later in this chapter should behave satisfactorily.

Examining the 32-bit platforms: Windows 95 and Windows NT

Although Windows 95 and Windows NT have major differences, we combine them in this section because many of the server applications that run under one also run under the other.

Advantages

One of the most apparent advantages of these 32-bit environments is speed. Applications written to operate under a 32-bit operating system generally run faster than 16-bit applications.

Another advantage lies in the fact that Windows NT (see Figure 3-2), and Windows 95 (see Figure 3-3) to a lesser extent, are true multitasking environments. These systems will not bog down the way that 16-bit operating systems do during the operation of more than one application.

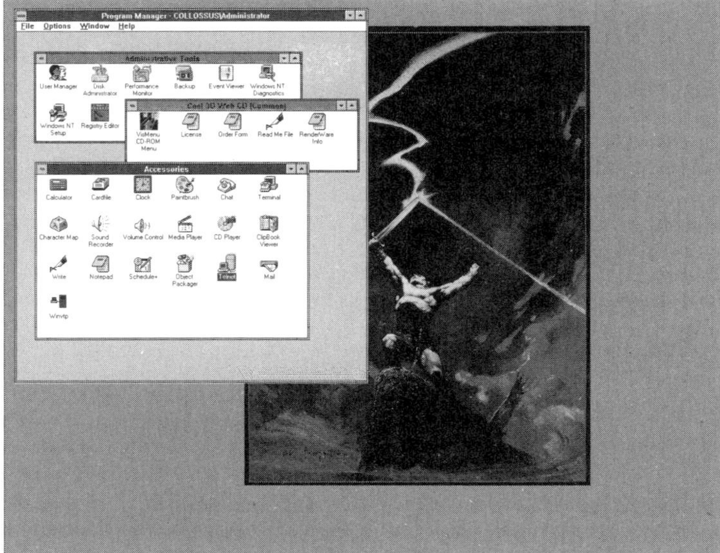

Figure 3-2: The Windows NT user interface is similar to the Windows 3.1*x* user interface and is therefore somewhat familiar.

Finally, an advantage lies in the similarity between the user interface for the 16-bit Windows operating systems and the interface for the 32-bit Windows operating systems. Because the Windows interface for the 16-bit systems is the most used interface today, users are familiar with it. You probably are not going to have a major problem changing your computing habits to work with Windows NT or Windows 95.

Figure 3-3: Windows 95 is expected to replace Windows 3.1 as the most used environment.

Disadvantages

Both software and hardware are slightly more expensive for Windows 95 than for the 16-bit operating systems. The Windows NT operating system software is considerably more expensive, and specific hardware requirements are much more expensive in some cases.

Final words on 32-bit platforms

Of the two platforms, the Windows NT platform is more stable and provides an excellent environment for a Web server. Windows 95, although not quite as stable, is less expensive.

Examining some of the software available for these platforms

Several server software applications are available for both the 16-bit and the 32-bit platforms. We next introduce you to and walk you through some of these applications.

Server software for Windows 3.1*x*

We begin with the 16-bit Windows 3.1*x* applications. We examine four applications, SerWeb, Web4Ham, WebServer, and Windows HTTPD 1.4, in alphabetical order.

SerWeb

SerWeb, a public domain server for both 16-bit and 32-bit Windows platforms, was written by Gustavo Estrella and ported to 32-bit Windows by Chris Alie.

The documentation states that Estrella wrote this program so that he could learn about Visual C++, learn about the World Wide Web, and learn how to program Winsock. The program offers few features, however.

Installing SerWeb is extremely simple.

1. **Download the file SERWEB03.ZIP and unzip it into the subdirectory where you want the program to reside.**

   SerWeb is available for download by anonymous FTP from

   ```
   ftp.cica.indiana.edu
   ```

   Unlike some of the other programs that we cover, no particular subdirectory is required. For simplicity's sake, we unzipped SERWEB03.ZIP to d:\serweb (as shown in Figure 3-4).

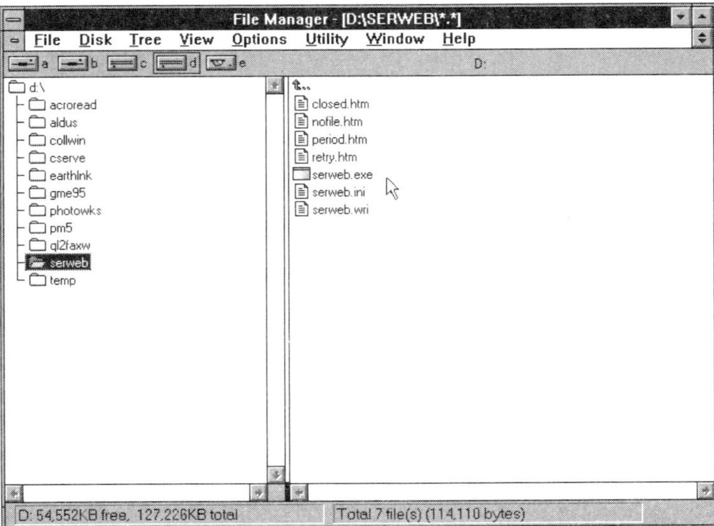

Figure 3-4: Unzip SERWEB03.ZIP into the directory where you want the program to reside.

Now that you've got the files unzipped, you'll notice a file named SERWEB.INI.

2. **Open this file using your favorite text editor (such as Notepad or Write).**

   You see a listing that's similar to Listing 3-1.

Listing 3-1: SERWEB.INI

```
[SERWEB]

PortNumber      = 80          ; Which Port to listen into
HowManyClients =  5      ; Allow up to 5 people to be⮐
on at the same time.

ClosedServer    =  0         ; 0 = OK to log in, 1 = not OK
PeriodAllowed  =  1         ; 0 = allow .. on the⮐
filenames, else don't..
PrintOut        =  1         ; Send output to status⮐
window: 1 = Yes, 0 = No

; Where to start sending from (ex - if you specify⮐
c:\data as your send dir, you can gewt c:\data\test,⮐
c:\data\other\test, but not c:\test
SendDir              = f:\www\serweb\intel

; Message files to send specific information ......
FileNotExistMsg   = f:\www\serweb\intel\nofile.htm
ClosedServerMsg   = f:\www\serweb\intel\closed.htm
PeriodAllowedMsg  = f:\www\serweb\intel\period.htm
```

3. **Edit the options in the initialization file as you prefer.**

   The defaults are shown in Listing 3-1. We'll walk through the options one by one.

   - `PortNumber = 80`. This option defines which port number the server will listen to for incoming messages and connections.

   - `HowManyClients = 5`. This option determines how many users can request files from the server at the same time. Adjust this setting depending on the speed of your machine.

- ClosedServer= 0. If you set this option to 0, the server sends the files requested by the user. If you set it to 1, the server sends the file designated by the ClosedServer option. Setting the option to 1 enables you to disable the server while you're running an application that's memory hungry and resource hungry or while you are upgrading some of your HTML files.

  Remember: we don't recommend that you use your server for anything else if you are running a 16-bit platform. Therefore, you have no reason to set the ClosedServer option to `1`.

- `PeriodAllowed = 1`. Setting this option to `0` enables the user to request files that have names that use two periods (..) on the path. An example of this is c:..\myfiles\private.txt. You can use this option to get to files outside of the SendDir subdirectory. For security purposes, we recommend setting this option to the default `1`, which doesn't allow these types of file requests.

- `PrintOut = 1`. The default `1` causes status messages to be printed. Setting this option to `0` prevents these messages from being printed and enables the system to run a little bit faster.

- `SendDir = f:`. This option defines which subdirectory holds the files that are to be sent out. For example, because we installed SerWeb at D:\SERWEB, we would need to change the default to reflect this. Then, when a user requests a file such as INDEX.HTM, the server will try to get this file from D:\SERWEB\INDEX.HTM. Now, if you don't care whether people can access all of your files, leave the default the way it is. We strongly recommend, however, that you keep the server-related files in a subdirectory all to themselves and set this option accordingly. It's simply good security for your system.

- `FileNotExistMsg = f:\serweb\nofile.htm`. This option designates the name of the file that is to be sent to the user by the server when the file that the user has requested doesn't exist. You should change this setting to reflect the location of your files, as discussed in the explanation for the SendDir setting. One other note: The file that is sent to the user should, in our opinion, be an HTML file that contains a hyperlink to your DEFAULT.HTM page.

- `ClosedServerMsg = f:\serweb\closed.htm`. Here is where you designate the name of the file that is to be used when the server is offline, as discussed in the explanation of the ClosedServer setting.

- `PeriodAllowedMsg = f:\serweb\period.htm`. This file will be sent to the user if he or she requests a .. in the path but the server doesn't allow it. This setting was discussed in the explanation of the PeriodAllowed setting.

4. **Now that you've changed the SERWEB.INI file to work with your computer, save the file and then copy it to your \WINDOWS\ subdirectory.**
5. **Edit the files NOFILE.HTM, CLOSED.HTM, PERIOD.HTM, and RETRY.HTM so that they refer to your Web site.**
6. **Define SerWeb to the Windows Program Manager, as in Figure 3-5.**

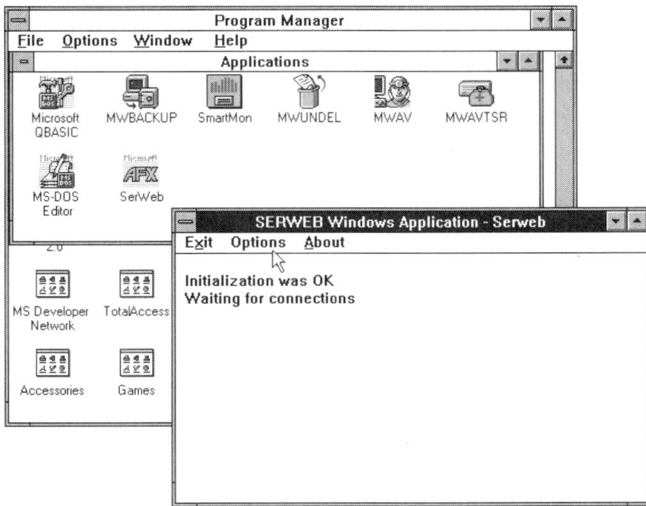

Figure 3-5: SerWeb is ready to run.

7. **Create your HTML files and store them in the same subdirectory where you placed the default files that you edited as part of the configuration.**

SerWeb is ready to run. We next turn our attention to another of these 16-bit Windows server applications.

Web4Ham

Web4Ham is a simple Web server that runs on 16-bit Windows platforms. Gunter Hille wrote the program to learn more about asynchronous file transfers over the Internet.

Specific features of this particular version include

- The ability to handle up to five client sessions
- Detailed log files of sessions in the SDF format
- The creation of private directories for special hosts and domains
- Paradox 4.0 table database interfaces

Installing Web4Ham is relatively simple.

1. **Unzip WEB4HAM.ZIP into the WEB4HAM subdirectory on your hard drive.**

   We installed the program on drive D.

2. **Load WEB4HAM.INI into the text editor of your choice so that you can edit it.**

   You can use Notepad, Wordpad, or Write. We'll walk you through the modifications that you need to make. The unmodified file is shown in Listing 3-2.

Listing 3-2: WEB4HAM.INI

```
[INIT]
DataDir  = c:\web4ham
LogFile  = .\web4ham.log
ErrFiles = .\weber
HTTPort  = 80
Debug    = 0
Iconic     = 0
LogAll     = 0
RxTimeout=30
;
;left hand side must be valid file name (8+3 chars)
;
[PROGRAMS]
PDXDEMO.SH   =.\WEB2PDX.EXE DEMO

;
; keep this order: special hosts first!
```

```
; change entries starting 134.
[255.255.255.255]
; dedicated hosts
127.0.0.1       = c:\web4ham
134.100.9.166     = c:\web4ham

[255.255.255.0]
;dedicated class C subnets
135.100.9 = c:\web4ham\classc

[255.255.0.0]
;class B subnets
136.100    = c:\web4ham\classb

[255.0.0.0]
;class A subnets
137.0      = c:\web4ham\classa

; all other hosts will have access to default DataDir

; we have to specify content-type here
; as new suffixes might be defined
;
[SUFFIXES]
HTM=text/html
PS =text/postscript
TXT=text/plain
DOC=text/msword
RTF=text/rtf
GIF=image/gif
JPG=image/jpeg
MPG=video/mpeg
WAV=audio/wav
AU =audio/ulaw
MID=audio/x-midi
ARC=file/arc
HQX=file/hqx
LHA=file/lharc
EXE=file/pcexe
TAR=file/tar
UUE=file/uuencode
ZIP=file/zip
ZOO=file/zoo
Z  =file/tar.z
```

3. **Edit the file.**

   The first part of this file is the `INIT` section. We'll now examine each option of this section, discuss the defaults, and explain the changes that we've made in our setup procedure.

   - `DataDir = c:\web4ham`. This option sets the default data directory for the server. Place all of your HTML files in this and lower subdirectories. In our example, this entry would read `DataDir = d:\web4ham`.

   - `LogFile = .\web4ham.log`. This option sets the complete path and filename for the server log file. Make sure that you specify the full path and filename. Our example would be `d:\web4ham\web4ham.log`.

     All user requests are written to this log file. Each request creates at least one line to be written to the log file. These lines consist of four items. The first item represents the date in the format year, month, day (YYYYMMDD). The second item is the time in the format hour, minute, second (HHMMSS). The third item is the IP address of the user. Finally, the last item is the first line of the user's request. An example might look like the following:

```
19960115,214716,"127.0.0.1","Web4Ham/0.14 started."
```

     This log file may also have error messages from the Winsock interface. The log file is written in SDF format.

   - `ErrFiles = .\weber`. This option sets the path to where the error files can be found. The server comes with a complete set of files containing error messages. These files are labeled WEBER200.HTM, WEBER201.HTM, and so forth. You can change the name to any name with fewer than eight characters, but the extension .HTM is mandatory. We recommend that you leave the names as they are until you become more familiar with the operation of this server software. In our example, these error files are in `d:\web4ham\weber`.

   - `HTTPort = 80`. This option defines which port number the server will listen to for incoming messages and connections. The default is `80` for all servers.

   - `Debug = 0`. This is a debug tool that the author of the program needed during the programming and debugging phase of the project. Always leave this option set to `0`.

- `Iconic = 0`. This option determines whether a window is created to show user requests or not. The default is `0` and shows user requests in a window. Setting this option to `1` allows the server to start without opening a window.

- `LogAll = 0`. The default, `0`, shows only the first line of the user's request. Setting the option to 1 allows all lines sent by the user to be shown.

- `RxTimeout=30`. If the next packet of information has not arrived before the number of seconds set by this option, the server will disconnect from the user. The default is `30` seconds.

The next section of WEB4HAM.INI is the PROGRAMS section.

- `PDXDEMO.SH = .\WEB2PDX.EXE DEMO`. The left side of this statement must be the name of a specific search engine. The extension `.SH` is mandatory for search engines. The right side gives the path to the program that will be executed by the server. There also will be an optional argument at the end of the statement. In this case, it is `DEMO`.

The next section of the WEB4HAM.INI file is the Netmasks section.

```
; keep this order: special hosts first!
; change entries starting 134.
[255.255.255.255]
; dedicated hosts
127.0.0.1        = c:\serweb
134.100.9.166    = c:\serweb

[255.255.255.0]
;dedicated class C subnets
135.100.9 = c:\serweb\classc

[255.255.0.0]
;class B subnets
136.100= c:\serweb\classb

[255.0.0.0]
;class A subnets
137.0   = c:\serweb\classa
; all other hosts will have access to default DataDir
```

Keep in mind that all directories must be considered as root directories for the specified host. This means that anyone can have access to these directories on this server. What you are doing with this section of the initialization file is setting up a level of user access.

The next section of the WEB4HAM.INI file is the `SUFFIXES` section. Basically, if the user generates a query, the MIME contents type is returned in the response. The contents type is based on the suffix of the file and the MIME type of the string following the equal sign in this section.

Take a look at the following excerpt from the WEB4HAM.INI file. The server doesn't know whether the user can view any specific type and therefore will send the file without any conversion attempts. You can also add types to this list as you feel necessary.

```
[SUFFIXES]
HTM=text/html
PS =text/postscript
TXT=text/plain
DOC=text/msword
RTF=text/rtf
GIF=image/gif
JPG=image/jpeg
MPG=video/mpeg
WAV=audio/wav
AU =audio/ulaw
MID=audio/x-midi
ARC=file/arc
HQX=file/hqx
LHA=file/lharc
EXE=file/pcexe
TAR=file/tar
UUE=file/uuencode
ZIP=file/zip
ZOO=file/zoo
Z  =file/tar.z
```

That's all you need to do to the WEB4HAM.INI file.

4. **Save the file and exit the text-editing program.**

   All necessary initialization for this server is performed in this file. Keep this file in the same directory as the server program itself. We keep both WEB4HAM.EXE and WEB4HAM.INI in D:\WEB4HAM.

5. **Define Web4Ham to the Windows Program Manager.**

6. **Create your HTML files and store them in the subdirectory where you placed the program files.**

Web4Ham is now ready to run. We next turn our attention to a third 16-bit Windows server application.

WebServer

WebServer is one of the Quarterdeck products that is designed to make Web publishing easier. Other Quarterdeck products are WebAuthor, WebCompass, and Mosaic.

Quarterdeck's WebServer is provided on the *Creating Cool Interactive Web Sites CD-ROM.* This software is encrypted. You will be able to access all product features from the CD-ROM after registering and paying for WebServer through Quarterdeck. Or, check Quarterdeck's Web page at `www.quarterdeck.com` to see if a trialware version of WebServer is available for downloading. See the appendix for more details.

We go into considerable detail on the operation, setup, and configuration of this software for the Windows 95 platform in Chapter 5, so we are not going to discuss it further at this time. We next turn our attention to the last software package to be discussed in this chapter.

Windows HTTPD

Windows HTTPD is an HTTP/1.0-compatible server that enables you to make hypertext and other documents available to Web browsers. HTTPD stands for Hypertext Transfer Protocol Daemon. All this really means is that Windows HTTPD is a type of information server that uses the HTTP protocol.

Windows HTTPD is based on NCSA HTTPD for UNIX. The UNIX version was written first, and later Robert Denny ported it to Windows. Keep in mind that this server is for the 16-bit Windows 3.1*x* and will not work with either Windows 95 or Windows NT.

Windows HTTPD is one of the easiest servers to install, but we highly recommend that you read the included documentation in addition to our explanation that covers the next few pages. The documentation file is named OVERVIEW.HTM.

Before we discuss the installation and setup of Windows HTTPD, you need to look at some of the features of this particular server.

- Windows HTTPD was, and is, designed to be a small, fast server. The program has modest memory and resource requirements; therefore, it can serve documents with little or no slowdown. It doesn't require the installation of Win32s, and it uses the asynchronous network I/O that's recommended for Winsock 1.1.

- According to the documentation, this server is capable of supporting up to 16 simultaneous transactions. The program handles concurrent user requests in a true multithreaded mode, overlapping network I/O and external script execution. If more than 16 requests are made concurrently, any users after the first 16 receive a message that the server is too busy for the moment.
- A particularly nice feature of this program is that if you don't make any changes to the recommended installation, the server will run as soon as it's loaded onto your hard drive.
- Windows HTTPD is compliant with both the HTTP/1.0 and HTTP/0.9 protocols. As a result, the program can serve HTML and multimedia documents to Web browsers using either of these versions.
- With this program, your documents are served from a single unified directory structure. Should you need to move documents from one directory to another, or even to another server, Windows HTTPD enables you to point users to the new location with little difficulty, and, in most cases, the user will not even notice the change.
- Windows HTTPD also enables you to create HTML catalogs of your directories so that users can tell what's in them. The catalogs can either be part of a document, or you can have the server generate them on the fly. You also can add and configure icons mapped to the various file types, add descriptions of the various files, and even add README files for each directory listed.

- One of the best features of this program is this server's internal support of the Common Gateway Interface (CGI), Version 1.1, for the execution of scripts at the request of online users. We explain CGI fully in Chapter 10. For now, we just want you to understand that this server uses two methods to provide CGI support. The first method is by creating a DOS virtual machine and executing the CGI environment there. This DOS CGI interface can be reconfigured to allow the use of QBASIC, Perl, or other programming languages instead of a DOS shell. The second and more preferred method is by directly executing a Windows application that can handle the variables and files itself. The Windows CGI interface provided with the program works nicely with Visual Basic and is recommended for this type of CGI, or back-end, development.
- Windows HTTPD supports both the CGI script and the POST method of HTTP, so the server can handle HTML forms.
- The server program also provides a preinstalled facility that provides for the presentation of image maps on your Web site.
- Security is handled through the control of access to the various document trees on the server. Access is controlled both through host filtering and through user authentication.
- The program's internal diagnostic tracing option makes finding the causes of problems easier.
- Finally, user activity can be viewed through the use of an onscreen animated icon.

To use Windows HTTPD, we suggest that you use, at the very least, a 486/66 with 8MB RAM running Windows 3.1. You also need to have a TCP/IP package installed on your machine and either a network or SLIP/PPP connection. We also recommend that if you are going to use Visual Basic to provide script support (something we highly recommend), you need the required Visual Basic run-time libraries.

If you're using Visual Basic 2.0 for Windows for scripting, you need the run-time library file VBRUN200.DLL. If you're using Visual Basic 3.0 for Windows for scripting, you need the run-time library file VBRUN300.DLL. If you're using Visual Basic 4.0 for scripting, you need VBRUN400.DLL.

One last note before we get to the installation procedure: Windows HTTPD is not free. You can evaluate it for 30 days for free, but then commercial users have to pay a registration fee. The license agreement (in the file LEGAL.HTM) that is distributed with the software explains the evaluation period and the registration requirement. Educational and noncommercial users should read the license agreement carefully and contact Robert Denny about any questions.

You can download Windows HTTPD from the server's home page at

```
http://www.city.net/win-httpd/
```

You may want to check this location on a regular basis just to keep aware of what new features have been added to Windows HTTPD. The following steps describe how to get Windows HTTPD working on your system:

1. **Create a new directory on the hard drive where you want to store the program.**

   In our case, the directory is D:\HTTPD\.

2. **Uncompress the zipped distribution file.**

   If you use PKZIP to decompress the file, you must use Version 2.04g or a later version. The command we would type would be

   ```
   pkunzip d:\httpd\whttpd14.zip d:\httpd -d
   ```

   This directive preserves the directory structure by using the `-d` option of the PKUNZIP program. You need to make sure that you maintain the directory structure.

   Another way to unzip these files is to use a Windows-based utility, such as WinZip, as shown in Figure 3-6.

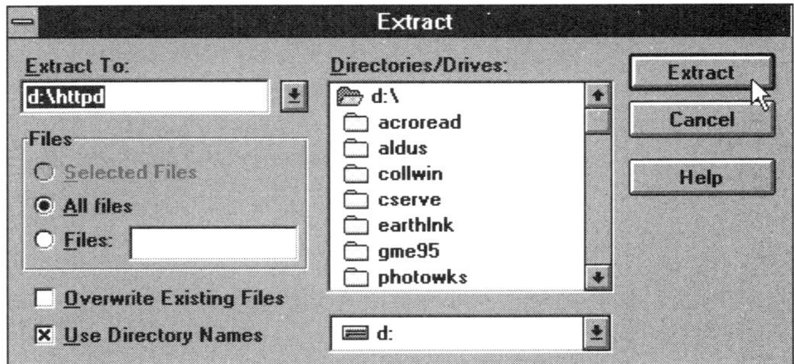

Figure 3-6: *Using WinZip to decompress the Windows HTTPD distribution file.*

Make sure that you select the Use Directory Names option in the Extract dialog box of WinZip.

3. **Edit the AUTOEXEC.BAT file and add a line to set the `TZ` variable to your time zone.**

   You need to add this line because the Common Log Format requires that times be recorded in Greenwich mean time (GMT). The `TZ` variable enables HTTPD to know what time zone your computer's local clock is set for.

   The line you add should read as follows:

   ```
   SET TZ=SSSNDDD
   ```

   The *`SSS`* is the three-letter abbreviation for your standard time zone. In our case, it is `CST` for central standard time. The *`N`* is the standard time offset of your time zone from GMT. In our case, it is `5`. Finally, *`DDD`* is the three-letter abbreviation for daylight savings time in your time zone. In our case, it is `CDT`. So our line reads as follows:

   ```
   SET TZ=CST5CDT
   ```

4. **If you installed the program in C:\HTTPD, reboot your computer to have the AUTOEXEC.BAT changes take effect.**

   The server will now run. If it doesn't, or if you didn't install the program to C:\HTTPD (as in our case), you may need to make a few other modifications. The first change that you may need to make concerns the server's use of back-end scripts in a DOS window. The demo page and many examples that are in the documentation may fail if there isn't enough environment space. Add the following line to the `[NonWindowApp]` section of your SYSTEM.INI file in the \WINDOWS\ subdirectory:

```
CommandEnvSize=8192
```

Another thing you need to make sure of, no matter where you install this server, is that you have the correct run-time libraries for Visual Basic and QuickBASIC, if you use them.

5. **Finally, create an icon for the server by selecting the Program Manager group window where you want the server to reside, choosing File⇨New, and then selecting Program Item and OK. Enter the location of and information about the server and click OK.**

   The icon for your server is now in place.

The next thing that you need to do is to make sure that you have Winsock software in place and operational. If you are using Windows for Workgroups 3.11, you already have this software; otherwise, you have to add a Winsock package to your system.

Make sure that the server and Winsock package are both running. The server will use the Domain Name System (DNS), if possible, to identify itself and the host names for users logging on. After you've double-clicked on the HTTPD icon, if DNS isn't available, HTTPD could take up to 30 seconds to initialize. After the server has minimized itself to an icon, the program is ready to go.

One of the most likely causes of errors at this point is that the time zone isn't set properly. If you have a problem, check the time zone setting first. If you don't have any problems, what you should see on your screen is something that looks similar to Figure 3-7.

If you have problems getting HTTPD to load correctly, you need to make modifications to the configuration files. There are four files that you may need to modify: the server configuration file, the server resource map, the global access configuration file, and the MIME types configuration file. We look at the server configuration file first.

Figure 3-7: Windows HTTPD is now ready to go.

The HTTPD server configuration file is called HTTPD.CNF and is in the \httpd\conf\ subdirectory. Listing 3-3 presents the unmodified version of HTTPD.CNF.

Listing 3-3: HTTPD.CNF

```
#------------------------------------------------------------
#
#   HTTPD.CNF
#
# Main server configuration for NCSA WinHttpd V1.3 (Windows)
#
# This is the main server configuration file. It is best to
# leave the directives in this file in the order they are in, or
# things may not go the way you'd like.
#
# Do NOT simply read the instructions in here without under↩
standing
# what they do, if you are unsure consult the online docs. You↩
have
# been warned.
#
```

```
# NOTE: path defaults are relative to the server's installation
#       directory (ServerRoot). Paths should be given in Unix
#       format (using '/').
#
# Bob Denny <rdenny@netcom.com> 13-Aug-94
#
#------------------------------------


# ServerRoot: The directory the server's config, error, and↵
log files
# are kept in. This should be specified on the startup↵
command line.
#
# Format: ServerRoot <path>
#
# ServerRoot c:/httpd/

# Port: The port the standalone listens to. 80 is the network↵
standard.
#
# Port 80

# Timeout: The timeout applied to all network operations. If↵
you are on
# a slow network, or are using a SLIP or PPP connection, you↵
might try
# increasing this to 60 sec.
#
# Format: Timeout nn    (seconds)
#
# Timeout 30

# ServerAdmin: Your address, where problems with the server↵
should be
# e-mailed.
#
# Format: ServerAdmin <email addr>
#
# ServerAdmin www-admin

# ErrorLog: The location of the error log file. If this does↵
not start
```

(continued)

Listing 3-3 *(continued)*:

```
# with / or a drive spec (recommended!), ServerRoot is➥
prepended to it.
#
# Format: ErrorLog <path/file>
#
# ErrorLog logs/error.log
# TransferLog: The location of the transfer log file. If this➥
does not
# start with / or a drive spec (recommended!), ServerRoot is➥
prepended to it.
#
# Format: TransferLog <path/file>
#
# TransferLog logs/access.log

# ServerName allows you to set a host name which is sent back➥
to clients for
# your server if it's different than the one the program would➥
get (i.e. use
# "www" instead of the host's real name). Make sure your DNS is➥
set up to
# alias the name to your system!
#
# Format: ServerName <domain name>
#
# no default
```

If you installed HTTPD on drive D, as we did, or on any drive other than the software-recommended drive C, you need to change certain locations in this configuration file. When editing this file, remember that all paths must be given in UNIX format. Unlike MS-DOS format, which uses the back slash (\ ) in directory paths, the UNIX format uses the forward slash (/). Another thing to keep in mind as you are editing this file is that all of the options are commented out at this point, so make sure that you delete the # sign in front of each line that you are changing.

- The first change is in the `ServerRoot` option. This option sets the directory where HTTPD can be found. When the server starts, it searches for the configuration file in the ServerRoot directory. Keep in mind that only one ServerRoot option is allowed in the server configuration file.

  The default for this option is `ServerRoot /user/local/etc/httpd`. The directory designated in this option should be the absolute path on your server. In our case, the path is `D:/httpd/`.

- The next change you may need to make is in the `Port` option. This option sets the port that the server will listen to for users. This number can be anywhere between 0 and 65536.

  Most ports that are below port 1024, with the exception of port 80, are reserved. Most servers run on port 80, which is the default for this option. There can be only one Port statement in the configuration file. We edited the file to remove the comment, so our Port option reads `Port 80`.

- You may want to change the `Timeout` option also. This option sets the maximum amount of time that the server will wait for a response from a user. The syntax for this option is `Timeout (`*`time`*`)`, where *`time`* is measured in seconds.

  The default for this option is `30`. This amount of time should be plenty in most cases, but if the server, or any users, are on extremely slow SLIP or PPP links, you may want to increase this amount. The configuration file can have only one `Timeout` directive. We edited our configuration file to remove the comment symbol, so our `Timeout` option reads `Timeout 30`.

- The `ServerAdmin` option enables you to specify your e-mail address, where complaints, comments, and server errors can be reported. The syntax for this option is `ServerAdmin` *`<email addr>`*.

  The configuration file can have only one `ServerAdmin` statement, but you do not have to include a `ServerAdmin` statement. If you do not place one in the file, nothing is assumed, and no address is listed.

- The `ErrorLog` statement sets the name of the file where the server will log the errors it encounters as it operates. These errors include user timeouts, scripts that fail to produce output, user configuration files that attempt to access things that they don't have permission to access, segmentation violations or bus errors that result from server bugs, and user authentication problems.

  The syntax for this statement is `ErrorLog` *`file`*, where *`file`* is the name of the file where the errors are logged. You can use either a full path name or a partial path name relative to what was declared in `ServerRoot`. The default for this option is `ErrorLog logs/error.log`. The configuration file can have only one ErrorLog statement. In our case, the statement reads `ErrorLog d:/httpd/logs/error.log`.

One final comment concerning the `ErrorLog` option: You can turn off error logging by typing **ErrorLog NUL:**. We do not support or recommend this option, however. Turning off error logging is a mistake that will come back to haunt you.

- The next directive that you may want to take a look at is the `TransferLog` statement. This directive tells the server where to record user accesses. The file where user accesses are recorded, known most often as the access log, conforms to the Common Log Format, which is a format used and produced by many other servers.

The syntax of this statement is `TransferLog` *`file`*, where *`file`* is the filename where transfers will be logged. This filename can either be a full path name or a partial one relative to ServerRoot.

The default for this statement is `TransferLog logs/access.log`. The configuration file can have only one TransferLog statement.

We modified this statement for our server to read `TransferLog d:/httpd/logs/access.log`.

- The final option that you may want to change in this configuration file is the `ServerName` option. This statement sets the host name that the server will return when creating redirection URLs.

  The syntax for this statement is `ServerName` *`NAME`* where *`NAME`* is the full host name that you want returned as the server address. The configuration file can have only one `ServerName` directive. If you don't specify a `ServerName`, the server will retrieve it through system calls.

  We modified our ServerName statement to read `ServerName www.VREvolution.com`.

The next file to examine is the server resource map configuration file. This file is in the \conf\ subdirectory. In our case, the file is at d:\httpd\conf\srm.cnf. Listing 3-4 shows what the unmodified file looks like.

Listing 3-4: SRM.CNF

```
#------------------------------------------------------------
#
#   SRM.CNF
#
# Server resource configuration for NCSA WinHttpd V1.3 (Windows)
#
# The settings in this file control the document layout and↵
name specs
# that your server makes visible to users. The values in the↵
comments
# are the defaults built into the server.
#
# NOTE: path defaults are relative to the server's installation
#       directory (ServerRoot). Paths should be given in Unix
#       format (using '/').
#
# Bob Denny <rdenny@netcom.com> 13-Aug-94
#
#------------------------------------------------------------
#
```

```
# DocumentRoot: The directory out of which you will serve your
# documents. By default, all requests are taken from this⮐
directory, but
# aliases may be used to point to other locations.
#
# DocumentRoot c:/httpd/htdocs

# DirectoryIndex: Name of the file to use as a pre-written HTML
# directory index. This document, if present, will be opened⮐
when the
# server receives a request containing a URL for the⮐
directory, instead
# of generating a directory index.
#
# DirectoryIndex index.htm

# AccessFileName: The name of the file to look for in each⮐
directory
# for access control information. This file should have a name⮐
which is
# blocked from appearing in server-generated indexes!
#
# AccessFileName #haccess.ctl

# ========================
# Aliasing and Redirection
# ========================
#
# Redirect allows you to tell clients about documents which⮐
used to exist in
# your server's namespace, but do not anymore. This allows⮐
you to tell the
# clients where to look for the relocated document.
#
# Format: Redirect fakename url
#

# Aliases: Add here as many aliases as you need, up to 20. One⮐
useful
# alias to have is one for the path to the icons used for the⮐
server-
# generated directory indexes. The paths given below in the⮐
AddIcon
# statements are relative.
#
```

(continued)

Listing 3-4 (continued):

```
# Format: Alias fakename realname
#
Alias /icons/ c:/httpd/icons/

# ScriptAlias: This controls which directories contain DOS⮐
server
#               scripts.
#
# Format: ScriptAlias fakename realname
#
ScriptAlias /cgi-dos/ c:/httpd/cgi-dos/
ScriptAlias /cgi-bin/ c:/httpd/cgi-dos/

# WinScriptAlias: This controls which directories contain Windows
#               server scripts.
#
# Format: WinScriptAlias fakename realname
#
WinScriptAlias /cgi-win/ c:/httpd/cgi-win/

# =========================
# MIME Content Type Control
# =========================
#
# DefaultType is the default MIME type for documents which the⮐
server
# cannot find the type of from filename extensions.
#
# DefaultType text/html
DefaultType text/plain

# AddType allows you to tweak MIME.TYP without actually editing⮐
it, or to
# make certain files to be certain types.
#
# Format: AddType type/subtype ext1
#

# ReadmeName is the name of the README file the server will look⮐
for by
# default.  The server will first look for name.htm, include it⮐
if found,
# and it will then look for name.txt and include it as⮐
plaintext if found.
```

```
# NOTE: Do not include an explicit extension, it is an error.
#
# Format: ReadmeName name
#
ReadmeName #readme

# ===========================
# AUTOMATIC DIRECTORY INDEXING
# ============================
#
# The server generates a directory index if there is no file➥
in the
# directory whose name matches DirectoryIndex.
#
# FancyIndexing: Whether you want fancy directory indexing or➥
standard
#
# FancyIndexing on

# IconsAreLinks: Whether the icons in a fancy index are links as
# well as the file names.
#
# IconsAreLinks off

# AddIcon tells the server which icon to show for different➥
files or filename
# extensions. In preparation for the upcoming Chicago version,
you should
# include explicit 3 character truncations for 4-character➥
endings. Don't
# rely on the DOS underpinnings to silently truncate for you.
#
AddIcon /icons/text.gif     .html   .htm    .txt    .ini
AddIcon /icons/image.gif    .gif    .jpg    .jpe    .jpeg➥
.xbm    .tiff   .tif    .pic    .pict   .bmp
AddIcon /icons/sound.gif    .au     .wav    .snd
AddIcon /icons/movie.gif    .mpg    .mpe    .mpeg
AddIcon /icons/binary.gif   .bin    .exe    .bat    .dll
AddIcon /icons/back.gif     ..
AddIcon /icons/menu.gif     ^^DIRECTORY^^
AddIcon /icons/dblank.gif       ^^BLANKICON^^

# DefaultIcon is which icon to show for files which do not have➥
an icon
```

(continued)

Listing 3-4 *(continued)*:

```
# explicitly set.
#
DefaultIcon /icons/unknown.gif

# AddDescription allows you to place a short description after⮐
a file in
# server-generated indexes. A better place for these are in⮐
individual
# "#haccess.ctl" files in individual directories.
#
# Format: AddDescription "description" filename
#

# IndexIgnore is a set of filenames which directory indexing⮐
should ignore
# Here, I've disabled display of our readme and access control⮐
files,
# plus anything that starts with a "~", which I use for⮐
annotation HTML
# documents. I also have disabled some common editor backup⮐
file names.
# Match is on file NAME.EXT only, and the usual * and ?⮐
meta-chars apply.
#
# WARNING: Be sure to set an ignore for your access control⮐
file(s)!!
#
# Format: IndexIgnore name1 name2...
#
IndexIgnore  ~* *.bak *.{* #readme.htm #haccess.ctl
### END ###
```

Again, remember that you need to use the UNIX-style forward slashes instead of the MS-style back slashes in the path names. We walk through each of the statements in this file and describe what changes need to be made for the software to operate now. Don't forget that all of the statements in the file listing have been commented out and that the # sign needs to be removed to make your changes to these statements take effect.

- The first statement that you need to check is the `DocumentRoot` directive. This statement determines the directory from which the server will serve files to users. This statement affects how users will access files on the server.

  The syntax for this statement is `DocumentRoot DIR`. `DIR` represents the absolute path to the directory where you have stored your Web documents. Remember that the configuration file can have only one `DocumentRoot` directive.

  If you don't enter anything for this directive, the default is used, `DocumentRoot /user/local/etc/httpd/htdocs`.

  We changed this statement to read `DocumentRoot d:/httpd/htdocs`.

- The next statement to be considered is the `DirectoryIndex` directive. This directive sets the file that the server looks for when a user requests a directory. It can return a prewritten index, or it can generate an index from the file system.

  The syntax for this statement is written as `DirectoryIndex` *`file`* where *`file`* is the filename of the given prewritten index file. If you don't specify this statement, the server assumes the default, `DirectoryIndex index.htm`. The configuration file can have only one `DirectoryIndex` statement.

- The `AccessFileName` statement sets the name of the file the server will look for to find access control files. The default access control file begins with a # sign to hide these files from directory indexes.

  The syntax for this statement is `AccessFileName` *`file`* where *`file`* is a filename. If you don't specify this statement, the default, `AccessFileName #haccess.ctl`, is assumed. The configuration file can have only one `AccessFileName` directive.

You need to make some other modifications to this file if you changed the hard drive that the file was to be installed on. Because we installed the server on drive D instead of on drive C, we made the following changes:

- The `Alias` directive has one entry currently. We changed this entry from `Alias /icons/ c:/httpd/icons/` to `Alias /icons/ d:/httpd/icons/`.

- The two entries under `ScriptAlias` need to be changed as follows: Change `ScriptAlias /cgi-dos/ c:/httpd/cgi-dos/` to `ScriptAlias /cgi-dos d:/httpd/cgi-dos` and `ScriptAlias /cgi-bin/ c:/httpd/cgi-bin` to `ScriptAlias /cgi-bin d:/httpd.cgi-bin`.

- The next change needs to be made to the `WinScriptAlias` directive. Here `WinScriptAlias /cgi-win/ c:/httpd/cgi-win/` needs to be changed to `WinScriptAlias /cgi-win/ d:/httpd/cgi-win/`.

The next file that you need to look at is the Global Access Configuration file, \httpd\conf\access.cnf. Listing 3-5 is the unmodified file.

Listing 3-5: ACCESS.CNF

```
#------------------------------------------
#
#  ACCESS.CNF
#
# Global access configuration for NCSA WinHttpd V1.3 (Windows)
#
# This is server global access configuration file. It is best to
# leave the directives in this file in the order they are in, or
# things may not go the way you'd like.
#
# Do NOT simply read the instructions in here without⮐
understanding
# what they do, if you are unsure consult the online docs.⮐
You have
# been warned.
#
# Bob Denny <rdenny@netcom.com> 13-Aug-94
#
#------------------------------------------
#
# The following access configuration establishes unrestricted⮐
access
# to the server's document tree. There is no default access⮐
config, so
# _something_ must be present and correct for the server to⮐
operate.
#
# This should be changed to whatever you set ServerRoot to.
#
<Directory c:/httpd>
Options Indexes
</Directory>

# This should be changed to whatever you set DocumentRoot to.

<Directory c:/httpd/htdocs>

# This may also be "None", "All", or "Indexes"
```

```
Options Indexes

# This controls which options the #HACCESS.CTL files in
directories can
# override. Can also be "None", or any combination of
"Options", "FileInfo",
# "AuthConfig", and "Limit"

AllowOverride All

# Controls who can get stuff from this server.

<Limit GET>
order allow,deny
allow from all
</Limit>

</Directory>

# You may place any other directories you wish to have access
# information for after this one.
```

The following changes need to be made to the ACCESS.CNF file:

- Change `<Directory c:/httpd>` to the drive where you stored the server software. We changed it to `<Directory d:/httpd>`.
- We also changed `<Directory c:/httpd/htdocs>` to `<Directory d:/httpd/htdocs>`.

The final file that we want to discuss, but make no changes to, is the MIME Types Configuration file. The MIME types configuration file is in \httpd\conf\ as MIME.TYP. We've provided the contents of this file in Listing 3-6.

Listing 3-6: MIME.TYP

```
# Edited by Bob Denny <rdenny@netcom.com>
# 07-May-1994
# Per comments received from Kevin Altis
#
application/activemessage
application/andrew-inset
application/applefile
application/atomicmail
```

(continued)

Listing 3-6 *(continued)*:

```
application/dca-rft
application/dec-dx
application/mac-binhex40
application/macwriteii
application/msword              doc
application/news-message-id
application/news-transmission
application/octet-stream        bin
application/oda                 oda
application/pdf                 pdf
application/postscript          ai eps ps
application/remote-printing
application/rtf                 rtf
application/slate
application/mif                 mif
application/wita
application/wordperfect5.1
application/x-csh               csh
application/x-dvi               dvi
application/x-hdf               hdf
application/x-latex             latex ltx
application/x-netcdf            nc cdf
application/x-sh                sh
application/x-tcl               tcl
application/x-tex               tex
application/x-texinfo           texinfo texi txi
application/x-troff             t tr roff
application/x-troff-man         man
application/x-troff-me          me
application/x-troff-ms          ms
application/x-wais-source       src
application/zip                 zip
application/x-bcpio             bcpio
application/x-cpio              cpio
application/x-gtar              gtar
application/x-shar              shar
application/x-sv4cpio           sv4cpio
application/x-sv4crc            sv4crc
application/tar                 tar
application/x-ustar             ustar
#
```

```
# Added for PC stuff
#
application/x-lzh               lzh
application/x-gzip              gz
#
audio/basic                     au snd
audio/x-aiff                    aif aiff aifc
audio/wav                       wav
image/gif                       gif
image/ief                       ief
image/jpeg                      jpeg jpg jpe
image/tiff                      tiff tif
image/x-cmu-raster              ras
image/x-portable-anymap         pnm
image/x-portable-bitmap         pbm
image/x-portable-graymap        pgm
image/x-portable-pixmap         ppm
image/x-rgb                     rgb
image/x-xbitmap                 xbm
image/x-xpixmap                 xpm
image/x-xwindowdump             xwd
message/external-body
message/news
message/partial
message/rfc822
multipart/alternative
multipart/appledouble
multipart/digest
multipart/mixed
multipart/parallel
text/html                       html htm
text/plain                      txt
text/richtext                   rtx
text/tab-separated-values       tsv
text/x-setext                   etx
video/mpeg                      mpeg mpg mpe
video/quicktime                 qt mov
video/msvideo                   avi
video/x-sgi-movie               movie
```

Don't touch the contents of this file at this time unless you know what you are doing.

Run the software and then use your Web browser to open INDEX.HTM. If you've made all the proper changes to the configuration files, or you installed to drive C and accepted all the defaults, you should see something similar to Figure 3-8 on your screen.

Figure 3-8: Windows HTTPD's INDEX.HTM.

In Chapter 6, where we cover writing your own HTML pages, you learn how to modify Windows HTTPD's default pages, as well as any other Web page.

We have finished the brief overview of the 16-bit Windows server applications. We next turn our attention to the 32-bit Windows server applications.

Server software for Windows 95 and Windows NT

The 32-bit Windows 95 and NT applications include Alibaba, FolkWeb, HTTPS, Internet Office Web Server, SerWeb, SPRY Safety Web Server, and W4-Server, WebServer, and WebSite. We examine them in alphabetical order, some more extensively than others. The reason some get more explanation than others is that they require more extensive coverage.

Alibaba

Written by Michael Koffer, Alibaba is a server that is compatible with Windows NT and Windows 95. Some of the many features that the software offers are

- Multithread capabilities
- HTTP 1.0 protocol
- A variety of CGI compatibilities

- GET, POST, and HEAD commands
- A configurable network port
- Aliases
- Directory ignores
- Definable MIME types
- Access logging
- Error logging with selectable levels
- Image maps
- HTTP access control

See the software's documentation for a full list of features. Alibaba is available in both Windows NT and Windows 95 versions. The file for the Windows NT version is called ALINT.ZIP, and the file for the Windows 95 version is called ALI95.ZIP. Make sure that you have the most up-to-date version. As we write this chapter, the current version is 1.2.

You can download either of these applications, as well as find out more about this server software, at

```
http://alibaba.austria.eu.net/
```

Figure 3-9 shows the Alibaba home page.

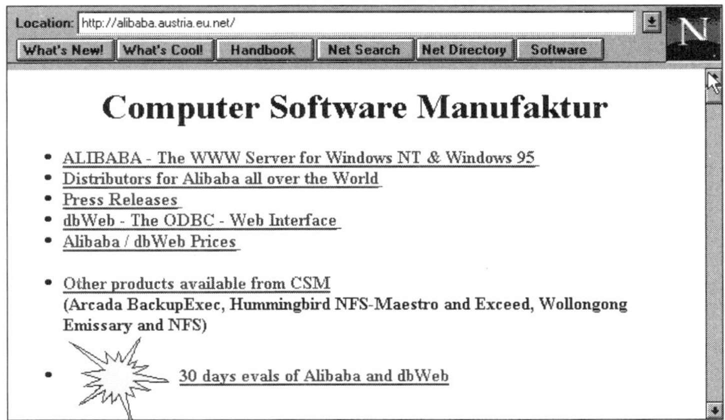

Figure 3-9: More information about Alibaba is available at its home page.

Installation is relatively simple.

1. **Download the zipped file for the version you want and move it into a temporary subdirectory.**

   We moved it to our \TEMP\ subdirectory.

2. **Decompress the zipped file.**

3. **Run SETUP.EXE.**

   SETUP.EXE installs all the necessary files to your hard drive.

One change that you may need to make with the installation after SETUP is complete is the addition of two lines to the SYSTEM.INI file. These two lines are

```
[NonWindowsApp]
CommandEnvSize=8192
```

If your SYSTEM.INI file already has a `[NonWindowsApp]` section, as did ours, just add the second line. We used Notepad to make this change.

After the software is installed, you need to make some configuration changes, depending on your hardware. Although you can edit these configuration files with any text editor, such as Notepad or Wordpad, we recommend that you use Alibaba's control panel application. Using these dialog boxes is easier than working directly with the configuration files in Notepad.

You click on buttons in the Alibaba–Settings window to go to dialog boxes where you can change the settings in the configuration files. After you make the changes you want, you click on OK to return to the Alibaba–Settings window.

We next walk you through these options and discuss them as we go along.

- **Server Startup.** Click on the Server Startup button in the control panel application to see a screen that's similar to Figure 3-10.

  You can start Alibaba as a system service, which is checked by default, and as a console application, which can be useful under Windows 95. Make sure that both boxes are checked and click on OK.

- **Network Settings.** The default port for the server is Port 80 (see Figure 3-11), but you can use other ports. Keep in mind that several ports are reserved. Your best bet is to leave your server on Port 80 or move it to Port 8080, the experimental port.

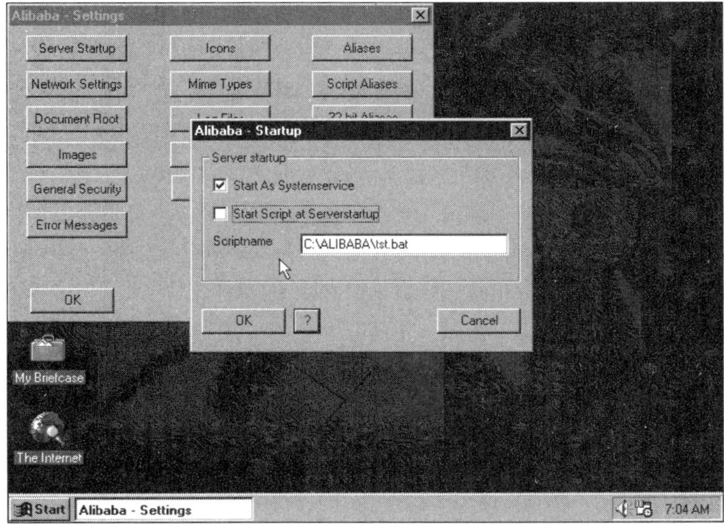

Figure 3-10: The Alibaba Startup option window.

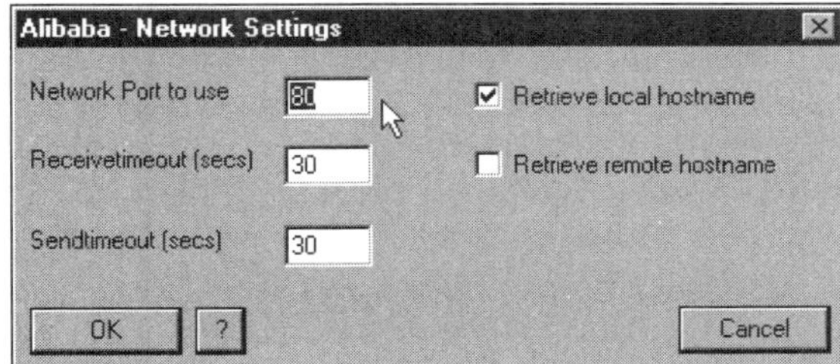

Figure 3-11: In the Network Settings window, you set the Port number that your server will use.

In this window, you also can change the Send and Receive timeout lengths, and you can determine whether the server will retrieve the local and remote host names. Choose the options you want and click on OK. We recommend that you accept the defaults until you know more about how to use this server.

- **Document Root.** If you have installed Alibaba on any drive other than drive C, you need to modify the Document Root (see Figure 3-12). You also can change the name of the Index Filename here if you want to. In the Server Administrator text box, you enter the name that you want to give yourself. (We entered `webmaster@VREvolution`.)

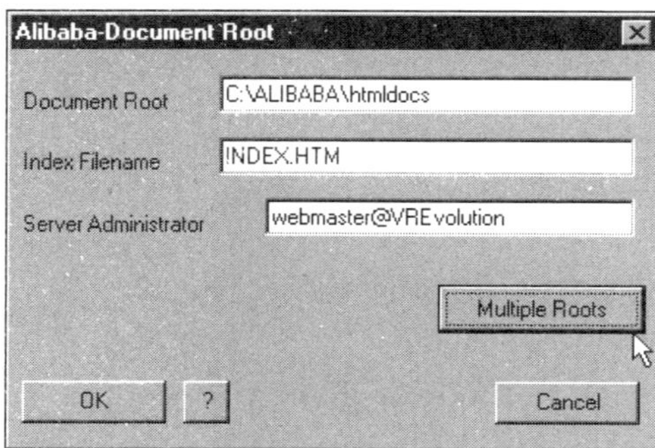

Figure 3-12: In the Document Root window, one of the things that you determine is your name as the Server Administrator.

Finally, you can click on the Multiple Roots button to see a window where you can change the IP address listed in the window to your server's IP address. You then click on OK to return to the Document Root window and then click on OK again to exit this window and return to the control panel application.

- **Images.** If you changed the hard drive where you loaded Alibaba from the initial defaults presented by the installation, you need to modify the Images option window, which is shown in Figure 3-13, to reflect the change in the drive. Otherwise, you can leave these options alone. This window simply tells the server what directory to look in for image maps. We go into image maps in more detail in Chapter 11.

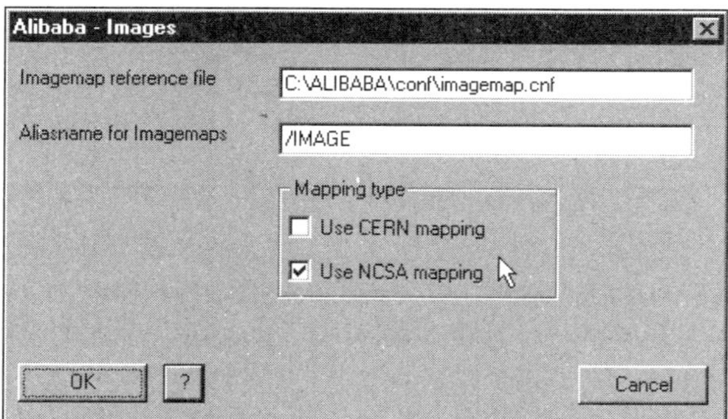

Figure 3-13: The Images window enables you to determine whether you want to use CERN or NCSA mapping for image maps on your server.

Also, you need to determine whether you want to use CERN mapping or NCSA mapping for your image maps. Keep in mind that Alibaba allows up to 1,000 image maps per server.

- **General Security.** You click on the General Security button to go to the Access window (see Figure 3-14). We recommend that you not change the settings in this window until you get used to using Alibaba.

  Two buttons, the Specified Clients and Ignore Files at DirBrowse buttons, enable you to specify clients who are exempt from certain security features and to specify files that are invisible to the directory commands. Make any modifications that you want and then click on OK.

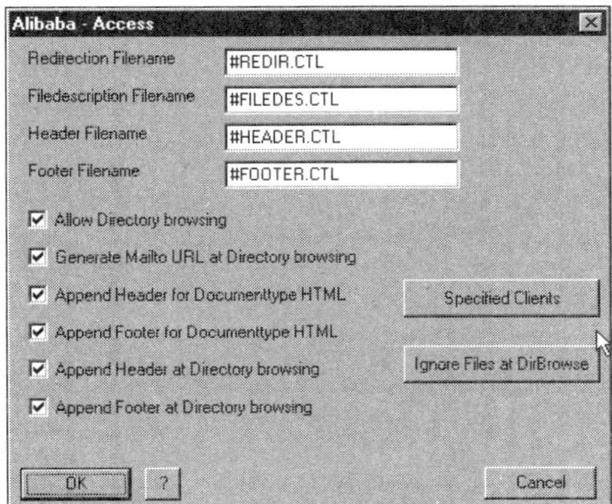

Figure 3-14: Security for your server is maintained in the Access window.

- **Error Messages.** The ERROR MESSAGES window (see Figure 3-15) is one of the most convenient, yet potentially dangerous, features of this server. You can use it to modify the error message that will be displayed to users if they experience a problem. We recommend that you leave the error messages as they are until you've had more experience with the server software.

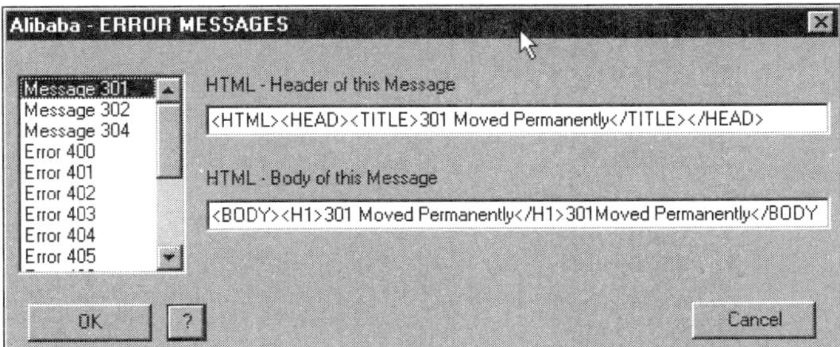

Figure 3-15: You can use the ERROR MESSAGES options window to change the error messages that are displayed to your users.

- **Icons.** In the ICONS window (see Figure 3-16), you can add or delete the icons that symbolize the file types in directory listings.

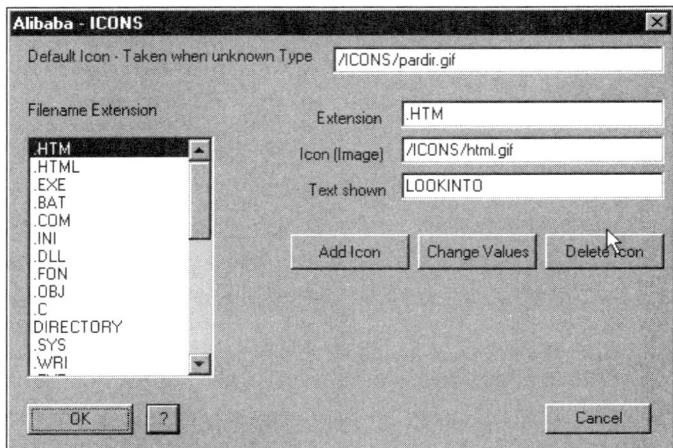

Figure 3-16: *The ICONS window controls how various file types are displayed in server directory listings.*

Keep in mind that you can have, at most, 199 icon definitions and that you need to use continuous numbering.

- **MIME Types.** In the MIMETYPES window (see Figure 3-17) you define MIME types.

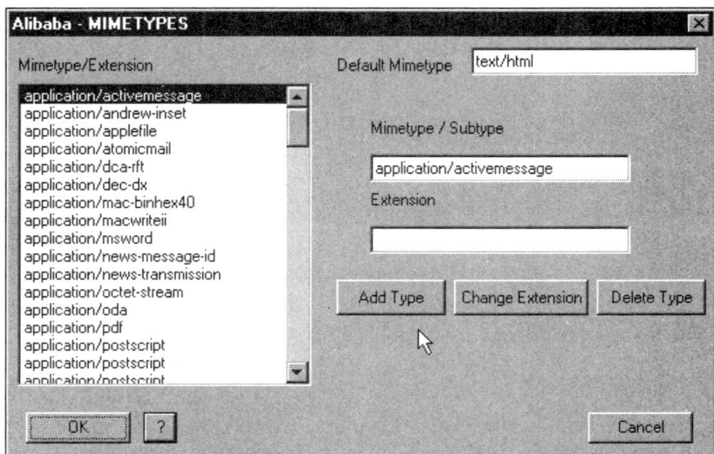

Figure 3-17: *Depending on how interactive you want your site to become, you may need to modify or add MIMETYPES in this window.*

If you decide to add many of the capabilities that we discuss later in this book to your server, you need to modify this options window at that point.

- **Log Files.** In the LOGFILES window (see in Figure 3-18), both Use Access Logs and Use Error Logs are checked by default. Don't change them unless you want to have problems with the server. Also make sure that the paths to both the access logs and the error logs are correct. For the Error Level of Log setting, we recommend that you use the default, which is 3.

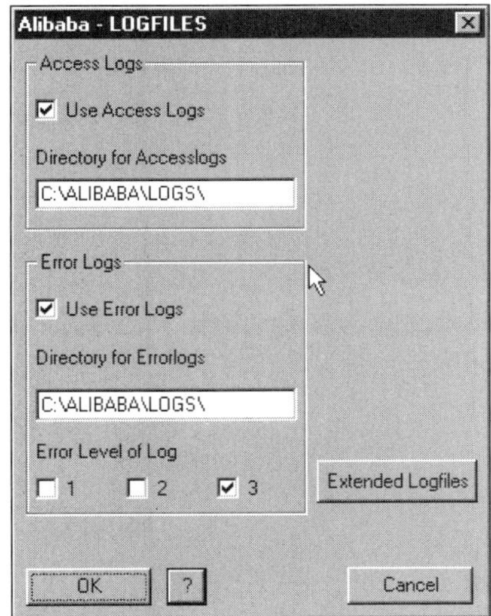

Figure 3-18: You need to make sure that the LOGFILES options are correct.

Click the Extended Logfiles button in the lower right of the window to see the EXTENDED LOGS window, as shown in Figure 3-19. The default for Use Extended Logs is unchecked, but we recommend that you check this box, after you've made sure that the path for the log is correct, to provide yourself with the extended logs option. Then, if you have any problems later with your server, you can check the logs to find out what those errors and problems were.

Click on OK to return to the LOGFILES option window, and then click on OK again to return to the control panel application.

- **SSI.** Clicking on this button on the control panel brings up the Server Side Includes option window, as shown in Figure 3-20.

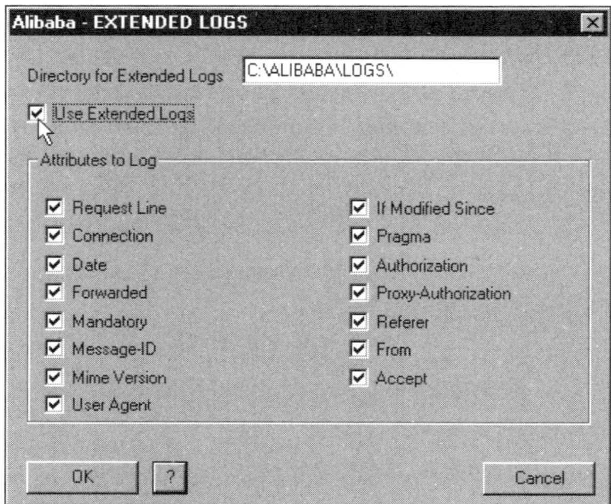

Figure 3-19: *We highly recommend the use of the Use Extended Logs option with Alibaba.*

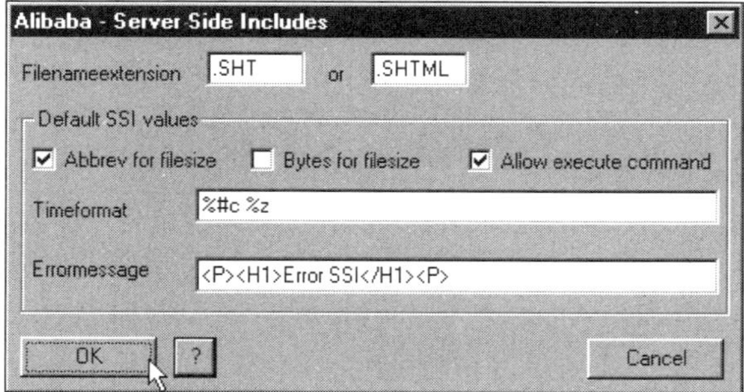

Figure 3-20: *Alibaba's control panel enables you to modify how your server will handle Server Side Includes.*

- **Dir Index.** In the Directoryindex window (see Figure 3-21), you can modify the way your server directories are presented to the user by your server.
- **Aliases.** The ALIASNAMES options window (see Figure 3-22) enables you to define aliases for directory paths. Don't forget to modify the path statements of these aliases if you installed Alibaba on a drive other than drive C.

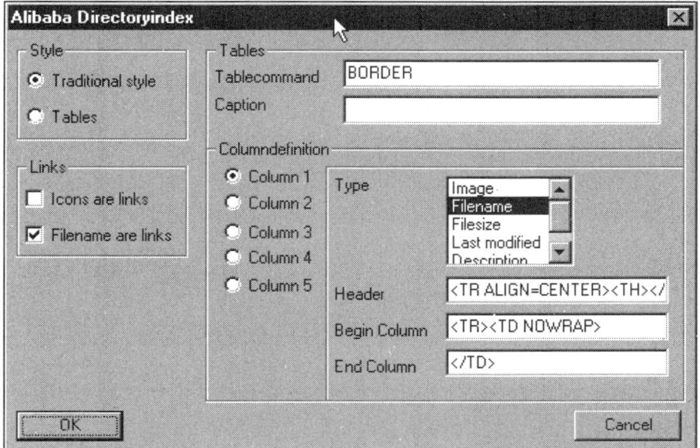

Figure 3-21: The Directoryindex option window enables you to modify how the server presents directories to your users.

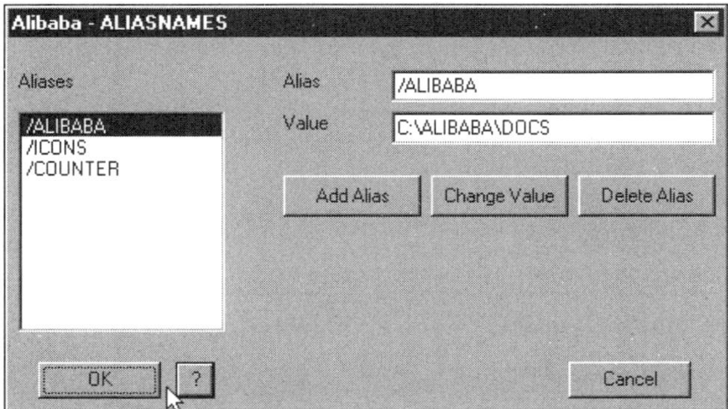

Figure 3-22: The ALIASNAMES options window.

- **Script Aliases, 32-bit Aliases, WinScript Aliases, and CGIDLL Aliases.** The SCRIPTALIAS options window (see Figure 3-23), the 32bit ScriptAlias options window (see Figure 3-24), the WINCGI options window (see Figure 3-25), and the DLL Alias options window (see Figure 3-26) are all much the same as the ALIASNAMES options window.

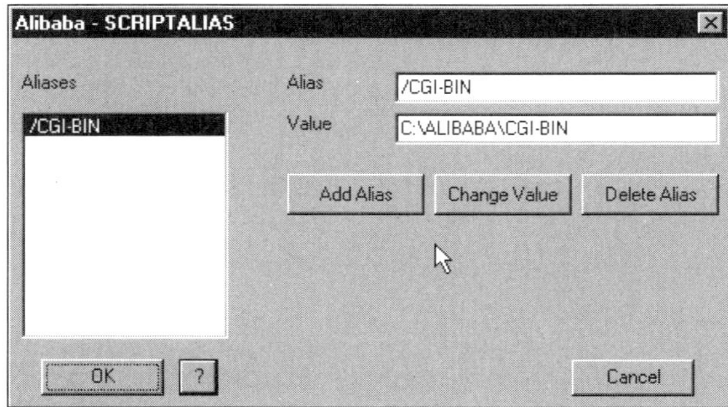

Figure 3-23: The SCRIPTALIAS options window.

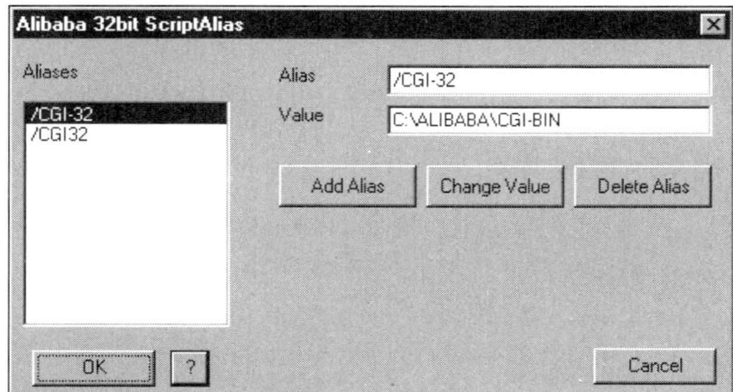

Figure 3-24: The 32bit ScriptAlias options window.

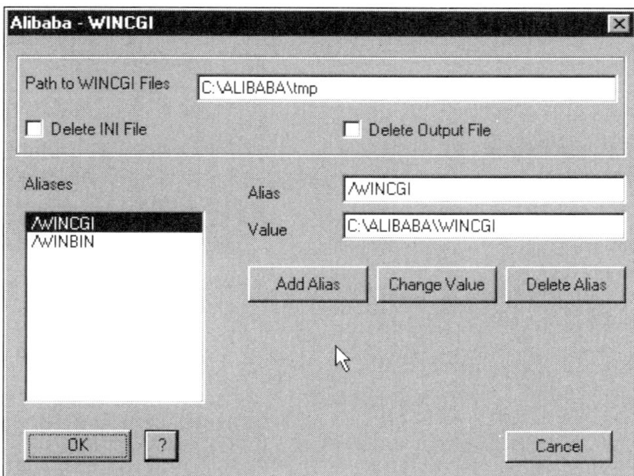

Figure 3-25: The WINCGI options window.

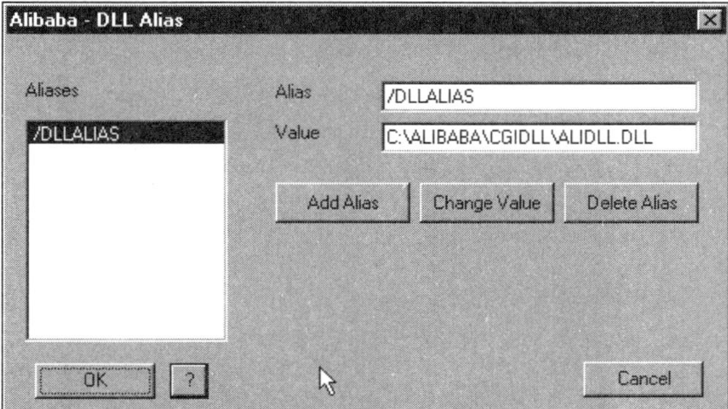

Figure 3-26: The DLL Alias options window.

Again, don't forget to modify the path statements of these script aliases if you installed Alibaba on any drive other than drive C.

Alibaba provides two methods for maintaining and controlling user access on the server. The first method is through the use of the well-known #HACCESS.CTL files. You need to use your favorite text editor to edit these files. This method is tedious and prone to mistakes for beginners, so we don't recommend it.

The second method is by using Alibaba's Authorization Tool (see Figure 3-27). Double-clicking on any of the entries brings up options. For example, double-clicking on the first entry brings up a window that is similar to Figure 3-28.

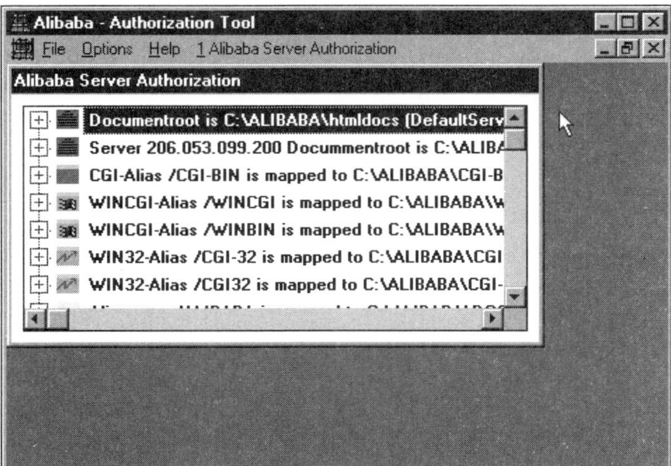

Figure 3-27: Use Alibaba's Authorization Tool to maintain and control user access on your server.

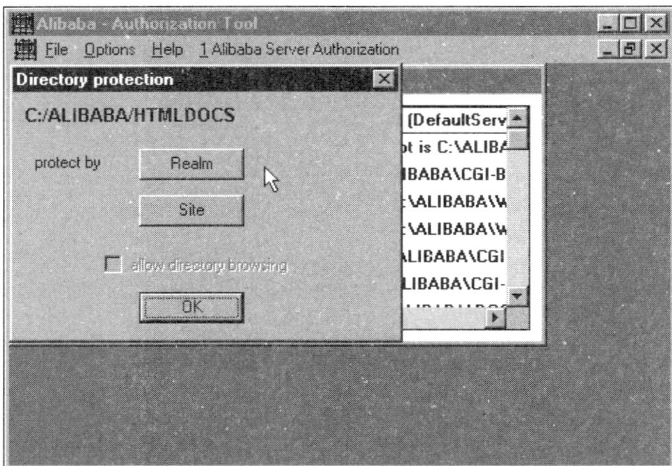

Figure 3-28: Each directory can be protected by realm or by site.

Each of the entries represents a variety of subdirectories on the server. You can protect these subdirectories by realm (see Figure 3-29) or by site (see Figure 3-30). If you protect the subdirectories by realm, then all of the subdirectories included in an entry have the same access control. If you protect them by site, you determine the level of access control separately for each subdirectory.

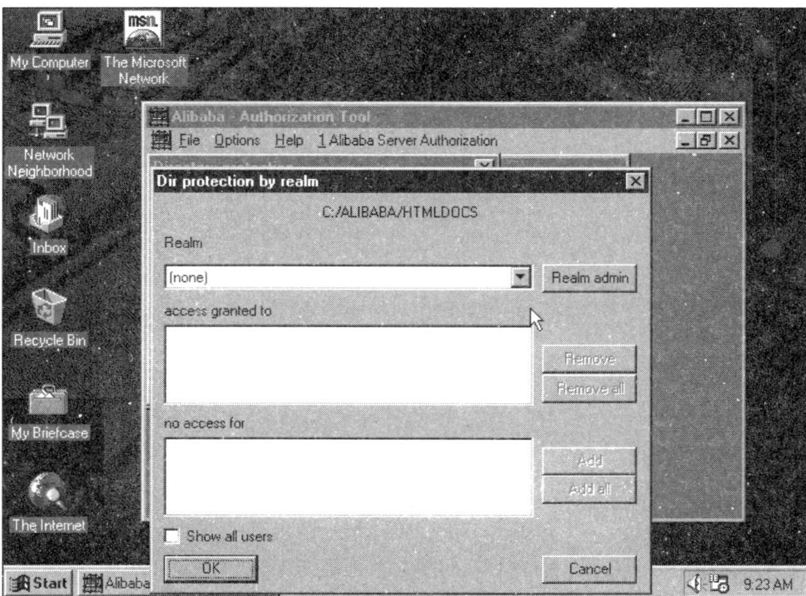

Figure 3-29: You can choose to have the directories protected by realm.

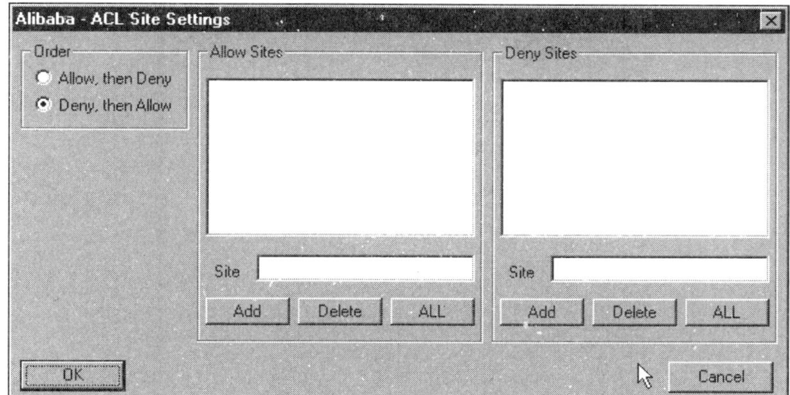

Figure 3-30: Your other option is to protect the directories using the ACL Site Settings window.

The Alibaba Authorization Tool also enables you to view files that may be kept in these directories to determine what kinds of access may be needed for these files.

INDEX.HTM, your home page on Alibaba's Web server software, is under the first entry in Figure 3-31. Double-clicking on INDEX.HTM, or any other file, in Alibaba's Authorization Tool, launches that file using the default associations on your computer. In our case, the default association for .HTM files is Microsoft Internet Explorer, as shown in Figure 3-32.

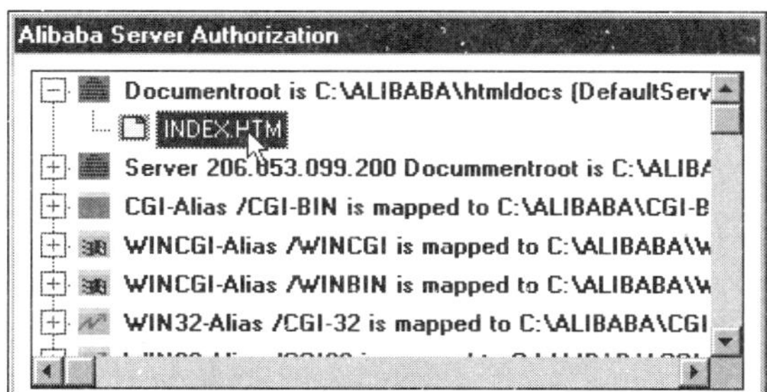

Figure 3-31: INDEX.HTM is found under C:\ALIBABA\htmldocs.

Figure 3-32: *Alibaba's INDEX.HTM as displayed in Microsoft Internet Explorer.*

Alibaba also provides an interesting Statistic Tool for your site. You can set the properties for your statistic reports using the Properties window.

Alibaba works well in conjunction with either Visual Basic 3.0 or Visual Basic 4.0. Alibaba includes some sample applications in both versions of Visual Basic.

FolkWeb WWW Server

FolkWeb WWW Server is a shareware server written by Larion and Irina Vasilkovsky and made available by ILAR Concepts of San Francisco, California. This full-featured server is fully compatible with HTTP 1.0 protocol and is designed to take advantage of the multithread capabilities and CGI that are available in both Windows 95 and Windows NT.

FolkWeb WWW Server is shareware, so you need to pay for it if you decide to continue using it.

The minimum hardware and software requirements include

- An IBM-compatible 486 or higher CPU
- A minimum of 8MB of RAM
- Windows 95 or Windows NT 3.51 or higher
- A minimum of 3MB of free hard drive space
- TCP/IP drivers for Windows 95 or Windows NT 3.51 or higher

- A minimum of a VGA graphics adapter and monitor
- A mouse or other pointing device supported by your Windows operating system

FolkWeb server provides the following features:

- Full Win32 multithreading capabilities
- Support for GET, HEAD, and POST request methods
- Built-in image-map support
- Built-in database connectivity
- Access authentication for users and groups
- Full Windows CGI Version 1.1 protocol support
- Aliasing
- Access logging
- Error logging
- MIME Type mapping

For a full discussion of the features available with this server, please refer to the software's documentation.

The installation of FolkWeb is relatively simple.

1. **Using Explorer, open up the subdirectory where FULL95.ZIP resides.**
2. **Decompress FULL95.ZIP into a temporary directory and then double-click on the SETUP.EXE file.**

   The first dialog box that you see looks similar to Figure 3-33.

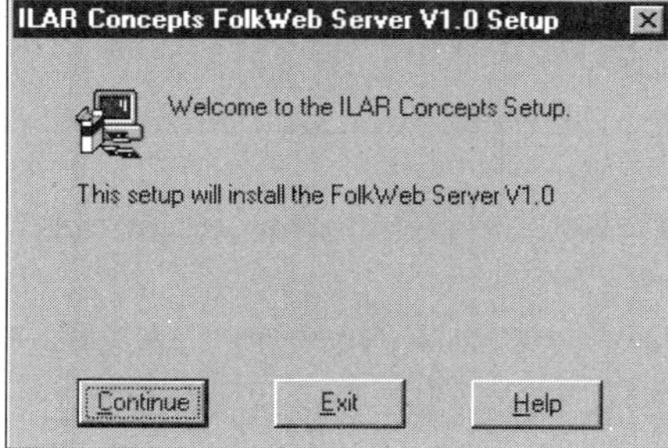

Figure 3-33: FolkWeb Server Setup is a relatively easy process.

3. **Click on the Continue button to be prompted for the server network name, as in Figure 3-34.**

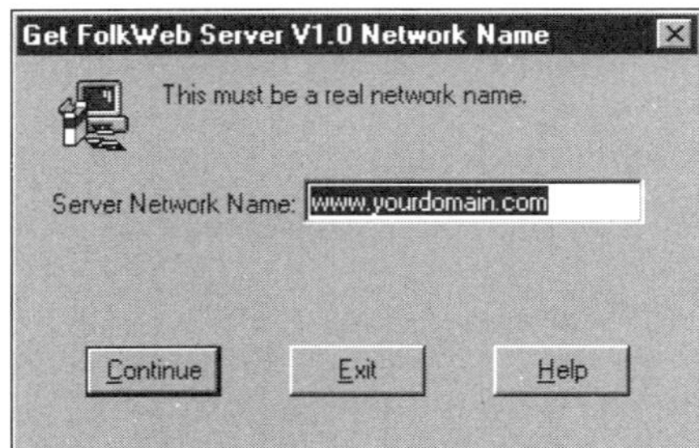

Figure 3-34: *Enter your server network name as prompted.*

4. **Enter the domain name for your server network name and click on the Continue button.**

   The setup program asks for your e-mail address.

5. **Enter your e-mail address and click on the Continue button.**

   You see a screen that looks similar to Figure 3-35.

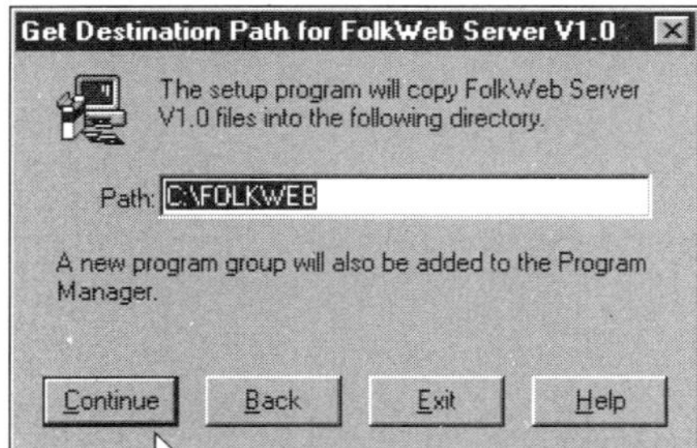

Figure 3-35: *Install FolkWeb to the drive and directory where you want to store it.*

6. **Designate the drive and directory where you want to install FolkWeb and click on Continue.**

   You will probably want to accept the default drive and directory, but you can change them if you need or want to.

   The necessary files for FolkWeb to operate are installed to the drive and directory that you designate, and you soon have something similar to Figure 3-36 on your screen.

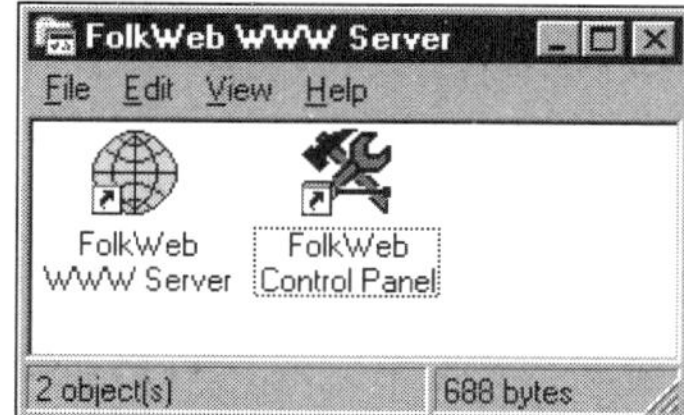

Figure 3-36: *The FolkWeb WWW Server program group.*

7. **Double-click on the FolkWeb Control Panel.**

   This tool enables you to easily maintain the server. You can change the settings in eight different categories: Server, Network, Logging, Mapping, Access, Groups, Users, and Directory.

   Figure 3-37 shows the modifications that you can make to the Server tab area. You can change the server directory, the resource directory, your e-mail address, your default resource, and the buffer length.

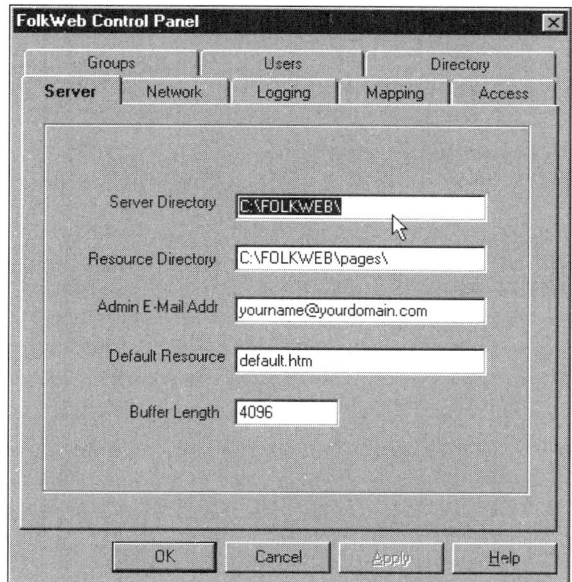

Figure 3-37: *You can make modifications to the Server page.*

Figure 3-38 shows the Groups page, where you can create new groups, remove groups from the group lists, add users to groups, and remove users from groups.

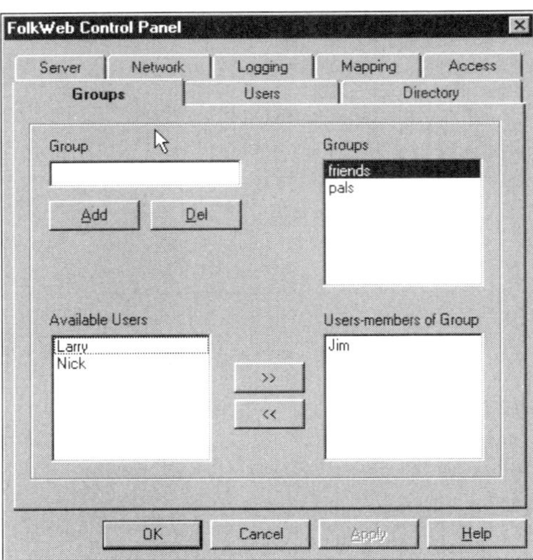

Figure 3-38: You can use this page to add and delete groups and users.

Figure 3-39 shows the Network page, where you can change the Server Network name, TCP service port, the timeout interval, and the maximum number of timeouts the server will accept and allow.

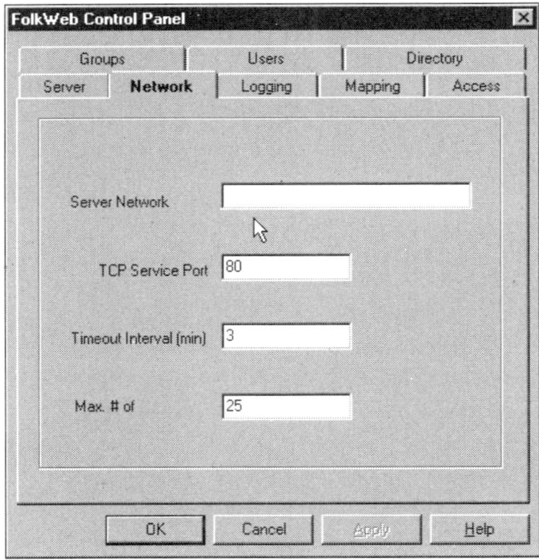

Figure 3-39: You can change the Server Network name on this page.

Figure 3-40 displays the Users page, where you can modify the passwords of your users to increase security on your Web site.

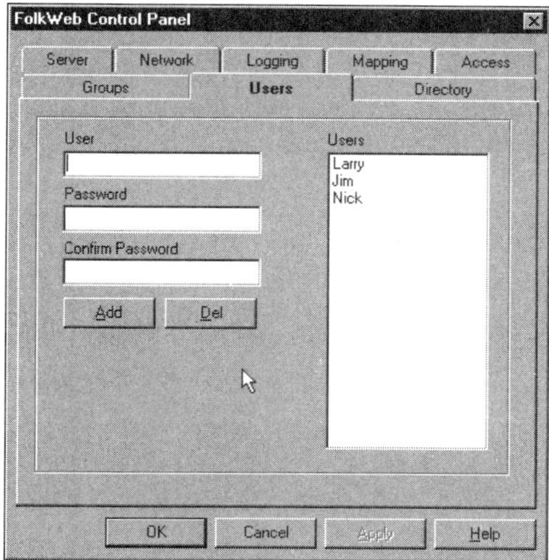

Figure 3-40: *You can use this page to increase security for your site.*

Figure 3-41 shows the Logging page, which controls the location where you place access and error logs. You also can choose not to enable logging of these two files. We recommend that you always log both access and errors. Unless you've installed FolkWeb on a drive other than C, or in a directory other than \FOLKWEB\, you shouldn't need to make any modifications here.

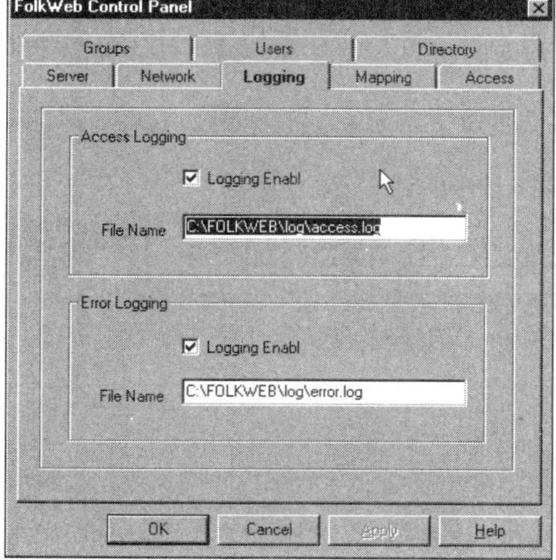

Figure 3-41: *No matter what Web server software you use, logging is one of the most important aspects of running a site.*

Figure 3-42 displays the Mapping page, where you can set mapping and URL aliases. Use this page if you want to hide the real locations of your resources. FolkWeb enables you to map URL To Path, EXT To MIME, URL To Doc, Path To URL, and Doc To Doc. This URL mapping can be a great asset to both you and your users. Read the FolkWeb documentation for more information on how you can use this capability.

Figure 3-43 shows what the Directory page of FolkWeb's control panel looks like. On this page, you can map an image to an extension, set default images, set parent directory images, and set child directory images.

Lastly, Figure 3-44 displays the Access page of FolkWeb's control panel application. The controls here enable you to add and delete realms, set access authentication by users and groups, or prohibit access by using IP filtering.

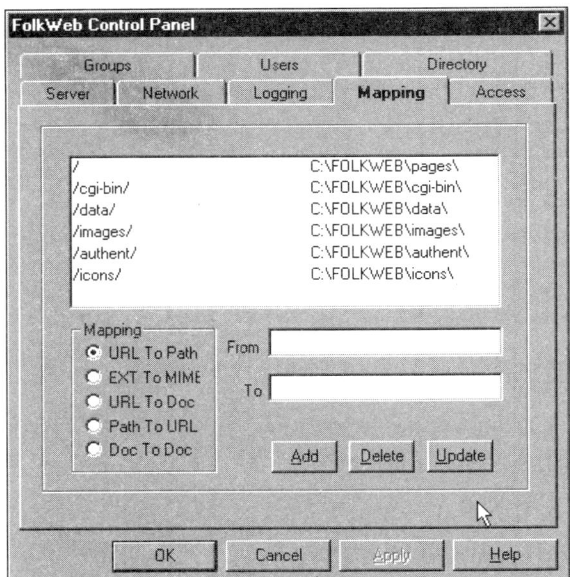

Figure 3-42: Hide the real locations of your files by using the Mapping page of FolkWeb's control panel.

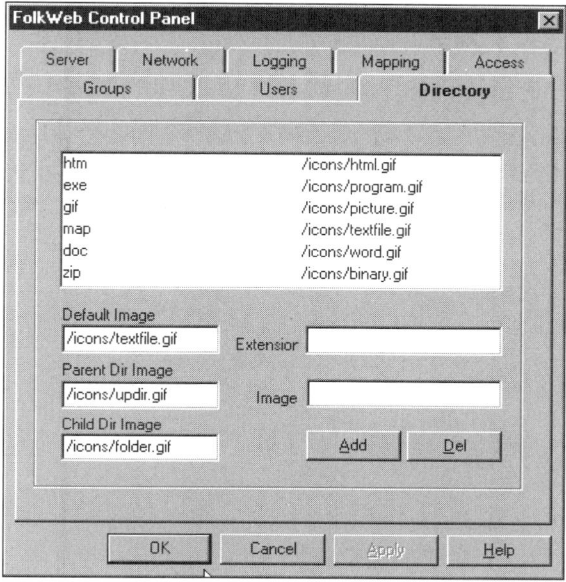

Figure 3-43: Using the Directory page of FolkWeb's control panel, you can add new mappings to your Extension Image list.

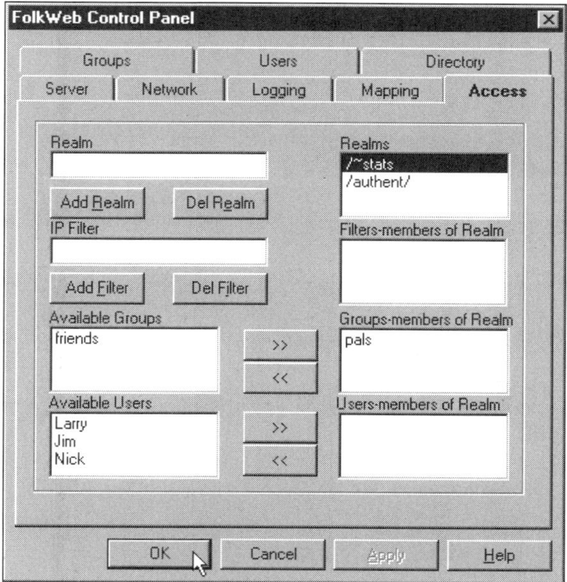

Figure 3-44: You can further control access to your site by using the Access page of FolkWeb's control panel.

8. **After you make whatever modifications you need by using FolkWeb's control panel application, click on the OK button.**

   Your changes are saved, and you exit the application.

To start FolkWeb Server, click on Start and then choose Programs⇨FolkWeb WWW Server⇨FolkWeb WWW Server from the Windows 95 interface. FolkWeb Server starts, as shown in Figure 3-45.

Figure 3-45: FolkWeb WWW Server is ready to respond to users.

You can now use FolkWeb WWW Server for a 30-day evaluation. Keep in mind that this software is shareware, and you need to pay for it if you decide to use it.

HTTPS

HTTPS is a freeware server from the European Microsoft Windows NT Academic Centre in Edinburgh, Scotland. The software is designed to run under the Windows NT operating system. The current version at the time of this writing was Version 0.99.

The newest version of this software is available for download at

```
http://www.emwac.ed.ac.uk
```

Download the file HSI386.ZIP.

Software and hardware requirements for this system include the following:

- An IBM-compatible 486 or higher CPU
- Windows NT 3.1 final release (or higher) with TCP/IP software installed

- At least 16MB of memory
- A network connection

If you plan to install, operate, manage, or deinstall the HTTP Server software, you need to read the manual for this software. The manual is available online at

```
http://emwac.ed.ac.uk/internet_toolchest/https/contents/htm
```

The files for HTTPS, including files for the manual in PostScript (.PS), Microsoft Word (.DOC), and Microsoft Write (.WRI) formats, are listed in Table 3.1.

Table 3-1 HTTPS Files

Filename	The File's Function or What the File Contains
HTTPS.EXE	The HTTP server itself
HTTPS.CPL	The Control Panel applet
HTTPS.HLP	The Control Panel help file
HTTPS.DOC	The user manual in Word for Windows format
HTTPS.PS	The user manual in PostScript format
HTTPS.WRI	The user manual in Windows Write format
EGSCRIPT.ZIP	Sample CGI script programs
COPYRITE.TXT	The copyright statement for the software
READ.ME	A summary of new features

If you have problems installing this software on your system, you can check a couple of different avenues for assistance. First, the manual is available online and in HSI386.ZIP. In addition, a FAQ is available at

```
http://www.emwac.ed.ac.uk/html/internet_toolchest/https/faq.htm
```

Because this version of the program is free, there is no technical support. When we sent a message to `emwac@ed.ac.uk` to ask whether the program would run on a Windows 95 system, we received an automatic reply that basically said to read the manual.

The program's creators do offer a "Professional" version of HTTPS that is marketed through third parties and does have tech support. We have not been able to find out whether this server will run on a Windows 95 platform, so try it at your own risk.

Internet Office Web Server

Internet Office Web Server is a nonsecure HTTP server from SPRY Internet software products. Internet Office Web Server is a Windows NT platform product that can be administered with Windows 95. A demo of this software is available at the SPRY Web site and in numerous Internet-related forums on CompuServe.

Follow these steps to install Internet Office Web Server:

1. **Decompress it into a temporary subdirectory.**
2. **Double-click on SETUP.EXE.**

   The program begins with a splash screen that looks similar to Figure 3-46.

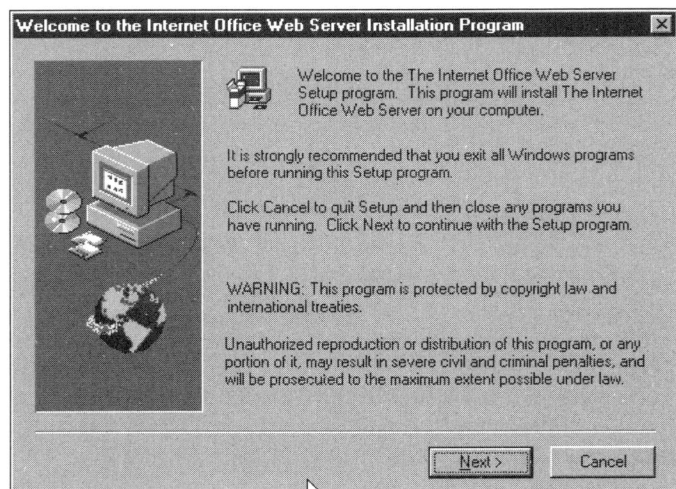

Figure 3-46: Click on Next to begin installing Internet Office Web Server on your Windows 95 system.

3. **Click on the Next button to start the installation of the system administrator to your hard drive.**

   You are soon asked, as in Figure 3-47, for your name and the name of your company.

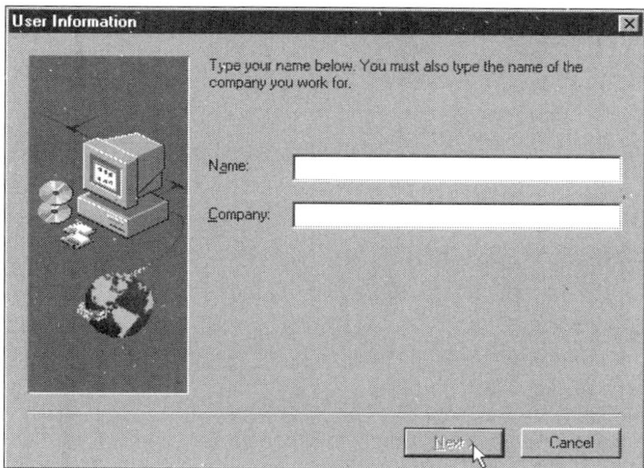

Figure 3-47: Type your name and your company name when the installation program requests them.

4. **Type your name and company name and then click on Next.**

   The next dialog box asks you to identify the location where you want to install the server software (see Figure 3-48). You can change the hard drive and the subdirectory where you want the program to install the server. In order to lessen the number of changes that you need to make later in the installation and configuration process, however, we suggest that you leave at least the subdirectory as is.

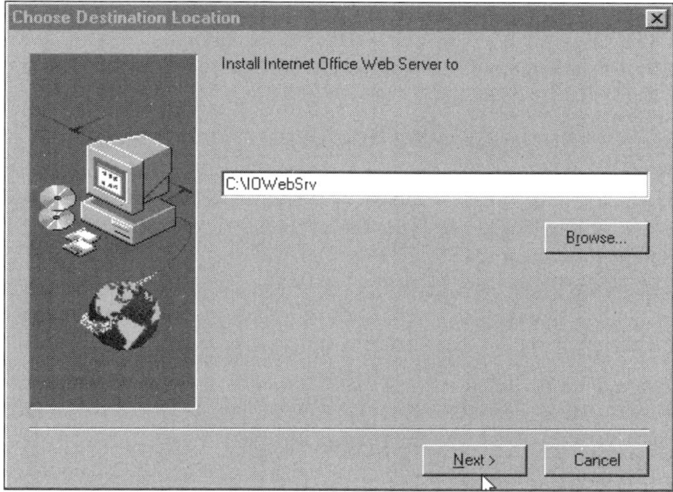

Figure 3-48: Unless you are going to change the drive letter or subdirectory where you want the server located, click on the Next button.

5. **Click on the Next button and move on to the next dialog box, as shown in Figure 3-49.**

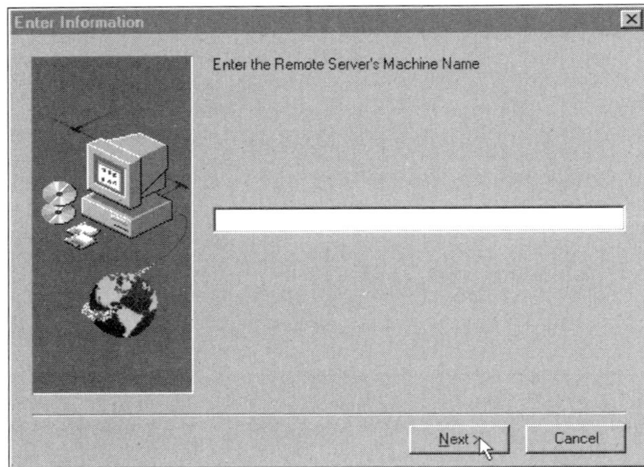

Figure 3-49: Type the Remote Server's Machine Name and then click on the Next button.

6. **Type the Remote Server's Machine Name and then click on the Next button.**

   You see the final installation window, as shown in Figure 3-50.

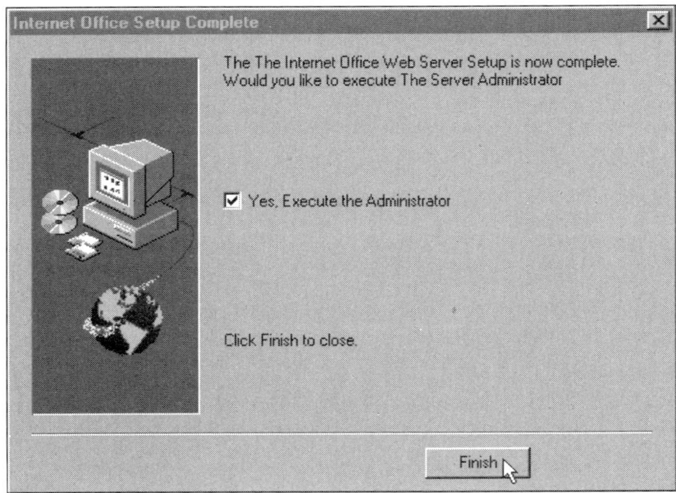

Figure 3-50: Check Yes to execute the Server Administrator and then click on the Finish button.

7. **Make sure that the Yes, Execute the Administrator box is checked and then click on the Finish button.**

Internet Office Web Server is now installed on your system. Check the README file and the online user's manual for information on changes that you need to make in order for this NT program to be administered from a Windows 95 system.

SerWeb

As we stated earlier in the chapter when discussing 16-bit applications, SerWeb is a public domain server for both 16-bit and 32-bit Windows platforms. The server was written by Gustavo Estrella and ported to 32-bit Windows by Chris Alie.

SerWeb is available for download by anonymous FTP from

```
ftp.cica.indiana.edu
```

The documentation states that Estrella wrote this program to learn about Visual C++, learn about the World Wide Web, and learn how to program Winsock. The software has only a few features.

The installation of SerWeb for the 32-bit platform is basically the same as for the 16-bit platform.

1. **Download the file SERWEB03.ZIP.**
2. **Unzip the file into the subdirectory where you want the program to reside.**

   Unlike some of the other programs we've discussed, SerWeb does not require you to use a particular subdirectory. For simplicity's sake, we unzipped the file to D:\SERWEB (as shown in Figure 3-51).

Figure 3-51: Unzip SERWEB03.ZIP into the directory where you want the program to reside.

Now that you've got the files unzipped, you'll notice a file named SERWEB.INI.

3. **Open SERWEB.INI using your favorite text editor (such as Notepad or Write).**

   You see a listing similar to Listing 3-7.

Listing 3-7: SERWEB.INI

```
[SERWEB]

PortNumber       = 80          ; Which Port to listen into
HowManyClients =  5       ; Allow up to 5 people to be
on at the same time.

ClosedServer     =  0          ; 0 = OK to log in, 1 = not OK
PeriodAllowed  =  1          ; 0 = allow .. on the
filenames, else don't..
PrintOut          =  1          ; Send output to status
window: 1 = Yes, 0 = No

; Where to start sending from (ex - if you specify
c:\data as your send dir, you can gewt c:\data\test,
c:\data\other\test, but not c:\test
SendDir              = f:\www\serweb\intel
```

```
; Message files to send specific information ......
FileNotExistMsg    = f:\www\serweb\intel\nofile.htm
ClosedServerMsg    = f:\www\serweb\intel\closed.htm
PeriodAllowedMsg   = f:\www\serweb\intel\period.htm
```

4. **Edit the options in this initialization file to match your installation.**

   The defaults are shown in the file in Listing 3-7. We'll walk through the options one by one:

   - `PortNumber = 80`. This setting defines which port number the server will listen to for incoming messages and connections.

   - `HowMany Clients = 5`. This option determines how many users can request files from your server at the same time. Adjust this depending on the speed of your machine.

   - `ClosedServer = 0`. If you set this option to `0`, the server sends the files requested by the user. If you set it to `1`, the server sends the file designated by the ClosedServer option. Setting the option to `1` enables you to disable the server while you're running an application that's memory hungry and resource hungry or while you are upgrading some of your HTML files.

   - `PeriodAllowed = 1`. Setting this option to `0` enables the user to request files that have names that use two periods (..) in the path. An example of this is c:..\myfiles\private.txt. You can use this option to get to files outside of the SendDir. For security purposes, we recommend setting this option to the default `1`, which doesn't allow these types of file requests.

   - `PrintOut = 1`. The default `1` causes status messages to be printed. Setting this option to `0` prevents these messages from being printed and enables the system to run a little bit faster.

   - `SendDir = f:`. This option defines which subdirectory holds the files that are to be sent out. For example, because we installed SerWeb at D:\SERWEB, we would need to change the default to reflect this. Then, when a user requests a file such as INDEX.HTM, the server will try to get this file from D:\SERWEB\INDEX.HTM. Now, if you don't care whether people can access all of your files, leave the default the way it is. We strongly recommend, however, that you keep the server-related files in a subdirectory all to themselves and set this option accordingly. It's simply good security for your system.

- `FileNotExistMsg = f:\serweb\nofile.htm`. This option designates the name of the file that is to be sent to the user by the server when the file that the user has requested doesn't exist. You should change this setting to reflect the location of your files, as discussed in the explanation for the SendDir setting. One other note: The file that is sent to the user should, in our opinion, be an HTML file that contains a hyperlink to your DEFAULT.HTM page.

- `ClosedServerMsg = f:\serweb\closed.htm`. Here is where you designate the name of the file that is to be used when the server is offline, as discussed in the explanation of the ClosedServer setting.

- `PeriodAllowedMsg = f:\serweb\period.htm`. This file will be sent to the user if he or she requests a .. in the path but the server doesn't allow it. This was discussed previously in the explanation for the PeriodAllowed setting.

5. **Now that you've changed the SERWEB.INI file to work with your computer, save the file and then copy it to your \WINDOWS\ subdirectory.**
6. **Edit the files NOFILE.HTM, CLOSED.HTM, PERIOD.HTM, and RETRY.HTM so that they refer to your Web site.**
7. **Define SerWeb to the Windows 95 Program Manager.**

   SerWeb is now ready to run, as shown in Figure 3-52.
8. **Create your HTML files and store them in the same subdirectory where you placed the default files that you edited as part of the configuration.**

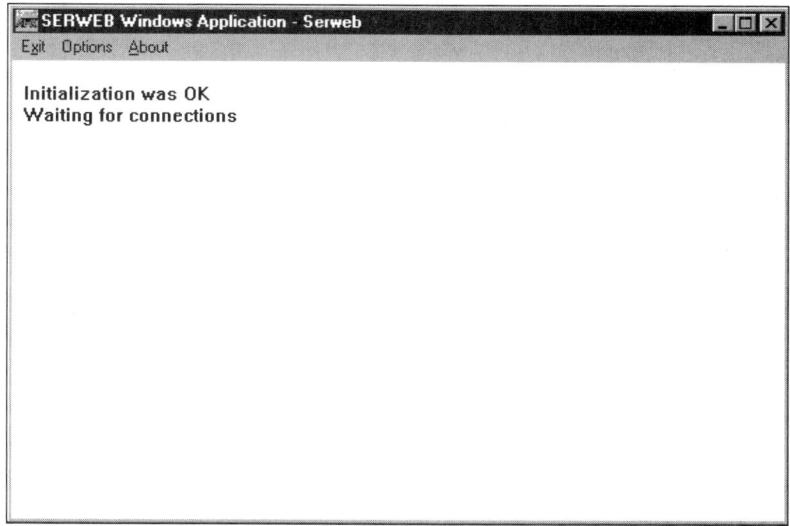

Figure 3-52: SerWeb is now ready to run.

SPRY Safety Web Server

SPRY Safety Web Server is another of SPRY's offerings for the Windows NT platform. SPRY Safety Web Server provides all the features of SPRY Web Server, which include a full-featured HTTP server, SQL, connectivity, a proxy server, complete access control, and multiple server support. In addition, SPRY Safety Web Server provides more comprehensive security measures.

SPRY Safety WEB Server also includes the following:

- SoftQuad's HoTMetaL PRO editing software for HTML authoring
- Architext Excite Text Indexing Server text indexing and search engine
- CompuServe's Internet Office, a suite of Windows-based TCP/IP applications

SPRY Web Server

SPRY Web Server is another version of SPRY's Web Server software. It is similar to Internet Office Web Server in both installation and operation, so we don't go into detail about the setup procedures. This software is designed for operation with Windows NT but can be administered from a Windows 95 machine.

You can download SPRY Web Server from SPRY's Web site at

```
http://www.spry.com
```

CompuServe has recently purchased SPRY, and a number of changes are being made in the Web sites and software.

W4-Server

W4-Server was written by two students in the Netherlands and distributed by Antelope Software. The two students wanted to start their own server but couldn't afford to buy server software from the United States. They ended up taking time off from their university studies to write the professional version of this freeware server.

Version 2.0 of W4-Server is available in a variety of Internet-related forums on CompuServe. The features of this version include

- The authors claim that this software provides no backdoors, so it is completely safe and secure. (Some hackers might consider this a taunt and therefore attack your server just to prove that it's not safe and secure.)
- The software takes up less than 80K of memory.
- You can still use Internet Explorer or Netscape to access the Internet to read your mail, and so on.
- Every action along with the Client IP, date, and time, is logged into the software's log file.
- The software's authors suggest that you don't need to worry about file protection because users can get files from only one subdirectory. (Again, this might be waving a red flag in front of the hacker bulls.)
- The number of users logged on to your server is always visible, even when the server's window is minimized.
- The software supports NCSA image maps.
- The server supports forms.
- The registered version provides access to the use of WWW Transport Data Protocol (WTDP).
- The software has one of the least expensive registration fees of those discussed.

Users can see only those files under the \DOCS\ subdirectory. This subdirectory is seen as the root directory for your hard drive by the W4-Server software. As a result, if the software is installed using the defaults, users can see only those files contained in or below the C:\WINDOWS\W4SERVER\DOCS subdirectory.

Another safety aspect is that W4-Server recognizes only the GET and POST commands. Anything else is ignored. The software's authors state that there are no backdoors. W4-Server doesn't use passwords either. You can't access the server from remote machines in any manner, according to the authors. We're not sure that this isn't just a call for hackers to try to attack your server.

Finally, no files can be sent to the server except those generated by the WTDP files. Only forms filled out and sent back can be processed. The server determines what happens with the data on the server-machine. Any file not recognized by the WTDP file is ignored.

Installation of W4-Server is a straightforward process:

1. **Open the subdirectory where you've decompressed the zipped file and double-click on SETUP.EXE.**

   Your screen soon looks similar to Figure 3-53.

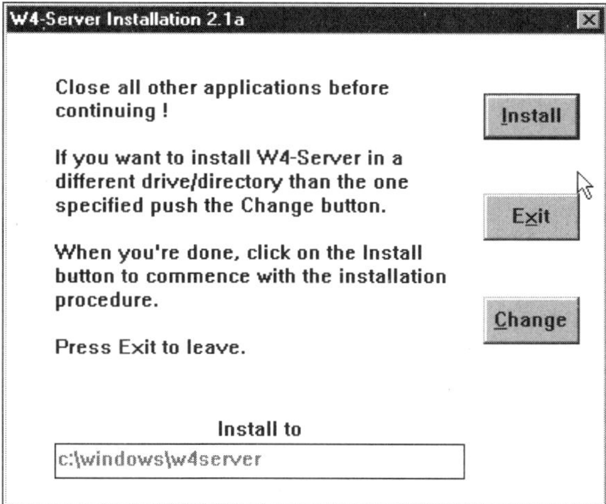

Figure 3-53: The W4-Server installation program recommends where to install the program.

The installation dialog box gives you the option of accepting the default location for the server program or changing it. As with most of the other server applications, we highly recommend accepting the default location until you become more familiar with the program's operation. If you want to change the installation directory, click on the Change button.

2. **When the installation directory that you want to use is in the text box, click on the Install button to see the Program Group dialog box shown in Figure 3-54.**

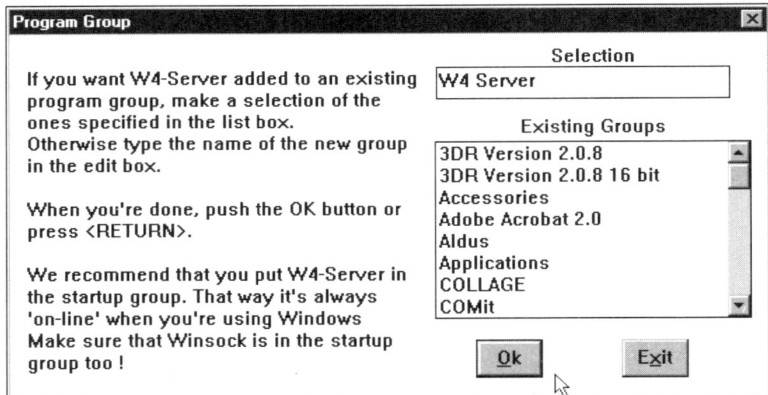

Figure 3-54: Choose the program group where you want to place W4-Server.

This dialog box gives you the opportunity to select which program group you want the server software to be placed in. It also makes the recommendation that you place both the server software and your Winsock software in the startup group. This location guarantees that the server will be online whenever you're using Windows.

The dialog box offers W4-Server as the name of your program group as the default. You can accept this default, select a program group from those listed in the Existing Groups box, or type the name of the new group you want to create in the Selection box.

3. **After you have completed everything you want to do here, click on OK and go on to the next dialog box (see Figure 3-55).**

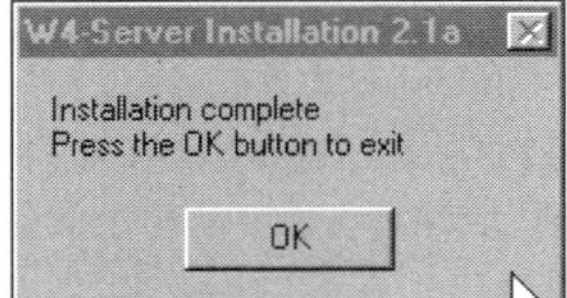

Figure 3-55: The W4-Server program group is created, and installation is complete.

The installation is completed.

4. **Click on OK, and then you can start the server.**

WebServer

WebServer is one of the Quarterdeck products that is designed to make Web publishing easier.

Quarterdeck's WebServer is provided on the *Creating Cool Interactive Web Sites CD-ROM.* This software is in encrypted form. See a more complete explanation earlier in this chapter in the WebServer discussion under "Server software for Windows 3.1*x*."

This version of Quarterdeck's WebServer is a 16-bit application that will run as such under both Windows NT and Windows 95. Quarterdeck plans to release a new 32-bit version of WebServer for both platforms sometime in 1996.

Because we go into considerable detail on the operation, setup, and configuration of this software in Chapter 5, this will be it for our discussion of Quarterdeck's WebServer application in this chapter. We next turn our attention to the last software package to be discussed in this chapter.

WebSite

WebSite is a server software application for Windows NT and Windows 95 produced by O'Reilly & Associates. The server's setup program will install the application to either platform and adjust to either environment.

The software and more up-to-the-minute information concerning WebSite are downloadable from WebSite Central.

```
http://website.ora.com
```

This demo version of the application is fully functional except that the software has a built-in expiration date and there is no technical support for this version.

Some of the features of WebSite are

- Compatibility with both Windows NT and Windows 95
- Full CGI with Visual Basic Toolkit
- Built-in maintenance tools

- Remote administration
- Multihoming capability
- Included Image Map Editor
- Integrated search engine
- Integrated key word indexing
- Wizards

WebSite provides a great deal of flexibility in configuring your Web site, but there are some minimum hardware and software requirements. The minimum hardware requirements, and some recommendations for improving on them, follow:

- An 80386 or higher CPU is required. An 80486 or Pentium machine is recommended.
- A minimum of 12MB of RAM is required for the Windows NT platform, and a minimum of 8MB of RAM is required for the Windows 95 platform. For the Windows NT platform, 16MB of RAM are recommended, and for the Windows 95 platform, 12MB of RAM are recommended.
- A minimum of 5MB of hard drive disk space is required.
- A minimum of VGA graphics is required, and SVGA graphics are recommended.
- A floppy drive for 3 1/2-inch disks is required for the purchased version of this software.
- A network connection through a network card or modem is required. Although a minimum of a 9600 baud rate is required, we recommend nothing less that 28.8 Kbps.

The minimum required software includes Windows NT 3.5 with long filenames enabled or Windows 95.

You need to make sure that you have the TCP/IP protocol stack installed and running. Also make sure that your system Date and Time are set to the correct date, time, and time zone.

You may want to consider adding the following software applications to those that come with this server:

- A graphics viewer program, such as LView, for GIF and JPEG files
- An audio player program, such as WHAM, for audio files

- A video viewer program, such as MPEGPlay, for MPEG files
- An HTML editor, such as the Internet Assistant add-on for Word for Windows
- A GIF editor, such as Photoshop
- The Visual Basic development environment
- A Perl programming language that's compatible with your operating platform

The version of WebSite available for download includes the WebSite server and server administration software; the WebSite applications WebView, Image Map Editor, and WebIndex; a copy of Enhanced NCSA Mosaic; the WebSite server self test; and other Web documents. These components are installed by the installation program.

Follow these steps to install the software:

1. **Decompress the downloaded file into a temporary file.**
2. **Double-click on SETUP.EXE to see something similar to Figure 3-56.**

Figure 3-56: WebSite's installation software installs the server and various tools.

The Welcome screen in the WebSite setup program has three buttons: Install, Exit, and Help. If you have questions about the installation process, click on Help. If you don't want to continue the installation process, click on Exit.

3. **Click on Install to begin the installation process as in Figure 3-57.**

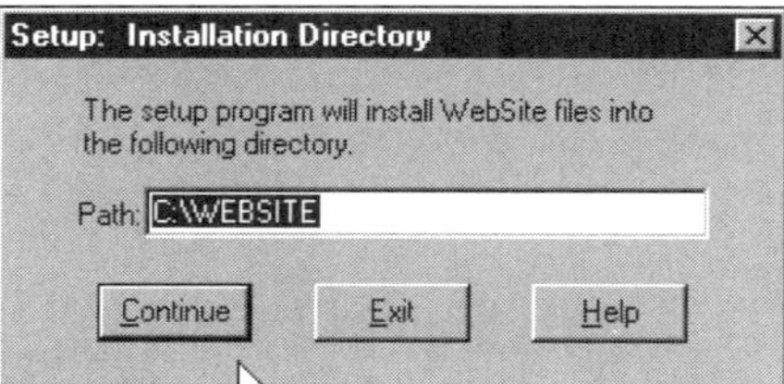

Figure 3-57: Choose where you want WebSite to be installed.

4. **Accept the default location (C:\WEBSITE) or type the name of the hard drive and subdirectory where you want WebSite to be installed.**

5. **Click on the Continue button to move on to the Server Configuration dialog box shown in Figure 3-58.**

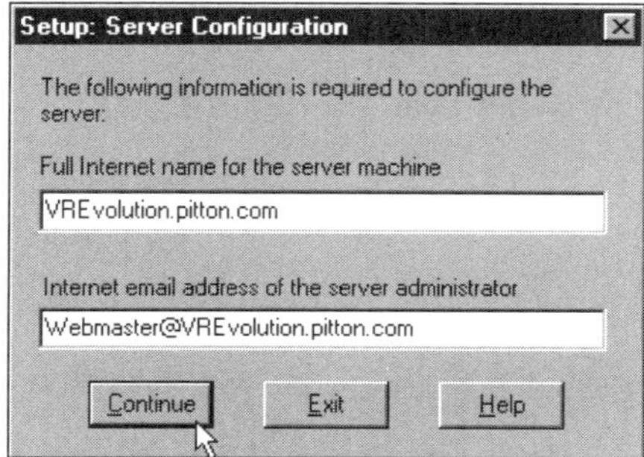

Figure 3-58: Designate the name of your server and your e-mail address in this dialog box.

6. **Enter the fully qualified domain name of the server in the first text box.**

   We entered **VREvolution.pitton.com**.

7. **In the second text box, enter the full Internet e-mail address of the person who will be responsible for this server.**

We entered **Webmaster@VREvolution.pitton.com**. Keep in mind that this address can be any address and isn't necessarily restricted to an address on the computer where WebSite is being installed.

8. **Click on the Continue button and move on to the Home Page setup dialog window shown in Figure 3-59.**

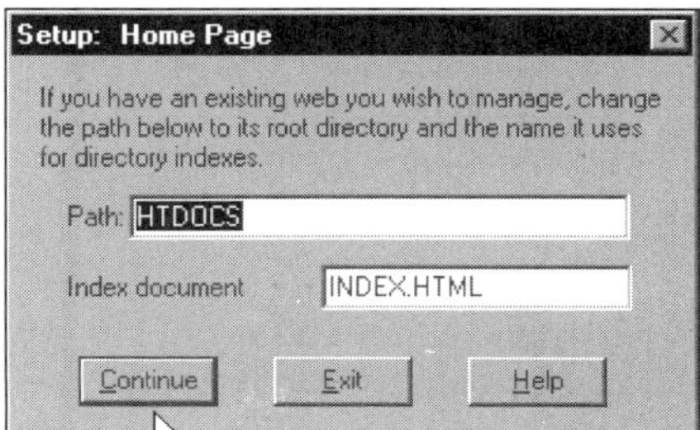

Figure 3-59: *If you have a previously established Web site on your computer, change the path and index document here.*

If you have a previously established Web site, WebSite enables you to manage and administer the site by changing the path and index document at this point. If you don't have a previously existing Web site, accept the default path and index document name.

9. **Change the path and index document or accept the default path and index document name.**

10. **Click on the Continue button to have WebSite's installation program begin installing the program files to your hard drive.**

    As the installation proceeds, command windows may open and close, but this is completely normal. When Setup is completed, a final dialog box appears, with recommendations about what steps to take next.

11. **Click on the OK button to close Setup.**

The WebSite server is launched, and the WebSite Program Group is displayed on your desktop, as in Figure 3-60. If you want to have the server start automatically when you start up your computer, move the WebSite server icon to your startup group.

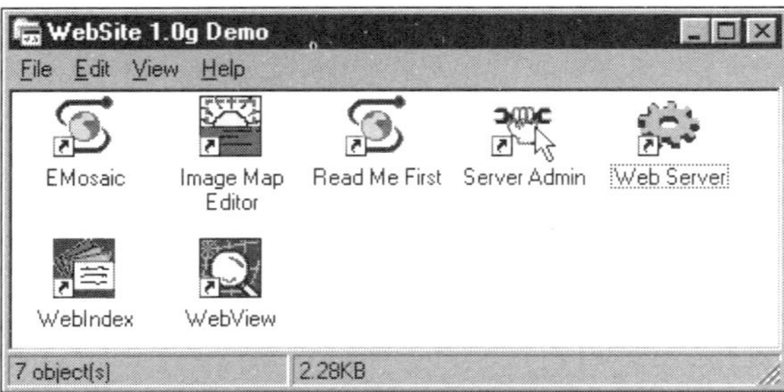

Figure 3-60: The WebSite Program Group as seen running on a Windows 95 platform.

Before you test the server to make sure that everything is working correctly, take a look at the WebSite Server Administration tool.

1. **Double-click on the Server Admin icon in the WebSite Demo Program Group to see the Server Admin General properties page (see Figure 3-61).**

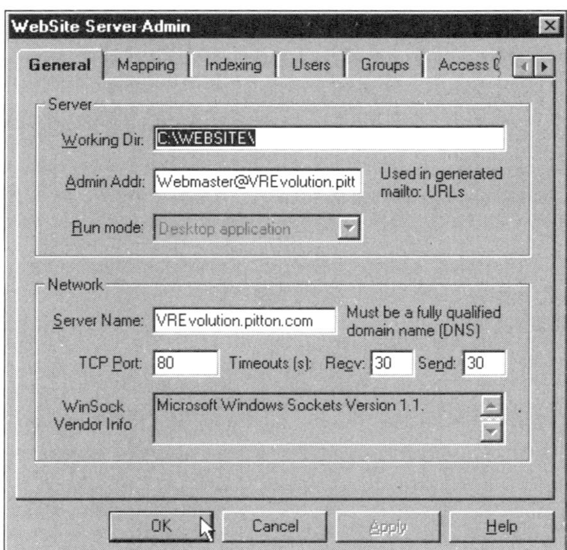

Figure 3-61: The General properties page.

You should not need to change the information on this page if you entered it correctly during the installation process.

- The Working Directory, which is sometimes called the server root, is where WebSite was installed.
- The Administrator's Address indicates the complete e-mail address of the person who is responsible for this Web site. This address is the one that you typed in during installation.
- Run mode tells you how the WebSite software will run the next time it is started. Under Windows NT, this drop-down list offers three choices: Desktop Application, System Service with Icon, and System Service without Icon. Under Windows 95, you can't run the software as a service, so this item is dimmed, and the software runs as a Desktop Application.
- The Server Name is the fully qualified domain name of the server. You entered this information during the setup procedure. This name is not necessarily the same as the computer's name.
- The TCP/IP port is the port number that your server is using. The default is port 80. Don't change this number unless you know what you are doing.
- The Timeouts settings for receive and send are fairly standard settings. You may want to increase these settings to 60 seconds each if you are using a PPP/SLIP connection and users complain that your server is slow.
- The Winsock Vendor Info box lists the Winsock programs detected on your system. WebSite uses Microsoft's Winsock Version 1.1, and you cannot change this field.

Little of the information on this page is changed very often. If you change the values here, the changes don't take effect until you have closed the program and restarted it.

2. **Click on the tab for the Mapping page, as shown in Figure 3-62.**

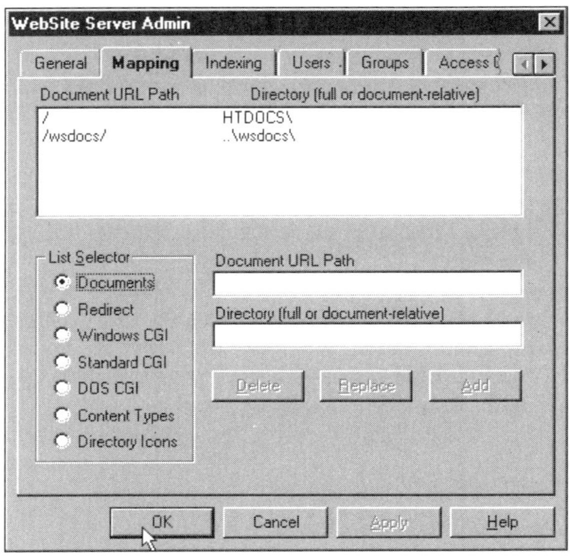

Figure 3-62: The Mapping page.

You can change URL paths from this page.

3. **Click on the tab for the Indexing page, as seen in Figure 3-63.**

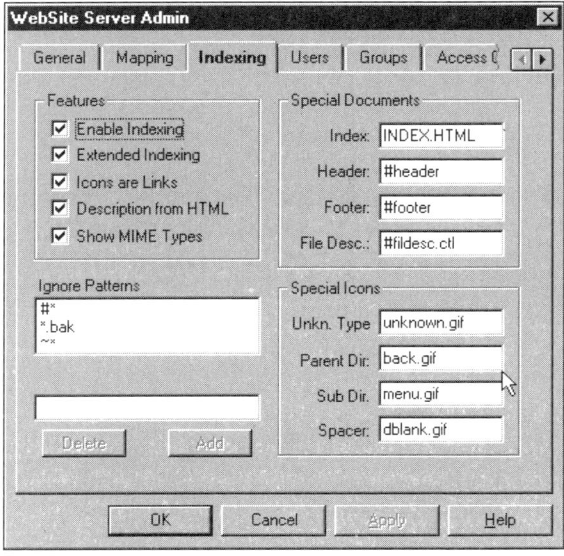

Figure 3-63: The Indexing page.

From this page you can customize how your directory listings are presented to users on the Web. You can provide indexes with icons and hyperlinks or not. You can also change the name of your home page for this server in the Special Documents section.

4. **Click on the tab for the Users page.**

   The Users page, as shown in Figure 3-64, is where you can modify the passwords of your users, thereby increasing the security of your server.

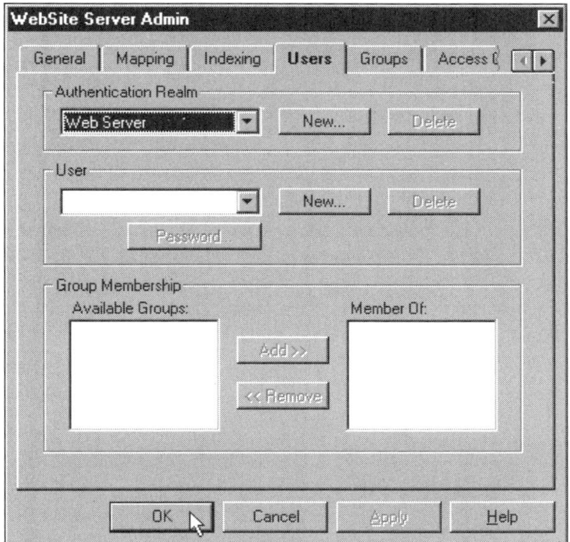

Figure 3-64: The Users page.

One thing to keep in mind as you are moving through these pages is that you cannot undo changes that you make on some of these pages (the Indexing and Users pages, for example) without restarting your computer. When you moved from the Indexing and Users pages, you should have seen a message box that looks similar to Figure 3-65. You can prevent this message from coming up again by checking Don't display this in the future. Click OK to make the message box go away.

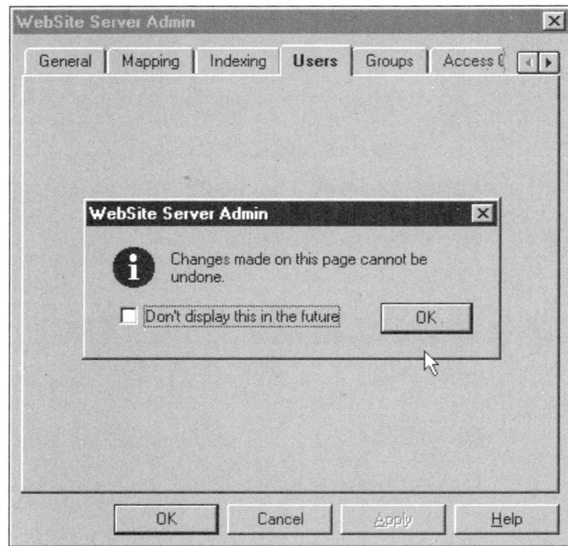

Figure 3-65: The changes you make on some pages can't be undone.

5. **Click on the tab for the Groups page, which is shown in Figure 3-66.**

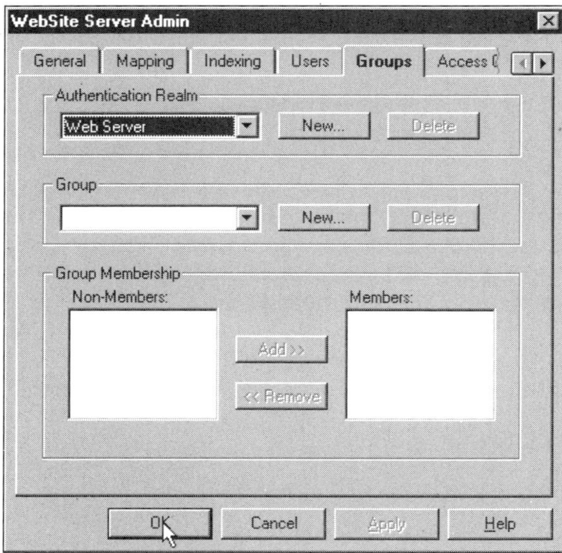

Figure 3-66: The Groups page.

You can create special groups of users and then give them greater or less access to your server than other groups of users.

6. **In order to look at the Access Control page and other pages available in the Server Administration dialog box, click on the right-arrow button in the upper right of this window, as shown in Figure 3-67.**

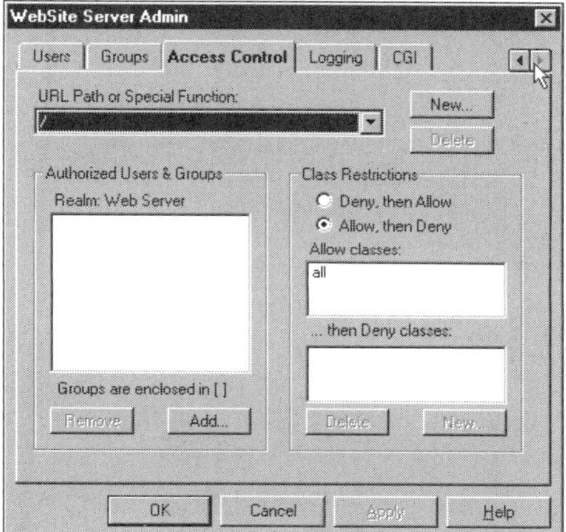

Figure 3-67: The Access Control page.

7. **Click on the Logging tab to move to the Logging page, as shown in Figure 3-68.**

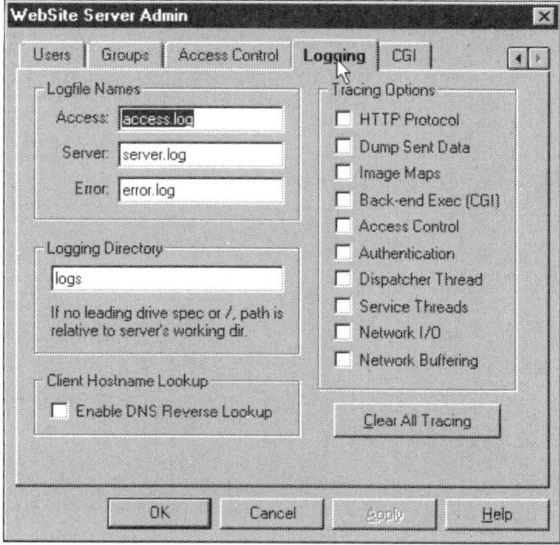

Figure 3-68: The Logging page.

Make sure that these log file names are correct and that any tracing options you want to use are turned on before moving on to the final tab.

8. **Click on the CGI tab to move to the CGI page, as shown in Figure 3-69.**

   You don't want to make any modifications to the options available on this page until you have gained considerable experience both with the server software and with CGI. We go into more detail concerning CGI in Chapter 10.

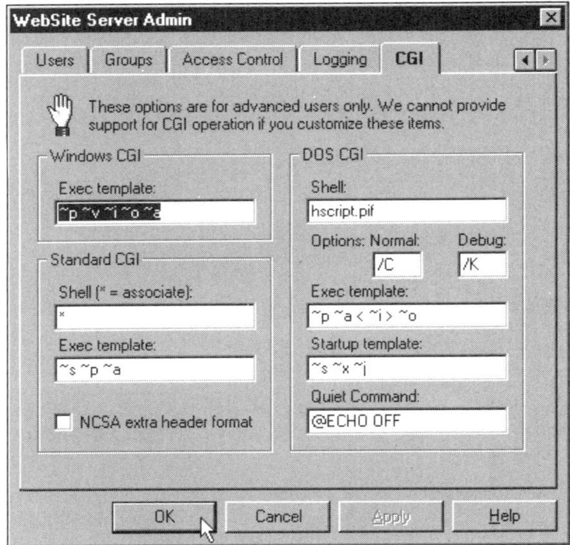

Figure 3-69: The CGI page.

9. **After you finish examining the options on the CGI page, click on OK to exit the Server Administration application.**

Your next task is to test the server to make sure that it is operating properly. You'll probably want to make sure that the server is running, view a document from the server, and then view the document from another computer.

When you exited the Setup program, the server was launched and minimized as an icon. The icon looks like that in Figure 3-70.

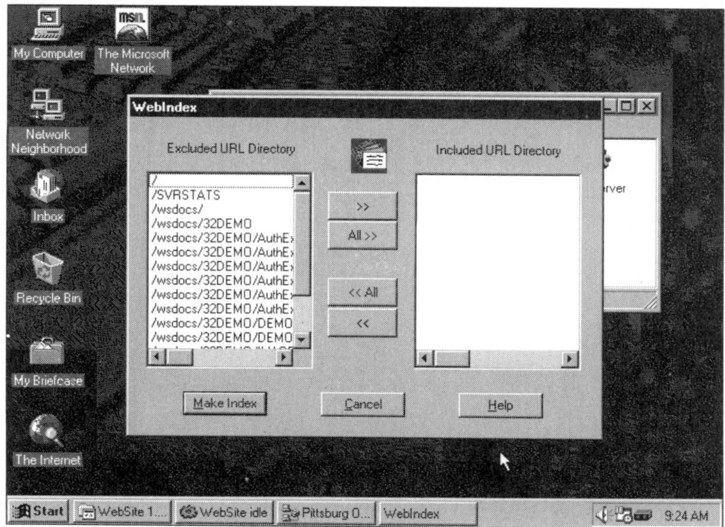

Figure 3-70: The WebSite idle icon is in the taskbar.

If you see this icon, the server is working. The next thing to check is whether you can view a document on your server.

1. **Double-click on the Read Me First icon in the WebSite Program Group.**

   Mosaic is launched, and you see the README file. This doesn't prove that the server is working, though.

2. **Click on the hypertext link <u>home page</u>.**

   If the server and computer are set up correctly, you see the temporary WebSite home page in your browser's window.

   Now you need to check the server using the IP address.

3. **Open the URL for your server, using the Web browser.**

   If your server's domain name is registered with DNS, you can test the server using the domain name.

   Now that you know that the server is working this much, you need to access your server and view a document from another computer.

4. **From another computer, start your Web browser.**

5. **Aim the second computer's Web browser at the URL for your server, using the IP address.**

If your server's domain name is registered with DNS, you can use the domain name.

6. **Click on the WebSite icon to bring up the server window, as shown in Figure 3-71.**

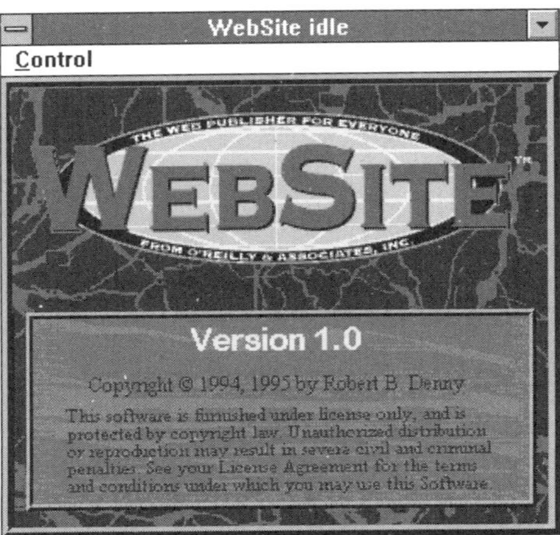

Figure 3-71: *WebSite is ready for your users.*

You have 60 days to test the WebSite server software. During that period, you should be able to determine whether it will satisfy your needs.

We have covered some of the major 16-bit and 32-bit servers in this chapter. Before we finish the chapter we need to look at VREvolution's Site Diary.

VREvolution Site Diary: Installment 3

In deciding which server to choose for VREvolution's Web site, we considered several variables:

- What kind of hardware are we using for our server?

  VREvolution's server is on a 486DX2 with 16MB of RAM. This system has both a 5 1/4-inch floppy drive and a 3 1/2-inch floppy drive, a 2X CD-ROM, SVGA graphics, a 28.8 Kbps modem, and 1.5GB of hard drive space available. Internet service is obtained for the server through Pittsburg Online with a dedicated telephone line.

- What kind of software platform are we using on our server?

  The platform running on this system is Windows 95.

- How much traffic do we expect on our server?

  We anticipate moderate use of this Web site, so we would like to be able to accommodate at least eight simultaneous hits.

- What kind of interactive applications do we plan to offer?

  VREvolution will offer virtual reality and 3-D graphics, audio and video, and other interactive applications from the site as is possible, given the bandwidth.

- What programming languages are we planning to use?

  VREvolution uses Microsoft Visual C++ 4.0 and Microsoft Visual Basic 4.0. We also experiment with other options, such as Microsoft Internet Suite (codenamed Blackbird), Java, the Borland and Symantec tools for Java use, various forms of CGI, and VRML.

Our responses to these questions provided us with a good start in determining which server application to use. First, because our platform is Windows 95, our choices were limited to servers that operate from this platform. Those servers include Alibaba, FolkWeb, SerWeb, VBServer, VRServer, W4-Server, WebServer, and WebSite.

Our next concern was whether these servers are capable of a minimum of eight simultaneous hits. According to the documentation, all of them are capable of at least eight simultaneous hits.

Of the eight Windows 95-compatible server applications we've discussed, only one, WebSite, advertises itself as having a Visual Basic Toolkit to use while working with CGI. Quarterdeck's WebServer's help files say that Visual Basic is usable for most simple applications, and WebServer includes several sample applications with the distribution files. FolkWeb Server comes with example applications written in Visual C++. Although the other server applications don't specifically refer to Visual Basic or Visual C++, all of them do refer to being able to use some sort of CGI applications.

We decided to install and operate VREvolution's server using Quarterdeck's WebServer software. We discuss the full setup and operation of this server in Chapter 5.

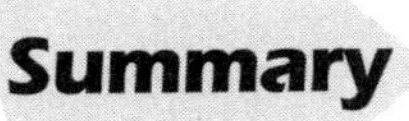

In this chapter, you first examined the various Web server software available for 16-bit platforms.

Your next step was to examine the Web server software available for 32-bit platforms.

Finally, you read about the process by which we chose which server software to use for VREvolution's Web server.

It is time now to look at Part II of this book. In Chapter 4, we look at a few security issues that you need to consider if you are going to run your own Web site.

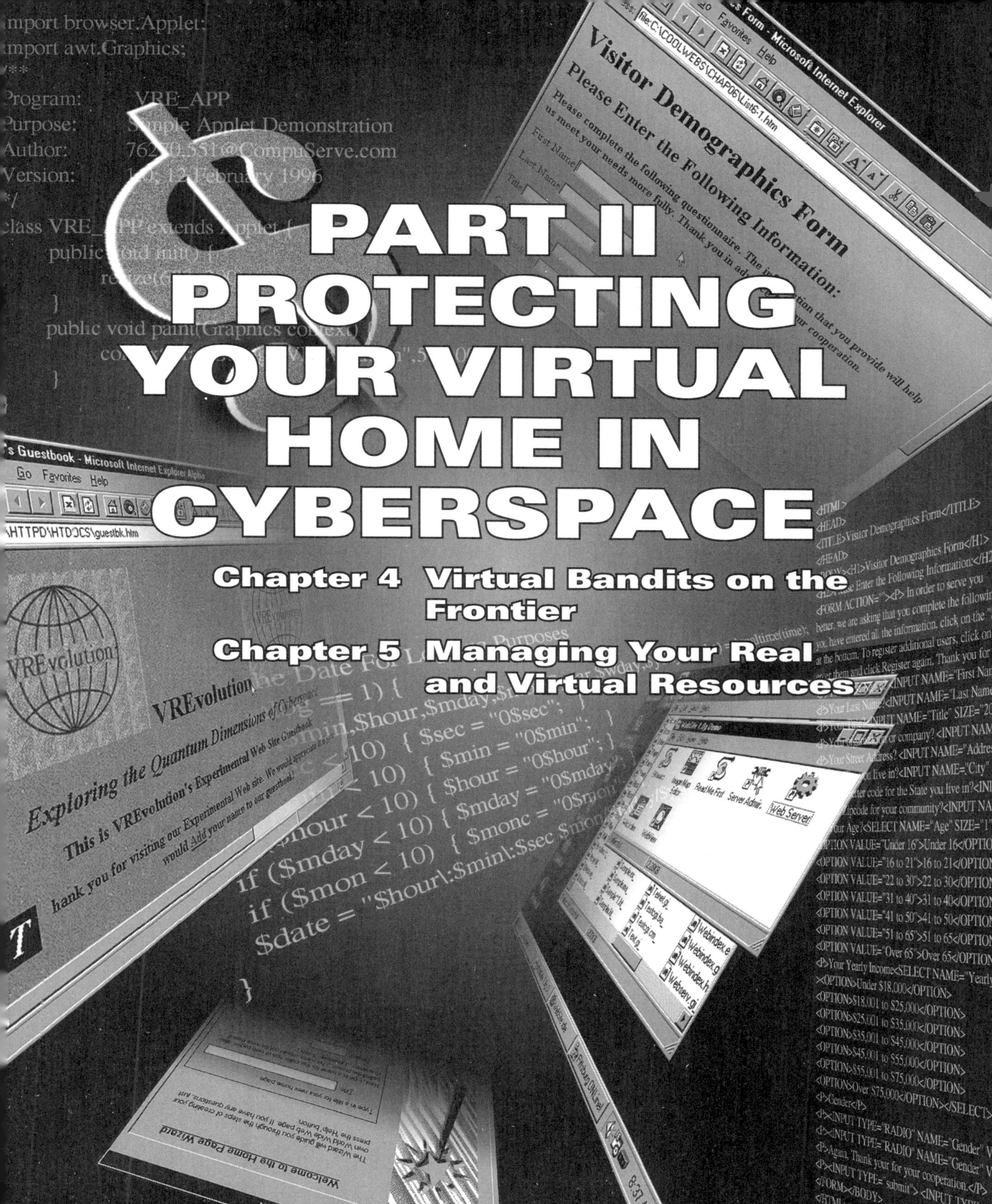

PART II PROTECTING YOUR VIRTUAL HOME IN CYBERSPACE

Although fun and exciting, operating your own Web server demands time and resources that you need to be aware of. In Part I of this book, we looked at service providers, created Web pages on some of those service providers, and installed and examined a variety of Web server software and platforms.

In this part of the book, we turn our attention to the concepts of protecting and managing your resources.

We'll begin by looking at the dangerous side of the cyberspace frontier: viruses, Trojan horses, and unauthorized access to your server and Web site.

Later, we discuss setting up a server's physical network parameters and directory structure, using and configuring the server-generated directory indexes, configuring the MIME types necessary for launching viewers, implementing password security and access for the server.

Virtual Bandits on the Frontier

In This Chapter

What is security?

Protecting your site from viruses

Protecting your site from hackers

Looking at the VREvolution Site Diary

Before we get started with this chapter, maybe we ought to say a few things about what this chapter is not. First, this chapter is not a discussion of Internet and World Wide Web security methods. You can get far more in-depth coverage of those topics in Doug Lowe's *Networking For Dummies,* 2nd Edition, and *Client/Server Computing For Dummies,* David Vaskevitch's *Client/Server Strategies,* 2nd Edition, or David Stang and Sylvia Moon's *Network Security SECRETS,* all from IDG Books Worldwide, Inc.

No, in this chapter we look at what "real" needs you may have for security procedures. Some readers may think that some of the following is romanticized, while at the same time calling for more and more security measures on their Web sites. We suggest that when you set up stronger and stronger security measures you are simply protecting yourself from the evil within. If this idea is slightly confusing, please read on.

Oh What a Beautiful World

In a perfect world, security would not be necessary. Everything would be open. There would be no secrets. People would have access to any information they wanted.

In a commercial world, everything is private. Anything of value is owned, and therefore private, and therefore in need of protection and security. Everything is closed in a commercial world. There is a cost for access to anything and everything. The reason for this cost is that everything has value and thus must be protected and kept secure from those who cannot afford it. Those who can't afford this information don't need it because they are not worthy of it.

In the beginning, the Internet was open, wild, and free. It was much like the American West during the mid- to late-1800s. Until civilization and commercialization began to contaminate the American West, there was little crime. We use the word *civilization* to reflect the concept proliferated by the white invaders of this continent, not the indigenous Native American population. Crimes, for these invaders, weren't named until things were private, land became property, and companies had secrets. What was done to the Native Americans was not a crime until civilization changed and made it so. Actions were not called crimes until they endangered some commercial and capitalistic concept.

When we say that a crime does not exist until it is named, we mean that until something is given a name, it doesn't really exist. As an example, although we don't mean to associate crime with children, we often name children long before they are born. Even when we don't give them actual names, we call them names such as "the child," "it," the "rug rat," and other terms of affection. Nothing, a crime included, exists until it is named.

The Internet was much the same. There was little need to name crimes until civilization and commercialization began to raise their ugly heads. Suddenly, doors closed and locked. Freedom of speech became tempered by the concept that "I" should be able to say anything "I" want but "you" shouldn't be able to say something "I" don't like.

Privacy became a buzzword signifying private property. The concept is that "you" should not have the right to information about me that you might obtain by invading "my" privacy, "my" private property. At the same time, "you" shouldn't have the right to keep "me" from exercising my right to information about you by invading "your" privacy, "your" private property.

Spokespersons, public relations practitioners, and demagogues from both sides of the political spectrum seek to influence us with their messages. To do this, they need information about us, making them guilty of what some of them fight against. Some self-appointed Internet privacy guardians even argue that this coming battle in cyberspace over privacy issues will be the central civil rights issue of the 1990s. The reason for this is that government and business see the Internet and the Web as a means of gathering information about the country's population.

It seems as if there should be some middle ground, some negotiated, reasonable solution. How this can be accomplished is a good question. When it comes to privacy, rights, and freedoms — concepts that some would argue don't exist in the first place — there seems to be no middle ground. Perhaps the acceptance of all viewpoints without objections is the answer.

Protecting Us from Ourselves

This is the current situation we face in cyberspace. People, companies, and governments are staking claims to virtual and imaginary landscapes, saying that those cyberspaces are now real and private property and, therefore, valuable. You, too, in reading this book, may have decided to claim your homestead on the cyberfrontier. You are about to help bring civilization to the virtual.

Civilization meaning *private property*. The world of "mine." And, because we believe that we should have privacy but others should not, we set up walls to protect ourselves from others who feel the same. The result is that we spend time and resources protecting things that may not need protecting.

Web browsers even notify us that the Web and the Internet may not be safe for private information, as shown in Figure 4-1.

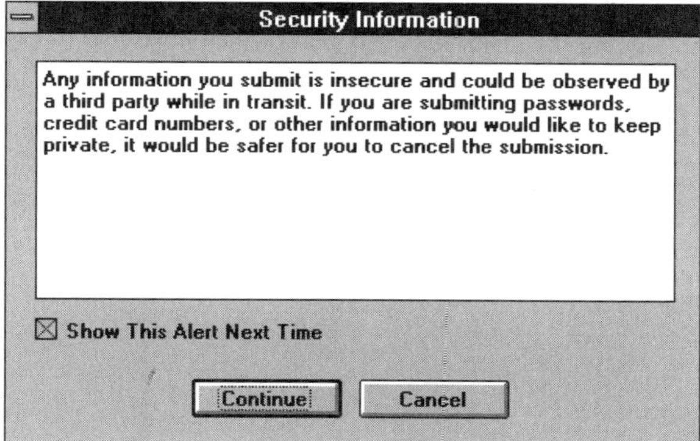

Figure 4-1: Internet communication is not really secure.

Although the network may not be secure, how is a potential thief to know which message is yours among all the messages traveling across the Internet at any point unless you've drawn attention to yourself? Yes, technology enables potential thieves to monitor everything that comes from your site and wait to find what they want. We've all seen movies of the police, the FBI, and other law enforcement agencies doing this. We just want to ask the question, what movie have you been watching that makes you so paranoid?

Does your Web site really need security?

Web and Internet security experts tell you that you need security. But, then, they are slightly biased. After all, they make their living by recommending the installation of security systems on corporate computers and Web sites. Interestingly enough, à la *Sneakers,* some of the better known, so-called security experts got their start by breaking into business, private, and government computers.

The point is, does your Web site really need security? For the most part, the answer depends on what you are placing on your site, what the purpose of your site is, and how exposed your site is.

What's on your site?

Before we go further, we need to make a distinction between sending something over the Internet and having something stored at your Web site. Everything on the World Wide Web is on the Internet, but everything that is on the Internet is not necessarily on the World Wide Web. Much data that people worry about has no business being on the Web; nor does it have any business being on any computer that is connected to the Internet.

Different kinds of data require different types of protection, and depending on what your data is, you may be required by law to protect it.

One textbook on Internet security uses a psychiatrist's client treatment records as an example of information that you need to protect. We question what this type of information would be doing on a Web site or on a computer that is connected to the Internet. Who, besides the psychiatrist, needs to see this information, and why would anyone choose a Web site as a place to store such information?

Other examples given in Internet security books concern a publicly traded company's unpublished financial reports, employee medical records, detailed specifications for a business's next project, final bids on business proposals, personal notes, and government classified information. Again, what are these types of information doing on a Web site?

It is understandable that a situation may occur where a company may send unpublished reports from one office to another over the Internet. Chances are that the data in the reports would be completely safe unless someone is intercepting every message sent from that company. If sending documents over the Net is not the usual practice, the chances of anyone's waiting to catch a message are minuscule. Now, if you are completely paranoid, use Federal Express. They're good people.

The best security advice that anyone can give you about the Internet and the World Wide Web is to not put something that you don't want strangers to see on a computer that's connected to the Internet or the Web.

Remember, too, that unless you call attention to yourself and your site by advertising, public relations, and so on, the chances that anyone will visit your site are pretty remote. As in Edgar Allan Poe's story, "The Purloined Letter," sometimes the best place to hide something is out in the open. Of course, hiding it seems to contradict the purpose you have for setting up the Web site in the first place.

What's the purpose of your site, anyway?

Most of you are interested in setting up a Web site to distribute information about yourself, your company, your product, or your services. The only information that you would put on this site is information that you want people to know.

This means that there is little chance that you would be placing your own medical records, or those of your employees, on your Web site. You probably wouldn't want to place any company secrets there either, seeing as how placing secrets on a public site isn't likely to maintain their secrecy.

The purpose of the Web is to disseminate information. If you're going to establish a Web site, don't try to hide information on the computer that is hosting the site.

Who are you protecting data from?

Five kinds of people may visit your Web site.

- **The people whom you put the site up for in the first place, the people whom you want to visit your site.** The truth is, the more security you have on your site, the more difficult you make it for these people to get the information that you want them to have.
- **Curious thrill seekers who happen upon your site.** This category could include anyone. Basically, they have no special computer skills and really aren't willing to expend a great deal of energy trying to break your security, but they won't ignore things that you put in front of them.
- **Pirates, who are sometimes called *hackers*.** The term *hacker,* which originally referred to someone who is very knowledgeable about computers, is now often used to refer to someone who tries to break into someone else's computer for malevolent purposes. In all likelihood, the only reason a pirate will even bother with you is that you have achieved some notoriety and visibility. These individuals have considerable skills and resources and, if your site seems to present a challenge, you could get a visit from one of them. The best protection against these individuals is to not present them with a challenge.

- **Industrial spies.** The only reason for an industrial spy to show up at your Web site is that it contains corporate secrets. If you keep such information off your Web site, you don't need to worry about them.
- **Government security agents.** These people have the expertise and funding to defeat most, if not all, security measures. If security agents are from unfriendly nations, they could become violent to get the information they want. Our question again is, what movie have you been watching that makes you think that these people would be interested in your Web site? If, by some chance, they are interested in your Web site, you must not be very smart to have placed the kind of sensitive data that they are interested in on your Web site in the first place.

Protecting your site from real dangers

There are two areas of "real" danger that you need to be aware of and may need to protect your Web site from.

Viruses and Trojan horses

The first area of "real" danger for your Web site lies in viruses and Trojan horses. Of course, unless you've been hiding on the dark side of the moon during the past five years or so, you've already heard all about viruses and Trojan horses.

How can you protect your site and your server from them? The same way you protect your computer.

- Obtain and use a good virus-protection program. Keep it up to date.
- Use only shrink-wrapped software, purchased retail, on your server platform.
- If you use downloaded software, download it only from the primary sites for this software.
- If your server is going to accept uploads, move the uploads to other machines that are not connected to the server and test them for viruses there.
- In effect, check each and every disk and file before you use it on the server.

Viruses and Trojan horses can cause problems, but diligent efforts on your part can prevent these problems from becoming major headaches for you and your visitors. Also, the security precautions you need to have in place to protect yourself from viruses and Trojan horses will not be major inconveniences for you and your users.

Unauthorized access to your server

There are four ways by which you can prevent unauthorized access to your server:

- Hiding your logs and configuration files
- Hiding your server
- Restricting access via software
- Using screening routers

Keep in mind that all four methods work against your goal of exposing your message to the public. Use these methods only if your goal is not to provide information to the public.

Hiding your logs and configuration files

For all our talk about running an open Web site, there is one part of your server that you don't want anyone getting into: your configuration files.

Unless you are running a completely public server, you need to restrict certain directories and capabilities on your server to certain users or to yourself. Hide both your error logs and your configuration files by placing them in directories that are not accessible to the general public.

Hiding your server

Hiding your server means that you are simply making it less visible and, therefore, less likely to be discovered. The following techniques can make your server less visible:

- **Run your server on a nonstandard port.** The Web standard is port 80. Most, if not all, browsers assume that port 80 is being used if no port is specified in the URL. Using a nonstandard port is an advanced technique, and you need to make sure that the port you choose doesn't conflict with other Internet services.
- **Give your server an unusual name.** The standard method of naming a server is to name it something such as WWW.VREVOLUTION.COM. Now, if we were trying to hide our server, we might name it something weird, such as JUNKHEAP, or, better yet, not name it at all. Browsers can access servers by IP addresses alone.
- **Don't let your server show up in the access logs of others.** What this means is, don't run your Web browser from the same machine from which your server runs. If you do, your server will show up in the access log of every server you access.

Using software features to restrict access

Most, but not all, Web server software provides a variety of different security measures and features. One of the simplest methods of access restriction is to use the `Limit` directive of your software to limit access to a specific directory or deny access to specific Internet addresses.

Using routers to prevent access

A router screens traffic between your network and the Internet. Routers can block traffic based on port addresses or source and destination addresses.

Final notes on denying access

Again, we want to remind you that the purpose of the Internet was, and is, to provide information to other people. The methods of denying access that we discuss in this chapter go against this entire philosophy.

VREvolution Site Diary: Installment 4

Because of our belief that the Web should be as open as possible, we made security for VREvolution's Web site as unobtrusive as possible. The only forms of protection determined necessary and important were those to prevent viruses and Trojan horses and those to prevent unauthorized access to the directory structures, access logs, and error logs.

We also decided not to keep any secret or personal information of any kind on the Web site server.

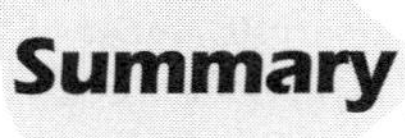

In this chapter, you've considered the issues of privacy and rights of access.

You looked at some of the security measures that you can put into place and discovered that in making the site more secure, you raise the inconvenience level for the site visitor.

Finally, you considered the question of site security in relationship to the purpose for your Web site.

In the next chapter, you begin looking at the various kinds of server software that are available.

Managing Your Real and Virtual Resources

In This Chapter

Installing Quarterdeck WebServer along with VREvolution
Configuring Quarterdeck WebServer along with VREvolution
Setting up your Web site along with VREvolution

In this chapter, we walk you through the setup of Quarterdeck's full commercial WebServer product.

The question arises as to why you should read this chapter if you have decided to use a different server software application. This software is similar to other httpd based server applications in many respects. As a result, you can use the settings described in this chapter for other applications.

VREvolution Site Diary: Installment 5

What happened to the rest of the chapter? you ask.

The answer is, this is it.

Our purpose in this chapter is to walk you through, step by step, the procedures that we went through in setting up the Web server for VREvolution. The entire chapter, therefore, is the VREvolution Site Diary.

We begin this Site Diary, and the chapter, by examining why we chose Quarterdeck's WebServer software for our site.

Selecting software for VREvolution's server

In the Site Diary for Chapter 3, we discuss some of our reasons for selecting Quarterdeck's WebServer for VREvolution's server software. We looked at five issues before making our selection:

- What kind of hardware are we using for our server?
- What kind of software platform are we using on our server?
- How much traffic do we expect to hit our server?
- What kinds of interactive applications do we plan to offer?
- What programming languages are we planning to use?

Our decisions about hardware, software, and our needs

We next look at how we answered those questions and explain the reasons for our choices.

- We decided to run our server on a 486DX2/66 with 16MB of RAM. This system has a 5 1/4-inch drive and a 3 1/2-inch drive and two hard drives that together offer 1.5GB of storage space. It also has a 2X CD-ROM and SVGA graphics. A 28.8 Kbps modem rounds out the system. We obtained Internet service for our server through the use of a dedicated telephone line that is connected to Pittsburg Online!

  Our reasons for choosing this system were partly financial. Its cost is reasonable, yet it meets our needs. This means that we can replace items that fail easily.

  Also, because this book concerns itself with setting up your Web site as inexpensively as possible, this hardware is readily available, and most people will be able to buy something similar, if not superior, locally.

- We decided to run Windows 95 on this system.

  Our reasoning here was twofold. First, from a practical point of view, most systems that you can buy off the shelf today come with Windows 95 preinstalled. Second, we decided that we wanted a 32-bit operating system because of its more stable operating environment (which means fewer GPFs), but we did not want to go to the expense of Windows NT.

- Because we anticipated moderate use of our site, we wanted to be able to accommodate at least eight simultaneous hits.

  Here, our reasoning stemmed from our estimate that, as a small company, our site was probably not going to generate more hits than any other small company's site. We decided that being able to accommodate at least eight simultaneous hits should be sufficient.

- Because the purpose of VREvolution is to teach people about virtual reality and cyberspace, VREvolution offers interactive virtual reality and 3-D graphics applications at its site.

  Another factor in our decision stems from our interest in audio and video production, multimedia production, and other interactive applications. As a result, we also have these types of applications at our site.

- Although we use a variety of languages in our programming efforts, our primary programming tools are Microsoft Visual Basic 4.0 and Microsoft Visual C++ 4.0.

  We also offer VRML applications and information at our site, and we experiment with Sun's Java, Microsoft's FrontPage, and Microsoft's Internet Suite.

Why we chose WebServer

We need to look now at how Quarterdeck's WebServer software meets our needs and how our system meets the requirements of WebServer.

- WebServer requires at least a 486/33 CPU with a minimum of 4MB of RAM. Quarterdeck recommends a 486DX2/66 with a minimum of 8MB of RAM.

  Our 486DX2/66, with 16MB of RAM, surpasses Quarterdeck's minimum requirements. It also matches the recommended CPU requirement and surpasses the recommended memory requirement.

- WebServer requires at least 2MB of hard drive space and requires 4MB if the system requires LAN Workplace files.

  Our 1.5GB of hard drive space allows sufficient space for the required files. Because we are using Windows 95, which has its own TCP/IP files, we do not need the LAN Workplace files.

- WebServer requires a working connection to a network.

  Before you say, "Well, duh! Really?" stop and think about it. Because we are discussing setting up a Web site on the Internet and the World Wide Web, you may not consider the fact that you can use this software to set up an in-house, corporate network.

- WebServer requires Windows 3.1 or greater.

  As stated previously, using Windows 95, which is a newer version than Windows 3.1, enables us to avoid having to use the LAN Workplace files.

- WebServer requires a network stack that is compliant with Winsock 1.1.

  The Winsock that is included with Windows 95 is compliant with Winsock 1.1.

- WebServer supports up to 16 simultaneous network connections.

  Our criteria was that our server needed to be able to take at least eight simultaneous hits. WebServer meets twice that criteria.

- WebServer is compatible with both the HTTP 0.9 and HTTP 1.0 protocols, so it is fully compatible with the World Wide Web and anything that uses either protocol.

The software also supports CGI Version 1.1 (discussed in Chapter 10) for executing DOS scripts, Windows-based applications, or Mosaic forms. Finally, Quarterdeck has made the software capable of running clickable image maps (discussed in Chapter 11).

- For Windows servers, the most popular programming languages are the DOS command shell, Visual Basic, C, and C++. WebServer, by providing both DOS and Windows CGI directories, allows for the use of the DOS shell for DOS CGI scripts or Visual Basic or C/C++ programs for Windows CGI scripts.

  As stated previously, Microsoft Visual Basic 4.0 and Microsoft Visual C++ 4.0 are our preferred programming languages. Because WebServer provides for the use of either language in CGI application programming, the server meets our needs to the letter.

One final word here on why we chose WebServer. As you can see from the preceding discussion, WebServer meets the needs we listed. However, several of the software applications we discuss in Chapter 3 also meet these requirements. Why, then, did we finally choose WebServer?

The answers to this question are ease of use and low cost. We found the maintenance requirements and cost factors of WebServer to be lower on both counts than for other software applications.

The next step is to install WebServer on our Windows 95 machine.

Installing the software

As we state in Chapter 3, WebServer is one of Quarterdeck's products that is designed to make Web publishing easier. Other such products from Quarterdeck include Quarterdeck Mosaic, WebCompass, WebAuthor, and Internet Suite.

See the appendix for details on accessing the encrypted, full-featured version of Quarterdeck's WebServer on the accompanying CD-ROM. You may wish to check Quarterdeck's Web page at `www.quarterdeck.com` to see if a trial version is available.

Commercial product features

The features of the commercial software are similar to those of the trialware version. Those features include

- An easy-to-use, graphical user interface that allows for customization of the administration and logging, document management, user access, script management, and network configuration functions of your server
- Concise online help
- Written documentation
- Web page samples
- Support for up to 16 simultaneous connections
- Multithreaded design that eliminates the need for a dedicated server machine
- Image map support
- Form support
- Activity logging
- Winsock 1.1 compliance
- Asynchronous processing support

As we mentioned earlier, WebServer has an easy-to-use, automated installation program that will complete most of the necessary server configuration process for you. In fact, this software is ready to run immediately after installation. We walk through the installation process for the commercial product next.

The software installation process

This commercial version of Quarterdeck's WebServer is a 16-bit application that runs under both Windows NT and Windows 95. Quarterdeck has announced plans to release a new 32-bit version of WebServer for both platforms late in 1996.

In the next several pages, we walk you through the installation of this software on our hardware. We used the commercial product that came on two floppy disks. You can follow along and make any substitutions necessary in the drive designations. The first few steps will be different for you if you install WebServer from the CD-ROM. (See the appendix.)

1. **Start Windows 95.**
2. **Insert the Quarterdeck WebServer Installation disk #1 into the 3½-inch floppy drive.**
3. **Click on the Windows 95 Start button.**

4. **Click Run.**
5. **Type** A:\INSTALL.EXE **and click on the OK button, as in Figure 5-1. (If your 3 1/2-inch floppy is drive B, type** B:\INSTALL.EXE **instead.)**

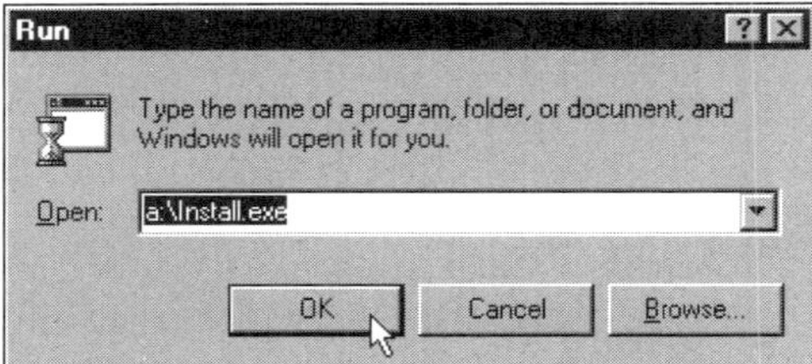

Figure 5-1: The Run dialog box.

The installation program begins, and you soon see an information screen such as the information screen in Figure 5-2 that summarizes the installation requirements for the software.

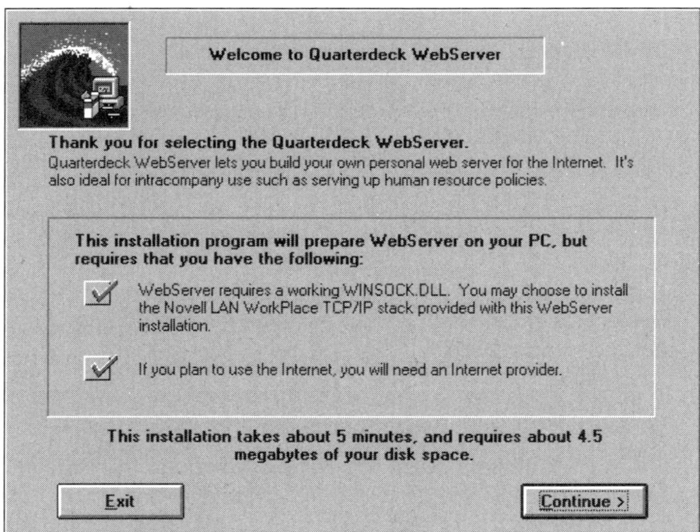

Figure 5-2: The Quarterdeck WebServer installation requirements screen.

6. **Click on the Continue button.**

   What happens next depends on whether you already have Winsock-compliant TCP/IP software installed. Because we're installing this server software onto a Windows 95 platform, you see the dialog box in Figure 5-3.

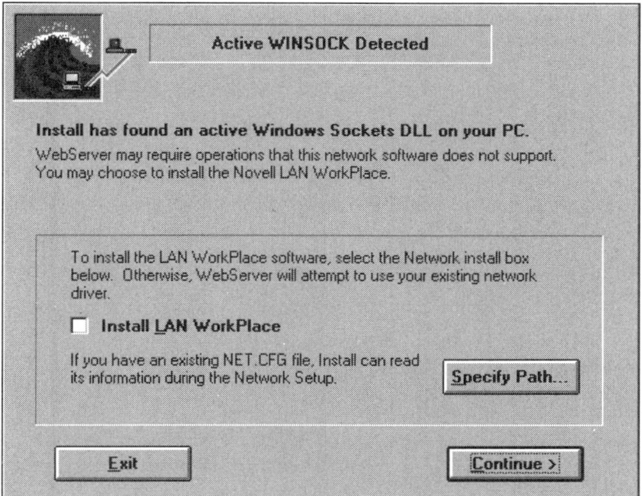

Figure 5-3: The installation program has detected Windows 95's TCP/IP software.

Because there is already an active Winsock, you don't need to replace it with the LAN WorkPlace software. If, for some reason you are not installing this software onto a Windows 95 platform, follow the onscreen directions or the manual's directions carefully for installing the LAN WorkPlace.

7. **Click on the Continue button.**

   You see something that looks like Figure 5-4 on your screen.

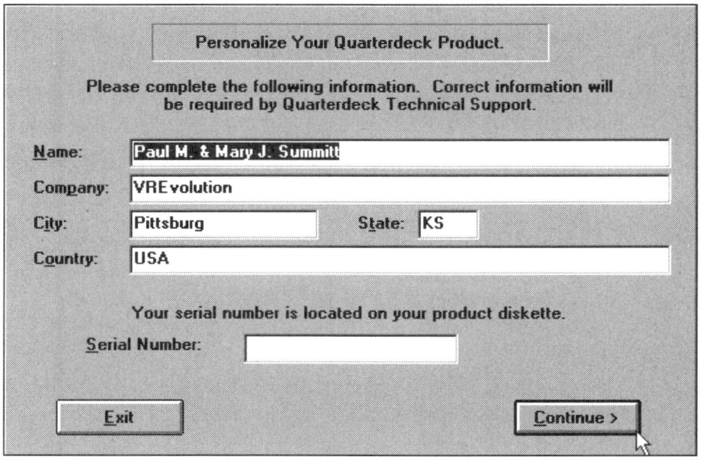

Figure 5-4: Enter your user information in the text fields of this dialog box.

8. **Fill out the information fields in the dialog box.**

   You need to enter your serial number in the last text field. Your serial number is on the label of Installation disk #1.

9. **Click on the Continue button.**

   The installation dialog box shown in Figure 5-5 appears. From this dialog box, you can determine what drive and subdirectory to install the product in and what program group to place the program icons in.

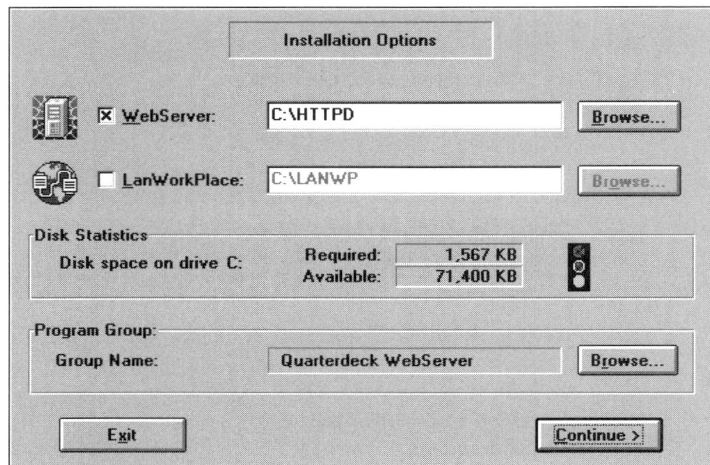

Figure 5-5: The Quarterdeck WebServer Installation Options dialog box.

This dialog box tells you how much space is required for installation and how much space is available on that drive. If you don't have enough space, either change the drive where you want to install the software or click on the Exit button and then free up the required amount of space.

10. **Make sure that the WebServer check box is checked so that the software will be installed.**

    You also can change your mind at this point and install the LAN WorkPlace TCP/IP product instead of your current Windows 95 Winsock application. If you are running Windows 95, we recommend that you keep your current Winsock and accept the program's recommended defaults, as we have done.

11. **Click on the Continue button.**

    If you're installing the commercial version over a previous installation of the trial version, you'll be asked whether you want to overwrite your existing configuration files or sample HTML files. Check the appropriate boxes if you want to upgrade these files.

    If you are installing for the first time (or you have uninstalled the trial version as we have done), you see the Installation User Options dialog box that is shown in Figure 5-6. If you are installing over a previously installed version, the program will use the information you provided earlier.

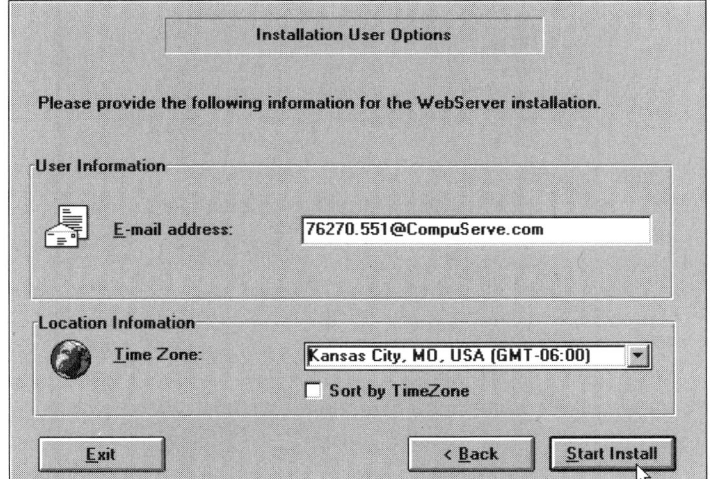

Figure 5-6: Give the server your e-mail address and set the time zone.

12. **Type the e-mail address that you want the server to use for users to send you e-mail and choose your time zone.**
13. **Click on the Start Install button.**

    The server software is installed to the hard drive that you've selected. You need to replace the installation disks when the program asks you to do so.

    When the program is finished installing, you see the window in Figure 5-7.

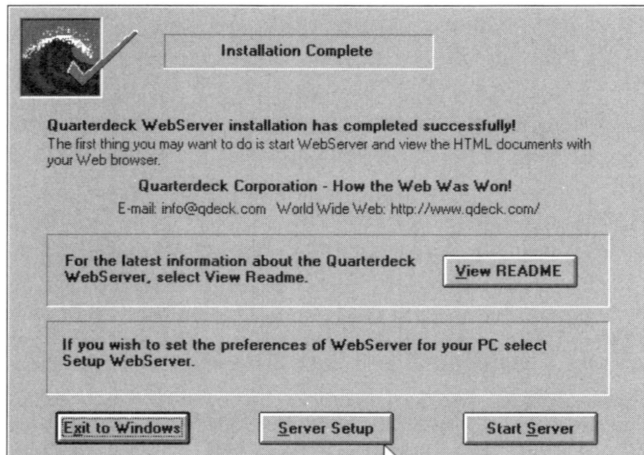

Figure 5-7: Read the README file for more information.

The installation is now complete. You'll probably want to read the README file for more information about the server software. Also, you'll want to write down the e-mail address (`info@qdeck.com`) and the Web page URL (`http://www.qdeck.com/`) for Quarterdeck. These locations are where you can get more information and perhaps have some of your questions answered. There's also a Quarterdeck forum on CompuServe. Just type **GO QUARTERDECK**.

At this point, you are ready to start, test, and exit the server software and then set any preferences you may have for the software.

Starting, testing, and exiting WebServer

Before you start the server software, make sure that you have a functioning network connection and that your Winsock and TCP/IP software are configured correctly and running.

Follow these steps to start and test WebServer:

1. **Double-click on the WebServer icon in the WebServer Program group, as shown in Figure 5-8.**

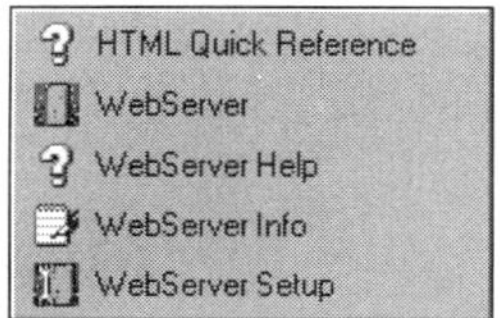

Figure 5-8: Double-click on the WebServer icon.

The WebServer window (see Figure 5-9) is displayed briefly and then minimized automatically to the bottom of the Windows 95 screen.

Figure 5-9: The Quarterdeck WebServer window.

If the server software doesn't start as expected, look in your C:\HTTPD\HTTPD.LOG file for an explanation.

In order to have the server software start automatically whenever you start Windows 95, copy the Quarterdeck WebServer icon to the Windows Startup group.

2. **Start your Web browser.**
3. **Type your IP address or your host name into the URL text box on your browser in the following format:** http://*address*.

   You see the file index.htm, which is the server's home page. There will be a link here to "server demonstration."
4. **Click the server demonstration link and check out the various links that have information on the following:**

   - Basic document retrieval
   - Document-based queries
   - Form-based queries
   - Directory tree navigation
   - File retrieval
   - Image maps
   - CGI

Take a few minutes to walk through these pages. Make sure that your server software is correctly configured to work with your setup.

After you check the software and know what changes you may want to make to the server configuration files, you need to shut down the server software.

1. **Maximize the WebServer icon so that you see the WebServer window shown in Figure 5-9.**
2. **Choose File and then choose one of the two ways to shut down the server software.**
    - Choose Exit for a graceful shutdown that allows the software to wait for any current active network requests to finish before shutting down the software and exiting.
    - Choose Force Exit to terminate any active network requests immediately and then shut down the software and exit. (Clicking on the *X* in the upper-right corner of the window has the same effect as choosing Force Exit.)

Setting WebServer's preferences

Next, you customize the WebServer software to meet your needs. The first thing that you need to do is choose the WebServer Setup icon from the Quarterdeck WebServer program group.

The first screen that you see looks similar to the WebServer Setup window shown in Figure 5-10.

From Quarterdeck's WebServer Setup dialog box, you can change the following preferences:

- Administration & Logging
- Directory Listings
- Aliasing & Redirection
- MIME Types & Encodings
- Network setup
- Access Permissions
- Script Management
- User Management

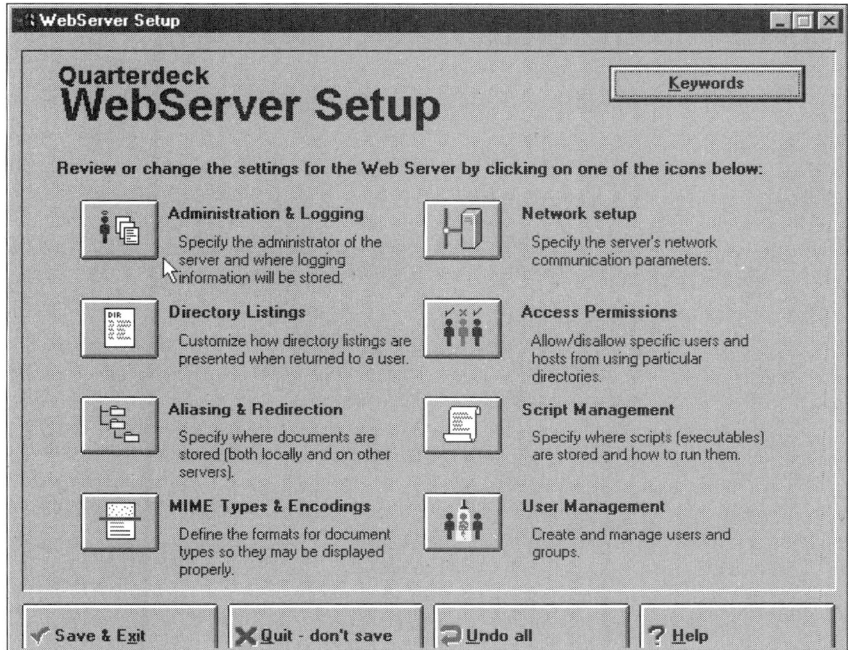

Figure 5-10: The WebServer Setup dialog box.

The dialog box includes a Keywords button and a Help button, which can provide considerable assistance.

In the next few pages, we work through the various setup options for WebServer. This information will give you a general idea of how to set up your preferences. Also, as we suggest earlier in the chapter, this information is applicable to other server software.

Quarterdeck makes it easy for you to set preferences. You simply click on the button for the category of preferences that you want to set, make the changes you want in the dialog box that appears, and then click on the Return to main menu button to return to the WebServer Setup dialog box.

Administration & Logging

When you click on the Administration & Logging button, you see a screen that resembles Figure 5-11. From this screen you can easily reconfigure your software installation options. Those options include such things as the server administrator's e-mail address, the location of log files, and the root directory for all of your documents. If the installation program installed the program's files to the default locations, you shouldn't need to make any modifications in this dialog box unless you specifically want to change things. We recommend that you stick with the defaults until you have more experience working with this software.

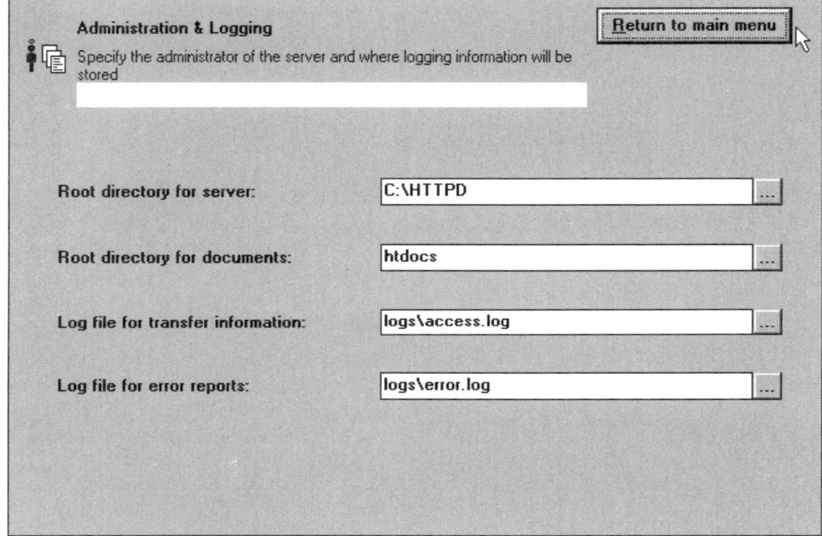

Figure 5-11: *Changing the Administration & Logging preferences is easy from this dialog window.*

Directory Listings

To customize how directory listings appear to users, click on the Directory Listings button. You see a dialog box like the one in Figure 5-12.

The server software can create directory listings that enable remote users to download files from your server simply by clicking on the filenames for these files. This feature eliminates the need to use FTP.

The configuration options that you select here determine whether your directory listings can include clickable icons or display HTML footnote files automatically at the bottom of the listings.

You can also enter the filename of your home page in the Override listing with file box.

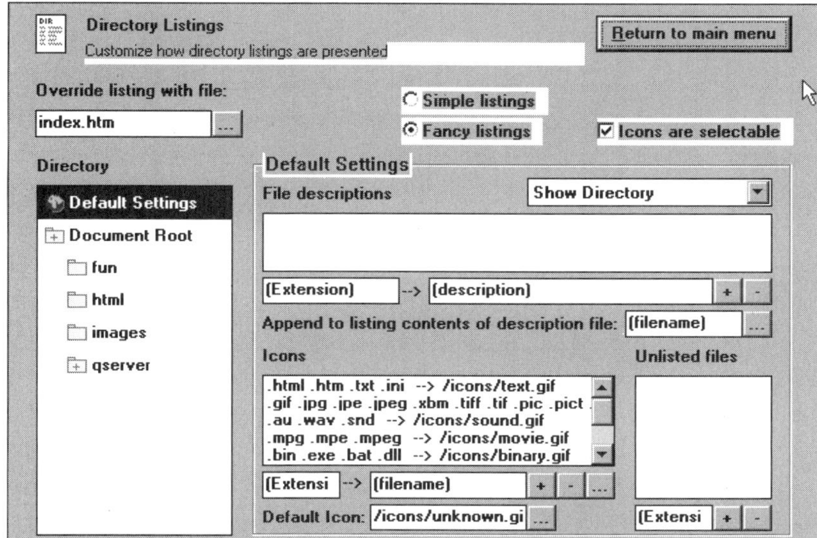

Figure 5-12: *Here you can customize how your directory listings are presented to your users on the Web.*

Another thing that you can do in this dialog box is improve the performance of WebServer. If you disable the Fancy listings feature, users can access your site faster. When icons are used in your directory listings, each icon requires a separate request from the user's Web browser. If you turn off the Fancy listings option, it reduces the number of requests made to the server and therefore speeds up the software. We left Fancy listings enabled on our server. Our decision was based on our efforts to provide a more graphical presentation on our site.

Aliasing & Redirection

Clicking on the Aliasing & Redirection button brings a dialog box that is similar to Figure 5-13 to your screen.

Your HTML pages will most likely contain hyperlinks to other files on your own server. Others may also have hyperlinks in their pages that point to files on your server. If you were to relocate some of your HTML files to other directories, or to other servers, all of those links would become invalid. Two things can prevent this from happening and keep the links working: aliasing and redirection.

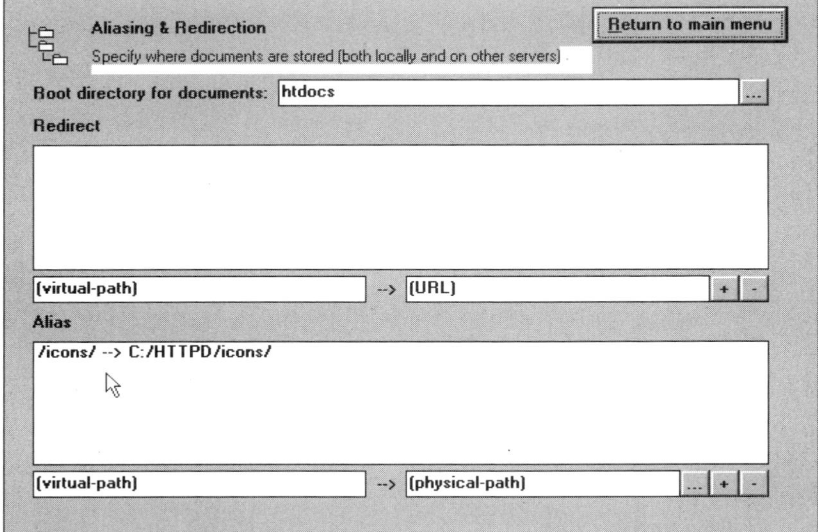

Figure 5-13: You can assign virtual paths to your physical paths and URLs from this dialog window.

- *Aliases* translate requests for one directory to another on the same server. In other words, aliases change the name of the old directory that is referred to in a hyperlink to the new directory where the files are actually located.
- *Redirection* is an extremely useful feature if you decide to relocate documents from one server to another. WebServer redirects any network requests for the old location to the new location automatically.

In the Aliasing & Redirection dialog box, you can assign virtual paths to your physical paths and URLs. We recommend that you not change anything here until you've developed more experience with the server.

MIME Types & Encodings

When you click on the MIME Types & Encodings button, you see a dialog box that looks like the one in Figure 5-14.

MIME types enable the browser and the server to communicate and cooperate when exchanging data. Both have to agree on what kind of data is being exchanged.

You'll use this window to add the VRML MIME extensions we discuss in Chapter 7. You will also define any other MIME types and encodings needed to handle whatever special applications you will be supporting with your server.

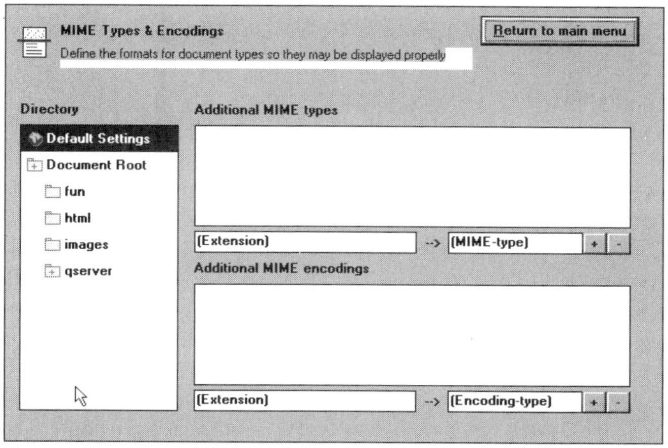

Figure 5-14: Here you can add, change, or delete the various MIME types available on your server.

Network setup

When you click on the Network setup button, you see a dialog box that looks like Figure 5-15. The options available here include technical network information such as the port number and the timeout interval. Make sure that you enter the correct host name for your server machine. For example, in the figure, we've entered just VREvolution. The full host name for the server should be `Pvrevolution.pitton.com`.

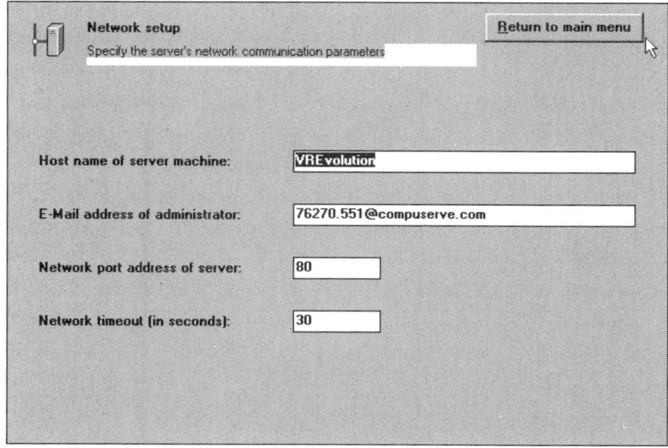

Figure 5-15: Confirm your network's communication parameters from this dialog window.

In the text box for the e-mail address of the administrator, give the address where you want to receive mail that contains comments about the server. For example, we've used our CompuServe address, but we could just as easily use `VREvolution@pitton.com`. Check with your service provider to make sure that you know what your mailing address should be.

You can change the network port address from this dialog box, but we recommend that you use the default port, 80, for your server.

Finally, you can modify the network timeout interval. If you are working with an exceptionally slow server, you may want to raise this number. Otherwise, leave it alone.

Access Permissions

Clicking on the Access Permissions button moves you to the dialog box shown in Figure 5-16.

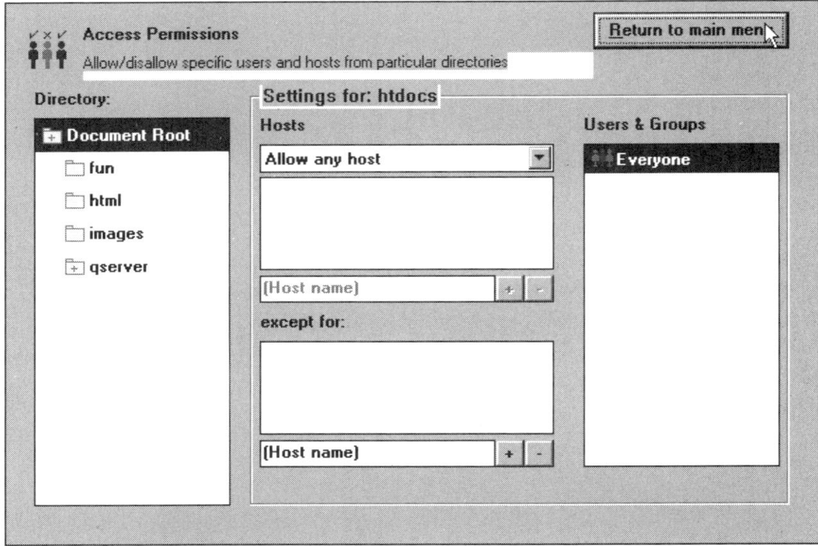

Figure 5-16: *Here you can determine who gets access to what on your server.*

You may or may not place information on your server that's not intended for public release. You may have information that you want only members of your company or other authorized users to have access to.

WebServer supports two methods of access restriction:

- Host name or IP address restriction
- Username/password authentication

The first method, host name or IP address restriction, allows only those people having addresses from a particular address to access an area of the server. For example, we could restrict a certain area of our server only to CompuServe users, another only to AOL users, and another only to users from pitton.com.

The second method, username/password authentication, requires that users provide usernames and passwords before your server will provide the restricted HTML documents.

The Access Permissions dialog box enables you to determine which of your users can have access to which documents on your server. This option may be important in the future. Until you've gained more experience with the server software, however, we recommend that you leave this feature as it is.

Script Management

From the main menu, click on the Script Management button to see a dialog box that is similar to Figure 5-17.

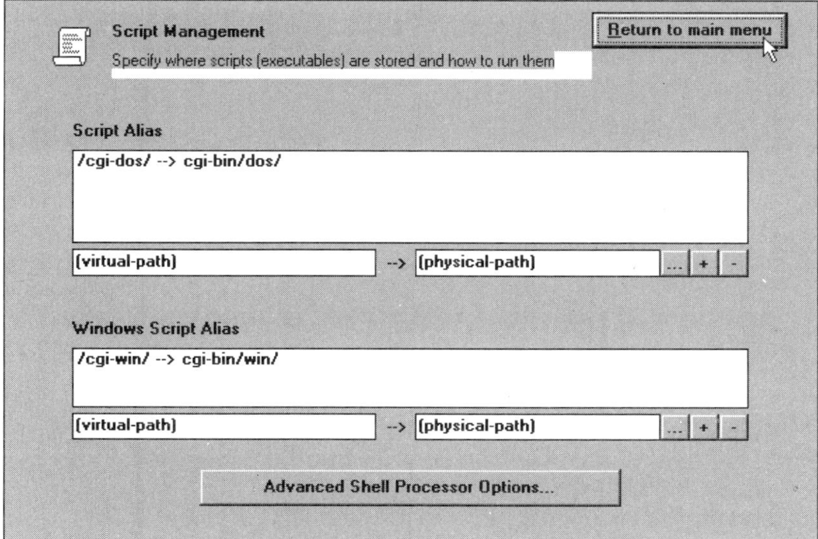

Figure 5-17: In this dialog box, you specify where your executables are stored and how they are run from the server.

You will more than likely be running scripts, or application programs, on your server. WebServer comes preconfigured with the appropriate directories for your custom script applications. If you decide to use WebServer, you'll return to this dialog box in Part IV of this book to assign aliases for your CGI scripts and Visual Basic programs.

User Management

Finally, click on the User Management button to see a dialog box that looks similar to Figure 5-18.

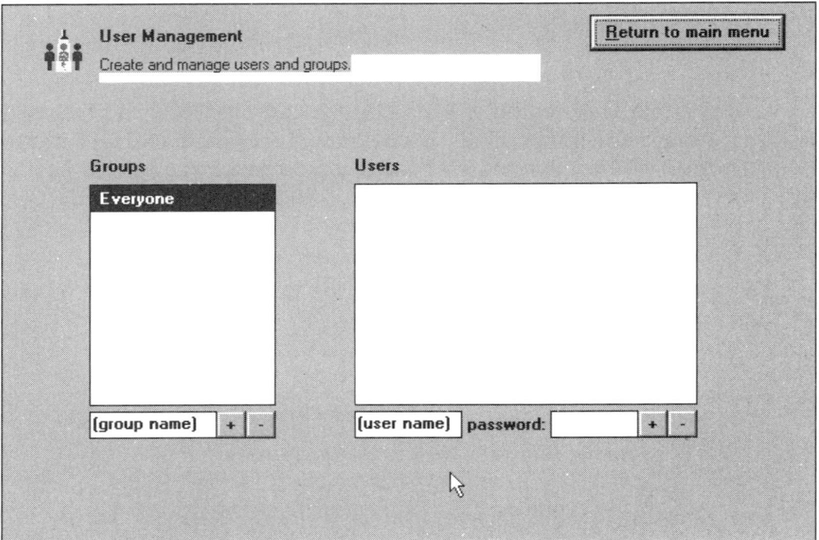

Figure 5-18: *WebServer's User Management dialog box enables you to maintain server security.*

Before you can impose the user-level access restrictions that we discuss in the explanation of the options in the Access Permissions dialog box, you need to define the usernames and passwords that you want WebServer to apply to any restricted documents you have.

In the User Management dialog box, you can assign users specific passwords to increase your server's security. This page enables you to add, modify, or delete users quickly and easily. You can even create groups of users and grant or deny the entire group access to documents at once.

If you are going to run an open Web server, you do not need to make any changes to this dialog box.

Saving and exiting

In the Quarterdeck WebServer Setup window, click on the Save & Exit button in the lower left of the screen. WebServer saves any changes that you've made to the configuration, and you exit the setup program.

One last possible change

The only other modification you may need to make concerns the Time Zone environment variable in your AUTOEXEC.BAT file. Although you set this variable during the installation process, you can modify this format to accommodate daylight savings time.

You can do this by changing the entry to the following format:

```
TZ=XXXYZZZ
```

Here's what the characters in italic mean:

- *XXX* represents a three-letter time-zone name, such as CST (central standard time).
- *Y* represents a signed (+ or -) number that gives the difference in hours between the local time zone and Greenwich mean time (or Universal Coordinated Time, UCT).
- Finally, *ZZZ* represents the three-letter time-code name, such as CDT (central daylight time).

For example, CST6CDT represents central standard time, six hours offset from UCT, central daylight time.

Restarting the server

The next thing that you want to do is rename your home page. To do that, you first need to restart WebServer by double-clicking on the WebServer icon in the WebServer Program group. After the WebServer window is minimized to the bottom of the Windows 95 screen, change the name of your home page to INDEX.HTM and store the file in the \httpd\ subdirectory.

Establishing the VREvolution presence

With the server software up and running properly, your next step is to establish a new presence with a new Web page. We decided to use some of the interactive technologies that are covered in this book to create a new series of Web pages for VREvolution.

We began with a relatively simple home page that included graphics, audio, animations, and links to more complicated pages to be housed on the site. We walk through the creation of this page in the next section.

Creating the page

We could have used a variety of tools to create the page, but we decided to use Internet Assistant for Word for Windows and the Source editing function of Microsoft Internet Explorer. This function of Internet Explorer allowed us to see the page as it would be displayed. We could also move back and forth quickly between the editing and Web views.

We began by using Internet Assistant for Word for Windows to create a basic page and then exiting Word and, running Internet Explorer, viewing the page we had created. We'll walk you through the HTML file.

The first HTML commands needed by the file are the <HTML> and <HEAD> commands.

```
<HTML>
<HEAD>
```

These commands are followed by the <TITLE> and "AUTHOR" information.

```
<TITLE>VREvolution Web Site Home Page</TITLE>
<META NAME="AUTHOR" CONTENT="Paul M. Summitt">
</HEAD>
```

With the HEAD completed, we can turn our attention to the body of this page.

```
<BODY>
<P>
```

Remember that the <P> command starts a new paragraph. The first thing that the viewer would actually see that we will program in is the background.

```
<BODY BACKGROUND="images/bkg14.gif">
```

This statement gives us a background on which to create the rest of the page. It finds the .GIF file in the images subdirectory on the server. We discuss the HTML particulars in Chapter 6.

The next command is specific to Microsoft Internet Explorer. In other words, people using other browsers such as Netscape will miss out on this. We used the following command to make audio play in the background when people visit our site:

```
<BGSOUND SRC="images/minuet.mid" loop=infinite>
```

This command causes the viewer's machine to play the minuet MIDI file that is in the images subdirectory if the proper MIDI player is installed on the computer with the Web browser. We discuss the use of audio more fully in Chapter 9.

The next part of our HTML file contains the display information for the VREvolution logo and motto:

```
<H1><center><IMG SRC="images/vre_logo.jpg"⮐
ALIGN=top>VREvolution<IMG⮐
SRC="images/vre_logo.jpg"</center></H1>
<P>
<H2><center><i>Exploring the Quantum Dimensions of Cyberspace<⮐
i></center></H2>
<P>
```

We then wanted to welcome any visitors to our site, but at the same time let them know that the pages found here would be constantly under construction. The use of the marquee is specific to users who are viewing with Microsoft Internet Explorer. Netscape and other browsers will see not the moving marquee but a static line of text.

```
<h4><center>Welcome to the VREvolution Web Site.</center></h4>
<p><center><img src="images/constlin.gif"</center></p>
<h6><center><Marquee width=50% direction=left⮐
align=middle border=0>
<b>These pages are currently under construction.⮐
Please excuse our mess.</b>
</center>
<p>
```

These statements create the marquee effect that produces the words that scroll across the screen.

We also wanted visitors to be able to check out our pages on other sites, so the next few statements in the page provide hyperlinks so visitors can simply click on these links and go directly to our other pages.

```
<h3>For More information on:</h3>
<p>
<h4><img src="images/dotblue.gif"ALIGN=BOTTOM><A↵
HREF="http://ourworld.compuserve.com/homepages/PSummitt/">↵
Creating Cool 3D Web Worlds with VRML</A>
<p>
<img src="images/dotblue.gif"ALIGN=BOTTOM>↵
<A HREF="http:/↵
www.webmaster.com/VREvolution/">VREvolution</A>
</h4>
<p>
```

These hyperlinks connect this Web page to our pages on CompuServe's server and to our pages on WebMaster's server.

Finally, the HTML file needs to close both the `<BODY>` and the `<HTML>` commands.

```
<p>
<h6><center><i>These pages copyrighted 1996,<b>VREvolution</↵
b>.<i>
</BODY>
</HTML>
```

Listing 5-1 shows the entire HTML file.

Listing 5-1: INDEX.HTM

```
<HTML>
<HEAD>
<TITLE>VREvolution Web Site Home Page</TITLE>
<META NAME="AUTHOR" CONTENT="Paul M. Summitt">
</HEAD>
<BODY>
<P>
<BODY BACKGROUND="images/bkg14.gif">
<BGSOUND SRC="images/minuet.mid" loop=infinite>
<H1><center><IMG SRC="images/vre_logo.jpg"
ALIGN=top>VREvolution<IMG↵
SRC="images/vre_logo.jpg"<center></H1>
<P>
<H2><center><i>Exploring the Quantum Dimensions of↵
Cyberspace</i></center></H2>
```

```
<P>
<h4><center>Welcome to the VREvolution Web Site.</cen
ter></h4>
<p><center><img src="images/constlin.gif"</center></p>
<h6><center>
<Marquee width=50% direction=left align=middle border=0>
<b>These pages are currently under construction.↩
Please excuse our mess.</b>
</center>
<p>
<h3>For More information on:</h3>
<p>
<h4><img src="images/dotblue.gif"ALIGN=BOTTOM><A↩
HREF="http://ourworld.compuserve.com/homepages/PSummitt↩
">Creating Cool 3D Web Worlds with VRML</A>
<p>
<img src="images/dotblue.gif"ALIGN=BOTTOM>↩
<A HREF="http://www.webmaster.com/VREvolution">↩
VREvolution</A>
</h4>
<p>
<p>
<h6><center><i>These pages copyrighted↩
1996,<b>VREvolution</b>.<i>
</BODY>
</HTML>
```

As we said, the page is constantly under construction. The first viewing of the page showed us a modification that had to be made immediately.

Looking at the page

Figure 5-19 shows what the page looked like after we finished creating the first version of it.

Notice that the background color of the marquee is gray instead of white as in the rest of the page's background. You can change the color easily.

Remember that the lines that create this marquee read as follows:

```
<h6><center>
<Marquee width=50% direction=left align=middle border=0>
<b>These pages are currently under construction.↩
Please excuse our mess.</b>
</center>
```

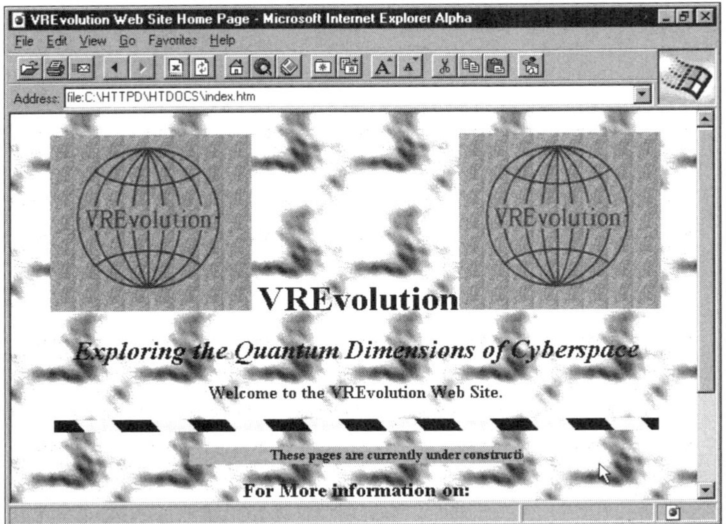

Figure 5-19: The VREvolution Web site home page (circa February 1996).

Change this code by adding `BGCOLOR=#ffffff`, as shown in the following snippet from the listing:

```
<h6><center>
<Marquee width=50% direction=left align=middle border=0
BGCOLOR=#ffffff>
<b>These pages are currently under construction. Please
excuse our mess.</b>
</center>
```

This statement changes the color of the background under the marquee to white. The white background to the marquee fits better with the background for the entire page now.

Future modifications to this page

As we said, the page is under construction. By the time you read this chapter, other modifications will include

- A VRML world (see Chapter 7)
- Java and JavaScript applets (see Chapter 8)
- More animations, audio, and video clips (see Chapter 9)

- CGI applications (see Chapter 10)
- Image maps, e-mail, databases, and search engines (see Chapter 11)
- User and usage statistics (see Chapter 12)

Summary

In this chapter, you've been exposed to the criteria by which you should select your server software.

You've also learned how to install Quarterdeck's WebServer software.

You learned how to modify the server software to accommodate your personal Web site.

This chapter concludes Part II of this book. You've now made many decisions concerning your Web site. With the conclusion of this part, you should have selected the Web server software that your site will use and you should have installed it on your platform.

Starting with Part III, we begin to examine more closely the various components of a Web page that enable you to create an interactive Web site. Chapter 6 covers HTML.

PART III
FURNISHING
YOUR VIRTUAL
HOME IN
CYBERSPACE
Chapter 6 HTML
Chapter 7 VRML
Chapter 8 Java
Chapter 9 Audio and Video Clips

There are many furnishings that you can use to spruce up your cyberhome: HTML, VRML, Java, and audio and video clips are just a few of them. In the next few chapters, we look at how you can use these tools to make your cyberhome more enjoyable both for yourself and for your visitors.

In this part, we examine how to use Hypertext Markup Language (HTML) to create your Web pages. The VREvolution Site Diary discusses which tools VREvolution has used to create its sites, where you can get these HTML authoring tools, and how to use them.

We also show you how to use the Virtual Reality Modeling Language (VRML) to create an interesting 3-D Web page. We look at some of the tools that are available, tell you where you can get them, and describe how to use them to create worlds for your Web site.

We also describe how to use Java to create some new and interesting interactive sites on the Web.

Finally, we wrap up Part III of this book by looking at and listening to video and audio clips.

HTML

In This Chapter

The development of HTML
Using HTML
Examining and choosing a Web-authoring tool
Installing and using Microsoft Internet Assistant
Installing and using SoftQuad's HoTMetaL
Installing and using WebMania!
Creating basic Web pages
VREvolution Site Diary

The heart of every Web page, what makes it all possible, is HTML. You know that HTML stands for *Hypertext Markup Language*. But what can you do with HTML?

This chapter covers the basics of HTML and describes how to create the documents that will explain to your cybervisitors what your Web site is about.

We begin with a brief explanation of what HTTP does and how it does it. After that, we briefly cover the use of HTML. This chapter will not be, however, the be-all-and-end-all explanation of how to use HTML to create a Web page. Plenty of other books do that. *Creating Cool Web Pages with HTML,* 2nd Edition, by Dave Taylor, and *HTML For Dummies,* 2nd Edition, by Ed Tittel and Steve James (both from IDG Books Worldwide, Inc.), are two books that you may want to take a look at. All we want to do in this chapter is give you enough background and skills so that you can create a Web page using some of the tools that we discuss here.

In the process, we look at some HTML editors, examine their strengths and weaknesses, tell you where and how to get them, and explain how to install and use the editors that are on the *Creating Cool Interactive Web Sites CD-ROM.*

The Development of HTML

The main purpose behind the development of HTML was to create a method of encoding plain ASCII text with complex hypermedia document control strings that focus the document more on structure than on appearance. Another important consideration was the need for these documents to be accessible by a wide variety of platforms so that anyone who accesses the Internet can access the documents, no matter what computer, operating system, or network they are using.

It's probably not a coincidence that HTML looks a lot like the industry standard, *Standard Generalized Markup Language (SGML).* HTML can be thought of as a subset, or perhaps an application, of SGML. SGML is found mainly on high-end workstations, where the creators of HTML spent a large proportion of their time. The creators of HTML were probably extremely familiar with SGML. HTML can be used in conjunction with SGML. HTML, however, isn't as extensive as the full SGML standard.

The Four HTML Versions

Currently, four different versions, or levels, of HTML coexist on the Web: Versions 0.9, 1.0, 2.0, and 3.0. In addition, both Netscape and Microsoft have added their own extensions to these versions, making things even more confusing in some ways.

Version 0.9 and 1.0

Versions 0.9 and 1.0 of HTML deal with the control of headings, lists, and character formatting. We've grouped these two versions together because there is very little change from 0.9 to 1.0. The original Mosaic 1.0 browser, which many of today's browsers were derived from, supported these versions. Most browsers, therefore, can read the Version 0.9 and 1.0 codes, and the commands available in these two versions are relatively easy to learn. In order for you to take advantage of the full implementation of graphics, sounds, Java, VRML, and other interactive capabilities, however, you need to learn the commands found in Versions 2.0 and 3.0, as well as the extensions provided by Netscape and Microsoft.

Version 2.0

Version 2.0 of HTML adds commands for menus and interactive forms. Most browsers can interpret Version 2.0's menu and form commands, but don't count on all browsers having that capability. Some users are still working with older browsers or are accessing HTML documents by using connections that don't provide full Web access. These visitors won't see your menus or forms if you use these commands.

Version 3.0

Version 3.0 of HTML is capable of supporting many new functions, including background bitmaps and the ability to create tables. Some of the more recent Web browsers have implemented many of Version 3.0's features. Don't expect, however, that all visitors will be using browsers that can handle these new features.

Netscape and Microsoft extensions

Both Netscape and Microsoft determined that the specifications of the various versions did not go far enough. Both, therefore, added their own extensions to the HTML specification to expand the capabilities of their browsers. Unfortunately, this has led to considerable differences in the ways that a page may look when viewed with one browser rather than another browser.

Using HTML

As we've suggested previously in this book, there are several places where you can find better and more in-depth explanations of how to use HTML. In this short HTML tutorial section, we stick mostly to Version 0.9 and 1.0 commands. In later chapters, we cover some of the commands that you can use to take advantage of the more interactive capabilities of HTML.

We group the Version 0.9 and 1.0 commands into eight basic categories: structural commands, text-flow commands, heading commands, character-formatting commands, list-formatting commands, special character escape sequences, in-line graphic commands, and anchor commands. In the following sections, we walk you through each of these categories and look at some examples of using these commands.

Structural commands

Structural commands define the parts of the Web document that you are creating. Table 6-1 shows some examples of these types of commands.

Table 6-1 Examples of Structural Commands

HTML Tag	Closing Tag	What the Command Does
<HTML>	</HTML>	Opens and closes an HTML Web file
<HEAD>	</HEAD>	Opens and closes formatting information
<BODY>	</BODY>	Defines the body of an HTML document

Other structural commands will probably be of interest and use to you later, but these three commands are the most important ones for now.

Text-flow commands

Text-flow commands assist in the formatting of the information within the HTML document. These commands don't require you to include closing tags. Table 6-2 shows some examples of text-flow commands.

Table 6-2 Examples of Text-Flow Commands

HTML Tag	What the Command Does
<P>	Indicates the end of a paragraph
 	Forces a line break
<HR>	Draws a horizontal line across the window

There are many other text-flow commands. These three are the ones you'll probably use the most.

Heading commands

Heading commands define headings and subheadings within your Web page. Just like the structural tags, heading tags come in pairs. One tag goes at the beginning of the heading, and the other goes at the end. Table 6-3 shows the six levels for heading tags.

Table 6-3 Heading Commands

HTML Tag	Closing Tag	What the Command Does
<H1>	</H1>	Opens and closes heading level 1
<H2>	</H2>	Opens and closes heading level 2
<H3>	</H3>	Opens and closes heading level 3
<H4>	</H4>	Opens and closes heading level 4
<H5>	</H5>	Opens and closes heading level 5
<H6>	</H6>	Opens and closes heading level 6

The type size and typeface for the display of each heading level depend on the browser that visitors use to access your document. The most important thing here is that heading level one is always the largest, and heading level six is always the smallest. Also, remember that heading tags terminate the current paragraph.

Character-formatting commands

This group of commands has two basic subcategories. The first subcategory deals with physical characteristics, and the second subcategory deals with logical characteristics. Keep in mind that these tags are always in pairs. Table 6-4 shows some of the character tags for physical characteristics.

Table 6-4 Examples of Character Commands for Physical Characteristics

HTML Tag	Closing Tag	What the Command Does
<B>	</B>	Creates **bold** text in a document
<I>	</I>	Creates *italicized* text in a document
<U>	</U>	Creates underlined text in a document

Keep in mind that these commands for physical characteristics have absolutely no effect on the formatting of anything outside of the opening and closing of the command. The commands operate to a large degree like the formatting of your word processor in that they don't change spacing or indentation.

The second subcategory of character-formatting commands includes a larger number of tags. These character tags for logical characteristics are more abstract than the tags for physical characteristics. Because of the large number of these tags, Table 6-5 illustrates just a few of them.

Table 6-5 Examples of Character Commands for Logical Characteristics

HTML Tag	Closing Tag	What the Command Does
<ADDRESS>	</ADDRESS>	Provides contact information for the author of the HTML document
<CITE>	</CITE>	Opens and closes citation information
<SAMP>	</SAMP>	Opens and closes sample outputs of commands

At the present time, many Web browsers interpret these character-formatting tags for logical characteristics the same way that they interpret the character-formatting tags for physical characteristics. The logical subcategory, however, should provide information about the nature of the text as well as about its appearance. Currently, there's no way to tell what any given visitor's Web browser is going to do with commands in the logical subcategory. If you can, however, use the logical subcategory rather than the physical one whenever possible. The reason for this is that someday it is hoped that the browsers will interpret these subcategories differently.

Another warning: Try not to use multiple categories on the same text. There's really no telling what the different browsers will do with your text if you do.

List-formatting commands

You can use list-formatting commands to create three basic styles of lists for your Web page: ordered lists, unordered lists, and definition lists. Table 6-6 shows some of the commands for these three styles and explains each type of list.

Table 6-6 Examples of List-Formatting Commands

HTML Tag	Closing Tag	What the Command Does
<OL>	</OL>	Opens and closes an ordered list where each item is numbered
<UL>	</UL>	Opens and closes an unordered or bulleted list
<DL>	</DL>	Opens and closes a definition list

You need to mark individual items within ordered and unordered lists with the tag <LI>. You mark text inside definition lists with the tags <DT> and <DD>, which define the text as terms or definitions, respectively.

Special character escape sequences

One of the most important considerations for HTML is that it be compatible with a wide variety of platforms. Most HTML documents, therefore, are created so as to display using the lowest common denominator of ASCII. Sometimes, however, especially in electronic publishing, you may need to use non-ASCII symbols. *Special character escape sequences* enable you to use non-ASCII symbols by encoding them into the HTML document. We've presented some of these symbols and their codes in Table 6-7.

Table 6-7 Examples of Commands for Special Character Escape Sequences

Escape Sequence	Displays as
`<`	<
`>`	>
`&`	&
`"`	"
`©`	©
`®`	®

A large number of escape sequences are available. You can find the entire list of escape sequences in the HTML 3.0 specifications at `http://www.hp.co.uk` or `http://www.w3.org`, as well as at other locations.

In-line graphics commands

Graphics images aren't really embedded in HTML documents. Instead, you use the `<IMG>` tag to refer to them in the HTML document, and the graphics image is stored in a separate file either on the same computer as the HTML file or on any addressable Web server. The basic format of the `<IMG>` tag is

```
<IMG SRC="URL" [ALIGN=TOP|MIDDLE|BOTTOM] [ALT="text"]>
```

When the browser views this tag, the graphics image stored at the location specified by the referenced URL is retrieved into the document and aligned according to the optional alignment parameters. The default alignment parameter is `BOTTOM`.

Another optional parameter for the `<IMG>` tag is the `ALT` parameter. You use the `ALT` parameter to specify certain text that is to be displayed in place of the image when the document is being viewed by character-only browsers.

Usually, the graphical browsers can handle a variety of different image formats, including JPEG and CompuServe GIF files.

Anchor commands

Anchor commands are used to designate and code *hyperlinks,* the words or, in some cases, bitmaps, that the user clicks on to get from one document to the next or to another location within the same document. Hyperlinked words are generally underlined, and their default color is usually blue.

The basic form of an anchor tag is

```
<A HREF-"URL"> your words</A>
```

where *your words* is what the user sees. The URL is the location of the hyperlink. This URL can be absolute, relative, or local:

- The URL is *absolute* if it contains the full host name and filename of the document that is to be displayed.
- The URL is *relative* if the path to the document is the same as the path of the original document.
- The URL is *local* if the file is on the machine that is running the browser instead of on the server.

Using a Simple HTML Editor

You can create a Web page by using any text editor that saves your files in ASCII format and enables you to save the file with the HTML extension (.HTM for 16-bit PCs). Of course, you have to be willing to memorize all the commands we explained on the preceding pages, as well as several hundred or so more commands.

Rather than memorize all those commands, another option is to download the latest specification for HTML that's currently available and then keep that 190+-page document next to you as you plan your Web pages at your computer.

A more reasonable method, and the one that we prefer, is to use one of the various HTML editors that are available in commercial, shareware, or public domain versions. In the next few pages, we look at some HTML authoring tools.

HTML authoring tools

Several HTML editors are available and distributed on the Internet for free. Other authoring tools come in both trial and commercial versions. All of these tools enable you to load and edit HTML files directly on your computer. The following sections describe some of these editors.

CU_HTML.DOT and other word processor templates

CU_HTML.DOT is a template that enables you to create HTML documents from inside Word for Windows. If you're a Word for Windows user, you get to use the same WYSIWYG screen that you're used to, and you can generate the resulting HTML file directly from Word. You also get to use your spell checker and grammar checker, as well as any of the other tools in Word that you've gotten used to.

Keep in mind though, that this add-on template comes with no support. The copyright for this software is owned by the Computer Services Centre of the Chinese University of Hong Kong. You can download the most up-to-date version of this template from `ftp.cuhk.hk` under the filename CU-HTML.ZIP. You can download other versions of this template, as well as other word processor add-ons, from the forums listed in Table 6-8.

Table 6-8 Where to Find Word Processor HTML Add-Ons on CompuServe

Filename	Word Processor	File Size	Forum
GTHTML.ZIP	WinWord 6.0	40,040 bytes	INETRE SOURCE
TAGWIZ.ZIP	WinWord 6.0	471,868 bytes	INETRE SOURCE
ANTHTM.ZIP	WinWord 6.0	99,831 bytes	WINMAG
WORDIA.ZIP	WinWord 6.0	1,093,313 bytes	WINMAG
WORDIA.ZIP	WinWord 6.0	1,041,040 bytes	IBMCOM
TXTSTY.ZIP	Ami Pro	6,772 bytes	LOTUSWP
AMIWEB12.ZIP	Ami Pro 3.0	56,359 bytes	LOTUSWP
INTASSIS.ZIP	WinWord 6.0	1,120,360 bytes	UKSHARE
WORDIA.EXE	WinWord 6.0	1,120,361 bytes	WINMAG
WORDIA.ZIP	WinWord 6.0	1,120,361 bytes	GERWIN

Table 6-8 Where to Find Word Processor HTML Add-Ons on CompuServe

Filename	Word Processor	File Size	Forum
AMIWEB.ZIP	Ami Pro 3.0+	105,236 bytes	WUGNET
CUHTML.ZIP	WinWord 2.0 or 6.0	69,970 bytes	WUGNET
WORDIA.ZIP	WinWord 6.0+	1,041,040 bytes	EURFORUM

HoTMetaL

Version 1.0 of HoTMetaL from SoftQuad is available on the *Creating Cool Interactive Web Sites CD-ROM.* Version 1.0 is a freely distributed, public domain version of this excellent program.

HoTMetaL is an excellent, professional-quality, HTML tool for beginners to use. It requires Windows 3.1. Although the program says that it requires at least 4MB of memory, with 8MB recommended, we discovered that it would not run on a 20 MHz 386SX with 6MB. It did run nicely, however, on a 66 MHz 486DX2 with 16MB.

Some of this program's extremely nice features are the capability to edit multiple documents at once, the capability to use templates to ensure consistency between documents, and the word-processor-like features that allow such powerful capabilities as search and replace.

This program sticks to the basic, standard features of HTML, so you won't be overwhelmed all at once. You also can simply hide the tags so that you can ignore them altogether.

Another feature enables you to create a simple outline of your Web page. This outline enables you to keep track of your page's links without going completely crazy.

Finally, as previously mentioned, HoTMetaL comes with templates (14 of them) that enable you to create typical documents such as home pages, registration forms, and hotlists, with little confusion and few problems.

In order to install HoTMetaL on your hard disk from the CD-ROM, you need to make sure that you have at least 5MB of free space on the hard drive that you're going to install it to. Your next step is to run the HoTMetaL installation program on the CD-ROM. Follow the simple directions found in the appendix to create the necessary directory and subdirectories on your hard drive.

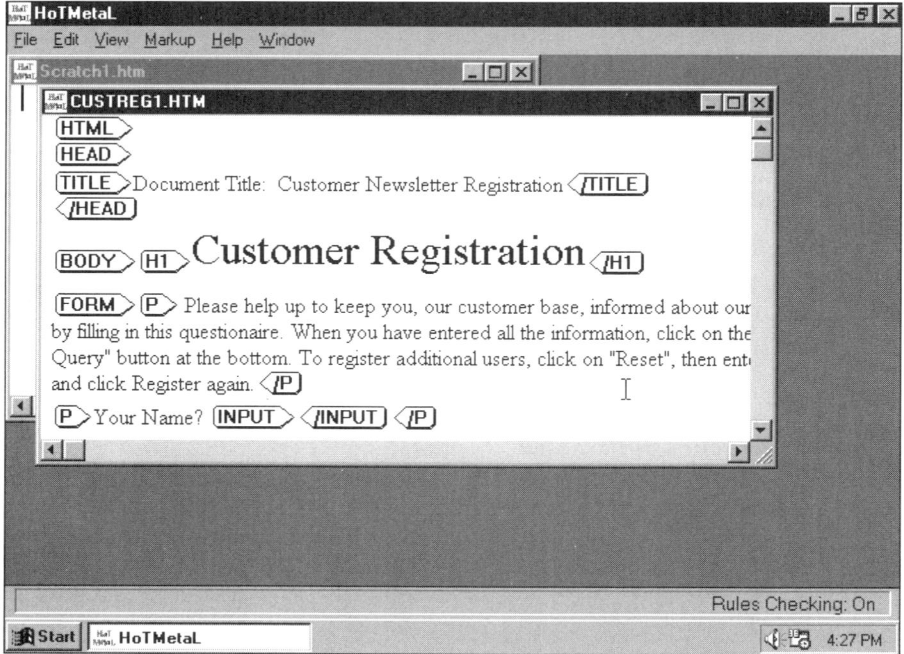

Figure 6-1: Keep in mind that HoTMetaL is fairly greedy when it comes to memory.

HoTMetaL is fairly memory greedy so, unless you have a great deal of RAM on your machine, don't try to run any other programs while you're using HoTMetaL (see Figure 6-1). You should keep this in mind especially when you are running HoTMetaL under Windows 3.1.

Remember, SoftQuad provides no support for Version 1.0, the freely distributed, public domain version that's on the *Creating Cool Interactive Web Sites CD-ROM.*

HTML Assistant

This simple, shareware, stand-alone HTML document editor was created in Visual Basic and, as with HoTMetaL, is also available in both a freeware version and a commercial version. The commercial version is called HTML Assistant Pro.

Most commands are accessible from the large button bar. Basically a text editor with additions that assist you in creating Web pages, HTML Assistant also includes a Test function that enables you to see what your pages will look like on the Web.

The features of this program vary, depending on whether you are using the freeware version or the commercial version. You can subscribe to a free e-mail newsletter for the program by sending an e-mail message to `harawitz@fox.nstn.ns.ca`. When you create the message, type the single word **subscribe** in the Subject field. You also can place comments in the content of the message.

The freeware version of HTML Assistant is available from the libraries and forums on CompuServe that are listed in Table 6-9.

Table 6-9 Where to Find HTML Assistant on CompuServe

Filename	File Size	Forum
HTMLAS.ZIP	206,616 bytes	PCEFORUM
HTMLAS.ZIP	167,678 bytes	INETRESOURCE
HTMLAS.ZIP	206,616 bytes	WUGNET
HTMLAS.ZIP	206,616 bytes	EURFORUM
HTMLAT.ZIP	206,616 bytes	EURFORUM
HTMLASST.ZIP	206,616 bytes	MUTFORUM

Remember that HTML Assistant is not WYSIWYG. It uses Mosaic or an OLE link to Cello in order to view files. Also, you need to be aware that Version 1.0, the downloadable version, is limited to editing files that are less than 32K.

You can purchase the commercial version of HTML Assistant by contacting Brooklyn North Software Works by phone at 902-835-2600 or by e-mail at `harawitz@fox.nstn.ns.ca`.

HTML Writer

This program has a very nice interface, with comprehensive menus, an attractive toolbar, and efficient shortcut keys. HTML Writer, like HTML Assistant, was created with Visual Basic 3.0.

HTML Writer is an easy-to-use, easy-to-learn, stand-alone Windows-based text editor that was created for using HTML to build and edit Web pages. As with HoTMetaL, HTML Writer comes with a collection of templates that can help in the speedy development of your Web pages.

You can download HTML Writer from several locations. Table 6-10 provides a list of the CompuServe Forums where you can find copies of HTML Writer.

Table 6-10 Where to Find HTML Writer on CompuServe

Filename	File Size	Forum
HWR9B4.ZIP	252,141 bytes	PCEFORUM
HW9B4A.ZIP	252,141 bytes	PCUKFORUM
HWR9B4.ZIP	252,141 bytes	EURFORUM
HTMLWR.ZIP	252,018 bytes	WUGNET
HTMWRT.EXE	242,286 bytes	GERWIN

Kris Nosack, HTML Writer's author, says his program is *donationware*. In other words, there are no restrictions on the program's use. You're free to use it as long as you want and as much as you want without ever feeling a pang of guilt because you haven't paid for it. If, however, you want to thank the author, you can send him $5 or $10. His address is 376 North Main Street, Orem, Utah 84057.

You also can reach Mr. Nosack and sign up to be on the mailing list to receive the HTML Writer newsletter at `html_writer@byu.edu`.

One final note—HTML Writer has its own home page, which is located at the following address: `http://wwf.et.byu.edu/~nosackk/htmlwrit.html`.

Microsoft Internet Assistant for Word for Windows

If you prefer integrated software whenever possible, as we do, we suggest Microsoft Internet Assistant for Word for Windows. This program add-on enables you to create and view Web pages in the word-processing program that you may have grown accustomed to using. In addition, its built-in browser capability enables you to go online from inside Word for Windows.

If you use Internet Assistant, you do not have to learn (or even see) the HTML codes for the Web page documents that you're creating. The program add-on includes a built-in browser that uses Word as its viewing screen. This feature enables you to cut and paste from any Web page to which you're connected to the page you're working on. You can also link your Web pages to other people's pages.

If you want to use the more advanced HTML features, Microsoft Internet Assistant requires that you edit these codes by hand. Also, one thing that you need to remember to do when using this program is to create a title field when you start a page (see Figure 6-2). Internet Assistant allows you to create a document without entering a title field, but all browsers require a title field on the page.

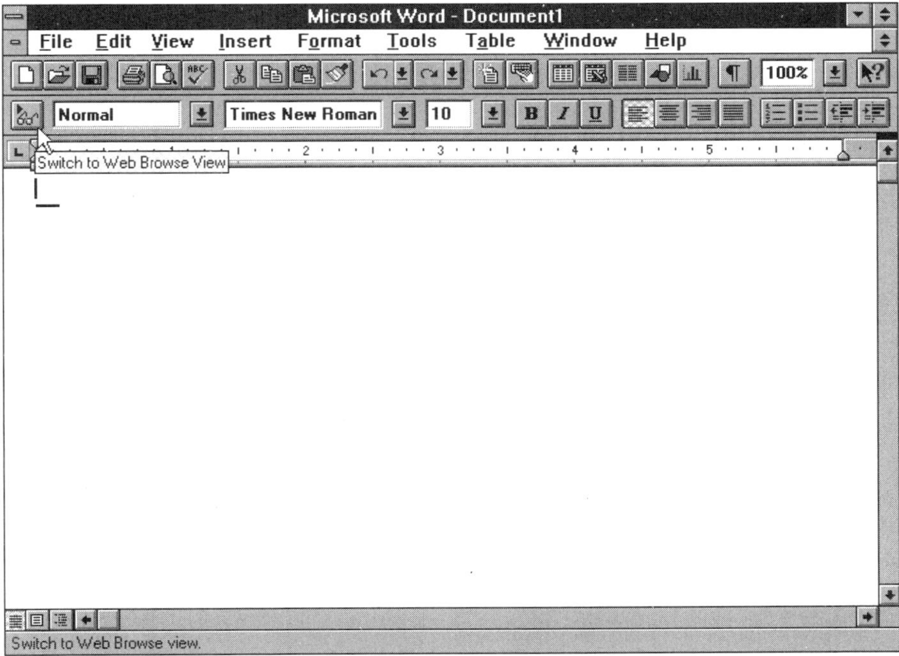

Figure 6-2: You need to remember to create a title field for each page when using Microsoft Internet Assistant for Word for Windows.

You can install Microsoft Internet Assistant for Word for Windows from the *Creating Cool Interactive Web Sites CD-ROM.* If you're installing from the CD-ROM, follow the directions in the appendix for easy installation.

You need to be aware of a couple of final things about Internet Assistant. First, any HTML tag that Internet Assistant doesn't recognize isn't displayed. Also, when you are editing your page, you cannot see some of the tags that you are creating, which makes editing difficult later.

WebMania!

WebMania! 1.0 is a product of Q&D Software Development in Chatham, New Jersey. Three versions of this program are available: a shareware version, a standard version, and a professional version. WebMania! requires no knowledge of HTML.

The shareware version of WebMania! 1.0 is included on the *Creating Cool Interactive Web Sites CD-ROM.*

The shareware version offers all of the features of the standard version, plus some of the features of the professional version, for a limited time period (about 30 days). After this initial evaluation period, some of the features may cease to function.

The standard version of WebMania! provides you with the ability to create HTML forms and to import individual responses to these forms. For each form that you create, the program creates a table where responses to the form are stored for easy viewing. Also, the program provides for the use of many different types of controls, such as radio buttons, check boxes, and list boxes.

The professional version of WebMania! has all of the features provided in the standard version, plus browser calling, outside help links, table creation, form copy, and batch response importing.

Installing WebMania! 1.0 to your hard drive is simple. Just follow the easy instructions in the appendix.

The first time that you run WebMania! you need to wait a few moments while the program creates its own database. Click on the OK button and wait. When the program is finished, you see Q&D's registration information. Click on the OK button and continue.

The first time that you run the program, after loading the program itself, the program loads the tutorial. This tutorial shows you the help files and gives you a short overview of how to use WebMania! Keep in mind that these help files are the only assistance that you'll get from Q&D until you've registered the software, so read them completely and carefully. You can print most of the pages, and printed documentation is available with the registered versions.

From WebMania!'s main toolbar, as seen in Figure 6-3, you can create or open a new page, create or open a new form, import or read responses to forms, or perform a wide variety of other Web page authoring functions.

Registering the WebMania! shareware program entitles you to full activation of the features listed in the Features list (found in the help files), free technical support by phone or e-mail, free upgrades to all subsequent shareware versions of this program, and the inclusion of a link from your Web site on Q&D's Web page.

Figure 6-3: WebMania!'s main toolbar enables you to access many HTML functions without having to learn HTML.

Web Weaver

Web Weaver is a stand-alone HTML editor that assists you with the creation and editing of HTML documents through automation. The program requires Windows 3.1 and VBRUN300.DLL. To find Web Weaver, refer to Table 6-11.

Table 6-11 Where to Find Web Weaver on CompuServe

Filename	File Size	Forum
WEBWEA.ZIP	39,359 bytes	PCEFORUM
WEBWEA.ZIP	77,474 bytes	PCUKFORUM
WEBWEA.ZIP	77,475 bytes	EURFORUM

Using the Tools on the CD-ROM

At this point, we want you to try using the tools that are on the *Creating Cool Interactive Web Sites CD-ROM* to create some interactive forms. Install the tool of your choice according to the instructions earlier in this chapter and then follow along with these minitutorials and learn about some of the more interactive capabilities of HTML.

Microsoft Internet Assistant for Word for Windows

In this exercise, we walk you through the process of creating a form for your Web page using Microsoft Internet Assistant for Word for Windows. Keep in mind that you are only creating the form. You are not doing anything with the information that may be typed into this form by your users.

To create the form, follow these simple steps:

1. **Start Microsoft Internet Assistant for Word for Windows.**

   To do this, if you have installed Internet Assistant, you simply start Microsoft Word for Windows.

2. **Choose File⇨New and then choose Html, as in Figure 6-4.**

3. **To create the new HTML file, click on the OK button.**

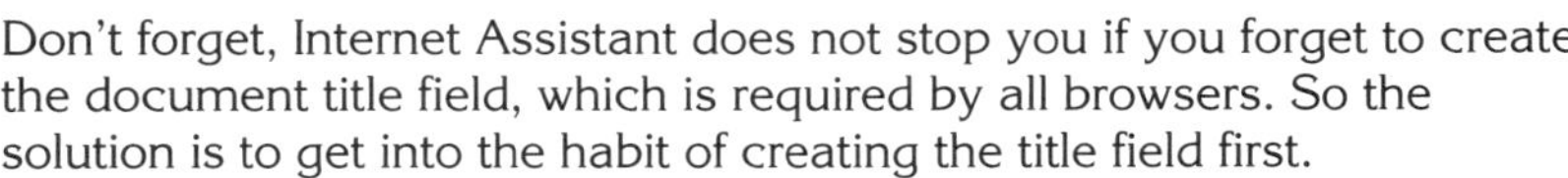

Don't forget, Internet Assistant does not stop you if you forget to create the document title field, which is required by all browsers. So the solution is to get into the habit of creating the title field first.

4. **To create a title field, click on the Title button on the desktop (see Figure 6-5).**

   You see a dialog box that asks you to enter the information that you want to include in the title (see Figure 6-5).

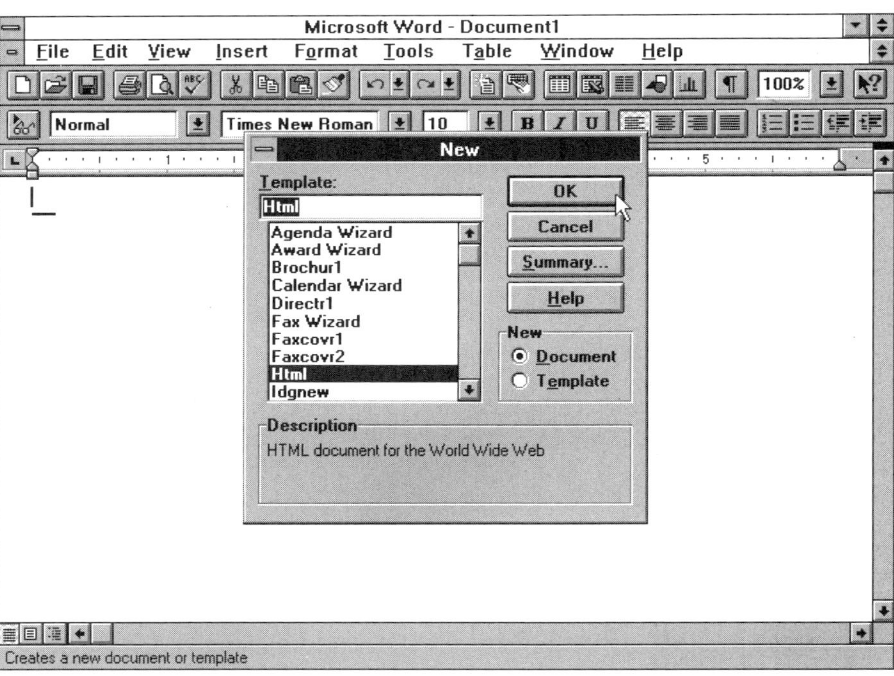

Figure 6-4: Choose New from the File menu to begin creating a new HTML document in the window that appears.

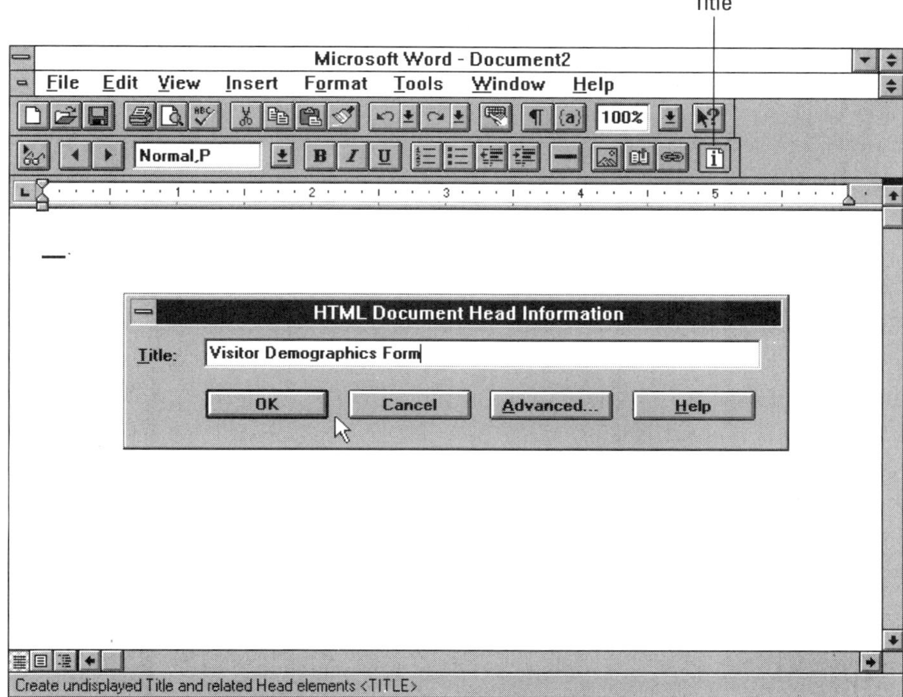

Figure 6-5: You enter the title information for your Web page in the HTML Document Head Information dialog box.

5. **Enter a title for your Web page.**

   For this example, enter **Visitor Demographics Form**.

   These two simple commands, New and Title, created the following HTML code in the document:

```
<HTML>
<HEAD>
<TITLE> Visitor Demographics Form</TITLE>
</HEAD>
```

Don't worry that there still doesn't seem to be anything on your Web page. Remember, one of the advantages of any one of these three programs is not having to deal with the code directly. Instead of concerning yourself with the mechanics of HTML itself, you can apply your creative energies to the aesthetics of the document. Let the computer and the program worry about the manual labor.

Some, if not most, browsers will pick up this title field and display it on the screen for anyone accessing your Web page. Some browsers, however, ignore this field. You'll want to make sure that anyone accessing your Web page knows who it belongs to.

First, you need to define the body of the document. Internet Assistant defines the body automatically, producing the following code after the previous lines all by itself:

```
<BODY>
```

Next, you tell anyone accessing your Web page, no matter what browser they're using, who the Web page belongs to. You want everyone to see the name of your Web page, so use the `<H1>` command to show the text in the largest font that a browser is capable of showing.

In Internet Assistant you change the style in the style drop-down box in the upper-left side of the desktop. Currently the style should be set to Normal, P.

6. **Change the style from Normal, P, to Heading 1, H1, as shown in Figure 6-6.**

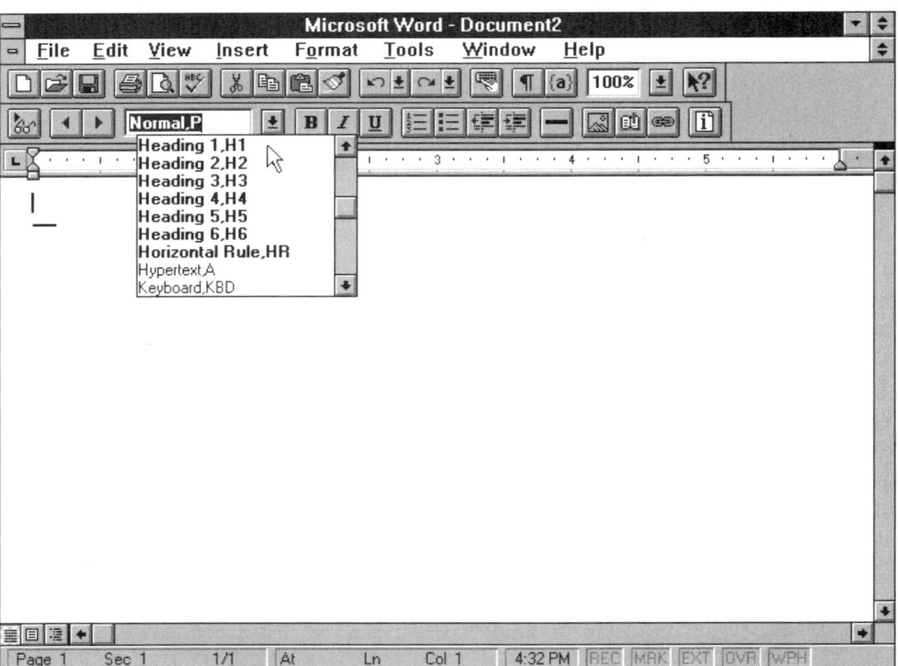

Figure 6-6: Change the style for your first paragraph to Heading 1, H1.

7. **Type the same information that you typed in the title field,** Visitor Demographics Form.
8. **Press Enter.**
9. **Select the style for the next line: Heading 2, H2.**
10. **Type** Please Enter the Following Information:.
11. **Press Enter.**
12. **Select the style for the next line: Heading 4, H4.**
13. **Type** Please complete the following questionnaire. The information that you provide will help us meet your needs more fully. Thank you in advance for your cooperation.

    You'll notice that the page isn't blank anymore. You should see something that looks like Figure 6-7.

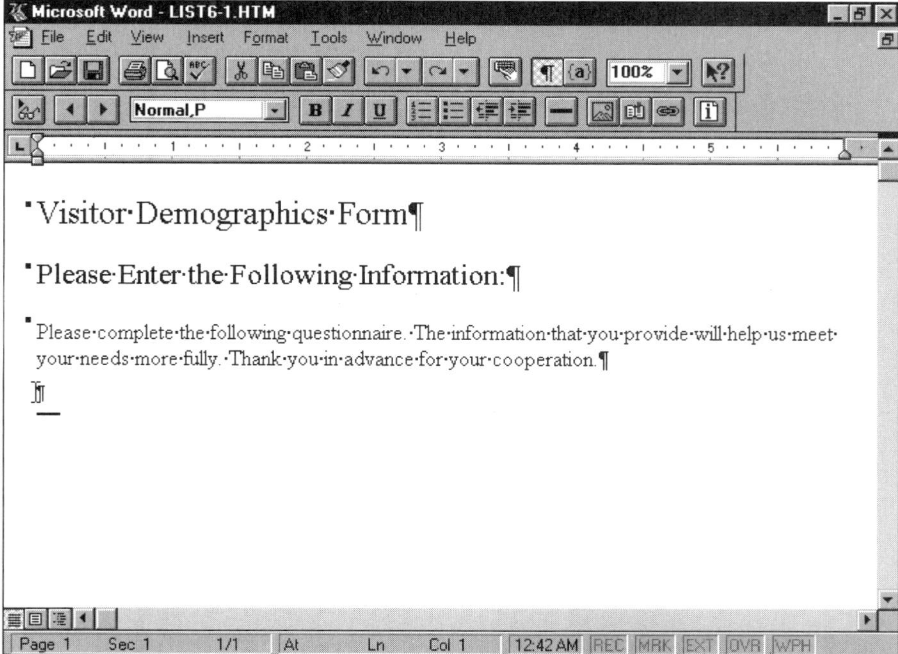

Figure 6-7: *Your page isn't blank anymore, is it?*

Next, you begin to create the form.

14. **Choose Insert⇨Form Field.**

    The first time you do this, you create an entire HTML form. A message telling you that you are creating a new form appears.

15. **Click on the Continue button.**

    You have something similar to Figure 6-8 on your screen at this point. Top-of-Form and Bottom-of-Form boundaries appear, as well as the Forms toolbar and the Form Field dialog box.

16. **Click on Cancel in the Form Field dialog box.**

    The first thing that you want visitors to enter is their first name.

17. **Type** First Name **at the cursor's location.**

18. **From the Forms toolbar, choose Text Form Field (see Figure 6-8).**

    A text form field appears in your document after the place where you typed **First Name**.

19. **Select the form field and double-click on it.**

    The Text Form Field Options dialog box opens (see Figure 6-9). In this dialog box, you can define the attributes of the form field itself.

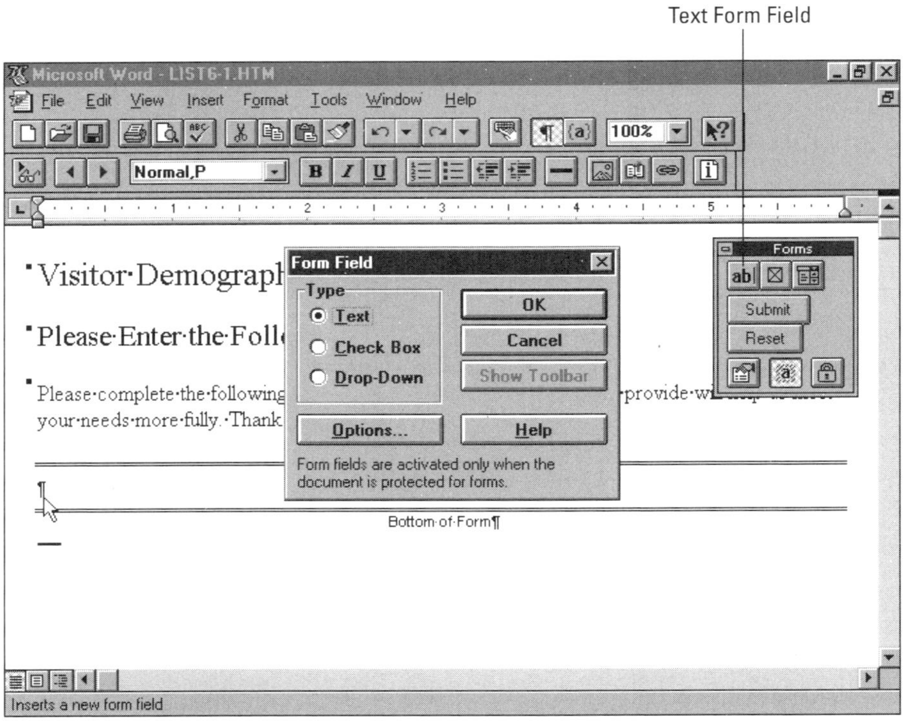

Text Form Field

Figure 6-8: The Form Field dialog box and the Forms toolbar.

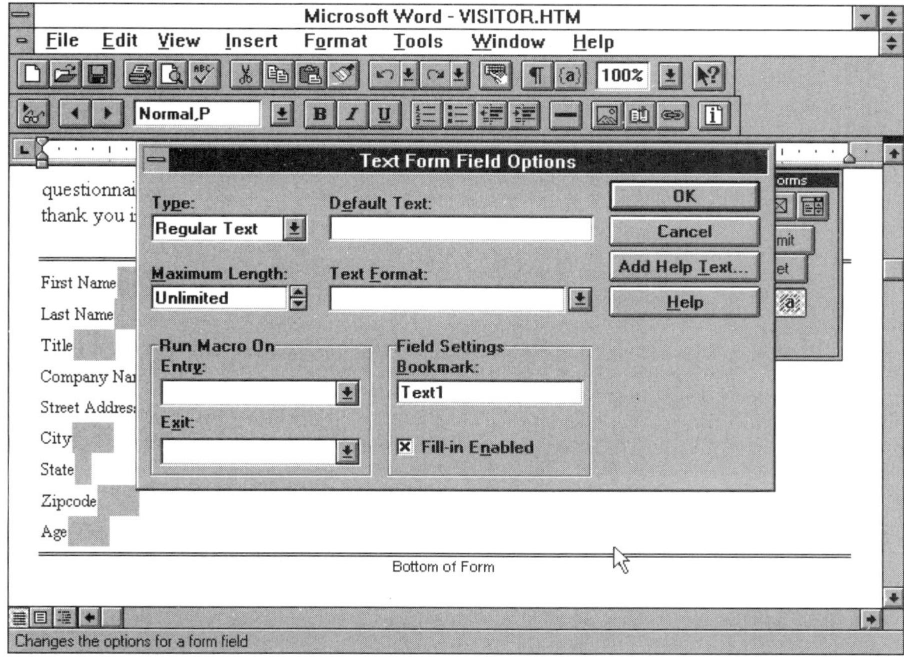

Figure 6-9: The Text Form Field Options dialog box.

The first attribute that you can change is Type. Usually you will leave this as Regular Text. The next change that you might make concerns the Default Text. Most of the time, you leave this box blank.

Next is Maximum Length. To define the maximum length of the First Name fill-in line, select the text in the Maximum Length dialog box and delete it.

20. **Type the maximum length that you want the First Name line to be.**

    The maximum length in the example is 12, but this field can go as high as 80 characters.

21. **Click on the Add Help Text button.**
22. **Choose Help Key (F1).**
23. **Select the Type Your Own button.**
24. **Type** First Name.

    This text is invisible to the person filling out the form, but it identifies the contents of this fill-in line when the form is returned to your Web server.

25. **Click on the OK button twice.**

26. **Now, repeat this process for the other fields in the form to create a form like the one in Figure 6-10.**

    The next item you want answered by Web site visitors is their age.

27. **Type** Age.

    At this point, rather than have visitors enter their specific ages, which some people have a problem doing, you can offer them a range of ages. To do this, you use a drop-down list.

28. **Choose Drop-Down Form Field from the Forms toolbar (see Figure 6-10).**

    A drop-down form field appears on the Web page. Select the form field and double-click on it. The Drop-Down Form Field Options dialog box opens, as shown in Figure 6-11.

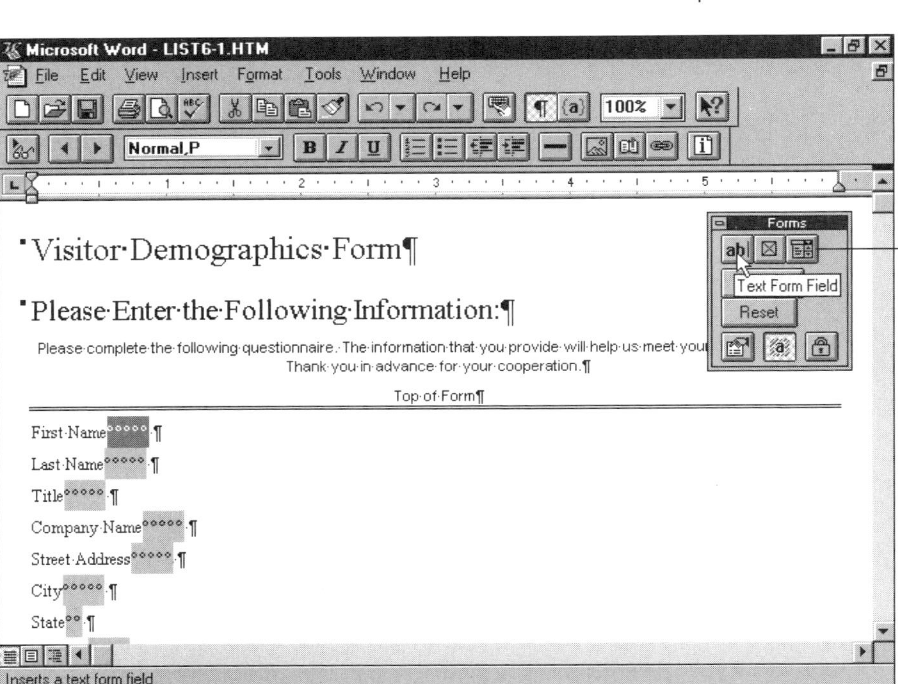

Figure 6-10: You can complete the form down to this point simply by repeating Steps 17 through 25.

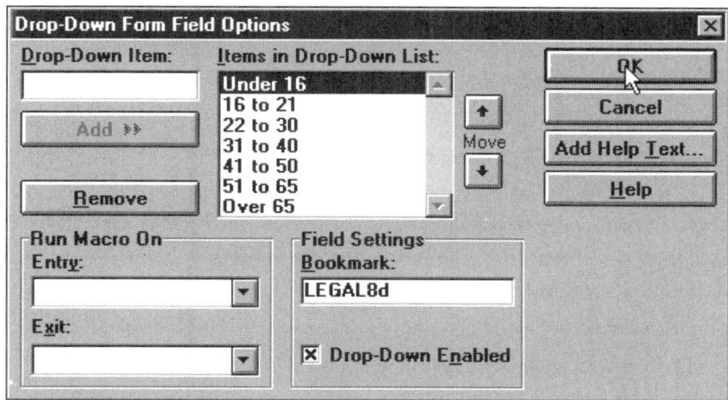

Figure 6-11: Here is where you enter the different age ranges that you want to offer to Web site visitors.

29. **In the Drop-Down Item text box, type** Under 16.

30. **Choose Add.**

    Under 16 is the first item in your drop-down list, and it appears in the Items in Drop-Down List text list.

    Repeat this process, adding **16 to 21**, **22 to 30**, **31 to 40**, **41 to 50**, **51 to 65**, and **Over 65** to the drop-down list.

Internet Assistant limits you to no more than 25 items per drop-down list. If you need more items in your list, use the HTML Markup command on the Insert menu to create the form field.

31. **Choose Add Help Text.**

32. **Select Help Key (F1).**

33. **Choose Type Your Own.**

34. **Type** Age.

    The purpose of *Age* is to identify the name of this drop-down list when the form is returned to your Web server.

    Click on the OK button here and again in the next window.

    Repeat this procedure for Yearly Income, using **Under $18,000**, **$18,001 to $25,000**, **$25,001 to $35,000**, **$35,001 to $45,000**, **$45,001 to $55,000**, **$55,001 to $75,000**, and **Over $75,000**. Your form now looks like Figure 6-12.

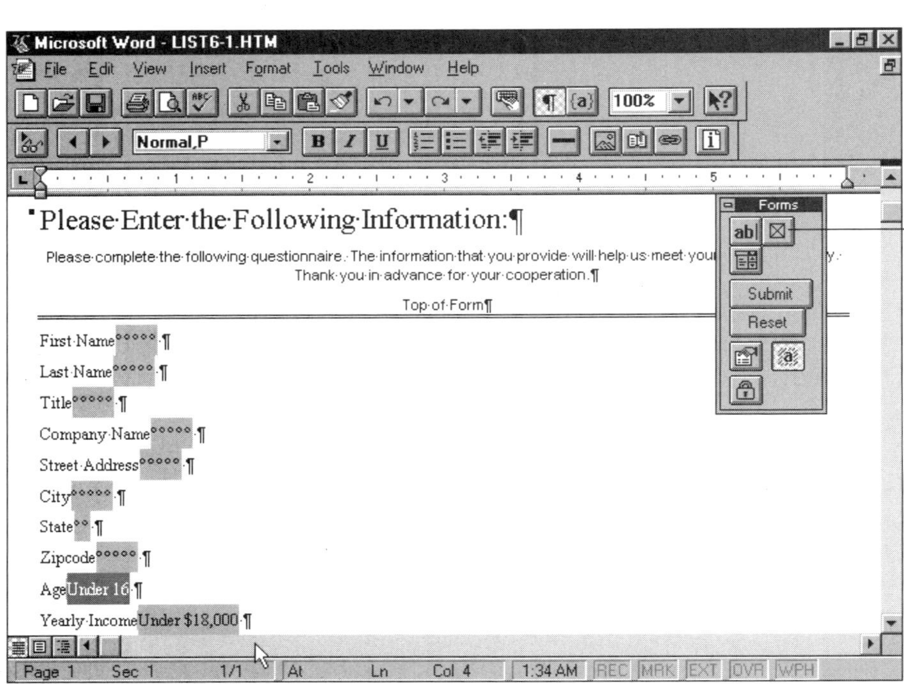

Figure 6-12: *The form is beginning to come together.*

The next item to add to the form is gender. We'll use check boxes for Female and Male.

35. **Type** Female.

36. **Click on Check Box Form Field in the Forms toolbar (see Figure 6-12).**

37. **Select the form field and double-click on it.**

    The Check Box Form Field Options dialog box opens.

38. **Under the Field settings in the Bookmark text box, add the string_RD to the bookmark name.**

    The current bookmark name should be Check1, so after you add this string it is Check1_RD.

39. **Choose Add Help Text and select the Help Key (F1) tab.**

40. **Choose Type Your Own and type the name of the form field in the text box.**

    In this case, the name of the form field is Gender.

41. **Now select the Status Bar tab.**
42. **Choose Type Your Own.**
43. **Type** Value="Female" **into the text box here.**
44. **Click on the OK button in this window and the next window.**
45. **Repeat this procedure and type** Male **where you typed** Female **previously.**

    The last two items that you need to include on the form are the Submit and Reset buttons.

46. **In the Forms toolbox, select the Submit button to bring up the Form Submit Button dialog box.**

    Your screen looks similar to Figure 6-13. Chapter 10 covers most of the information that you need to place in the Form Submit Button dialog box.

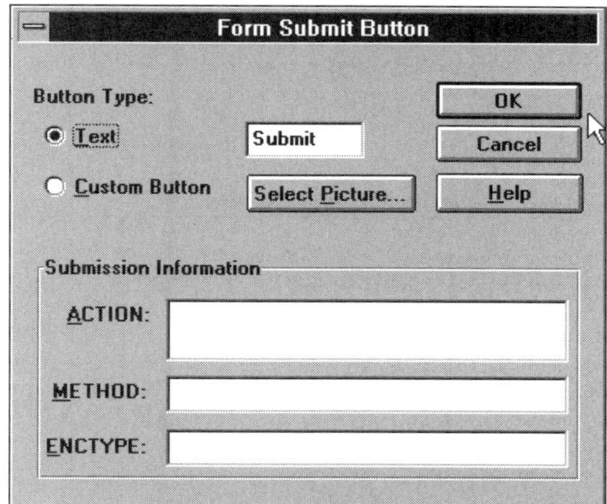

Figure 6-13: Chapter 10 covers most of the information that you need to place in the Form Submit Button dialog box.

47. **At this point, just click on the OK button.**
48. **Select the Reset button in the Forms toolbox.**

    A Reset button appears next to the Submit button.

Congratulations! You've created a basic Web page that includes a form. In order to look at the form, you first need to save it and then switch to the Web Browser view. You may also want to load it into another Web browser, such as Microsoft Internet Explorer, as in Figure 6-14, to see how it looks.

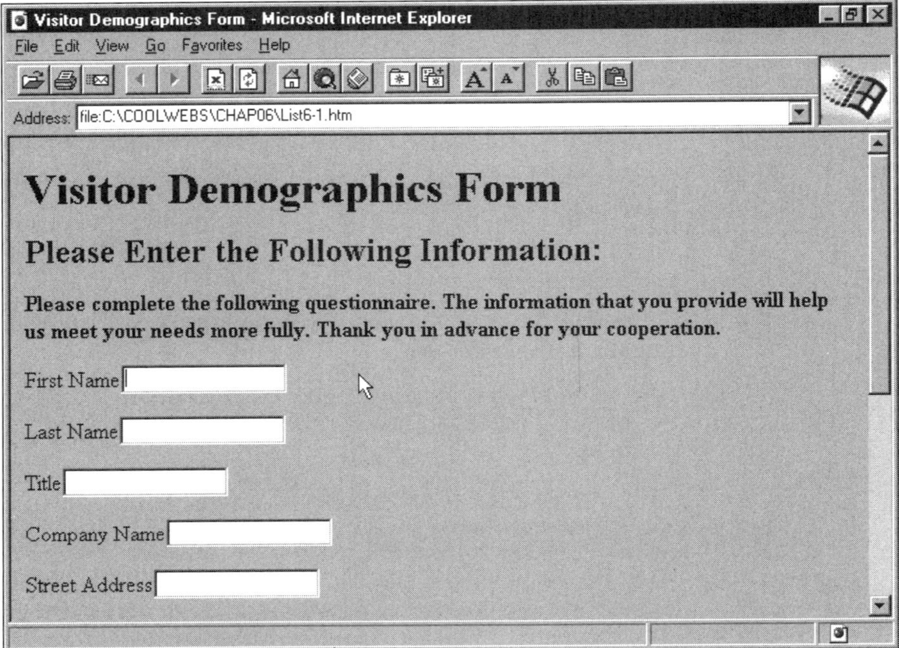

Figure 6-14: *VISITOR.HTM, as seen using Microsoft Internet Explorer.*

This form is VISITOR.HTM on the CD-ROM. Listing 6-1 is the entire HTML code for VISITOR.HTM, so you can see exactly what the code looks like.

Listing 6-1: VISITOR.HTM

```
<!doctype html public "-//IETF//DTD HTML//EN">
<HTML>

<HEAD>

<TITLE>Visitor Demographics Form</TITLE>

<META NAME="GENERATOR" CONTENT="Internet Assistant for Word⮐
1.0Z">
<META NAME="AUTHOR" CONTENT="Paul M. Summitt">
</HEAD>

<BODY>
```

```
<H1>Visitor Demographics Form</H1>

<H2>Please Enter the Following Information:</H2>

<H4>Please complete the following questionnaire. The↩
information that you provide will help us meet your needs more↩
fully. Thank you in advance for your cooperation.</H4>

<FORM >

<P>
First Name<INPUT NAME="First Name" VALUE="" MAXLENGTH="12" >
<P>
Last Name<INPUT NAME="Last Name" VALUE="" MAXLENGTH="25" >
<P>
Title<INPUT NAME="Title" VALUE="" MAXLENGTH="15" >
<P>
Company Name<INPUT NAME="Company Name" VALUE="" MAXLENGTH="40" >
<P>
Street Address<INPUT NAME="Street Address" VALUE=""
MAXLENGTH="45" >
<P>
City<INPUT NAME="City" VALUE="" MAXLENGTH="35" >
<P>
State<INPUT NAME="State" VALUE="" MAXLENGTH="2" >
<P>
Zipcode<INPUT NAME="Zipcode" VALUE="" MAXLENGTH="5" >
<P>
Age<SELECT NAME="Age" >
<OPTION>Under 16
<OPTION>16 to 21
<OPTION>22 to 30
<OPTION>31 to 40
<OPTION>41 to 50
<OPTION>51 to 65
<OPTION>Over 65</SELECT>
<P>
Yearly Income<SELECT NAME="Yearly Income" >
<OPTION>Under $18,000
<OPTION>$18,001 to $25,000
<OPTION>$25,001 to $35,000
<OPTION>$35,001 to $45,000
<OPTION>$45,001 to $55,000
<OPTION>$55,001 to $75,000
```

(continued)

Listing 6-1 ***(continued):***

```
<OPTION>Over $75,000</SELECT>
<P>
Female<INPUT TYPE="RADIO" NAME="Gender" Value="Female">
<P>
Male   <INPUT TYPE="RADIO" NAME="Gender" Value="Male">
<P>
<INPUT TYPE="SUBMIT" VALUE="Submit"><INPUT TYPE="RESET">
</FORM>

</BODY>

</HTML>
```

You have just created a simple page with a form. It is relatively basic HTML. You created the page in a reasonable amount of time with a reasonable amount of effort, using Microsoft Internet Assistant for Word for Windows. You'll notice that Listing 6-1 includes several HTML commands that we never said anything about in the steps for creating this page. The beauty of Internet Assistant and the next two authoring tools that we discuss is that they enable you to plan your work and format it without having to memorize a lot of code and commands. In the next few pages, you use SoftQuad's HoTMetaL to create the same page.

HoTMetaL

We begin the construction of the Web page using HoTMetaL with the assumption that you have installed HoTMetaL according to the instructions given in the appendix and that you have started the program. One of the ways that HoTMetaL is different from other Web-authoring tools is in its use of templates. For this Web page, you use the template CUSTREG1.HTM. Follow these instructions to create the Web page:

1. **Choose File⇨Open, change to the \Template\ subdirectory, and select CUSTREG1.HTM.**

   You see a screen that looks similar to Figure 6-15.

2. **Save this file under a different name, VISITOR2.HTM, so you don't mess up the template.**

3. **Modify the template's introductory text to reflect the Title, Headings, and the opening paragraph that are shown in Listing 6-2.**

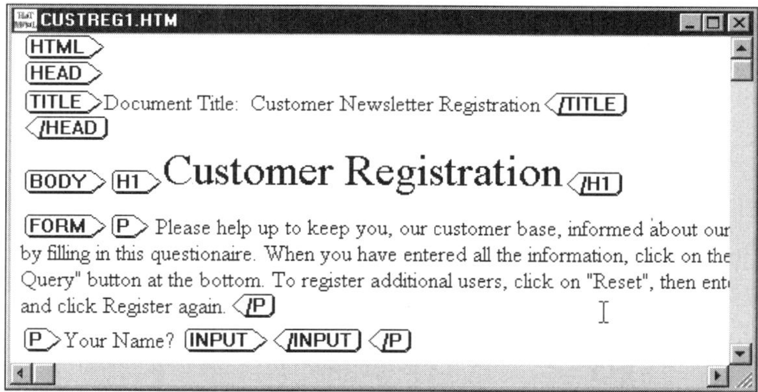

Figure 6-15: In HoTMetaL, you don't have to start with a blank page. You can use a template.

Listing 6-2: VISITOR2.HTM

```
<!DOCTYPE HTML PUBLIC "-//IETF//DTD HTML 2.0 plus SQ/ICADD
Tables//EN" "html.dtd"
>
<HTML>
<HEAD>
<TITLE>Visitor Demographics Form</TITLE>
</HEAD>
<BODY><H1>Visitor Demographics Form</H1>
<H2>Please Enter the Following Information:</H2>
<FORM ACTION=""><P> In order to serve you
better, we are asking that you complete the following
questionaire. When
you have entered all the information, click on the
"Submit Query" button
at the bottom. To register additional users, click on "Reset",
then
enter them and click "Register" again. Thank you for your coop
eration.</P>
<P>Your First Name? <INPUT NAME="First Name" SIZE="20"></P>
<P>Your Last Name?<INPUT NAME="Last Name" SIZE="30"></P>
<P>Your Title?<INPUT NAME="Title" SIZE="20"></P>
<P>Your organization or company? <INPUT NAME="Company"
SIZE="30"></P>
<P>Your Street Address? <INPUT NAME="Address" SIZE="40"></P>
```

(continued)

Listing 6-2 *(continued)*:

```
<P>The City you live in?<INPUT NAME="City" SIZE="30"></P>
<P>The 2-letter code for the State you live in?<INPUT⮐
NAME="State" SIZE="2"></P>
<P>The Zipcode for your community?<INPUT NAME="Zipcode"⮐
SIZE="5"></P>
<P>Your Age?<SELECT NAME="Age" SIZE="1" MULTIPLE="MULTIPLE">
<OPTION VALUE="Under 16">Under 16</OPTION>
<OPTION VALUE="16 to 21">16 to 21</OPTION>
<OPTION VALUE="22 to 30">22 to 30</OPTION>
<OPTION VALUE="31 to 40">31 to 40</OPTION>
<OPTION VALUE="41 to 50">41 to 50</OPTION>
<OPTION VALUE="51 to 65">51 to 65</OPTION>
<OPTION VALUE="Over 65">Over 65</OPTION></SELECT></P>
<P>Your Yearly Income<SELECT NAME="Yearly Income" SIZE="1"⮐
MULTIPLE="MULTIPLE"
><OPTION>Under $18,000</OPTION>
<OPTION>$18,001 to $25,000</OPTION>
<OPTION>$25,001 to $35,000</OPTION>
<OPTION>$35,001 to $45,000</OPTION>
<OPTION>$45,001 to $55,000</OPTION>
<OPTION>$55,001 to $75,000</OPTION>
<OPTION>Over $75,000</OPTION></SELECT></P>
<P>Gender</P>
<P><INPUT TYPE="RADIO" NAME="Gender" VALUE="Female">Female</P>
<P><INPUT TYPE="RADIO" NAME="Gender" VALUE="Male">Male</P>
<P>Again, Thank your for your cooperation.</P>
<P><INPUT TYPE="submit"> <INPUT TYPE="reset"></P>
</FORM></BODY>
</HTML>
```

Next, you create the text box for First Name.

4. **Choose Markup⇨Insert Element.**

   You see a menu of elements that you can insert into the document window. It looks similar to Figure 6-16.

5. **Move down the list of elements until you find P, Paragraph contains text.**

6. **Make sure that the Include Required Elements box is checked and click on the Insert Element button. The Insert Element window will now disappear and you'll be returned to the HTML window.**

7. **Make sure that you are between the** `P` **and the** `/P` **and type** Your First Name?

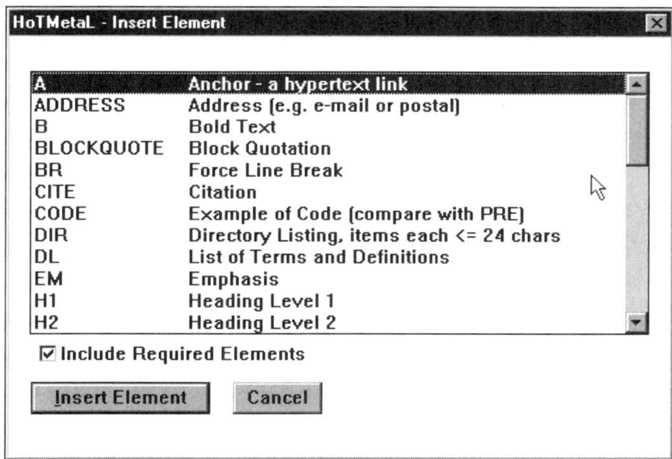

Figure 6-16: When you choose Insert Element, you see a menu of elements that you can insert into the document.

8. **Choose Markup⇨Insert Element again.**
9. **Move down the list of elements until you find Input, +Input to a Form (level 2, HTML2).**
10. **Make sure that the Include Required Elements box is checked and click on the Insert Element button.**
11. **Move the cursor to between the** `<INPUT>` **and** `<\INPUT>` **symbols and choose MARKUP⇨Edit SGML Attributes.**

    The Edit Attributes Window appears, as in Figure 6-17.
12. **Change the attributes of First Name to reflect what you see in Figure 6-17 and then click on Apply.**

    That's basically how you use HoTMetaL.
13. **Repeat Steps 4 through 12 for all of the information down to and including the Zip Code text box.**
14. **Delete the parts of the template that you don't need.**

    The next entry is Age. This entry is a little more difficult than the previous entries, but not much.
15. **Choose Markup⇨Insert Element again.**

    Move down the list of elements again until you find P, Paragraph contains text.
16. **Make sure that the Include Required Elements box is checked and click on the Insert Element button as you've done before.**
17. **Make sure that you are between the** P **and the** /P **and type** Your Age?
18. **Choose Markup⇨Insert Element.**

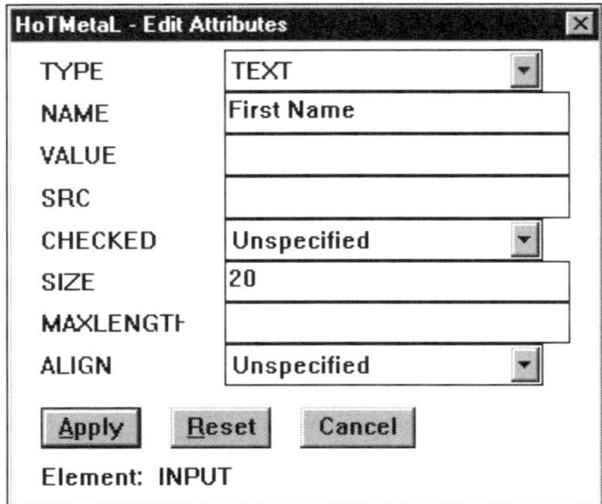

Figure 6-17: Change the attributes of the Input option to reflect what you see here.

19. **Move down the list of elements until you find Select + Form Selection List (level 2, HTML2).**

20. **Make sure that the Include Required Elements box is checked and click on the Insert Element button.**

    A dialog box appears, asking you whether you want to edit the required elements or edit the required elements attributes.

21. **Click on Stop and Edit.**

    You see the Edit Attributes window that is shown in Figure 6-18.

22. **Type** Age **for Name,** 1 **for Size, and** Multiple **for Multiple in the Edit Attributes Window, as shown in Figure 6-18, and click on the Apply button.**

23. **Move the cursor to inside the Select element.**

24. **Choose Markup⇨Insert Element again and choose Option.**

25. **Type** Under 16 **for the first Option element.**

26. **Repeat this Option element process for** 16 to 21, 22 to 30, 31 to 40, 41 to 50, 51 to 65, **and** Over 65.

27. **Follow Steps 17 through 26 again for the Your Yearly Income element.**

    This time use **Your Yearly Income** for the Name attribute, **1** for size, **Multiple** for Multiple and **Under $18,000**, **$18,001 to $25,000**, **$25,001 to $35,000**, **$35,001 to $45,000**, **$45,001 to $55,000**, **$55,001 to $75,000**, and **Over $75,000** for the seven options.

    The only elements left to create at this point are the Gender radio buttons.

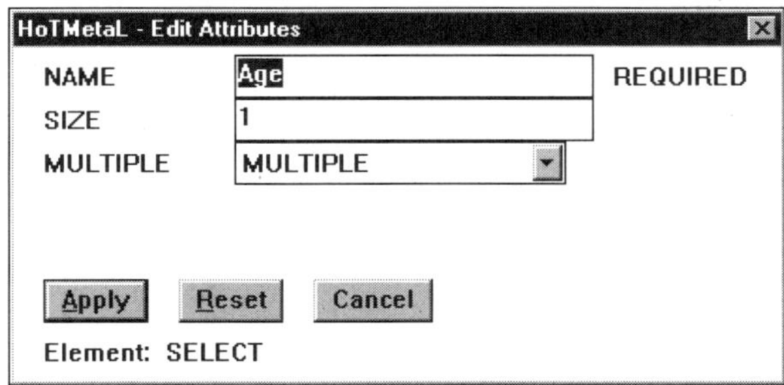

Figure 6-18: Make the modifications shown to the attributes for Name, Size, and Multiple.

28. **Choose Markup⇨Insert Element one last time.**
29. **Move down the list of elements again until you find P, Paragraph contains text.**
30. **Make sure that the Include Required Elements box is checked, and select the Insert Element button as you've done before.**
31. **Make sure that you are between the** `P` **and the** `/P`**, and this time type** Gender?
32. **Choose Markup⇨Insert Element again and insert a new paragraph after the last one.**
33. **Choose Markup⇨Insert Element again and insert an Insert element.**
34. **Choose Markup⇨Edit SGML Attributes and change the attributes as in Figure 6-19.**
35. **In the document window, move to the right of the Insert element and type** Female.
36. **Repeat Steps 32 through 35 for the Male radio button, using the following attributes: Name is** Gender, **Value is** Male.

    Don't forget to move to the right of this Insert element in the document window and type **Male**.

You have used SoftQuad's HoTMetaL to create the same form that you created with Microsoft Internet Assistant for Word for Windows. Figure 6-20 shows what the form looks like if you view it in Netscape.

HoTMetaL - Edit Attributes

TYPE	RADIO
NAME	Gender
VALUE	Female
SRC	
CHECKED	Unspecified
SIZE	
MAXLENGTH	
ALIGN	Unspecified

Apply Reset Cancel

Element: INPUT

Figure 6-19: Change this Insert Element to reflect the attributes shown here.

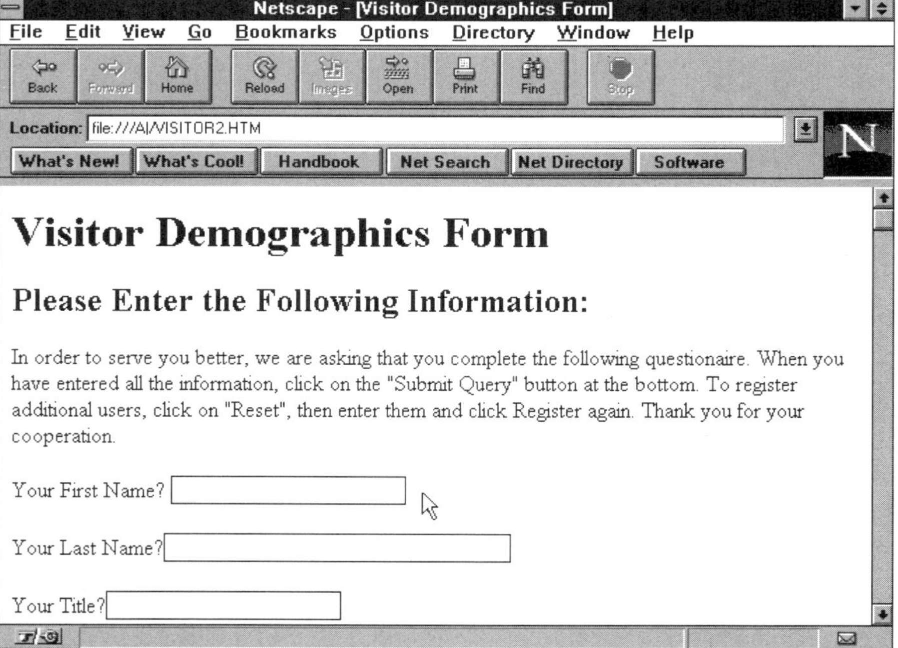

Figure 6-20: VISITOR2.HTM, as viewed with Netscape 2.0.

WebMania!

In this section, you create the same Web page and form one last time, but this time you use Q&D Software's WebMania!

We begin with the assumption that you have installed WebMania! according to the instructions in the appendix and that you have started the program.

1. **Select File⇨Forms⇨New.**

   In a moment, you see a screen that looks like Figure 6-21.

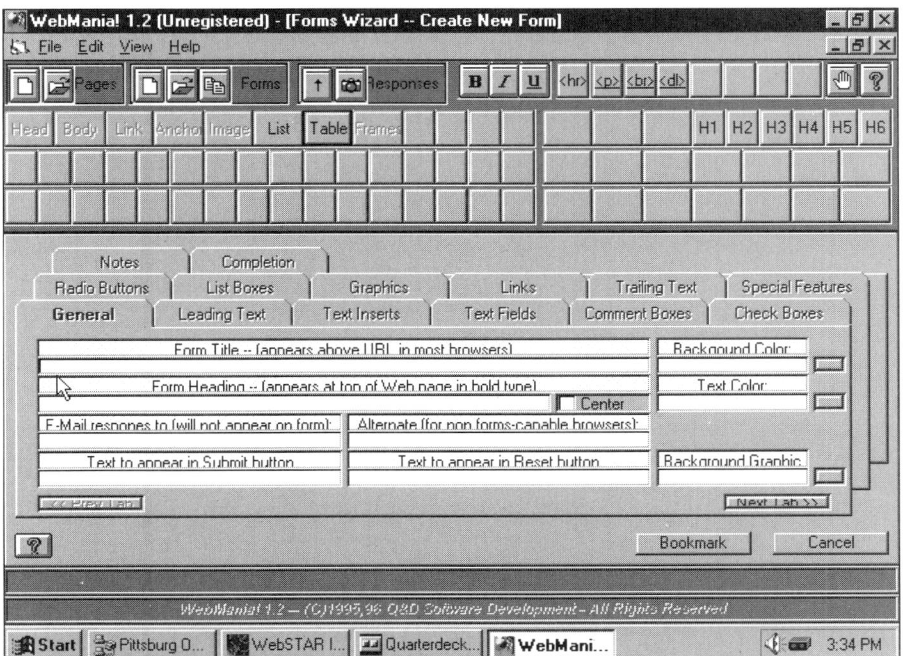

Figure 6-21: Creating a New Form using WebMania! is quite different from what you've experienced before.

   You see the Forms window, where you enter all the information about the form that you're about to create. The first tab in this window is the General Information tab, as pictured in Figure 6-21. You need to enter the form's title here.

2. **Type** Visitor Demographics Form **in the Form Title text box.**
3. **In the Form Heading text box, type** Visitor Demographics Form **again and center the Heading by checking the Center check box.**

4. **Type your e-mail address in the next box so that the responses will come to you and type in an alternative for visitors who use browsers that are not forms compatible.**

   Other options include changing the background color, changing the text color, and including a background graphic. If you include both a background color and a background graphic, most browsers will ignore the color and display the graphic.

5. **After you complete the changes in this box, click on the Next Tab button in the lower right of the General Information tab.**

   You go to the Leading Text tab.

6. **Type the following information:**

```
Please Enter the following information:
In Order to serve your needs more fully, we are asking
that you complete the following questionnaire. This
information is important in our being able to meet your
needs better and we thank you in advance for your
cooperation.
```

   Your screen looks like Figure 6-22.

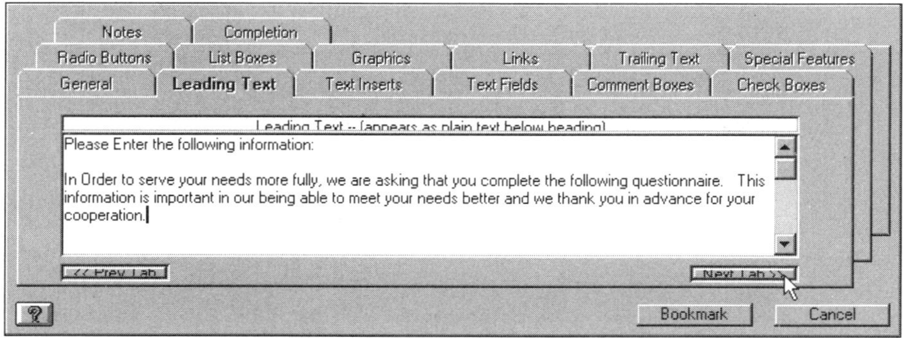

Figure 6-22: After you type the text, click on the Next Tab button.

7. **Click on the Next Tab button again to go to the Text Inserts tab.**

   This tab is quite different from what you have seen previously.

8. **Type the following text strings, pressing the down-arrow key after each text string.**

```
Your First Name?
Your Last Name?
Your Title?
Your Company or Organization?
Your Street Address?
Your City?
Your State's two-letter code?
Your Zip Code?
Your Age?
Your Yearly Income?
Your Gender?
```

After you enter this material, your screen looks similar to Figure 6-23.

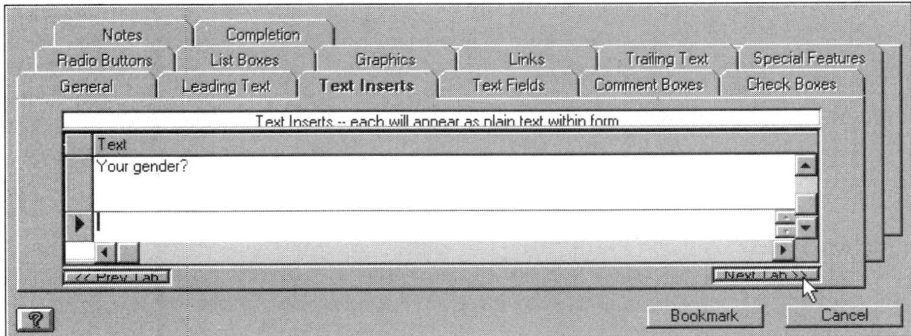

Figure 6-23: After you enter the text inserts, click on the Next Tab button again.

9. **Press the Next Tab button again to go to the Text Fields tab.**
10. **Type the following field names and size, pressing the down-arrow key after each entry.**

    For example, the first thing you would type is **First Name**. You would then press Tab. Then you would type **20** and press the down arrow.

```
First_Name     20
Last_Name      40
Title          30
Company        40
Address        30
City           30
State          2
Zipcode        5
```

The screen looks similar to Figure 6-24.

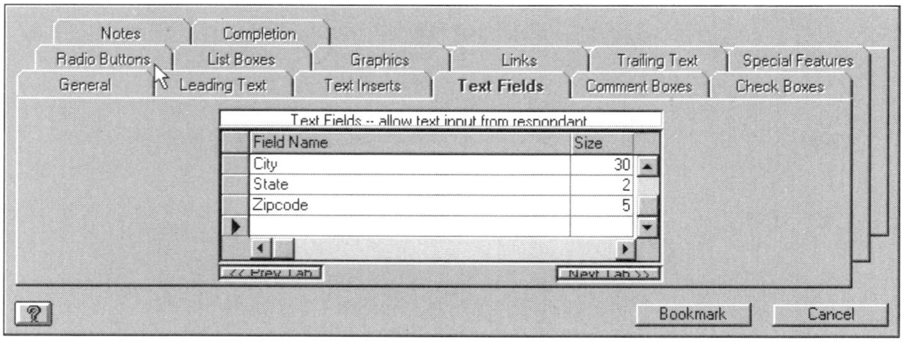

Figure 6-24: *After entering this information, you go to the Radio Buttons tab.*

11. **Press the Next Tab button three times or click on the Radio Buttons tab to go to the Radio Buttons tab.**
12. **In the Enter New Radio Group text box, type** Gender **and then click on the Add Group button.**

    Gender is added to the Radio Button Groups box.
13. **In the Enter New Button Name text box, type** Female.
14. **Click on Gender in the Radio Button Groups box on the left side of the screen and click on the Add Item button.**
15. **Repeat Steps 12 through 14 for Male.**

    Your screen looks similar to Figure 6-25.

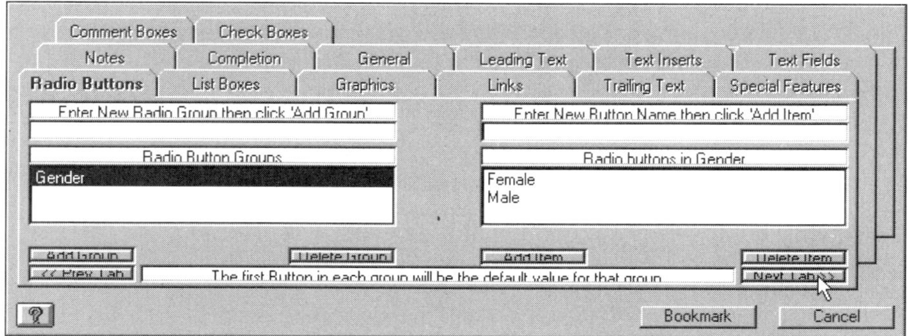

Figure 6-25: *After you complete the Radio Buttons tab, you press Next Tab to go to the List Boxes area.*

16. **Press Next Tab to go to the List Boxes area to create two List Boxes.**
17. **Type** Age **in the box for Enter New List Box then click 'Add Group' and then click the Add Group button.**
18. **Type** Income **in the box for Enter New List Box then click 'Add Group' and then click the Add Group button again.**
19. **Select Age in the List Boxes area on the left and then enter the following items in the box for Enter New List Box Item then click 'Add Item'.**

    Enter the items one at a time, clicking on Add Item after each item.

```
Under 16
16 to 21
22 to 30
31 to 40
41 to 50
51 to 65
Over 65
```

20. **Select Income in the List Boxes area and enter the following items in the same manner, clicking on Add Item after each item.**

```
Under $18,000
$18,001 to $25,000
$25,001 to $35,000
$35,001 to $45,000
$45,001 to $55,000
$55,001 to $75,000
Over $75,000
```

Your screen looks similar to Figure 6-26.

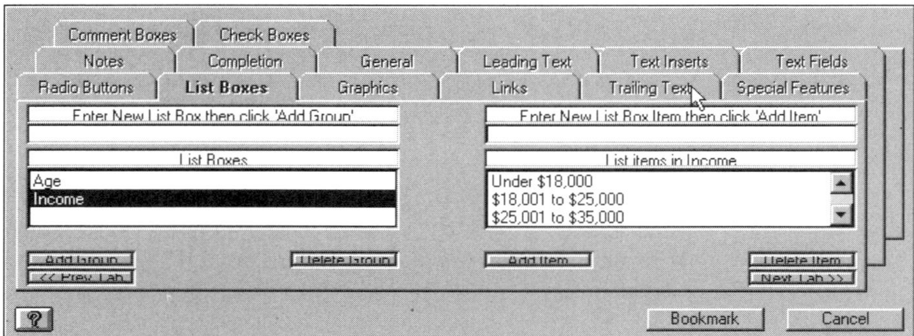

Figure 6-26: Your next destination after completing this form is the Trailing Text tab.

21. **Press Next Tab three times or click on the Trailing Text tab to move to the next area where you need to make modifications.**
22. **Type the following text:**

```
Again, thank you for your cooperation.
```

Your screen looks similar to Figure 6-27.

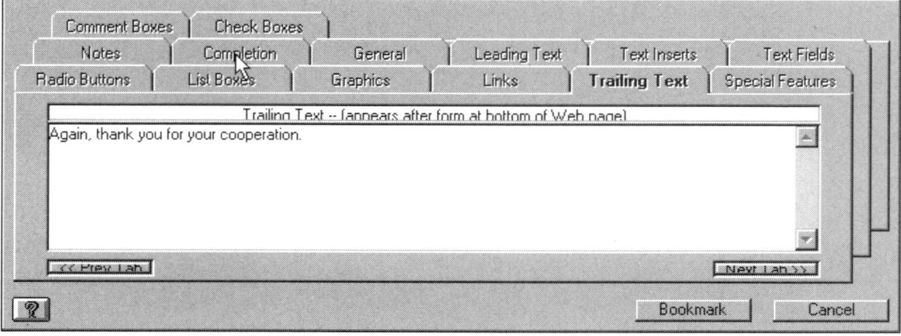

Figure 6-27: You're almost done.

23. **Press Next Tab to go to the Completion tab.**

    You're nearing completion of the form.

24. **In the Completion tab area, click on the Refresh Controls button.**

25. **Copy the controls sequentially from the left side (Controls List) to the right side (Sequence List).**

    After you transfer everything in the correct order, your screen looks like Figure 6-28.

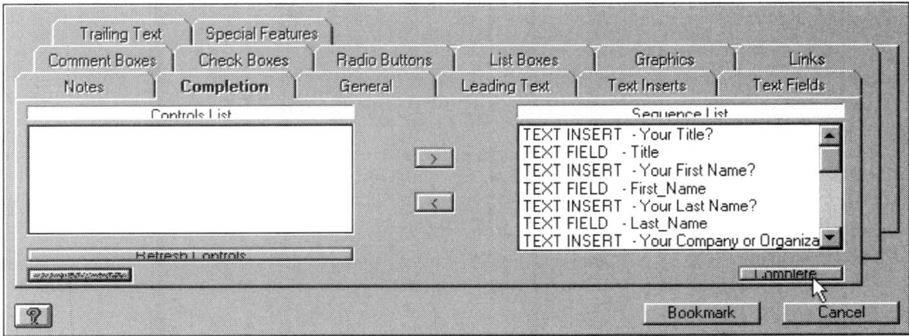

Figure 6-28: Now you are ready to complete the form.

26. **Click on the Complete button in the lower right of the Completion tab area.**

27. **Choose Yes when you are asked whether you are ready to generate the HTML file.**

    After the data has been saved, you are told that WebMania! will now create the HTML form.

28. **Click on the OK button, name the file VISITOR3.HTM, and click on the OK button again.**

Webmania! informs you after it finishes creating the form, and you can click on the OK button. Listing 6-3 shows what the code that WebMania! created for this form looks like.

Listing 6-3: VISITOR3.HTM

```
<html>
<head>
<title>Visitor Demographic Form</title>
</head>
```

(continued)

Listing 6-3 *(continued)*:

```
<body>
<center><h1>Visitor Demographics Form</h1></center>
<p>Please note: Although it is most unlikely that you will⮐
experience any problems responding to this form, certain non-⮐
standard browsers will not respond properly.  If you experience⮐
any difficulties, (or if you are not using a forms-capable⮐
browser) you may e-mail your response to this form to: <a⮐
href="mailto:76270.551@compuserve.com">76270.551@compuserve.⮐
com</a>.
<p>
Please Enter the following information:

In Order to serve your needs more fully, we are asking that⮐
you complete the following questionnaire. This information is⮐
important in our being able to meet your needs better and we⮐
thank you in advance for your cooperation.
<FORM ACTION="mailto:PSummitt@EarthLink.net" METHOD=POST>
<INPUT TYPE="hidden" NAME="Test1" VALUE="1">
<INPUT TYPE="hidden" NAME="Test2" VALUE="2">
<INPUT TYPE="hidden" NAME="WFTestWF" VALUE="1.0">
    <p>Your First Name?<br>
    <p><PRE>First Name:                    <INPUT TYPE="text"⮐
NAME="First_Name" SIZE=20></PRE>
    <p>Your Last Name?<br>
    <p><PRE>Last Name:                     <INPUT TYPE="text"⮐
NAME="Last_Name" SIZE=40></PRE>
    <p>Your Title?<br>
    <p><PRE>Title:                         <INPUT TYPE="text"⮐
NAME="Title" SIZE=30></PRE>
    <p>Your Company or Organization?<br>
    <p><PRE>Company:                       <INPUT TYPE="text"⮐
NAME="Company" SIZE=40></PRE>
    <p>Your Street Address?<br>
    <p><PRE>Address:                       <INPUT TYPE="text"⮐
NAME="Address" SIZE=30></PRE>
    <p>Your City?<br>
    <p><PRE>City:                          <INPUT TYPE="text"⮐
NAME="City" SIZE=30></PRE>
    <p>Your State's two-letter code?<br>
    <p><PRE>State:                         <INPUT TYPE="text"⮐
NAME="State" SIZE=2></PRE>
    <p>Your Zip Code?<br>
```

```
    <p><PRE>Zipcode:                          <INPUT TYPE="text"⮐
NAME="Zipcode" SIZE=5></PRE>
    <p>Your Age?<br>
    <p><SELECT NAME="Age">
        <OPTION SELECTED> Under 16
        <OPTION> 16 to 21
        <OPTION> 22 to 30
        <OPTION> 31 to 40
        <OPTION> 41 to 50
        <OPTION> 51 to 65
        <OPTION> Over 65
    </SELECT>
    <p>Your Yearly Income?<br>
    <p><SELECT NAME="Income">
        <OPTION SELECTED> Under $18,000
        <OPTION> $18,001 to $25,000
        <OPTION> $25,001 to $35,000
        <OPTION> $35,001 to $45,000
        <OPTION> $45,001 to $55,000
        <OPTION> $55,001 to $75,000
        <OPTION> Over $75,000
    </SELECT>
    <p>Your Gender?<br>
    <p><menu>
        <INPUT TYPE="radio" NAME="Gender" VALUE="Female"⮐
CHECKED>Female<br>
        <INPUT TYPE="radio" NAME="Gender" VALUE="Male" >⮐
Male<br></menu>
<p>
Again, thank your for your cooperation.
    <p><INPUT TYPE="hidden" NAME="WebFormID" VALUE="1">
    <p><INPUT TYPE="submit" VALUE="Submit" > <INPUT⮐
TYPE="reset"VALUE="Reset">
</FORM>
<p>
<hr><FONT SIZE=-2>WebMania!™ 1.0 Unregistered - (C)1995 Q&amp;D⮐
Software Development<br><a href="http://www.intac.com/~dversch⮐
">http://www.intac.com/~dversch/</a></FONT>
</body>
</html>
```

Figure 6-29 shows what VISITOR3.HTM looks like when viewed using Netscape.

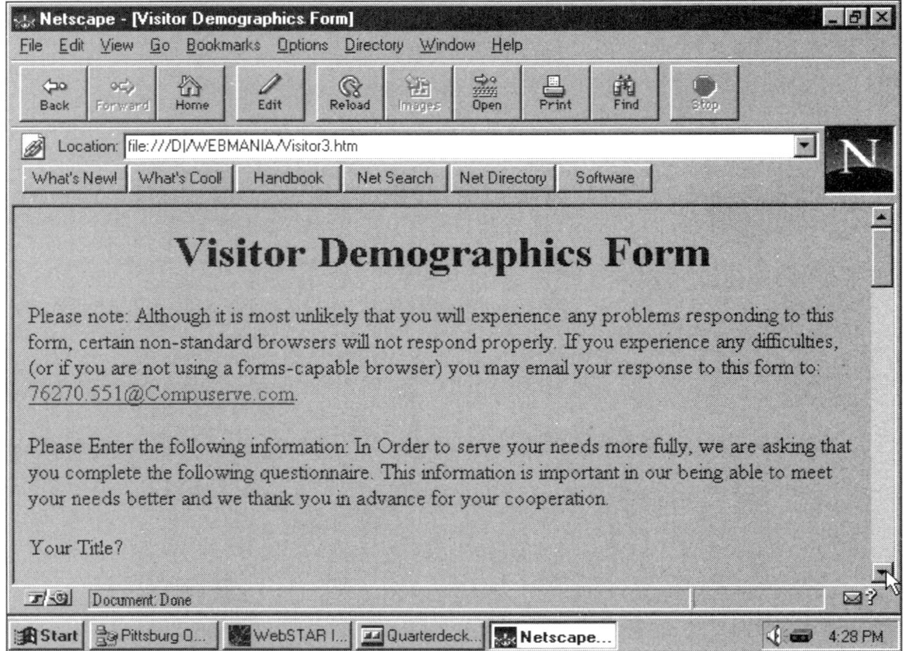

Figure 6-29: VISITOR3.HTM as seen using Netscape.

Final Comments Concerning Web-Authoring Tools

You have created the same form using three different Web-authoring tools. Each tool has advantages and disadvantages when compared with the others. Depending on only one of these helper tools will inhibit your total creativity.

Learning what is possible using HTML and being able to edit your pages by hand so you can fine-tune problem areas will greatly enhance your ability to create a cool and interactive Web site.

VREvolution Site Diary: Installment 6

The choice of a Web-authoring tool for HTML is a personal matter. It depends to a large degree on what you are used to using. Because we use Microsoft Word for Windows extensively in our writing, we find it easier to simply stay with what we are used to. As a result, we use Microsoft Internet Assistant for Word for Windows to create many of our Web pages.

At the same time, few of these Web-authoring tools offer compatibility with the newest and most interesting abilities of HTML and the other protocols that we will be using. The result is that many times we use one of these tools as a starting place but end up working in our favorite text editor.

Often, other tools offer capabilities that Internet Assistant, or one of the other tools described, does not have. So, as you cruise the Web and visit many of the Web sites we suggest, take a look at the source code to see what tools are being used.

You may, and probably will, find many sites that were created by using a simple text editor and a knowledge of HTML. Perhaps the best of both worlds is possible.

Use the Web-authoring tools and then use a text editor and your knowledge of HTML to fine-tune your Web pages by hand. This is the one technique that we have come to use the most.

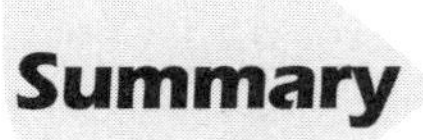

In this chapter, you examined some of the basics of HTML.

You've also looked at some Web-authoring tools.

Some of those Web-authoring tools are provided on the *Creating Cool Interactive Web Sites CD-ROM*.

Using the three Web-authoring tools, you walked through the creation of a Web page containing a simple form.

Finally, you found out how VREvolution determined which Web-authoring tools to use and why.

The next chapter deals with creating 3-D worlds for the Internet using VRML. The chapter is an easy and simple introduction to using VRML, just as this chapter is an easy and simple introduction to using HTML.

VRML

In This Chapter

Using the VRML programs

Visiting VRML worlds

Using Fountain to create VRML worlds

Using Virtus WalkThrough VRML to create VRML worlds

VREvolution's use of VRML

One of the most exciting new technologies on the World Wide Web is the Virtual Reality Modeling Language (VRML). In this chapter, we look at some of the tools that you can use to view, create, and offer VRML on your Web server.

This brief chapter touches on only some of the possibilities of VRML. We cover VRML in considerably more depth in our book, *Creating Cool 3D Web Worlds with VRML* (IDG Books Worldwide, Inc.).

VRML was created by Gavin Bell, Tony Parisi, and Mark Pesce. VRML helps give the Web a "there" feeling. It creates a three-dimensional "there" where you can move around and explore. Just as the Windows desktop metaphor changed the way we use personal computers, the VRML 3-D metaphor will change the way we use the Internet.

VRML creates a three-dimensional space in which you can navigate by using various keyboard entries or mouse clicks and movements. This new technology is the beginning of fictions that you have seen in films such as *Disclosure* and *Lawnmower Man*. The big difference, and hence why VRML is included in this book, is that you are no longer restricted to simply viewing the virtual world; you can now interact with that world, changing your viewing perspective, and possibly your intellectual perspective, on the data that you are exposed to.

We begin by looking at the VRML viewing tools that are on the *Creating Cool Interactive Web Sites CD-ROM.* Our next step is to look at the tools that make creating VRML worlds easier. We examine how you can use VRML worlds in various Web sites, and finally, we look at how VREvolution has used VRML on its sites.

Keep in mind that after you have installed the Web browser and VRML viewer of your choice, you can view any of the examples in this chapter by using that combination. You do not need to install each of the software packages, only the ones that you want to use.

Viewing VRML Worlds

Before you can understand the possibilities and limitations of VRML, you need to be able to experience it. This section of this chapter deals with the Web browser and VRML viewer combinations that are available. Please don't think that these options are the only ones. They simply are the ones that we deal with in this chapter.

Internet Explorer VRML add-ons

Microsoft Internet Explorer is Microsoft's Windows 95 Web browser. Version 2.0 of Internet Explorer is on the *Creating Cool Interactive Web Sites CD-ROM.* You'll find installation instructions in the appendix. You can also download a newer version of the browser for the platform of your choice when it becomes available from Microsoft's home page, as shown in Figure 7-1.

You can then go to another area in Microsoft's Web pages to download the VRML add-ons that enable you to explore 3-D worlds (see Figure 7-2).

Install either the software provided on the *Creating Cool Interactive Web Sites CD-ROM* or the version you've downloaded to your hard drive according to the installation instructions in the appendix. Configure your Windows 95 TCP/IP package to work with your Internet provider and check out Dennis McKenzie's Web site, which is shown in Figure 7-3.

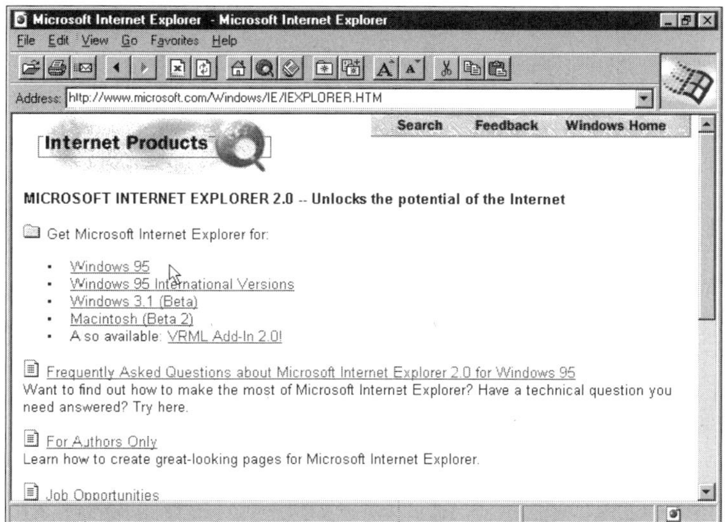

Figure 7-1: You can download Internet Explorer here.

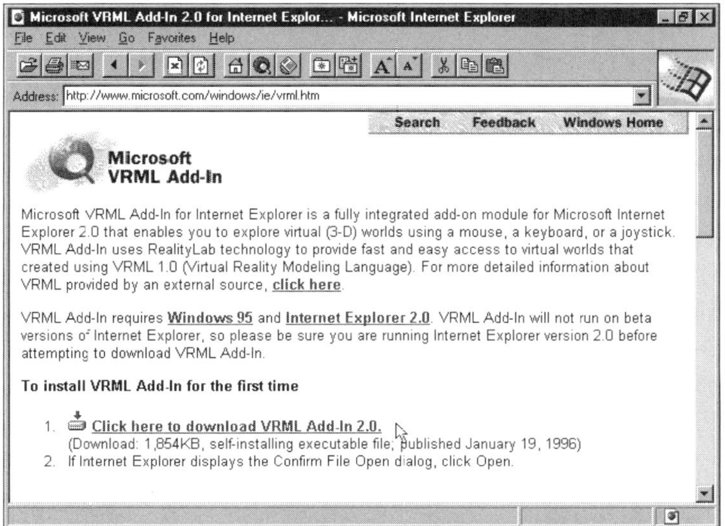

Figure 7-2: Download the Microsoft VRML Add-In for Internet Explorer.

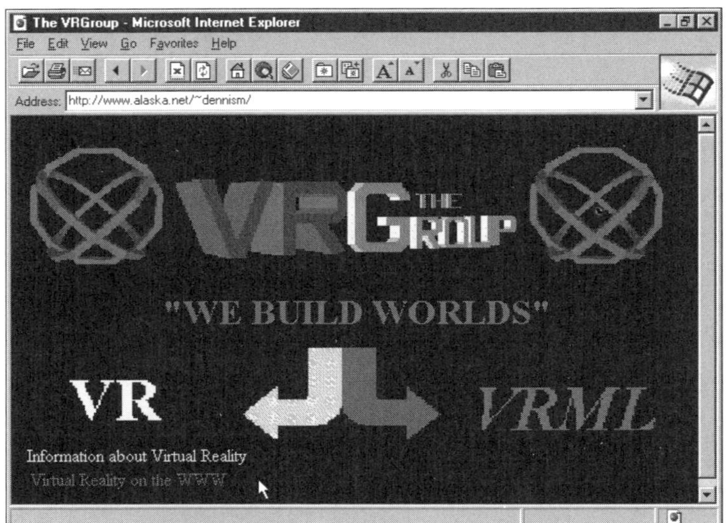

Figure 7-3: Dennis McKenzie's Web pages are the home of the VR Group.

Choose the VR hyperlink. Then move down the Web page until you see Our World. Double-click on this hyperlink and explore the VRML world that is similar to what is shown in Figure 7-4.

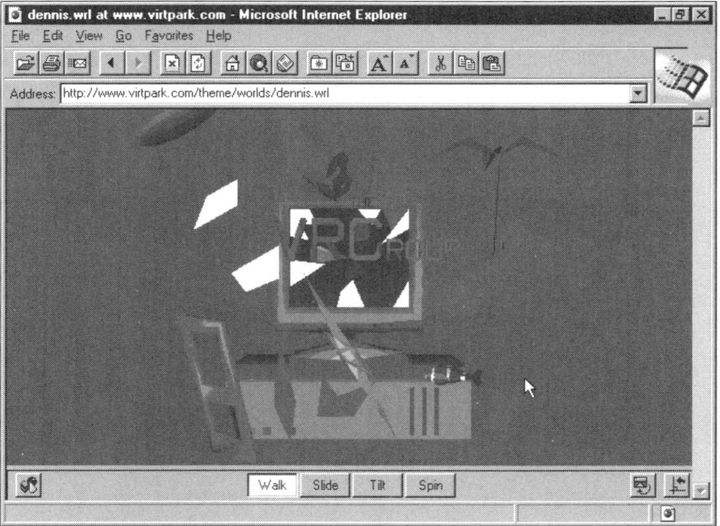

Figure 7-4: Dennis McKenzie's virtual reality.

Use your mouse to move around inside this virtual world. You can press the right button and move the mouse to move around the object. Pressing the left button enables you to move forward or backward from the object.

VRealm

VRealm is a VRML viewer created jointly by Portable Graphics and Integrated Data Systems (IDS), Inc. This viewer runs on the Windows NT and the Windows 95 platforms. The minimum hardware requirements to run VRealm include a 486/66 processor, 8MB of RAM, and a 256-color display driver and graphics card.

VRealm is included on the *Creating Cool Interactive Web Sites CD-ROM*. The newest version of this VRML viewer is available for download at `http://www.ids-net.com/ids/introduc.html`, as shown in Figure 7-5. For complete information on the IDS product line, contact IDS at `hotline@ids-net.com`, `sales@ids-net.com`, or phone 912-236-4374.

Installation instructions for VRealm are in the appendix. Turn there and install the software. You then need to configure this viewer to work with your Web browser in order to view VRML worlds. The recommended Web browser, according to the README file, is Netscape 1.22. We've installed VRealm and used it configured with Version 2.0 of Netscape with no problem.

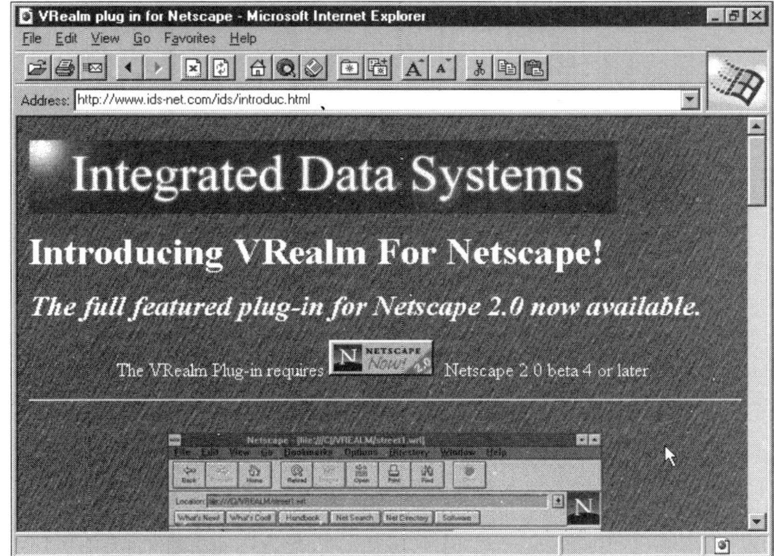

Figure 7-5: The VRealm beta is downloadable from this location.

To configure Netscape 1.22 for VRealm follow these steps:

1. **Choose Options⇨Preferences.**
2. **Choose the Helper Applications item in the drop-down list.**
3. **Click the New Type button.**
4. **In the Configure New MIME type dialog box, type** x-world **for MIME Type and** x-vrml **for MIME Subtype.**
5. **In the Extensions field, type** .wrl.
6. **In the Action group box, click on Launch Application.**
7. **In the text entry field, enter the location of the VREALM execution file.**

   In the example, the entry is C:\VREALM\VREALM.EXE.

VRealm is now ready to view 3-D VRML worlds. Check it by taking a quick look at IDSHOME.WRL. Figure 7-6 shows what you see on your monitor when you open this world. Be sure to read the README file for navigation information.

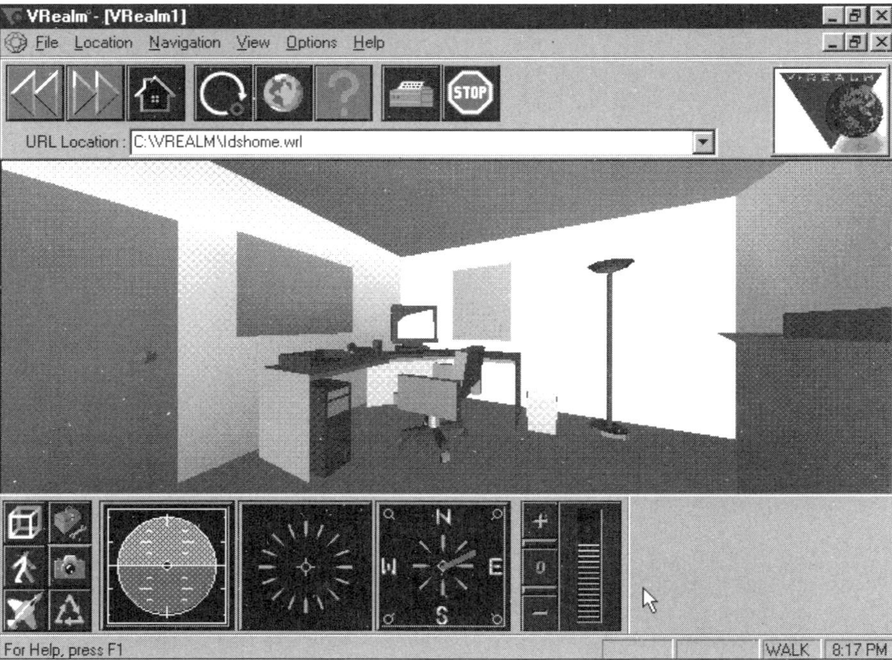

Figure 7-6: You can use VRealm to explore virtual worlds.

WorldView

WorldView is a VRML viewer created by Tony Parisi's company, InterVista Software, Inc. Parisi is one of the coauthors of the original VRML specification.

Both the Windows 3.1 and Windows 95 versions of WorldView are included on the *Creating Cool Interactive Web Sites CD-ROM*. The most up-to-date versions of WorldView for the various platforms are available for download from `http://www.webmaster.com/high/products/index.html`, as seen in Figure 7-7.

WorldView requires a minimum 486/50 processor with 8MB of RAM and a 256-color display driver and graphics card. The Windows 3.1 version also requires that Win32s be installed.

Turn to the appendix for installation instructions. The installation program will ask whether you want to install WorldView and where you want the program located. Follow the directions and answer the questions. The program and the necessary program group and icons will be installed.

Figure 7-7: The newest versions of WorldView are available from WebMaster.

WorldView must also be configured to work with your Web browser in order for you to view VRML worlds. WorldView comes preconfigured to work with Netscape. The WorldView readme file includes modification instructions for configuring WorldView for other browsers.

You also need to configure your Web browser to recognize VRML files and use WorldView to read them. To configure Netscape with WorldView, do the following:

1. **Choose Options⇨Preferences.**
2. **Choose the Helper Applications item from the drop-down list.**
3. **Click on the New Type button.**
4. **In the Configure New MIME type dialog box, type** x-world **for MIME Type and** x-vrml **for MIME Subtype.**
5. **In the Extensions field, type** .wrl.
6. **In the Action group box, click on Launch Application.**
7. **In the text entry field, enter the location of the WorldView execution file.**

   In the example, we typed **C:\WRLDVIEW\WRLDVIEW.EXE**.

Configuring WorldView to work with other Web browsers is a similar process. Be sure to read your Web browser's documentation for how to change or add these MIME types.

WorldView is now ready to view 3-D VRML worlds. Check it by taking a quick look at the worlds located at InterVista's Web pages.

Be sure to read the README file for navigation information. Explore some other VRML sites while you're out there. See how VRML is used by others to enhance their sites.

Now that you know how to view VRML worlds, you need to find out how to create them so that you can use them on your Web site.

Creating VRML Worlds

Fountain from Caligari and Virtus WalkThrough VRML are two of the tools that you can use to create VRML worlds. Both of them are on the *Creating Cool Interactive Web Sites CD-ROM*.

We're not artists, so don't expect our examples to be highly artistic. All we hope to do with these short tutorials is get you started working with these tools. We begin with Caligari's Fountain.

Using Caligari's Fountain

Fountain, from Caligari Corporation, is a VRML world-builder and browser.

The Beta version of Fountain is on the *Creating Cool Interactive Web Sites CD-ROM.* An up-to-date version of the software, as well as demos of other Caligari products, is available at Caligari's Web site, which is at `http://www.caligari.com`.

Installing Fountain is easy. We've provided full installation instructions in the appendix. Turn there and install the program. After that, you can create a simple world by following these instructions:

1. **Start Fountain by clicking on the icon.**

   Your screen looks like Figure 7-8. (You'll notice that there is a URL listed in the URL line despite the fact that you are not connected to the Web yet. Don't worry about this. The URL is there because the cursor is over a hyperlink that will take you to that location.)

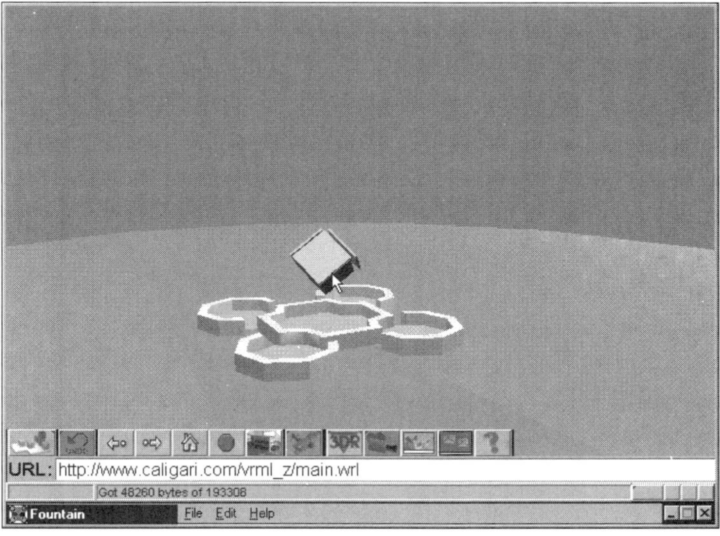

Figure 7-8: Fountain's user interface is easy to use.

2. **Click on the cube in the center.**

   You go online and are taken to `http://www.caligari.com/vrml_z/main.wrl`, which is shown in Figure 7-9. In the figure, again, the cursor is over a hyperlink and therefore the URL shown in the URL line is the URL for the hyperlinked world rather than for the world that you are in.

Figure 7-9: Fountain is a VRML viewer as well as an authoring tool.

3. **Click on the archway on the right side of the screen.**

   You are taken to LEARN.WRL, another world at Caligari's Web site, which is shown in Figure 7-10.

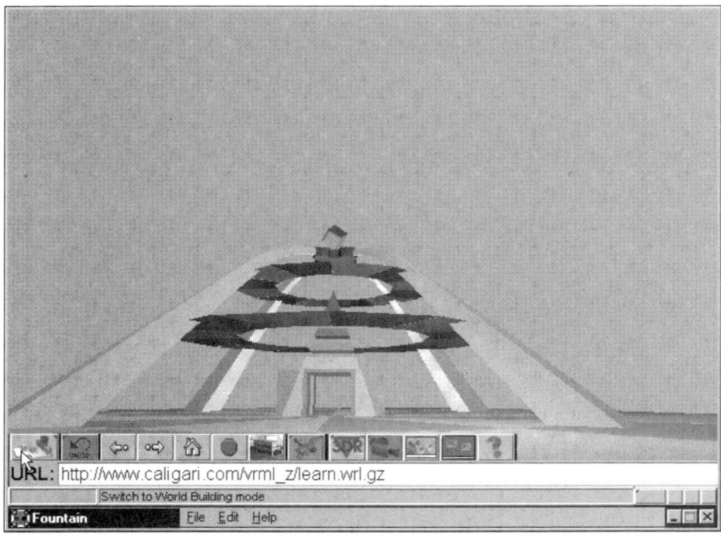

Figure 7-10: Each world can be tied to many other worlds.

Note that the cursor in Figure 7-10 is on the button that you use to switch between Fountain's browsing and world-building modes.

4. **Exit the program and then start it up again, but do not go online.**
5. **Click on the button mentioned in Step 3 that switches you to the world-building mode.**
6. **Choose File⇨Scene⇨New, as in Figure 7-11.**

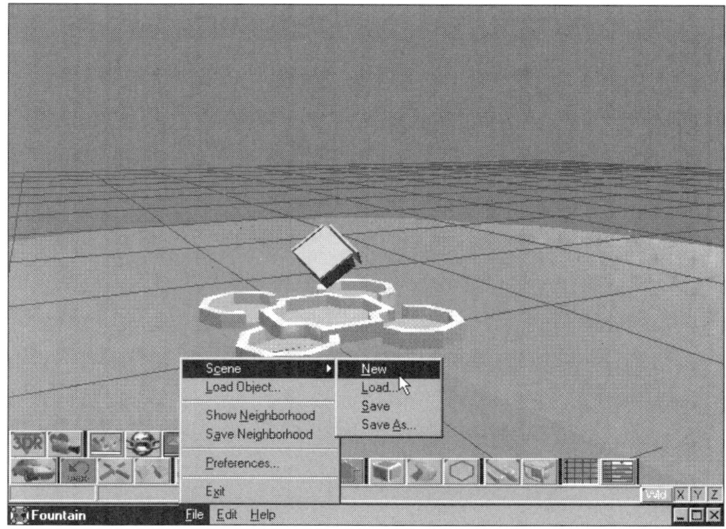

Figure 7-11: *To build something, you need to start with a clean screen.*

You see a new screen, where you can do your world building.

7. **Click on the primitives icon and then click on the Add Vertical Text icon (see Figure 7-12).**
8. **Type** Publications**, as we did, or a word of your choice.**

   We typed **Publications** because we were creating a VRML library of Paul's academic articles.
9. **Change to Fly mode by clicking the button that looks like an airplane (see Figure 7-12) and back away from the letters (see Figure 7-13).**

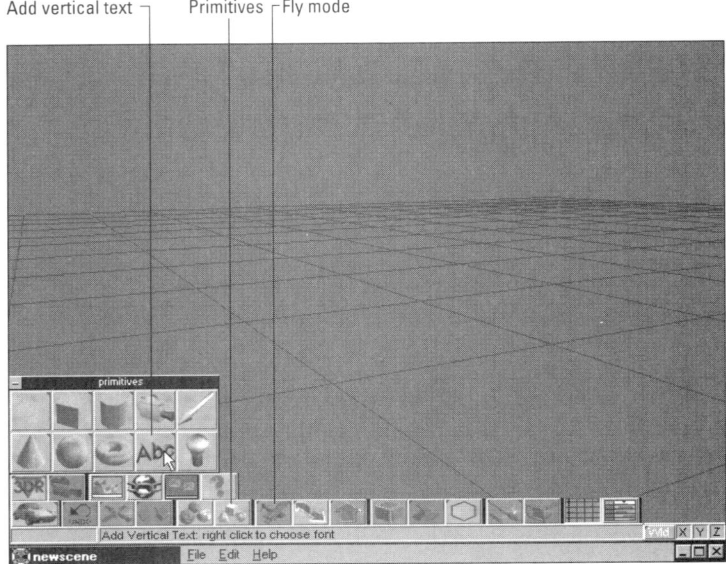

Figure 7-12: Add text to this new virtual world.

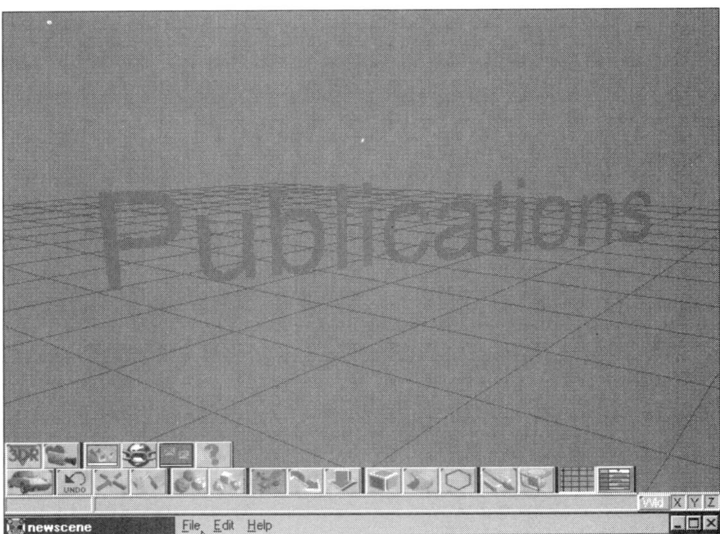

Figure 7-13: You have to pull back to see the entire world that you've created. This world contains one word.

10. **Switch to the viewer mode by clicking on the car in the lower left of the screen.**

11. **Save this world by clicking File⇨Scene⇨Save As, as in Figure 7-14.**

Figure 7-14: Save the file.

12. **Type** PUBS.WRL **or the name that you want to save the file under and then press the Enter key.**

    A dialog box that's similar to Figure 7-15 is displayed on your screen.

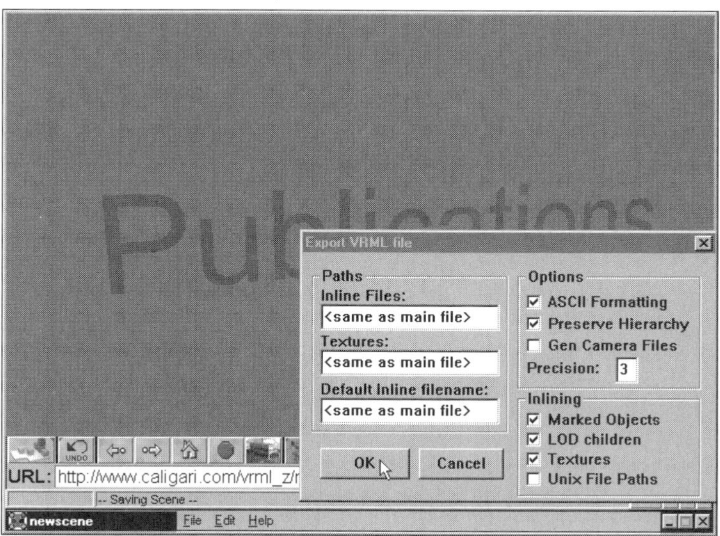

Figure 7-15: Choose your options and click OK to save the VRML file.

13. **Choose the options shown in Figure 7-15 and click on the OK button.**

    Your VRML file is saved.

You can see how we used this VRML world by aiming your Web browser at `http://vrevolution.pitton.com/pubs.htm`. We say more about how to use VRML in the overall construction of your Web site in the VREvolution Site Diary at the end of this chapter.

Using Virtus WalkThrough VRML

Virtus WalkThrough VRML, which is on the *Creating Cool Interactive Web Sites CD-ROM,* has a user interface that's easy to use (see Figure 7-16).

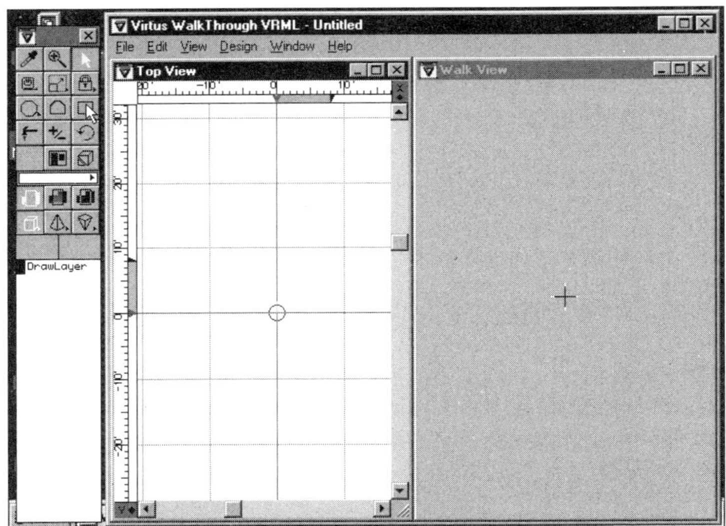

Figure 7-16: In this opening view, you look down on the objects that you create.

Installing WalkThrough VRML is simple.

1. **Run the Setup program on the CD-ROM and follow the necessary instructions.**
2. **After the installation is complete, double-click on the Virtus WalkThrough VRML icon to start the program.**

   After a brief identification screen that shows the copyright notice and the program version number, the WalkThrough VRML window opens, as shown in Figure 7-16.

The screen consists of three main windows: the Tools Pad on the left, the Top View, and the Walk View. Only one of these areas can be active at a time. You can tell which area is active by looking at the individual title bars. If the title bar is colored, then that window is active.

The program always begins with the Top View active. You can change which part of the screen is active by clicking inside the view that you want to switch to.

The Top View is one of six Design views possible in that window. The others are Left, Right, Front, Back, and Bottom. The Walk View is the 3-D version of what you've created. You view and design your virtual worlds in these two windows.

To give you an idea of how Virtus WalkThrough VRML works, you are now going to create a simple VRML world.

1. **Click on the Rectangle panel in the Tools Pad on the left of the screen, as indicated by the cursor in Figure 7-16.**
2. **Move the cursor to the Top View, just above the circle at the center of the axes.**
3. **Click and hold the left mouse button and move the cursor till you have drawn a small rectangle, as shown in Figure 7-17.**

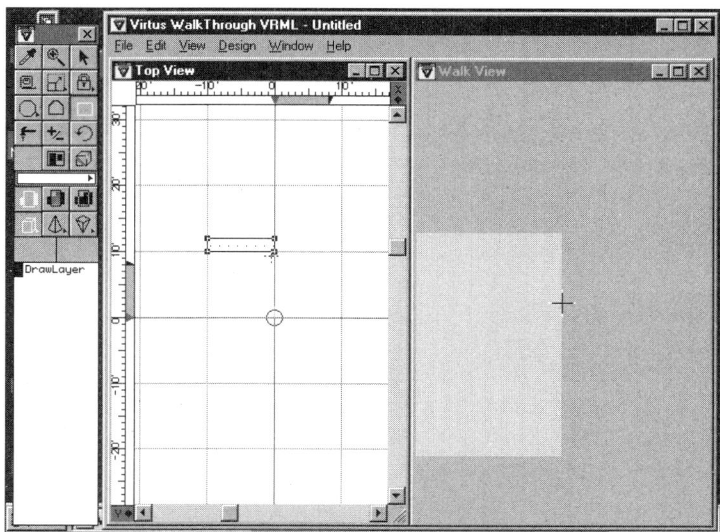

Figure 7-17: Notice the two-dimensional rectangle created in the Top View window and, although you can't tell it in the two-dimensional screen shot, the 3-D object in the Walk View.

4. Change your view by choosing View⇨Change View, as in Figure 7-18.

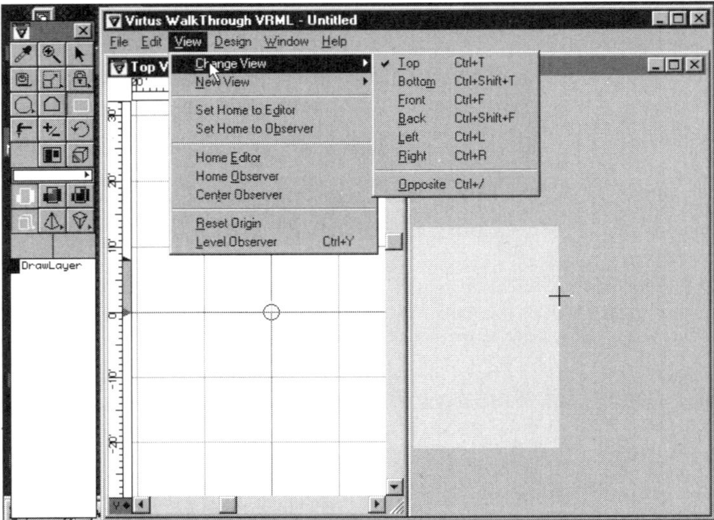

Figure 7-18: You can change your design view of the object easily.

5. Choose the Front View.
6. Click the enlargement icon (the icon under the cursor in Figure 7-19).

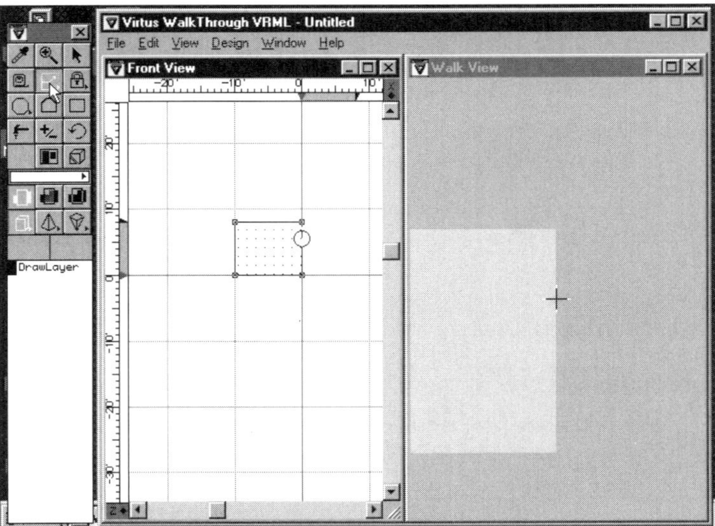

Figure 7-19: You'll want to enlarge the object now.

7. Place your cursor on the upper-left corner of the square and, pushing and holding the left mouse button, drag the top line upward to extend the height of the object. Your screen should look like Figure 7-20 now.

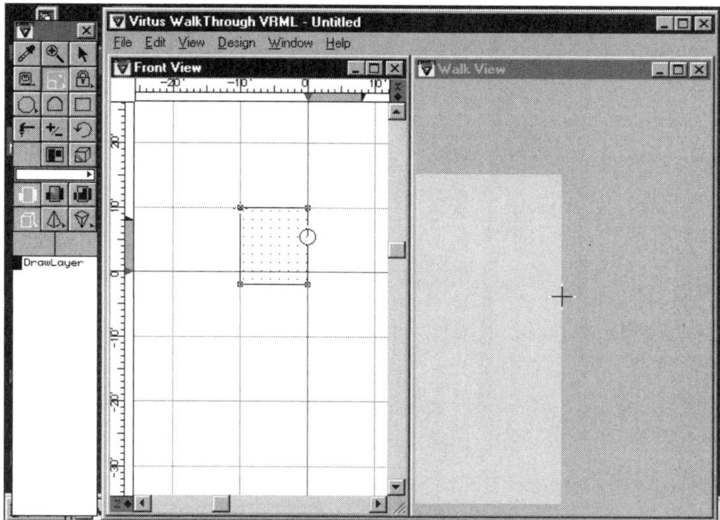

Figure 7-20: The square becomes a rectangle.

8. Switch back to the Top View and click the arrow icon, as in Figure 7-21.

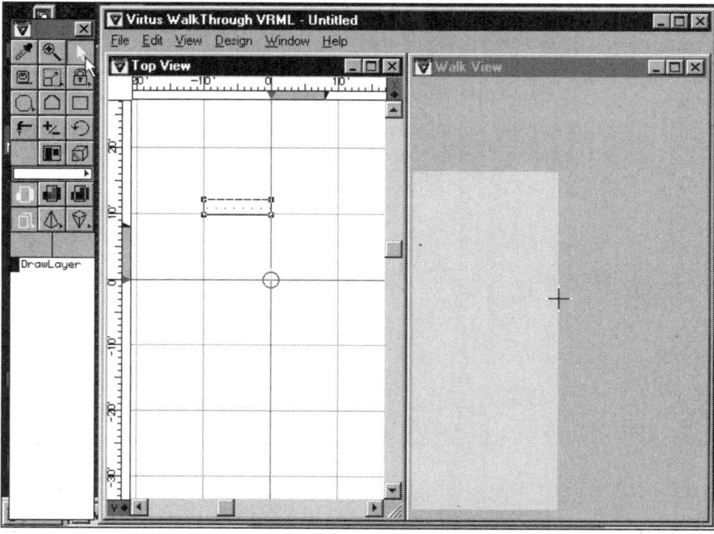

Figure 7-21: Choose the arrow icon from the Tools Pad.

9. Place your cursor on the circle and move it down as in Figure 7-22.

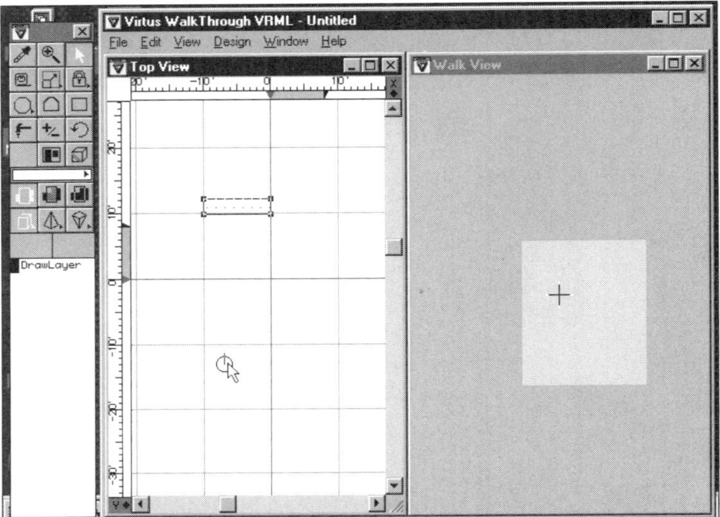

Figure 7-22: Moving the observation icon changes your view.

10. **Watch what happens in the Walk View on the right side of the screen as you move the circle in the Top View.**

    What you see before you are the beginnings of a VRML representation of a book.

11. **Continue to work with WalkThrough VRML and create a book for possible use later.**

Take your time and explore the creation of this virtual book. When you're finished, choose File⇨Export. Your only option with Virtus WalkThrough VRML is to export to a VRML file. Save the virtual book and exit the program.

Load your Web browser and VRML viewer again and check out the pages at `http://vrevolution.pitton.com/vrmltest.htm`. We say more about how you can use VRML to improve the appearance of your Web site in the VREvolution Site Diary.

VREvolution Site Diary: Installment 7

Because one of the purposes of VREvolution is to educate people about virtual reality, it was a given that VRML applications would be available from our site. We made this decision despite our opinion that under the VRML Version 1.0 specification, VRML is nothing more than 3-D graphics for the Internet. It is not yet virtual reality, but it is the closest generally available application there is.

As this chapter is being edited, the decision is being made on the direction for VRML Version 2.0's specification. From our observations of the discussions around this decision, despite six proposals, it looks like a choice between the Worlds Away proposal (backed by Sun, SGI, Netscape, and others) and the ActiveVRML proposal (from Microsoft). Early indications are that the Worlds Away proposal will be chosen, but Microsoft may go ahead with ActiveVRML as its standard anyway. The future of VRML as a Web standard seems in doubt.

In its current specification, VRML provides a means of presenting 3-D worlds over the Web. Using Microsoft Internet Explorer, you can embed a VRML world inside an HTML Web page. The use of Frames in Netscape 2.0 and the Microsoft Internet Explorer 3.0 Beta provide a similar method of splitting the HTML page and presenting text in one half of the document and the virtual world in the other half.

Of the authoring tools available, we decided to use those tools that enabled us to create our worlds quickly. Depending on what kind of VRML world we are trying to create at a given point in time, we tend to use Fountain for the creation of worlds that require text and WalkThrough VRML for basic geometric shapes. In the end, however, as with HTML, due to the ever-changing status of VRML and the Web in general, we have found that final tweaking of the worlds, as with the pages themselves, needs to be done by hand using a basic text editor.

Summary

In this chapter you've learned about a number of VRML viewers and have chosen to use one and configured it with your Web browser.

You've also had the opportunity to experiment with two VRML authoring tools.

You found out why we at VREvolution chose to create our 3-D Web worlds with a variety of tools but, in the final analysis, perform our final construction of the worlds by hand.

Next, you look at Java, which is one way to bring animation and interactivity to Web sites.

Java

In This Chapter

Exploring Java's possibilities
Visiting Java-empowered Web sites
Developing Java applications
VREvolution's Java explorations

One of the coolest possibilities for interactivity on the Web can be found in Sun's Java.

Animated Content on the Interactive Java Frontier

Java is a programming language that was developed by engineers at Sun Microsystems. Java brings animation and interaction to the Web and enables you to transform static Web pages into somewhat interactive applications. You use Java to create content your server can deliver to the user's computer where it will run.

The question of interactivity

Chapters 6 and 7 of this book deal with HTML (Hypertext Markup Language) and VRML, Virtual Reality Modeling Language. HTML is two dimensional and basically static. Other than forms and fill-in check boxes, HTML doesn't offer much in the way of interactivity.

VRML, on the other hand, is three dimensional, but, again, it is also basically static. You can move around the objects, but in the current VRML specification (1.0), the objects themselves don't move.

But what, specifically, is interactivity?

The word *interactivity* has become somewhat of a cliché in the computer field. It is used to describe everything from hangman and tic-tac-toe games to voyeuristic peep shows and shoot-'em-ups.

According to the dictionary, the word *interactive* means "to act upon one another." When discussing interactivity with regard to communication technologies, the level of interactivity refers to how much the user can affect, change, or influence the form, content, or composition of the environment in which the communication takes place.

What we are saying here is that if no change is possible, then no interactivity is possible. Change must be possible on both sides of the communication for the level of interactivity to be high. The level, or quality, of this interactivity is what helps to produce a sensorially rich mediated environment in which the communication can take place.

In HTML, hyperlinks enable users to select various pages for viewing in much the same way as channel changers enable television viewers to select channels for viewing. Such interactivity is limited to selecting what to view and nothing more.

The current specification of VRML (Version 1.0) enables users to change their viewpoint in regard to the world they are viewing, but users cannot make changes to the world they are viewing. Interactivity is somewhat higher here than with HTML but is still not to the level of an unmediated communication environment.

CGI programming, which we cover in Chapter 10, provides more interactivity by enabling you to customize your server's responses to the individual user. These programs aren't active all of the time, however. They require users to click buttons before their selections can be processed and then reacted to.

Java makes immediate and continuous user interaction possible. Java applets accept and respond to user input with customized feedback. A Java *applet* is a Java application, or program, that runs within the confines of a browser. Applets are just little applications The Java technology has the potential to create a richer and more interactive World Wide Web.

A short history

In early 1991, a small group of Sun Microsystems employees began work on what was known at that time as *the Green Project*. The original purpose of this project was to develop consumer electronic products that would be simple and maintenance free. The group determined that to accomplish their task they needed a platform-independent programming language that allowed the programs they created to run on any computer.

They began with C++, but the language wasn't able to do everything they needed, and the team soon abandoned it. James Gosling, one of the team members, began developing a new language for the project. At first this language was called Oak, but this name failed a trademark search, and the language was later renamed Java. In 1992, the language was combined with an operating system, a user interface, and hardware, and named *7 (Star 7). Star 7 was a small, hand-held, personal remote control device.

In 1993, the Green Project became FirstPerson, Inc. FirstPerson, then began development of proposals for Time-Warner's television video-on-demand set-top box but lost the bid to Silicon Graphics, Inc. About the same time, NCSA Mosaic 1.0, the first graphical Web browser, was released.

With the loss of the Time-Warner proposal and the failure of a proposed deal with 3DO, FirstPerson was dissolved in early 1994. The remaining staff began applying the Green Project technology to CD-ROM, online multimedia, and network-based computing. As the Web grew in popularity, the team turned its attention to developing a Web browser. By September 1994, they had finished WebRunner, a Web browser that was later renamed HotJava.

Sun executives were impressed and saw the possibilities of the new browser. In May 1995, Sun Microsystems formally announced Java and HotJava at Sun World '95 in San Francisco.

The HotJava Web browser

HotJava is the browser written in Java that enables you to view interactive content created with Java that is available on the Web. You can get HotJava only from Sun Microsystems at `http://java.sun.com/`, as shown in Figure 8-1. This browser is available only for Windows NT and Windows 95 and is of little use for the newer applets created under the Java release version.

Figure 8-1: *HotJava is available only at Sun's Web site.*

The HotJava user's guide is also available at this site, and you need to read the licensing agreements here. An overview of the browser also is available, as shown in Figure 8-2.

Some of the newer Beta versions of browsers such as Netscape 2.0 are Java enabled, using the Beta version of Java. You cannot use the new browsers to view Java applications created for HotJava. Similarly, you cannot use HotJava to view Java applications created for the new browsers.

Java's features

Think of Java as three interwoven components:

- The language necessary for writing the code of the application itself
- The architecture for running the programs written with the language
- The tools necessary for building, compiling, and running the applications

These three components, in combination, make up what is known as *Java*.

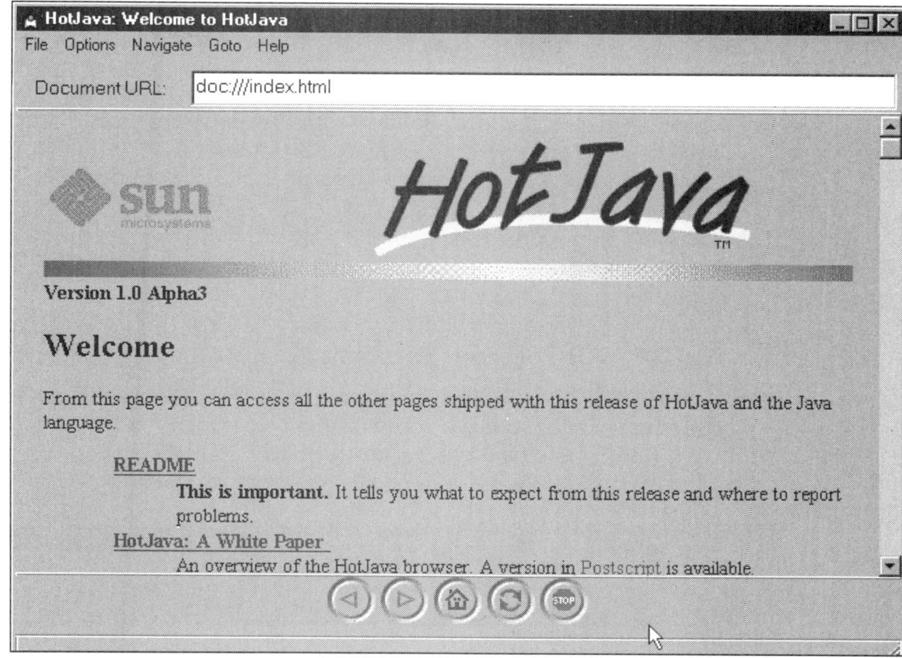

Figure 8-2: The HotJava Web browser.

Although Java was not directly born from C++, it can be thought of as an evolution of C++. Java looks and feels a great deal like C++. As a result, Java is object-oriented and familiar. Java also uses automatic garbage collection and thread synchronization.

Along with the similarities between C++ and Java, there also are differences. For example, Java has no structures, unions, defines, pointers, multiple inheritance, individual functions, goto, operator overloading, or automatic coercion. Many of these C++ features were dropped in Java to reduce the level of redundancy that exists within C++.

The next step for you is to get the software and begin learning how to build Java applets. An applet is like a little application. The applet allows you to create an environment for activities to take place on the user's own computer.

Getting and Using Java

In order to write Java applets, you need to obtain a copy of the Java Developer's Kit. You can download it from the same location, `http://java.sun.com`, where you got HotJava. To obtain the kit, you simply click on the Download icon, which has the cursor on it in Figure 8-3.

The Java Developers Kit (JDK) enables you to write applets that will transform your pages. Two documents come with the JDK: the COPYRIGHT file and the README file.

- The COPYRIGHT file contains information about the copyright and licensing.
- The README file contains information about the JDK, including why the JDK was made, what packages comprise the final applet API, and how to get in touch with Sun if you find bugs that you want to report.

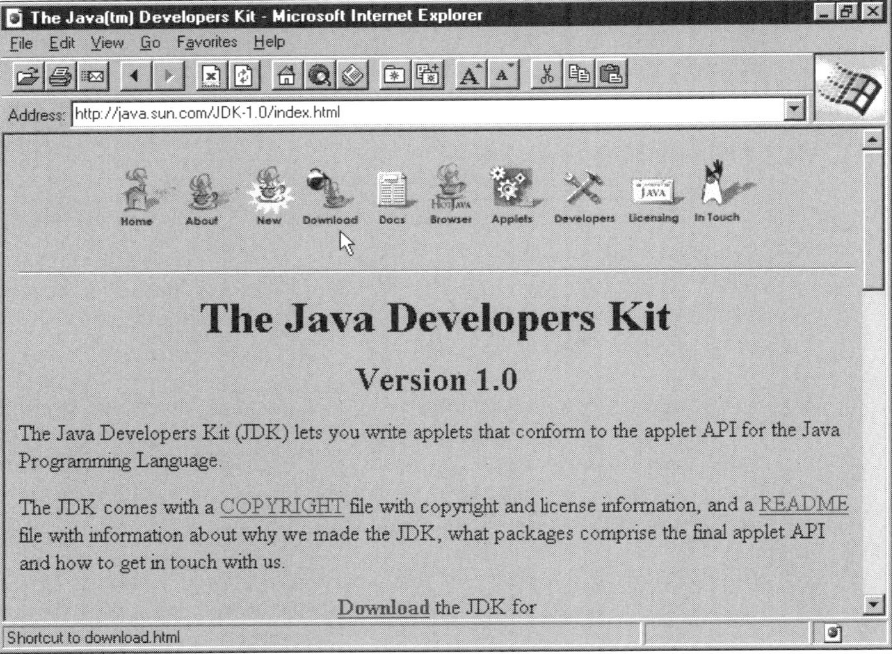

Figure 8-3: You need to download the Java Developer's Kit in order to write Java applets.

Copyright © 1996, Sun Microsystems, Inc. Used with permission.

You also want to download the documentation for the JDK (see Figure 8-4) from the same site where you obtained the JDK itself.

Setting up the Java SDK

You need to download the Java SDK Version 1.0 for Windows NT and Windows 95. This self-extracting file uncompresses and unpacks to just under 6MB. Here are the steps you need to follow:

1. **Download the distribution file from Sun's Web site.**

   The distribution file is a self-extracting archive.

2. **Place the distribution file in the root directory of drive C.**
3. **Uncompress the distribution file.**

   Because the file is a self-extracting archive, you simply double-click on the distribution file icon.

4. **Move the redistributable libraries to the \java\bin subdirectory.**

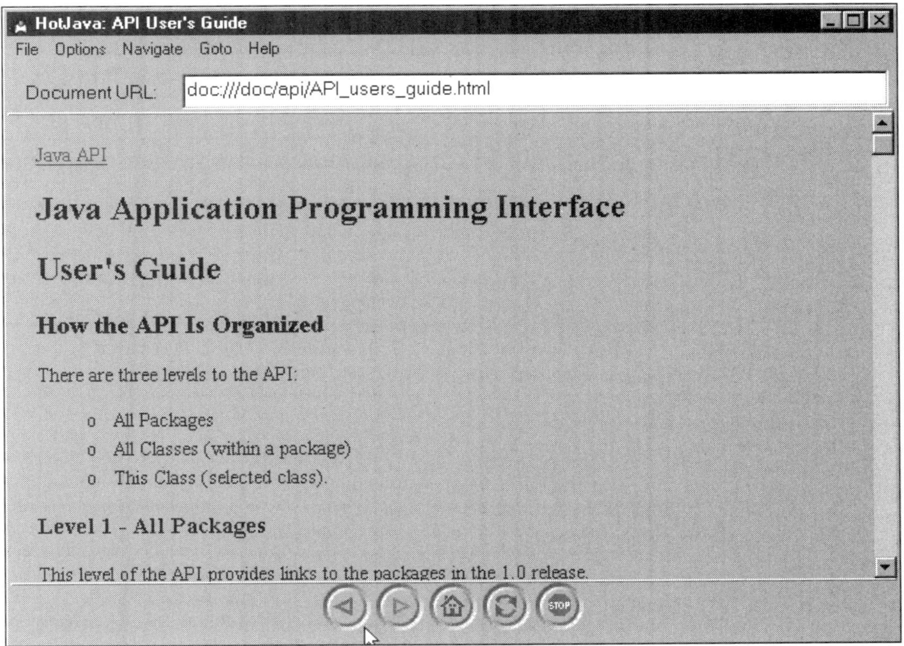

Figure 8-4: This is just one of the types of documentation available.

5. **You do not need to update your path statement in your AUTOEXEC.BAT file to include \java\bin.**

   You do need to set your `HOME` variable.

6. **Under Windows 95, add the statement** `set HOME=C:\` **to your AUTOEXEC.BAT file.**

7. **Save the file and reboot your machine so that the changes will take effect.**

8. **Create the configuration directory.**

   The configuration files are stored in the .HotJava directory inside your home directory. For Windows 95, you need to create the .HotJava subdirectory by running the statement `mkdir %HOME%.hotjava` in a Command Prompt window.

Your machine is now configured and ready for Java. You should have the files in Table 8-1.

Table 8-1 Java Files

File	Description
COPYRIGHT	A text file that contains the standard copyright notice
README	A text file that contains information about this specific release
\bin\	A subdirectory that includes the Java language tools
\demo\	A subdirectory that includes the Java demo programs
\include\	A subdirectory that includes the C\C++ header files for interfacing C\C++ to Java
\lib\	A subdirectory that includes the Java packages and platform-specific libraries
\src\	A subdirectory that includes the Java package sources (such as src.zip in the Win95/NT distribution)

Under the \bin\ subdirectory, you'll find the Java tools that are listed in Table 8-2.

Table 8-2 Java Tools

Tool	Description
appletviewer	A viewer that allows the running of Java applets without a Web browser
java	The Java language interpreter
javac	The Java language compiler

Table 8-2	Java Tools
Tool	**Description**
javadoc	The Java language structured documentation tool
javah	The C language code generator for interfacing C with Java
javap	The Java language disassembler
jdb	The Java debugger

Now that you've had the chance to see the various components of this product, we'll show you how to test it out.

Testing Java on your machine

Try Java out by following these steps:

1. **Double-click on the My Computer icon and open the C:\hotjava\bin subdirectory.**
2. **Double-click on the HotJava icon.**

   You see something similar to what you saw in Figure 8-2.
3. **Move down the page by dragging down the scroll box on the right side of the window until you see the hyperlink Cool HotJava Demos.**
4. **Click on this hyperlink to see something similar to Figure 8-5.**

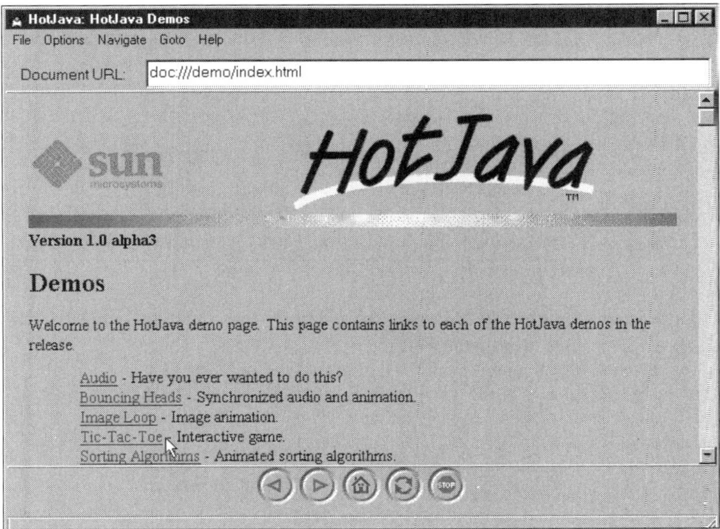

Figure 8-5: Try out the Tic-Tac-Toe HotJava demo.

5. **Click on the Tic-Tac-Toe hyperlink first.**

   The circle belongs to the computer and the *X* belongs to you. This game is set up so that you have a chance to win.

6. **Click on the lower-left space and place an *X* here.**

   The computer places a circle in the center.

7. **Place an *X* in the upper-right space.**

   The computer places a circle in the upper-left space.

8. **Block the computer by placing an *X* in the lower-right space.**

   The computer places a circle in the upper-middle space.

9. **Place an *X* in the lower-middle space to win, as shown in Figure 8-6.**

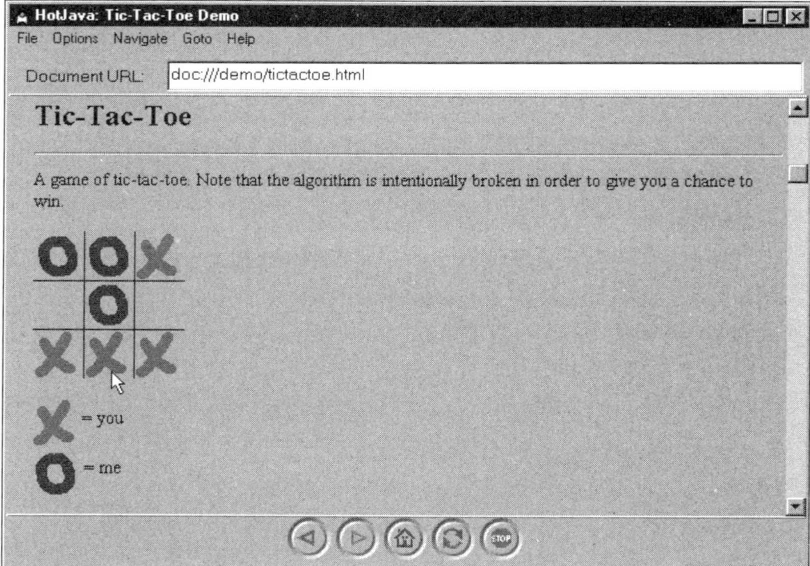

Figure 8-6: You can beat the computer in this HotJava Tic-Tac-Toe game.

10. **Click the left arrow in the lower-middle part of the screen to return to the screen shown in Figure 8-5.**

Choose the Bouncing Heads demo this time. Be prepared for an animated multimedia experience as four copies of the head of one of Sun's employees bounce over the screen.

Now that you've installed Java and HotJava, and you've checked out the system and made sure that everything is working correctly, check out some of the Java powered Web pages.

Visiting Java Powered Web Sites

Probably the most important Web site to explore is `http://java.sun.com`. Figures 8-1 and 8-3 are examples of the types of information available at this site.

Some Java sites

You can find similar sites at the following locations:

- `http://www.science.wayne.edu/java/`
- `http://www.javasoft.com`
- `http://dimensionx.com`
- `http://sunsite.unc.edu`
- `http://www.gamelan.com`

We examine the last site in this list in the following section.

WWW.GAMELAN.COM

Gamelan, pronounced *Gah'-meh-lonn,* proclaims itself as the directory and registry of Java resources. Examining the information available here suggests that this proclamation may not be too far off track.

Figure 8-7 shows how the Gamelan site looked in early 1996 using Microsoft's Internet Explorer. Examine this image carefully.

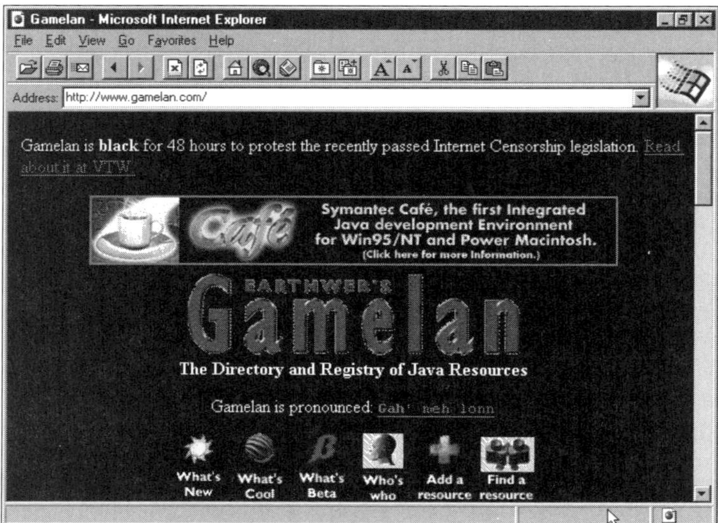

Figure 8-7: Gamelan's site as seen using Microsoft Internet Explorer.

Next, look at Figure 8-8, which shows Gamelan's site as viewed with Sun's HotJava Web browser.

Figure 8-8: Gamelan's site as viewed with Sun's HotJava.

Notice that certain graphics images that are present in HotJava don't show up in Microsoft Internet Explorer. At the same time, the black background that is so apparent in Microsoft Internet Explorer doesn't register in Sun's HotJava.

This is another example of how the Web and the Internet itself look different, depending on how you view them. If you use any of the versions of Mosaic or Netscape, you might also see slightly different versions, because the tool that you use to explore the Web can determine what you see or do not see.

More Java Pages

Since this is a discussion of Java enhanced pages, you should probably explore the following pages using either Sun's HotJava or Java enhanced Netscape 2.0.

1. **Whichever browser you are using, move down the page until you see the Communication hyperlink.**
2. **Click this hyperlink to see a listing of Java applets that looks similar to what you see in Figure 8-9.**

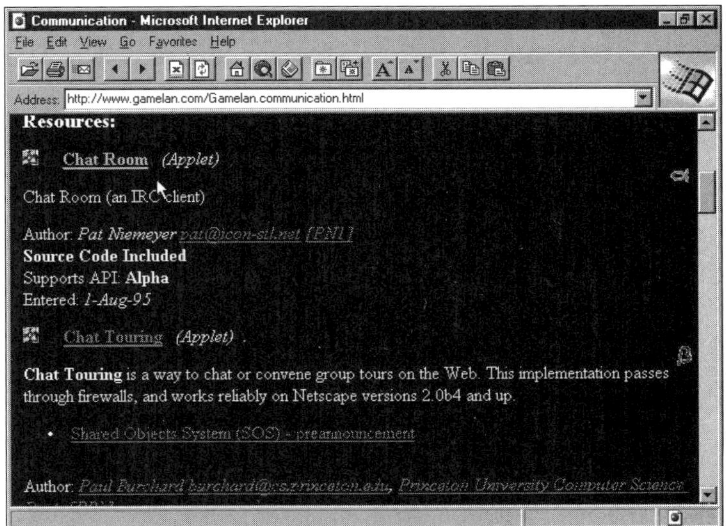

Figure 8-9: The Chat Room Java applet.

3. **Choose the Chat Room hyperlink, and, if you are using HotJava or some other Java-capable Web browser, you see something similar to Figure 8-10.**

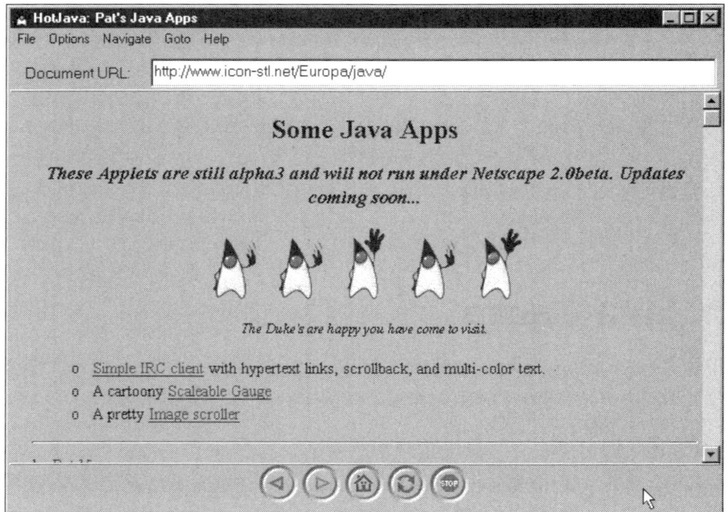

Figure 8-10: The animated Dukes welcome you to this Java page.

4. **Choose the second option, the Scaleable Gauge.**

   After a few moments, your screen changes.

5. **Move down the page slightly to see something similar to Figure 8-11.**

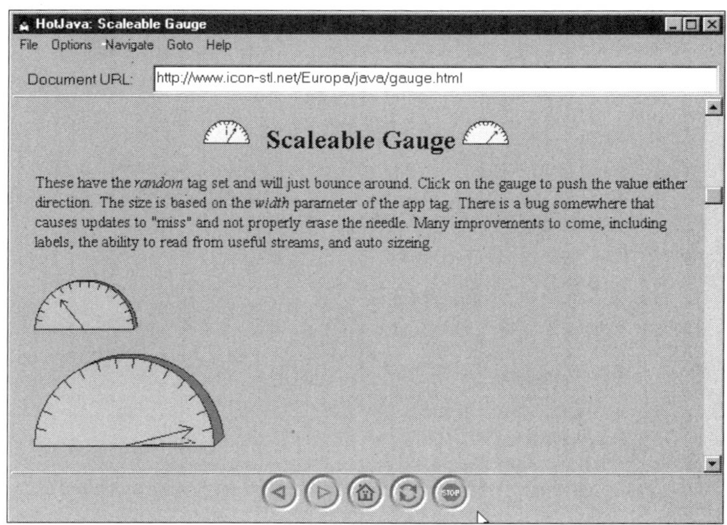

Figure 8-11: Check this page out! The gauges move.

6. **Click the back button at the bottom of the page to return to the page where the Dukes are waving at you.**
7. **Choose the Image scroller option.**

   After a slight delay while the information is transferred to your machine, you see an image that's similar to Figure 8-12.

Figure 8-12: Click on the image with your cursor and the map will move.

8. **Place your mouse cursor on any point inside the image.**
9. **Click and hold the left button to move to the edge of the image.**

   You'll notice that the image moves with your mouse.

   By the way, Pittsburg, Kansas, where we live, is under the arrow in Figure 8-12.
10. **Back yourself out to the Gamelan main screen again.**

    Many applets are available at this page, including graphing applets such as the one in Figure 8-13.

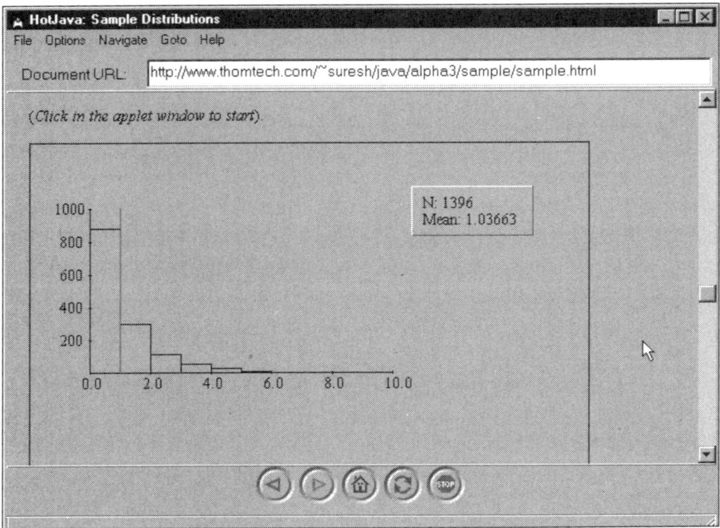

Figure 8-13: Online graphing is possible using Java.

Games such as Netris (see Figure 8-14), a 3-D Java version of the familiar computer game, also are accessible from Gamelan's site.

All right, we've given you a little history concerning Java; we've shown you how to obtain, install, and test Java on your machine; and we've explored some of the Web sites pertaining to Java. Next you write your own simple Java application.

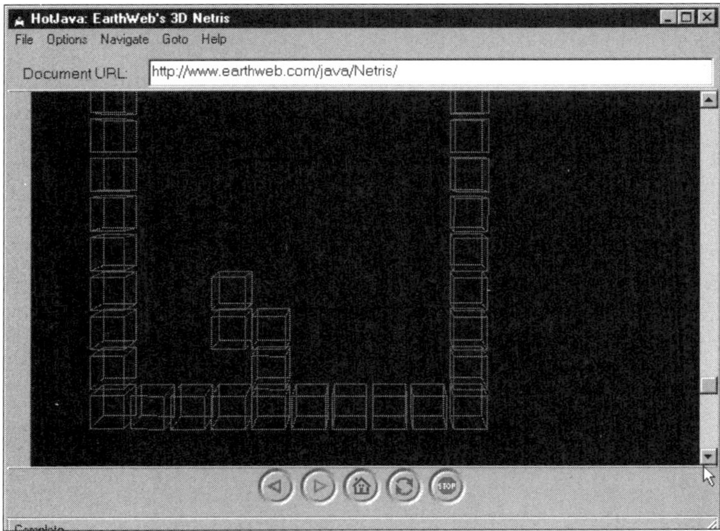

Figure 8-14: Netris, a Web version of Tetris.

A Simple Java Applet

Remember, whole books have been and are being written about how to program using the Java language. This chapter is not intended as a complete guide to writing Java applications. It is only a first stepping stone.

Java programming tools

Java consists of the following tools that enable you to write Java applications. When you downloaded the distribution files earlier in this chapter, you should have received all of these tools.

- **The HotJava Web Browser.** This Web browser was written entirely in Java and is used to view and interact with Java applications. Typing the command **HotJava** ***app*** from the command prompt (where ***app*** stands for the name of the Java code file) starts this application.
- **The Java Interpreter.** The interpreter is what makes the observation of Java content possible. This interpreter must be installed on the user's machine in order for the user to view this content. Typing the command **java** from the command prompt starts the Java interpreter.
- **The Java Compiler.** The compiler is what translates the human-readable Java source code into machine-readable code. Typing the command **javac** from the command prompt starts the Java compiler.
- **The Java Disassembler.** The dissassembler will print out information about a file created with the Java compiler. This file is called a *class file*. Typing the command **javap** from the command prompt starts the Java disassembler.
- **The C header and source file Generator.** The generator creates and generates all C header and source files for making methods. Typing either **javah** or **javah_g** from the command prompt initiates this application.
- **The Java Document Generator.** Given a specific source file, this application can generate a page of documentation for that application. Typing the command **javadoc** from the command prompt starts this application.
- **The Java Profiling Tool.** The profiling tool formats the output of the *-prof* option of the Java interpreter. Typing the command **javaprof** from the command prompt starts this application.

The Java package also includes a set of Java class libraries. These libraries are a package of predeveloped code applications that can be linked into your own individual applications. The libraries include

- **Language Foundation classes.** These classes provide the basic classes for strings and arrays.

- **Utility classes.** These classes provide utilities such as stacks, vectors, tables, and so on.
- **Input/Output classes.** These classes provide utilities for standard input and output, as well as standard file utilities.
- **Browser classes.** These classes provide utilities for working in conjunction with the HotJava browser.
- **AWT (Another Window Toolkit) classes.** These classes provide graphical interface tools for use in creating fonts, controls, buttons, and so on.
- **Network classes.** These classes provide utilities for accessing networks through such protocols as FTP, WWW, or telnet.

Together, the preceding tools and classes enable you to create five basic types of applications for use with Java. These types of applications are

- **Applets.** Again, an applet is a program that is included in an HTML page. To display it, you need a Java enabled browser.
- **Applications.** An application is a stand-alone program, written in Java, that can be executed independently of the Java-enabled browser. This independence is accomplished by having the Java interpreter installed on the user's machine.
- **Protocol handlers.** Protocol handlers are programs that can be loaded into the user's Java-enabled browser. These handlers interpret the protocols, which can be standard protocols, such as HTML, or programmer-defined protocols.
- **Content handlers.** Content handlers are programs that interpret file types defined by the Java programmer. They are loaded into the user's Java-enabled browser. The Java programmer must provide all required code for the browser to display and interpret these special formats.
- **Native methods.** Native methods are declared in a Java class but are implemented in another language. A *native method* is a procedure or function that is written in a language other than Java. The native method is then compiled to be binary compatible with the processor of a specific CPU rather than with the Java virtual machine.

Other tools you can use to work with Java

As Java has become more and more popular, tools have become available for working with the language. Before you create a simple application, here is some information about four of these tools.

Diva for Java

Diva, shown in Figure 8-15, is a product of Quintessential Objects, Inc. Diva enables you to edit and test Java applications in an Integrated Development Environment (IDE) that is based on Windows.

The product is currently in its alpha phase and is available for testing and evaluation purposes only. For further information and to download the latest version, go to `http://www.inch.com/~friskel/`.

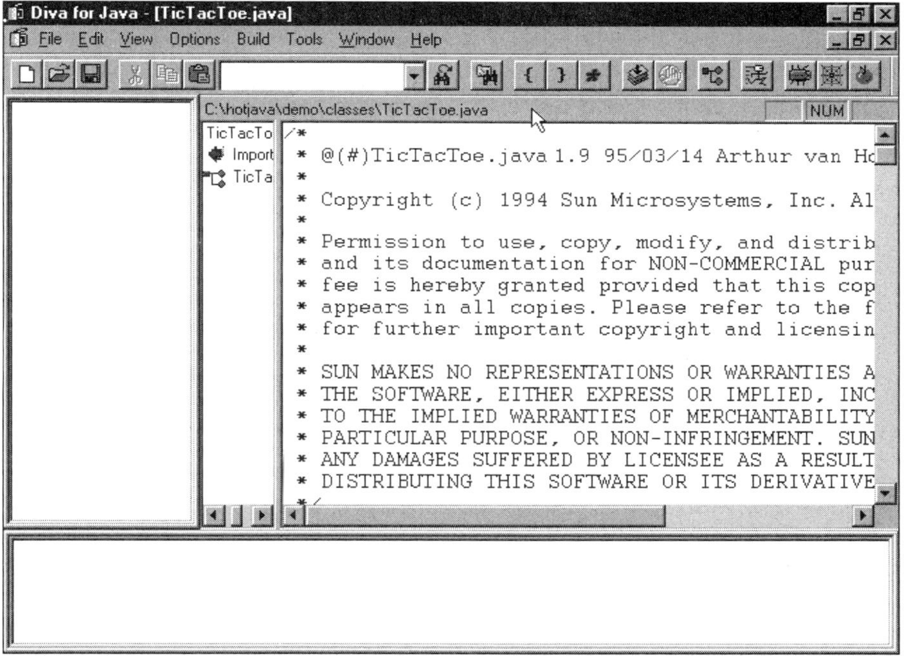

Figure 8-15: Diva provides an IDE for Java programming.

Borland's Latté

In November 1995, Borland International, Inc., announced that it would license Sun's Java language and also market Java development tools. Borland also announced that it would build a high-performance, visual rapid application development (RAD) environment for creating Java applications. This RAD environment would become a product code-named Latté and was to be developed completely in Java.

The first of the Borland products for Java was Debugger for Java, which was available from the Borland JavaWorld site during February and March 1996. Check Borland's site at `http//www.borland.com`.

In February 1996, Borland announced that Borland C++ 5.0 would include a fully integrated version of Sun's Java Development Kit and that the kit would be accessible from the Borland IDE.

JavaMaker

JavaMaker, which was written by Hee Chang Choi, provides a Java applet programming environment. This environment allows for an easy way to edit, compile, and run Java applets. Figure 8-16 shows ImageLoopItem.java after it has been translated from UNIX to DOS.

You can download JavaMaker from `http://net.info.samsung.co.kr/~hcchoi/`.

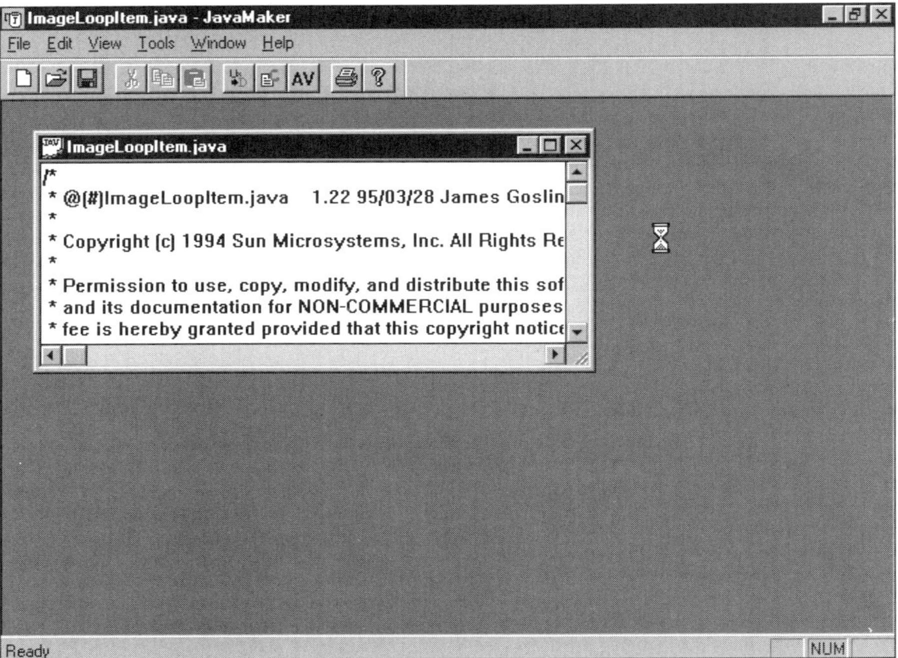

Figure 8-16: JavaMaker provides an easy-to-use application for Java programming development.

Symantec's Café

In December 1995, Symantec Corp. announced the release of the first Java development environment for Windows 95 and Windows NT. Symantec licensed Sun's Java language and, at first, gave the product the codename *Expresso*. Symantec later changed the product name to *Café*.

Information about Java and Café, as well as information on how to download your own copy of the beta release of Café, are available at Symantec's Web site (see Figure 8-17).

You need Symantec C++ Version 7.2 in order to take advantage of the Beta version of Café. There is also a version of Café Lite. For more information on this product, contact Symantec.

Figure 8-17: You can find information about Symantec's Java products at java central.

Writing Your Own Applet

Next, you create an applet for use with your Web site. Keep in mind that this exercise demonstrates basic capabilities and is not meant to be an example of anything more than a simple basic applet.

1. **Open a DOS window in Windows 95.**

   To open it, click on Start, choose Programs, and click on MS-DOS Prompt.

2. **Change to the \HOTJAVA\ subdirectory on your hard drive.**

3. **Name the Java application something that will represent what the application does.**

   For this sample application, you are going to make the Java language print something on the screen. In our case, the application is going to print the word *VREvolution,* so we opened a Java file to edit by typing **EDIT VRE.JAVA**.

4. **Type Listing 8-1, but change** `"VREvolution"` **to whatever you want to be displayed on the screen.**

Listing 8-1: VRE.JAVA

```
/**
Program:        VRE
Purpose:        Simple Demonstration
Author:         76270.551@CompuServe.com
Version:        1.00; 31 March 1996
*/

import java.awt.Graphics;

public class Simple extends java.applet.Applet {

    public void init() {
        resize(185, 100);
    }

    public void paint(Graphics g) {
        g.drawString("VREvolution", 50, 50);
    }

}
```

5. **Choose File⇨Exit, and when the dialog box asks whether you want to save the file, click on Yes.**

   You return to the DOS prompt.

6. **You need to compile the Java application next, so type the following at the command line:**

   ```
   javac VRE.java
   ```

   Don't forget that Java is case sensitive. `VRE.java` is not the same thing as `vre.java`.

   If you've typed everything correctly, you soon return to the DOS prompt.

7. **Type the following command at the DOS prompt:**

   ```
   applet VRE.htm
   ```

   Again, don't forget that Java is case sensitive.

   If everything goes according to plan, the word *VREvolution,* or text of your choice, is displayed in the applet viewer on your monitor.

So you've created you first Java applet, compiled it, and run it.

You're ready now to create a Web page that will contain the applet.

1. **Open the editor again and type Listing 8-2.**

Listing 8-2: VRE_APP.HTML

```
<HTML>
<!—Purpose: HTML file to hold reference to our⮐
applet. -->
<!—Author:  76270.551@CompuServe.com -->
<!—Version: 1.1; 31 March 1996 -->
<HEAD>
<TITLE>VRE_APP Web Interface</TITLE>
</HEAD>
<BODY>
<P>This is <applet code="VRE.class" width=100 height=100>
</applet>
<hr>
</BODY>
</HTML>
```

2. Save this file and close the DOS window.
3. View the file using the HotJava browser.

VREvolution Site Diary: Installment 8

As you've seen, you can use Java for a variety of purposes. Our simple example in the preceding section of this chapter just placed the words "This is VREvolution" on the screen. You could have used basic HTML to do the same thing.

As you've seen in the examples provided with the Java Development Kit and on the World Wide Web sites we visited, Java provides much more exciting capabilities than the ones demonstrated by this example. This chapter was meant only as a simple introduction to the possibilities of Java.

VREvolution's site uses many of the Microsoft extensions to the HTML specification for the creation of our pages. Microsoft Internet Explorer 2.0 and the Alpha for Internet Explorer 3.0 are not Java enabled. As a result, in the early days of the site construction, the site provided no pages containing Java applets. Later, when we decided to create two tracks, one containing pages designed for Microsoft Internet Explorer and one containing pages designed for Netscape, we began adding Java applets on the Netscape pages.

Summary

In this chapter, you examined what interactivity is.

You learned the history of Java and how the language came into being.

You tried out the HotJava Web browser.

The Java language and its features were examined.

We showed you how to get the Java Development Kit, set it up on your computer, and then test it to make sure that it was operating correctly.

You toured several Web sites that are Java-enabled so that you could see some possible uses for Java.

Finally, you wrote both an application and an applet in Java, compiled them, and then tested them.

Next, turn your attention to the possibilities of adding audio and video clips to your Web site.

Audio and Video Clips

In This Chapter

Audio, video, and animation

Visiting audio enhanced and video enhanced Web sites

Audio and video with HTML

The VREvolution Site Diary

By this part of the book, you should be getting the idea that the Web is a new communication medium. This chapter is about audio and video and how you can add them to your Web pages. We look at some examples of audio, video, and animation that are already available on the Web, and then we look at how you can add some of these types of applications to your pages.

One point we also want to make is that you can use other applications, such as Java and VBScript, to add audio, video, and animation. We cover only HTML and extensions to HTML in this chapter.

Talk about the Weather?

Sometimes, when you try to talk to someone, the only thing that you can really talk about is the weather. The Web enables you to examine current weather conditions anywhere in the world. In this case, we look at information on conditions in the United States.

Michigan State University provides a Web site where you can check the current weather conditions for a location near you in the United States. To check it out, point your Web browser at `http//wxweb.msu.edu/weatherinteractive.html`. Moving down the page, you'll find a place to identify the specific weather station that you want to obtain information from. The two closest locations to our home in Pittsburg, Kansas, are Joplin, Missouri (JLN), and Chanute, Kansas (CNU, see Figure 9-1).

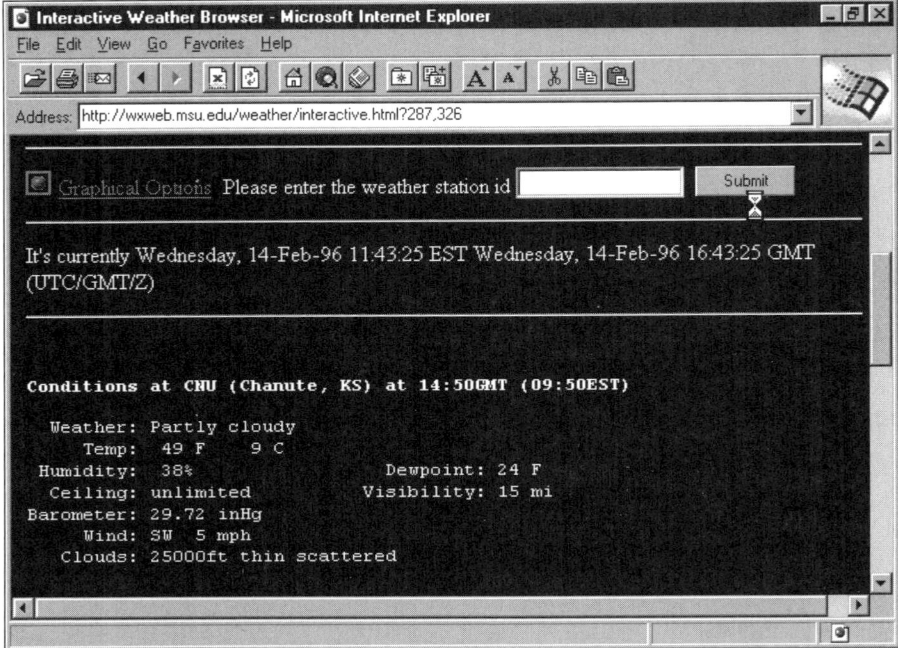

Figure 9-1: The weather conditions at Chanute, Kansas, on February 14, 1996.

Farther down the page is an interactive temperature map of the continental United States. When you click on the temperature for any specific location, you get a report of the current conditions for that location (see Figure 9-2). When you use this map, you don't have to know the location ID.

Planning on going to Las Vegas anytime soon? Check out the current conditions and forecast at `http://www.intellicast.com/weather/las/`. Here you will find KVBC meteorologist Nathan Tannenbaum's Las Vegas forecast. Both a .WAV file (to use if you have a .WAV player loaded and configured for your browser) and an .AU file (to use on the standard audio player that comes with Windows) are available. Pick one and listen to the current weather conditions and forecast (see Figure 9-3).

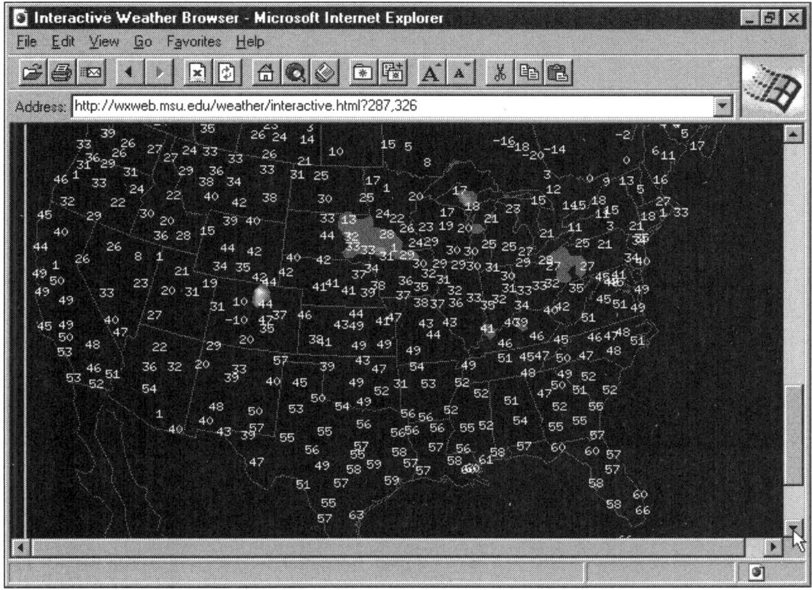

Figure 9-2: Click on any of these interactive locations for the current weather conditions.

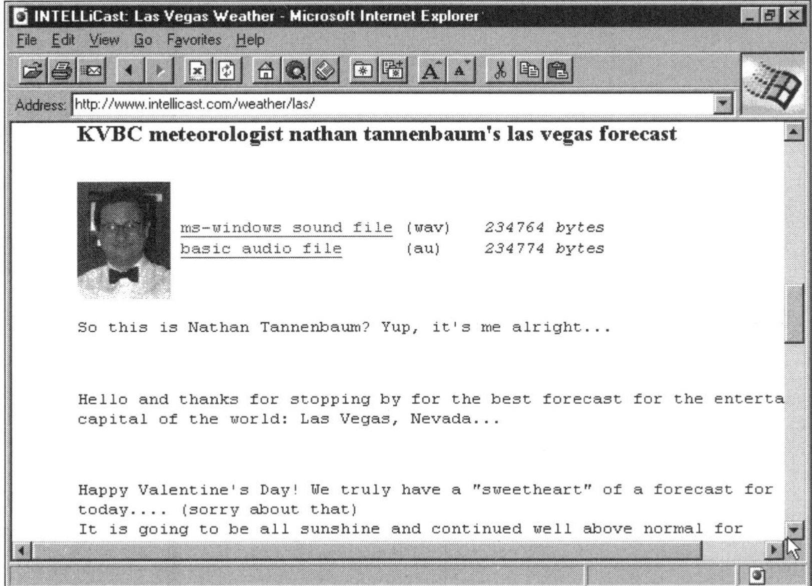

Figure 9-3: Click on one of the two sound files to hear the current Las Vegas weather conditions.

One of the most interesting uses of video on the Web is the live picture from San Diego. Aim your Web browser at `http://www.live.net/sandiego/Images/Current/latest_b.jpg`. The image in Figure 9-5 shows the current conditions at the airport in San Diego.

The benefits of using real-time video and graphics are readily apparent in these types of examples. Weather reports, however, are not the only up-to-the-minute types of reports that are available on the Web.

You can find out what the current weather is in Southern California at `http://www.intermind.net/im/weather.html`. Figure 9-4 shows the weather conditions from San Diego to San Francisco and from Las Vegas to Los Angeles.

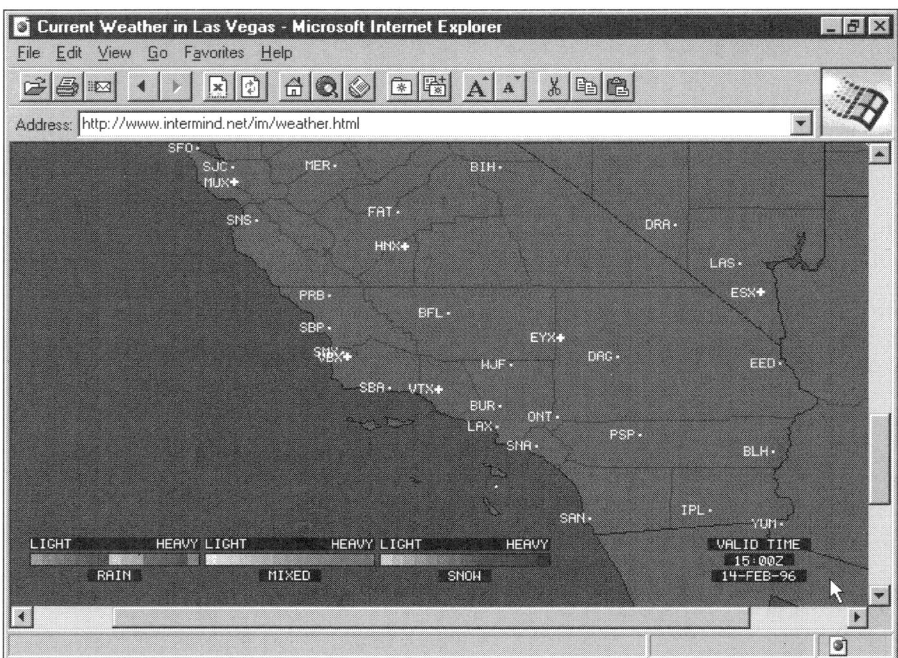

Figure 9-4: Check the weather conditions for Southern California at this Web site.

Figure 9-5: Check out what it's like in San Diego from the comfort of your computer and Web browser.

Or How about a Traffic Report?

How are the highways in your major metropolitan area? Traffic reports, such as the one shown in Figure 9-6, are available at `http://herman.tamu.edu/traffic.html`.

Traffic conditions for a number of California cities are available at `http://www.scubed.com/caltrans/caltrans.html`. You'll also find a hyperlink that leads you to a site offering traffic conditions in Chicago.

Weather and traffic audio and video aren't the only type of interactivity offered on Web sites.

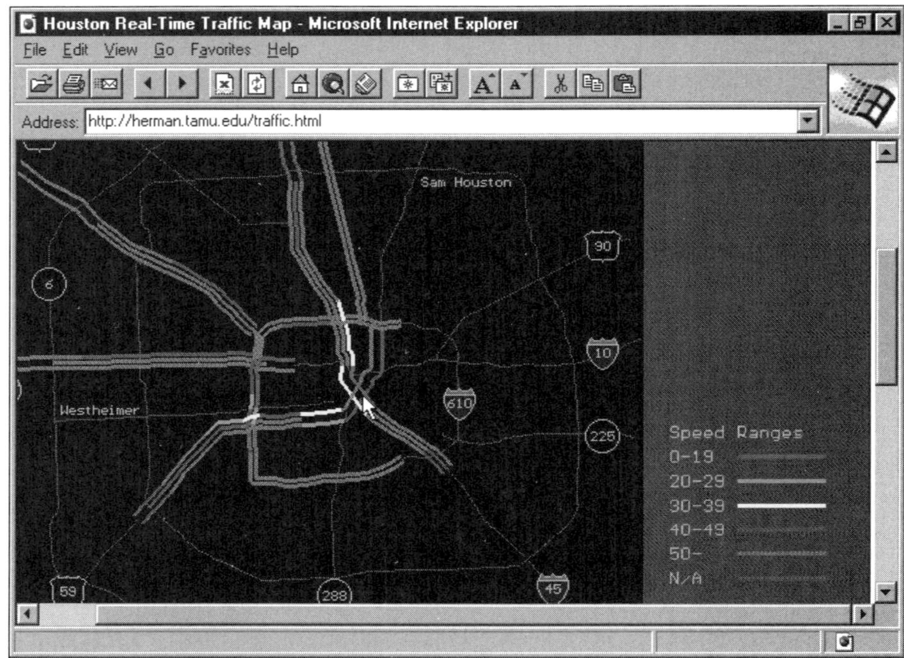

Figure 9-6: Traffic conditions for Houston are available at this site.

Talk about Music

Another topic for audio offerings is music. One interesting site that offers musical audio clips is the Heart of Mary Priory convent's Web site (see Figure 9-7).

The convent is in Denmark, and the pages are at `http://inet.uni-c.dk/~grant/kloster1.htm`. The nuns of this convent perform some of the finest religious music available on the Net (see Figure 9-8).

These demos run about ten seconds each. Click on one, and after waiting as the demo downloads, you can listen to this fabulous music. You may want to check this site using Microsoft Internet Explorer. It was selected by Microsoft as one of the top Internet Explorer sites during February 1996.

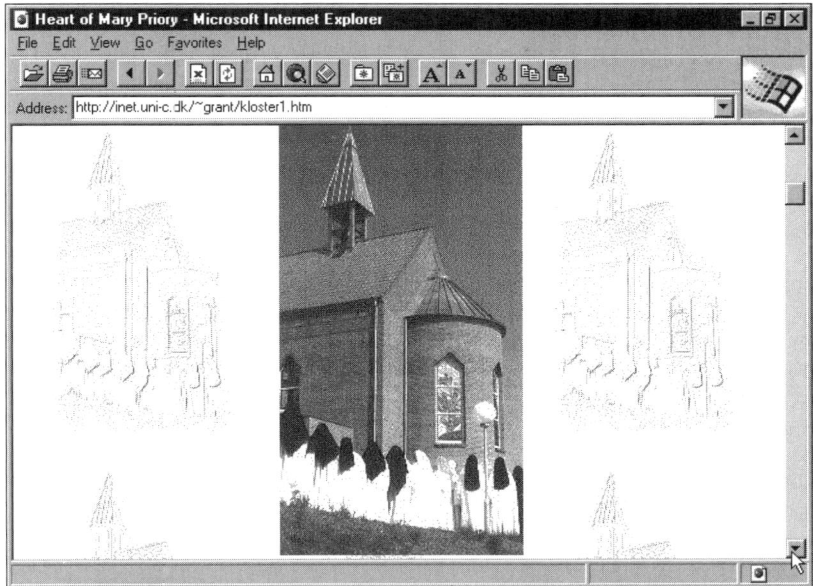

Figure 9-7: Ave Maria plays as you view this picture of the convent.

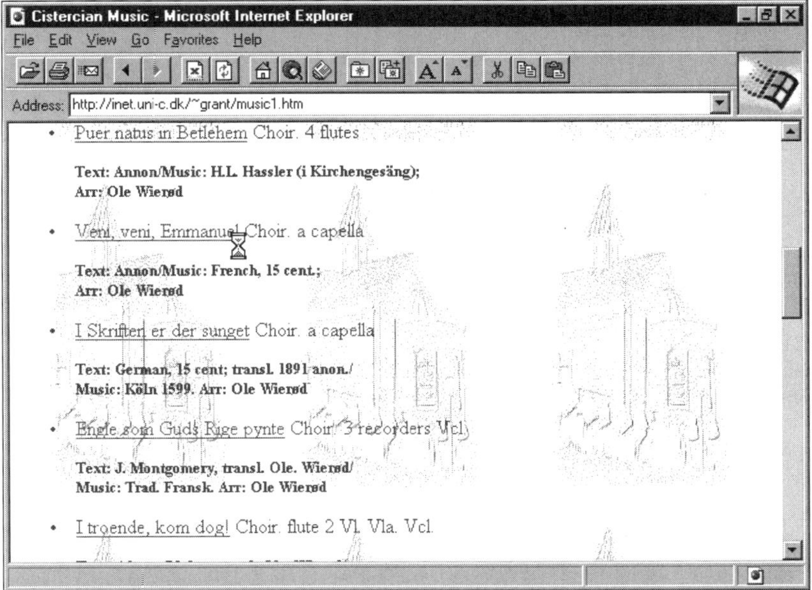

Figure 9-8: Several short demos of the nuns' music are available at this site.

More on Music

Another site chosen as one of Microsoft's top Internet Explorer sites during February 1996 was that of Open Mind Productions in the Netherlands. This site features innovative uses of inline video and fabulous music that has a slightly less heavenly aspect. When you begin loading this page, some interesting music starts to play. If your system is set up for it, the music will be in stereo.

The Open Mind Productions site (see Figure 9-9) is at `http://ourworld.compuserve.com/homepages/OpenMind/`. Alex van den Berg is General Manager of Open Mind Productions.

One interesting feature of this site is that it includes a hyperlink to Peter Gabriel's Real World Studios in Box, England.

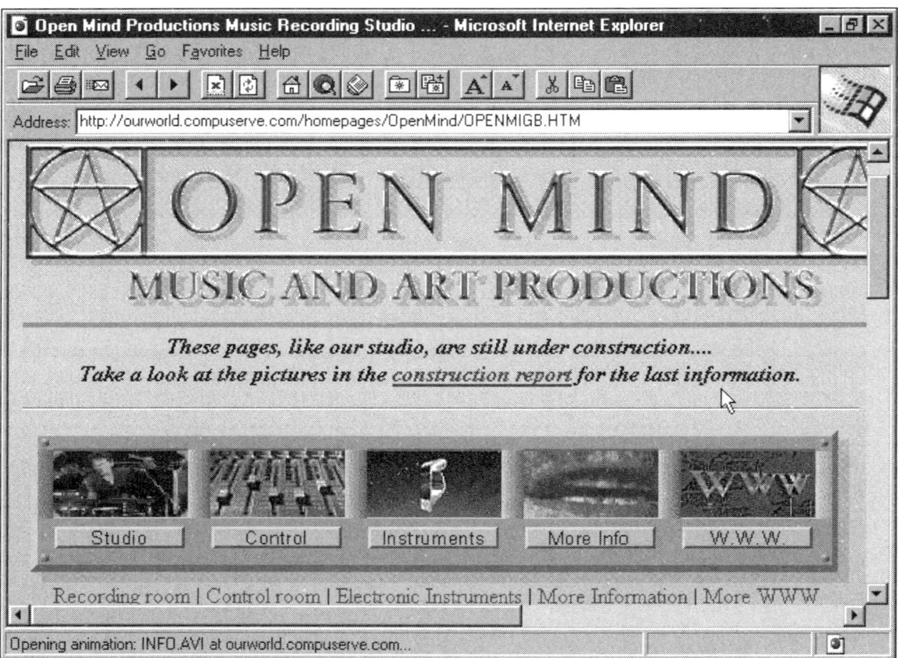

Figure 9-9: Open Mind Productions is an innovative Web site that includes both audio and video applications.

The Talk Is Rock

In the February 13, 1996, issue of the *WinNews Electronic Newsletter,* Microsoft said that KISW is one of its favorite Seattle radio stations. Exploring the KISW site at `http://www.kisw.com` can give you an understanding of why Microsoft likes it (see Figure 9-10). The site was designed and is managed by Web architect Joe Moss of HotLink Internet Consultants (`jmoss@hotlinknet.com`).

To truly experience and enjoy this site, you need to install the RealAudio software and configure it to work with your particular Web browser. RealAudio software allows for audio-on-demand for the Internet.

Two versions of RealAudio are currently available. Version 1.0 provides acceptable sound over a 14.4K baud modem connection. This version works with both Windows 3.1 and Windows 95. Version 2.0 is in the Beta stage at the time of this writing; it improves the sound and works with a 28.8K baud modem connection. Although versions are available for both Windows 95 and Windows 3.1, the Windows 3.1 version requires a minimum Pentium processor for operation, while the Windows 95 version operates with a 486 processor.

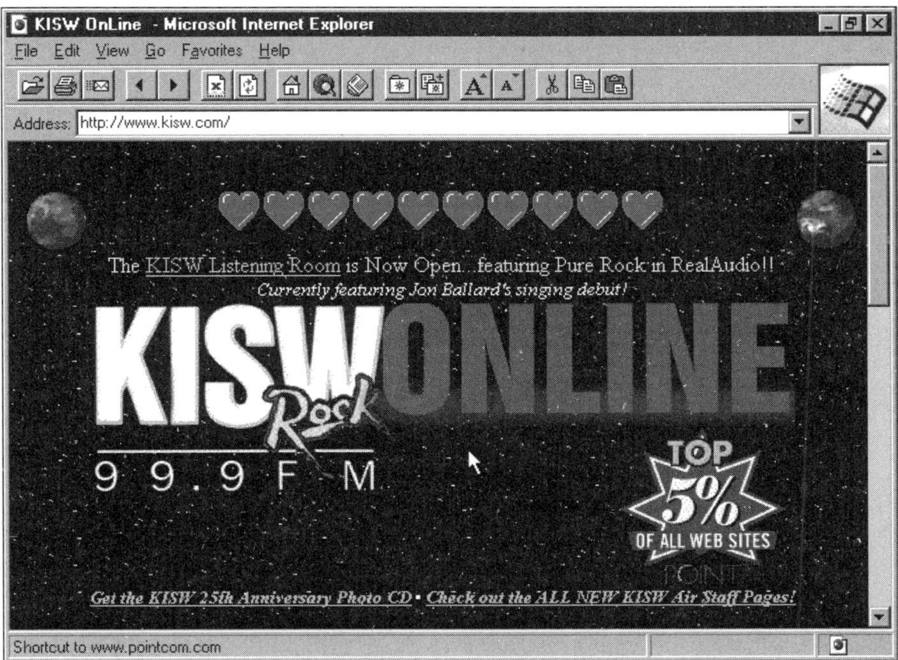

Figure 9-10: The Web site for KISW 99.9 FM, one of Microsoft's favorite Seattle radio stations.

The KISW ONLINE page contains a hyperlink to the RealAudio site, where you can download the RealAudio software, `http://www.realaudio.com/`. As you can see in Figure 9-11, the software for providing RealAudio from your Web server is also available for download from this site.

The KISW ONLINE page also contains a hyperlink to the KISW Listening Room, where you will find a listing of various songs that can be played. These songs are complete, and, if you have installed the RealAudio software, you can listen to them by simply clicking on the song and version that you want to listen to. If you choose one of the RealAudio versions and your software and hardware are installed properly, you start hearing the song you've chosen within a few seconds. In Figure 9-12, the ZZ Top song that we selected is being played.

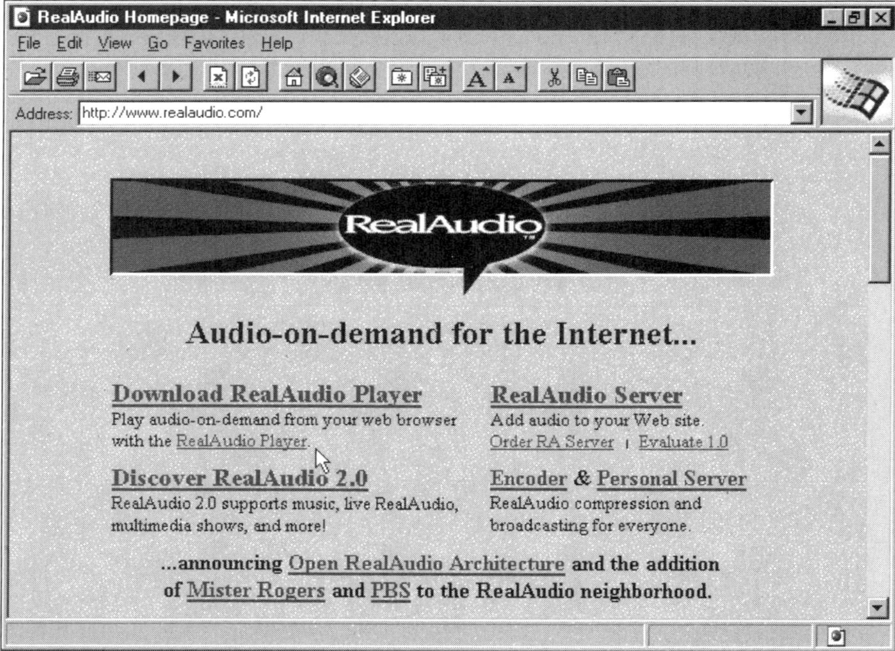

Figure 9-11: RealAudio software is available for download from the RealAudio Web site.

RealAudio is a trademark of Progressive Networks.

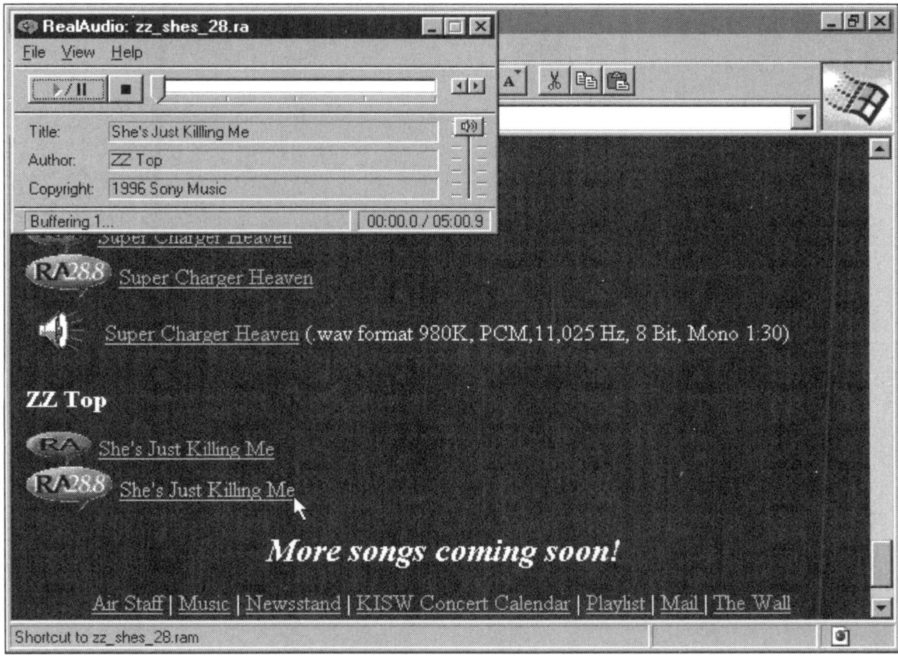

Figure 9-12: Paul likes the Texas rock of ZZ Top.

Microsoft HTML Extensions for Audio and Video

How do you include an audio clip or video clip in your Web site? That's what we're going to look at briefly in this section of the chapter. We begin by looking at the code for some pages at the sites we've just finished visiting. Keep in mind that these sites were configured using Microsoft extensions to HTML and are viewed best with Microsoft Internet Explorer.

If you've been using Microsoft Internet Explorer to visit the sites discussed in this chapter, you will find the pages you've visited in the \cache\ subdirectory under the directory where Internet Explorer is found.

Reload, or revisit, the Heart of Mary Priory Web pages. If you're looking in the Microsoft Internet Explorer \cache\ subdirectory, this Web page is kloster1.htm. Listing 9-1 lists the HTML code that plays "Ave Maria" if you have a MIDI player installed with your Web browser.

Listing 9-1: kloster1.htm *(excerpt)*

```
<TITLE>Heart of Mary Priory</TITLE>
<BODY BACKGROUND=priory.jpg>
<h1>Heart of Mary Priory<h1>
<br><h2>(Maria Hjerte Kloster)<br>and Sostrup⮐
Castle<h2><br><bgsound src="ave-harp.mid" loop=infinite><br>
```

As you will see in the real-life examples listed here, the command `bgsound src="FILE.mid"` statement plays the MIDI file. The *FILE* is the name of the MIDI file to be played at the particular Web site.

Load Open Mind Productions' home page (Openmigb.htm in your \cache\ subdirectory) and take a look at the beginning of this HTML file. Listing 9-2 shows the code for the audio playback.

Listing 9-2: Openmigb.htm *(excerpt)*

```
HTML>
<HEAD>
<TITLE>Open Mind Productions Music Recording Studio :⮐
HomePage</TITLE>
</HE<AD>
<BODY BACKGROUND="BACKGRND.GIF">
<BGSOUND SRC="STEAMY.MID"LOOP=INFINITE>
<CENTER>
```

In this case, the `bgsound src="FILE.GIF"` statement calls a MIDI file named `STEAMY.MID`.

Listing 9-3 provides an excerpt from Open Mind Productions' information page that also provides a musical background.

Listing 9-3: ACHTERGb.HTM *(excerpt)*

```
<HTML>
<HEAD>
<TITLE>Open Mind Productions : More info . . . </TITLE>
</Head>
<BODY BACKGROUND="BACKINFO.GIF">
<BGSOUND SRC="ACHTERGR.MID"LOOP=INFINITE>
```

Listing 9-4 is a final example from Open Mind Productions' Web site.

Listing 9-4: ANDEREgb.HTM *(excerpt)*

```
<HTML>
<HEAD>
<TITLE>Open Mind Productions : Other interesting sites </TITLE>
</Head>
<BODY BACKGROUND="BACKWWW.GIF">
<BGSOUND SRC="NOLIFE.MID"LOOP=INFINITE>
```

In Open Mind Productions' Web pages, you will also see some of the most interesting uses of video and animation. Examine the HTML code for the <IMG DYNSRC="*FILE*.AVI"> statements that create the moving images within the page.

The ANDEREgb.HTM file contains numerous statements of this type, as do other HTML files at the Open Mind Productions site. The Heart of Mary Priory's kloster1.htm page also contains this statement.

VREvolution Site Diary: Installment 9

In Chapter 2, we describe how we created a Web site on CompuServe's Web server using CompuServe's software. Here we show how we changed some of the code in the original Web pages to allow for the inclusion of audio and video files.

In Listing 9-5 you can examine the HTML code for the home page for our site on CompuServe's server.

Listing 9-5: HOMEPAGE.HTM

```
<!- Generated by the Home Page Wizard - CompuServe Inc. -⮐
Last Updated : Dec 26, 1995  12:07 ->

<html>
<!- The following HTML tags are the header and title tags.⮐
These tags allow you to specify a title for this page. -->
<head><title>Paul & Mary Summitt</title></head>

<!- The following HTML tag is the body tag.  This defines the⮐
body portion of this page or document. -->
<body background="tech_bak.gif">

<!- The following is an HTML headline tag.  Values for this tag⮐
range from H1 (largest) to H6 (smallest). -->
```

(continued)

Listing 9-5 *(continued):*

```
<center><h1>Paul &amp; Mary Summitt</h1></center>

<!— The following is an HTML horizontal rule tag (or line). -->
<hr align=center width=80% size=3>

<hr align=center width=90% size=3>

<!— The following HTML is just plain text. -->
<p><center>Hi!  We're Paul and Mary Summitt.  We're the authors↵
of IDG's newly released book</center></p>

<center><h2>Creating Cool 3D Web Worlds with VRML</h2></center>

<center><h5>(ISBN: 1-56884-796-3)</h5></center>

<p><center>You can find out more information about this new↵
book at:</center></p>

<!— The following HTML tag is the external link tag.  This↵
tag is a hot link to the specific URL (or location). -->
<br><center><UL><LI><a href="http://www.idgbooks.com/whats_hot/↵
Cool3D/">IDG's Home page</a></UL></center>

<hr align=center size=1>

<center><h5>You can find out more about us and our previous↵
writings at</h5></center>

<br><center><UL><LI><a href="http://www.webmaster.com/↵
VREvolution/">VREvolution</a></UL></center>

<!— The following HTML tag is the internal link tag.  This is a↵
hot link to another page in your project. -->
<br><center><UL><LI><a href="summitth.htm">The Summitt Quarterly↵
Newsletter</a></UL></center>

<hr align=center size=1>

<br><center><a href="mailto:76270.551@CompuServe.com">Contact↵
us:</a></center>

</body>
</html>
```

We want to add music to this page first. In order to do this, we will include the `bgsound src` statement after the `<body background="tech_bak.gif">` statement in the file. We'll use the MIDI file MINUET.MID as background music for this page. We type the following statement after the `<body background="tech_bak.gif">` statement.

```
<bgsound src= "minuet.mid" loop=infinite>
```

Now, anyone who accesses this page on our CompuServe site will hear the Minuet playing in the background if they have their MIDI player configured properly.

Video is similar. For example, to include a revolving planet earth that's similar to the one in some of the other Web pages in this chapter (Figure 9-10 for example), you place the following statement where you want the graphic to be:

```
<img dynsrc="earth.avi" src=earth.gif" width=50 height=50↩
loop=infinite>.
```

Summary

In this chapter, you examined the basics of adding audio and video to you Web site to create a more interactive experience for your visitors.

You examined a number of exciting and interesting sites.

You saw how VREvolution has included audio and video on one of its sites.

In the next chapter, you look at how to use various programming languages, such as C, C++, and Visual Basic, to create CGI scripts that enable you to bring interactivity to your Web site in a way that goes beyond simply using forms.

PART IV MANAGING YOUR CORNER OF CYBERSPACE

Chapter 10 The Common Gateway Interface (CGI)

Chapter 11 Databases, Search Engines, E-Mail, and Image Maps

Chapter 12 Web Site Usage Statistics

Chapter 13 Promoting and Advertising Your Web Site

Part IV discusses the use of the Common Gateway Interface (CGI) to add other forms of interactivity to your Web site. Using a variety of applications and programming languages, you learn how to add image maps to your site, create counter programs to count the number of visitors to your pages, create guestbook applications that let you know who stopped by, and use applications to find out how well your site is being used. Finally we look at how to let others know where your site is and how to encourage them to visit it.

The Common Gateway Interface (CGI)

In This Chapter

Defining CGI

Deciding which language to use for CGI Application Programming

Building your own CGI applications

VREvolution Site Diary

In this chapter, you examine CGI, which is the mechanism that enables the Web to be somewhat interactive. CGI provides for the operation of external applications under the Web server. In other words, it is a way that the HTTP server can "talk" to programs on your computer. These applications are called by the Web browser and look similar to ordinary URLs. The Web provides the structure and CGI provides the ability to turn static HTML pages into interactive Web documents.

So what can you use CGI for? Gathering information from visitors to your page is one aspect of CGI's use. You also can use CGI to provide animations or the time and date, find out how many users have visited a particular page, order pizza or other products, and list directories — just to name a few of CGI's other uses.

What Is CGI?

CGI stands for *Common Gateway Interface*. CGI is the default standard that programs and applications use to interface with Web server software. CGI supplies the transport services between the user's Web browser and the data and information that's available on the Web. CGI programs are extensions to the server itself. Instead of including various functions within the server software, CGI allows for the inclusion of various services that are not specifically part of the server software itself.

Think of the CGI program as being the doorway through which information is exchanged on the Web. In fact, this program determines whether the door is open or closed. These doorways can be used for a large variety of different purposes. Generally, however, they're used for handling `<ISINDEX>` and `<FORM>` HTTP requests.

In Chapter 6, you learn how to build a feedback form for your Web site. User information gained from these forms can be a valuable data source for feedback on your product or your server. But how can you use these feedback forms? How do you get the information from the visitor's entry on the form to some sort of usable format at your site? This is where CGI comes in.

How does CGI work?

Rather than building various new functions into the server software, the people who created the original HTTP server built a central, well-defined combination of HTTP functionality and the capability of extending this functionality through the inclusion of extended services. The application programming interface (API) is the means for extending this functionality.

The API allows any Perl, C, C++, Shell, or Visual Basic programmer access to CGI. You can find out more about this API by aiming your Web browser at `http://hoohoo.ncsa.uiuc.edu/cgi/interface.html` (see Figure 10-1).

One area of discussion at this location concerns the command line arguments and the CGI environment variables themselves.

Command line arguments and CGI environment variables

For information about the data request from the server to the script to be dealt with, a Web server uses either command line arguments or environment variables. A script is nothing more than a list of commands that tell the server what to do. These commands can be in the form of simple shell commands (similar to a .BAT file) or in the form of a full-blown program. We discuss the command line arguments first.

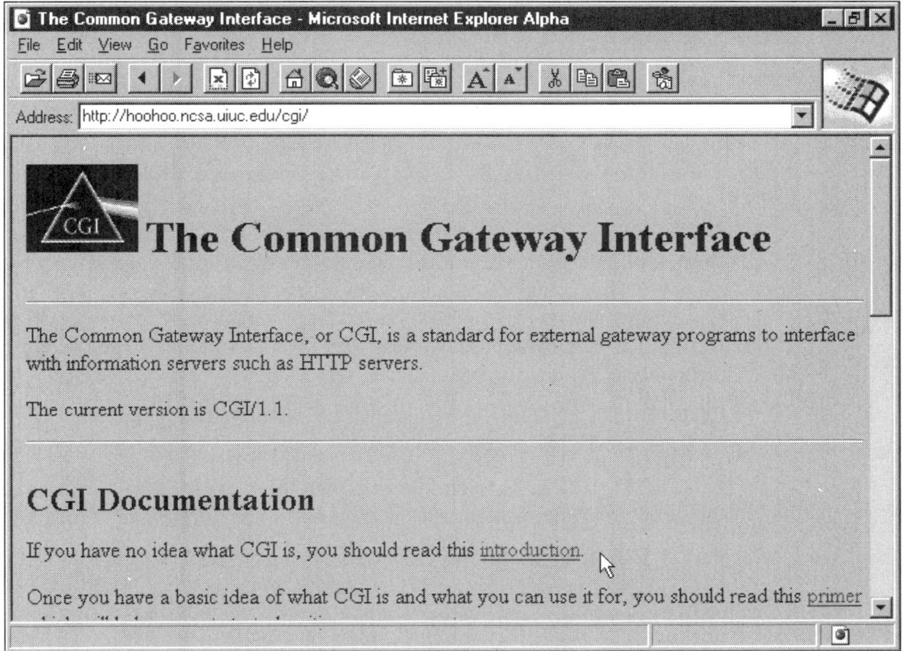

Figure 10-1: At this site you can find more information about CGI.

CGI command line options

Generally, the command line is used only in `<ISINDEX>` queries. It is not used in HTML forms. Therefore, the server has to have a way to know whether to use decoding. This is accomplished in the following manner in the case of forms: Upon being queried, the server searches the query information, as represented in the QUERY_STRING environment variable, for a noncoded = character. If it finds one, the command line is not used. This means that no decoding is performed. The query is then intact to be processed by the proper `FORM` submission decoder.

CGI environment variables

A CGI program accepts input from the user and returns information necessary for the completion of the expected task. The program uses environment variables to accomplish this. Environment variables are set when the server executes the CGI program. Some of these variables are not request-specific. In other words, these variables are set for all requests.

- **GATEWAY_INTERFACE.** This variable states which specific version of the CGI specification this specific Web server software complies with. The format for this variable is `CGI/revision`.

- **SERVER_NAME.** This variable holds the Web server's host name, DNS alias, or IP address.
- **SERVER_SOFTWARE.** This variable states the name and version of the Web server software that is being used. The specific format is `name/version`.

Other variables are specific to the particular request that is being made.

- **AUTH_TYPE.** This variable contains information pertaining to whether the Web server software supports user authentication and what script is protected thereby. This protocol-specific authentication procedure is used to validate your users' access to specific documents and files. The most common AUTH_TYPE is Basic and means that the client must authenticate itself with a user ID and password pair.
- **CONTENT_LENGTH.** This variable contains the length of the content defined by the CONTENT_TYPE variable.
- **CONTENT_TYPE.** This variable defines the type of data contained in the query. This works specifically with queries such as HTTP POST and PUT.
- **PATH_INFO.** This variable provides any extra path information that the client supplies so that scripts can be accessed by their virtual path names. The extra path information is provided in this variable, and the information is decoded by the server before it is passed to the CGI script.
- **PATH_TRANSLATED.** This variable causes the server to provide another version of PATH_INFO. The new version will take the path and do any virtual-to-physical mapping to it.
- **QUERY_STRING.** This variable contains information that follows the question mark in the URL that references this particular script. This information is called the query information and should not be decoded in any fashion whatsoever. As stated previously, this variable is always sent when there is query information, even when there is command line decoding.
- **REMOTE_ADDR.** This variable contains the IP address of the remote host that is making the request.
- **REMOTE_HOST.** This variable contains the host name of the server that is making the request. If the server doesn't have this information, it should set the REMOTE_ADDR variable and leave the REMOTE_HOST variable unset.
- **REMOTE_IDENT.** If your Web server software supports RFC 931 identification, this variable is set to the remote user name retrieved from the server. The specification recommends that this variable be limited only to logging procedures.
- **REMOTE_USER.** If the Web server software supports user authentication and the AUTH_TYPE variable is set, this variable contains the username that the user is authenticated as.
- **REQUEST_METHOD.** This variable defines the method that was used to make the specific request. In regard to HTTP, the methods include GET, HEAD, and POST.

- **SCRIPT_NAME.** This variable holds the virtual path to the script that is being processed. This variable is used for self-referencing URLs.
- **SERVER PORT.** This variable holds the port number that the request was sent to.
- **SERVER_PROTOCOL.** This variable names the specific information protocol and version from which the specific request was made. The format for this variable is `protocol/revision`.

Finally, two variables can be found in the header lines from the client:

- **HTTP_ACCEPT.** This variable contains a listing of the MIME types which the client will accept. Each item in this list must be separated by a comma, as in the HTTP specification. The format for this variable is *`type/subtype, type/subtype`*.
- **HTTP_USER_AGENT.** This variable defines the browser application that the client is using to send the request. The format for this variable is *`software/version library/version`*.

CGI script input and output

Now that you've seen the CGI environment variables and command line options, you need to look at CGI Script input and output.

CGI input scripts

When a request is made that has information attached after the HTTP request header, the information is delivered to the CGI application using standard input file descriptors. These HTTP request headers could include either HTTP POST or PUT commands. Keep in mind that all CGI applications follow this same pattern for reading data. Also, for all practical purposes, POST and GET are the only methods that are used. POST is the preferred method, and GET is the default. PUT allows the editing of the contents of given pages. Few, if any clients, are capable of using the PUT method.

The server sends the information in a packet whose length is specified in the variable CONTENT_LENGTH. The value in this variable defines the number of bytes of information to be sent by the server. Keep in mind that the server also specifies the type of data in the CONTENT_TYPE variable. The CONTENT_TYPE variable allows the application receiving the information to decide how to use the information after it's received. Also, the server isn't required to send an EOF (end-of-file) marker. The reason is that both the Web server software and the Web browser software assume that the reading will end as soon as the number of bytes specified by the CONTENT_LENGTH variable is reached.

CGI output scripts

A CGI application always responds when it receives something. The response, the application's output, is always sent to a standard output descriptor. This output is returned in the form of either a document generated by the script or instructions to the server to retrieve the desired output.

In most cases, these CGI scripts produce output that is interpreted and sent back to the user. This method is good because some scripts may not need to include full HTTP headers for each and every request.

Other scripts may not want to include the extra overhead that would be necessitated by the Web server software's parsing the output of these scripts. Instead, these scripts talk directly to the user. These scripts are distinguished from the others by CGI's requirement that the script name begin with `nph-` if the script doesn't want the server to parse its header. In these cases, the script is required to return valid responses to the user.

Another way that data can be returned is through the use of parsed header output. This form of output only requires Web server software to be made possible. In other words, no special additional software or programming is required. The Web server software itself is capable of handling this type of output.

The output of these CGI scripts always begins with a small header. This small header consists of text lines that are formatted in the same manner as HTTP headers and terminated by a blank line that includes a linefeed at the end.

Any headers that are not server directives are immediately sent back to the user's Web browser. The three server directives are

- **Content-type.** This is the MIME type of the type of document that is being returned.
- **Location.** This server directive specifies to your Web server software that a reference to a document is being returned rather than the actual document.

  If the argument to Location is a URL, the Web server software issues a redirect to the user's Web browser software.

  If this argument is a virtual path, the Web server software retrieves the document specified as if the user had requested that specific document originally.
- **Status.** This directive is used to give the Web server software an HTTP/1.0 status line to send to the user's Web browser. The format for this directive is *nnn xxxxx*, where *nnn* is the three-digit status code, and *xxxxx* is the reason string.

There is just not enough space in this book for us to fully explain all the aspects of the Common Gateway Interface. We turn our attention next to the various languages that can be used in the creation of CGI scripts.

Programming language possibilities

HTML pages, even pages using Version 2.0 and Version 3.0, are rather plain and static. CGI programs, which enable you to "hook up" your databases to the World Wide Web, are executed in real time and provide for the dynamic presentation of your information.

Because CGI programs are executables, using them is like letting other users run programs on your system from their computers. This type of access to your system isn't considered the safest thing you might do with your computer. To lessen the hazards involved, most CGI programs are kept in a separate subdirectory that is under the control of the Webmaster and usually not accessible to average users. We use the term *Webmaster* to refer to the person who operates the actual server. If you are operating your own server, then you are the Webmaster, and the next paragraph doesn't apply to you.

If, on the other hand, your site is located on another system, you need to contact your Webmaster in order to find out what you need to do to use CGI scripts and programs. There are several ways that your Webmaster can allow access to CGI scripts.

CGI programs can be written in any language that allows the resulting program to be executed on the system. The possible programming languages include, but are not limited to, C, C++, Fortran, Perl, TCL, and Visual Basic. Some of these languages provide for the creation of smaller executables. In fact, some require that the source be compiled before the program can be run.

Using the C programming language for CGI applications

C is a procedural programming language. In other words, a file of this nature describes a set of procedures that are to be followed that will perform the prescribed and expected outcomes. Each step is required in succession for this successful outcome.

C is also one of the so-called compiled programming languages. This means that the source code must be compiled before the program can be run.

An advantage of using C as your preferred CGI programming language lies in the ability of C to create an extremely tight and small binary executable. These compiled files are also capable of being executed much faster than files created in other interpreted languages.

Several public domain CGI source code libraries in C are available. Listing 10-1 demonstrates how to use the C programming language to create a CGI application.

Listing 10-1: CDEMO.C

```
#include <windows.h>
#include <stdio.h>

void main(int argc, char * argv[]) {
   FILE   *fin;
   FILE   *fout;
   char   *szInputFileName;
   char   *szOutputFileName;
   char   szTmp[160];


   if (argc != 2) {
       printf("Command line parm invalid.  Expecting
infile,outfile.\n");
       return;
   }

   // get pointer to input filename
   szInputFileName = argv[1];

   // get pointer to output filename
   szOutputFileName = strchr(szInputFileName,',');
   if (szOutputFileName==NULL) {
       printf("Command line parm invalid.  Expecting
infile,outfile.\n");
       return;
   }

   // terminate the input filename, adjust output filename
pointer
   *szOutputFileName = '\0';
   szOutputFileName++;

   // open the input file for read
   fin = fopen(szInputFileName,"r");
```

```
    if (fin==NULL) {
        printf("Could not open input file\n");
        return;
    }

    // open the output file for write
    fout = fopen(szOutputFileName,"w");
    if (fout==NULL) {
        printf("Could not open output file.\n");
        return;
    }

    fprintf(fout,"content-type: text/html\n\n");
    fprintf(fout,"<html>\n");
    fprintf(fout,"<head><title>CDEMO</title></head>\n");
    fprintf(fout,"<h1>CDEMO Environment Variables</h1>\n");
    fprintf(fout,"<ul>\n");

    while (fgets(szTmp,sizeof(szTmp),fin)) {
        fprintf(fout,"<li>%s",szTmp);

    }
    fprintf(fout,"</ul>\n");
    fprintf(fout,"</body></html>\n");

    fclose(fin);
    fclose(fout);
    _unlink(szInputFileName);

}
```

Figure 10-2 shows one location where you can find a library of C code for CGI programming.

A disadvantage of using C as your CGI programming language is the difficulty with which strings are manipulated by C. Most CGI applications involve the manipulation of string data. This manipulation usually requires much transformation, conversion, and translation as your data is changed from one form to another.

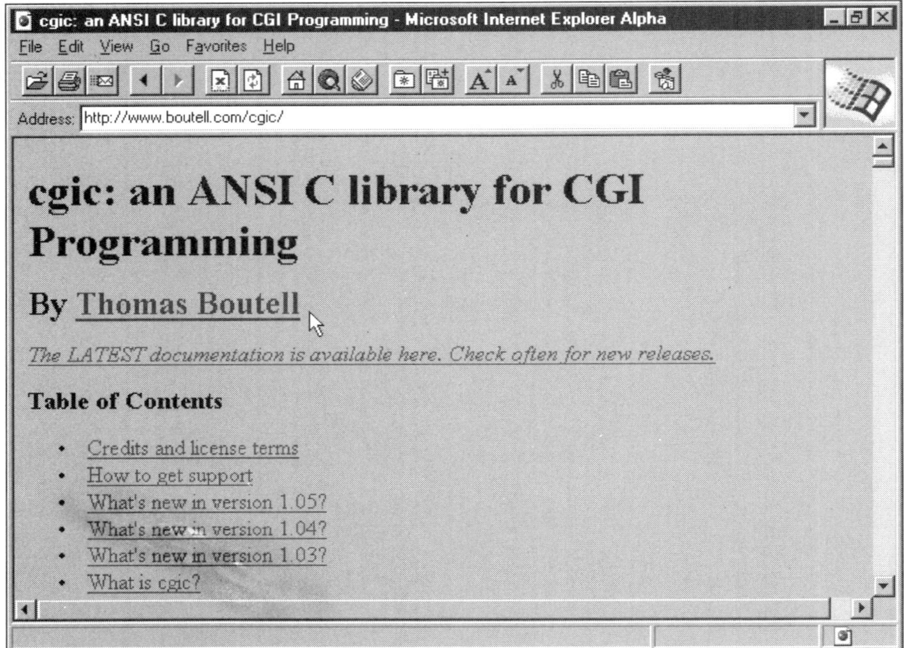

Figure 10-2: You'll find a library of CGI code in C at this Web location.

Using the C++ programming language for CGI applications

C++ is a superset of the C programming language. A big difference between C++ and C is that C++ is one of the object-oriented (OO) programming languages. A similarity between the two languages is that, because C++ is a superset of the C programming language, C++ is also another of the compiled languages.

Object-oriented languages offer many advantages because they provide both reusable and extensible classes. Such classes reduce the costs of future development.

A major disadvantage of using C++ is that it is object oriented. Object-oriented languages require a totally new way of thinking for people who are not familiar with object-oriented programming.

Another disadvantage is that few public domain CGI source code files are available. Figure 10-3 shows a location that offers a library of such source code files in C++. Contact information this library is as follows: Dragos Manolescu, Digital Computer Laboratory, Room 2413, 1304 W. Springfield Ave., Urbana, IL 61801. E-mail: `manolesc@cs.uiuc.edu`. WWW: `http://www.uiuc.edu/ph/www/manolesc`

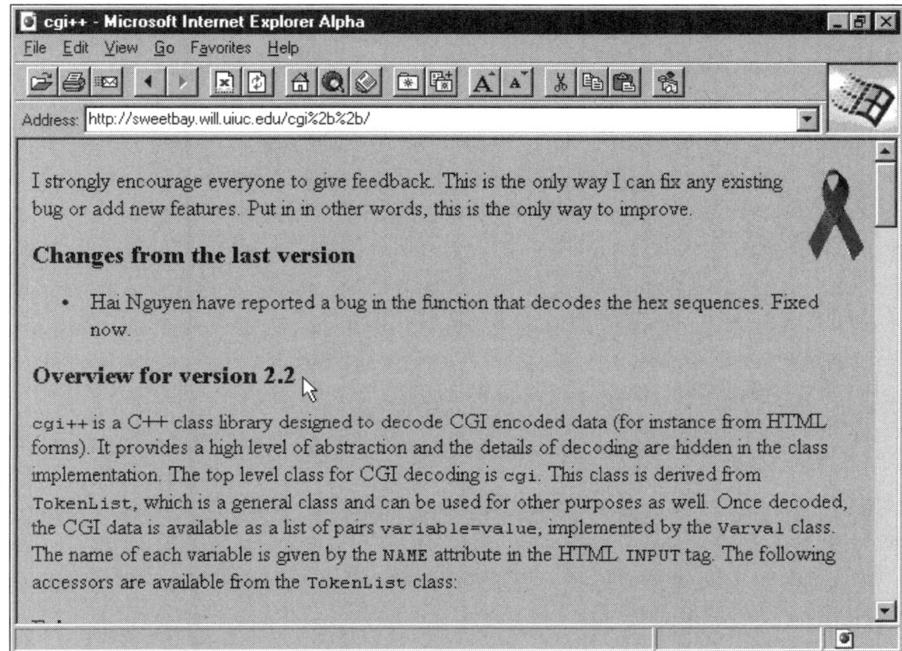

Figure 10-3: A C++ library for CGI is available at this location.

Using the Fortran language for CGI applications

Fortran is one of the early compiled languages for computers. Created in 1954 by IBM, *Fortran* stands for *formula translator*. It was, and still is, used extensively in scientific and engineering applications.

A few individuals and companies have used Fortran as their programming language for CGI. An interesting example of using Fortran as a CGI application is at `128.84.170.71`.

The page, located at 128.84.170.71, is an example of how a site's actual location can be hidden from view, as we discuss in Chapter 2. We have no idea where this page is located. All we have is an IP address. When we first began work with the VREvolution site and were having people check the site out, we gave only the IP address.

Listing 10-2 shows how the page at 128.84.170.71 is put together and how the Fortran program code helps to create the page.

Listing 10-2: CGI in Fortran!

```
<HTML><HEAD><TITLE>CGI IN FORTRAN!</TITLE></HEAD>
<BODY><H1>CGI IN FORTRAN!</H1>
The output of this page may <EM>look</EM> like
static HTML - but please take our word that it was
painstakingly output by a FORTRAN program!
<P>Check out:<PRE>
13:17:18
</PRE>the system time!<BR>
And here is the source
<B>PROGRAM</B> (not script!):
<XMP>
      PROGRAM CGI
      CHARACTER*8 T
      CHARACTER*70 A
      WRITE(6,*) "Content-type: text/html",CHAR(13),CHAR(10),
     1   CHAR(13),CHAR(10)
      WRITE(6,*) "<HTML><HEAD><TITLE>CGI IN FORTRAN!</TITLE>
</HEAD>"
      WRITE(6,*) "<BODY><H1>CGI IN FORTRAN!</H1>"
      WRITE(6,*) "The output of this page may <EM>look</EM>
like "
      WRITE(6,*) "static HTML - but please take our word that
it was
      WRITE(6,*) "painstakingly output by a FORTRAN program!"
      WRITE(6,*) "<P>Check out:<PRE>"
      CALL TIME(T)
      WRITE(6,*) T
      WRITE(6,*) "</PRE>the system time!<BR>"
      WRITE(6,*) "And here is the source "
      WRITE(6,*) "<B>PROGRAM</B> (not script!):"
      WRITE(6,*) CHAR(60),"XMP",CHAR(62)
      OPEN(10,FILE='cgi.f',STATUS='UNKNOWN')
100   READ(10,200,END=300) A
200   FORMAT (A)
      WRITE(6,*) A
      GOTO 100
300   CLOSE(10)
      WRITE(6,*) CHAR(60),"/XMP",CHAR(62)," Cute eh?"
      WRITE(6,*) "</BODY></HTML>"
      STOP
      END
</XMP> Cute eh?
</BODY></HTML>
```

Using the Perl language for CGI applications

Perl, which stands for *Practical Extraction and Report Language,* was created, written, and developed by Larry Wall. Perl is an interpreted language that is optimized for the easy manipulation of program files, text, and processes. Perl is one of the best of the interpreted languages because it performs string and binary data manipulation with ease.

Perl is extremely similar to C, yet it was designed for ease of use and efficiency. Most CGI applications are created with Perl. More than half of the publicly available CGI libraries on the Web are written in this language. For more information about Perl, go to `http:www.cis.ufl.edu/perl/` (see Figure 10-4).

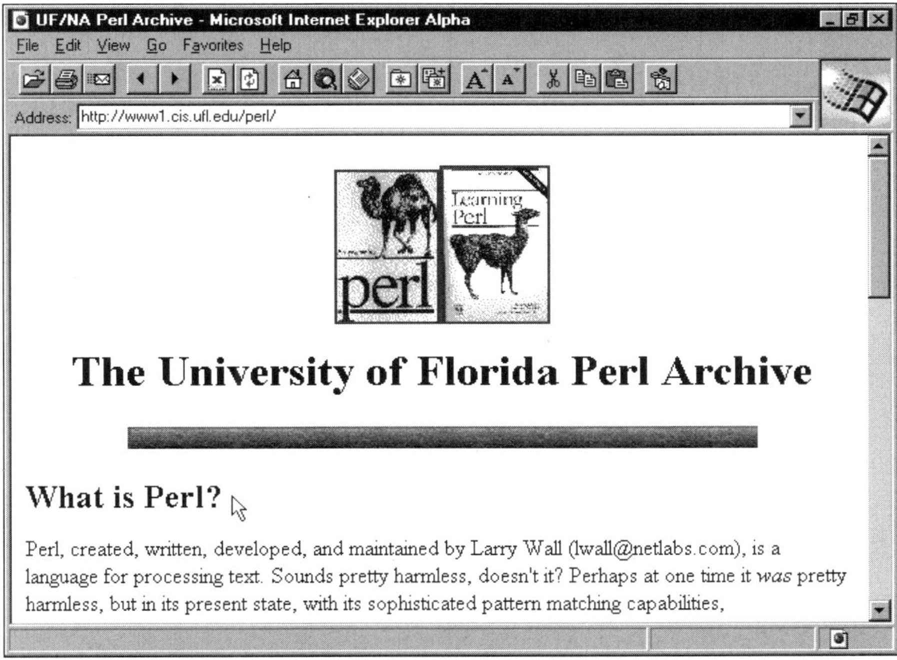

Figure 10-4: Perl CGI scripts are available at this site.

Matt Wright has made many examples of Perl CGI scripts available at `http://www.worldwidemart.com/scripts/`. Listing 10-3 shows one of those scripts, which is a counter program that is similar to the counter we show in Chapter 12. It counts the number of times that a given Web page is accessed.

Listing 10-3: Counter Script in Perl by Matt Wright

```
#!/usr/local/bin/perl

# Counter Script          Version 1.1.1
# Created by Matt Wright mattw@misha.net
# Created on: 10/27/95           Last Modified on: 1/11/96
# Scripts Archive:               http://www.worldwidemart.com/⮐
scripts/
# Consult the file README for more information and Installation⮐
Instructions.

##########################################################################
# Define Variables

  ### FILE AND DIRECTORY LOCATIONS, REFERERS ###

$count_file = "/path/to/count.txt";
$digit_dir = "/path/to/digit_dir";
$access_log = "/path/to/access_log";
$error_log = "/path/to/error_log";

$flyprog = "/path/to/fly/fly -q";
$fly_temp = "/path/to/fly_temp.txt";

$bad_referer_img = "http://www.host.com/path/to/bad_referer.gif";

@referers =
("www.worldwidemart.com","worldwidemart.com","206.31.72.203");

  ### IMAGE SETTINGS ###

$width = "24";
$height = "28";

$tp = "X";
$il = "1";

$frame_width = "8";
$frame_color = "0,0,0";

$dot = "X";
$logo = "X";
```

```
   #### OPTIONS ####

$uselog = "1";    # 1 = YES; 0 = NO

# Done
##########################################################################

# Get the Date For Logging Purposes
if ($uselog == 1) {
   ($sec,$min,$hour,$mday,$mon,$year,$wday,$yday,$isdst) =⮐
localtime(time);
   if ($sec < 10)  { $sec = "0$sec";   }
   if ($min < 10)  { $min = "0$min";   }
   if ($hour < 10) { $hour = "0$hour"; }
   if ($mday < 10) { $mday = "0$mday"; }
   if ($mon < 10)  { $monc = "0$mon";  }
   $date = "$hour\:$min\:$sec $mon/$mday/$year";
}

# Make Sure People Aren't Messing With the Counter From Other⮐
Web Pages
&check_referer;

# Get the Counter Number And Write New One to File
&get_num;

# If they Just want a transparent dot or a logo, give them that.
&check_dot;

# Determine Length of Counter Number
$num = $length = length($count);

# Set Individual Counter Numbers Into Associative Array
while ($num > 0) {
   $CHAR{$num} = chop($count);
   $num--;
}

# Determine the Height and Width of the Image
$img_width = (($width * $length) + ($frame_width * 2));
$img_height = (($frame_width * 2) + $height);

# Open the In-File for Commands
```

(continued)

Listing 10-3 *(continued)*:

```
open(FLY,">$fly_temp") || die "Can't Open In File For FLY⮐
Commands: $!\n";

# Create New Counter Image
print FLY "new\n";
print FLY "size $img_width,$img_height\n";

# If User Wants Frame, Print Commands to the In-File
&make_frame;

# Copy Individual Counter Images Commands to In-File
$j = 1;
while ($j <= $length) {
   print FLY "copy $insert_width,$insert_height,-1,-1,-1,⮐
-1,$digit_dir/$CHAR{$j}\.gif\n";
    $insert_width = ($insert_width + $width);
    $j++;
}

# If they want a color transparent, make it transparent
if ($tp ne "X" && $tp =~ /.*,.*,.*/) {
    print FLY "transparent $tp\n";
}

# If they want the image interlaced, make it interlaced
if ($il == 1) {
    print FLY "interlace\n";
}

# Close FLY
close(FLY);

$output = "$flyprog -i $fly_temp";
print "Content-type: image/gif\n\n";
print "$output";

# Remove Temp File
unlink($fly_temp);

# Log the Counter Access
if ($uselog == 1) {
    &log_access;
```

```
}

sub check_referer {
   if (@referers && $ENV{'HTTP_REFERER'}) {
      foreach $referer (@referers) {
         if ($ENV{'HTTP_REFERER'} =~ /$referer/) {
            $ref = 1;
            last;
         }
      }
   }
   else {
      $ref = 1;
   }

   if ($ref != 1) {
      print "Location: $bad_referer_img\n\n";

      if ($uselog == 1) {
         open(LOG,">>$error_log") || die "Can't Open User⮐
Error Log: $!\n";
         print LOG "$error: $ENV{'REMOTE_HOST'} [$date]⮐
$ENV{'HTTP_REFERER'} - $ENV{'HTTP_USER_AGENT'}\n";
         close(LOG);
      }

      exit;
   }
}

sub get_num {
   open(COUNT,"$count_file") || die "Can't Open Count Data⮐
File: $!\n";
   $count = <COUNT>;
   close(COUNT);
   if ($count =~ /\n$/) {
      chop($count);
   }

   $count++;

   open(COUNT,">$count_file") || die "Can't Open Count Data⮐
File For Writing: $!\n";
```

(continued)

Listing 10-3 (continued):

```
    print COUNT "$count";
    close(COUNT);
}

sub check_dot {

    if ($dot == 1) {
        # Open the In-File for Commands
        open(FLY,">$fly_temp") || die "Can't Open In File For⮐
FLY Commands: $!\n";

        # Create New Counter Image
        print FLY "new\n";
        print FLY "size 1,1\n";
        print FLY "fill x,y,0,0,0\n";
        print FLY "transparent 0,0,0\n";
        close(FLY);

        $output = "$flyprog -i $fly_temp";
        print "Content-type: image/gif\n\n";
        print "$output";

        exit;
    }
    elsif ($logo ne "X" && $logo =~ /.*tp:\/\//) {
        print "Location: $logo\n\n";

        # Log The Access
        if ($uselog == 1) {
            &log_access;
        }

        exit;
    }
}

sub make_frame {
    $insert_width = $insert_height = $frame_width;

    $insert_frame = 0;
```

```
    while ($insert_frame < $frame_width) {
        $current_width = ($img_width - $insert_frame);
        $current_height = ($img_height - $insert_frame);

        print FLY "line➥
0,$insert_frame,$img_width,$insert_frame,$frame_color\n";
        print FLY "line➥
$insert_frame,0,$insert_frame,$img_height,$frame_color\n";
        print FLY "line➥
$current_width,0,$current_width,$img_height,$frame_color\n";
        print FLY "line➥
$current_height,0,$current_height,$img_width,$frame_color\n";

        $insert_frame++;
    }
}

sub log_access {
    open(LOG,">>$access_log") || die "Can't Open User Access➥
Log: $!\n";
   print LOG "[$date] $ENV{'HTTP_REFERER'} - $ENV{'REMOTE_➥
HOST'} -  $ENV{'HTTP_USER_AGENT'}\n";
    close(LOG);
}
```

Using Tcl for CGI applications

Tcl, sometimes pronounced *tickle,* stands for *Tool Command Language.* Tcl is a simple scripting language that can be embedded in C applications because Tcl's interpreter is implemented as a C library.

An extension to Tcl is called *Tk* (pronounced *tee-kay*). Together, Tcl and Tk provide an easy-to-use system with relatively powerful graphical interface capabilities. The combination of Tcl/Tk is a programming system developed by John Ousterhout. You can find Tcl CGI scripts at `http://www.lbl.gov/~clarsen/projects/htcl/http-proc-args.html` (see Figure 10-5).

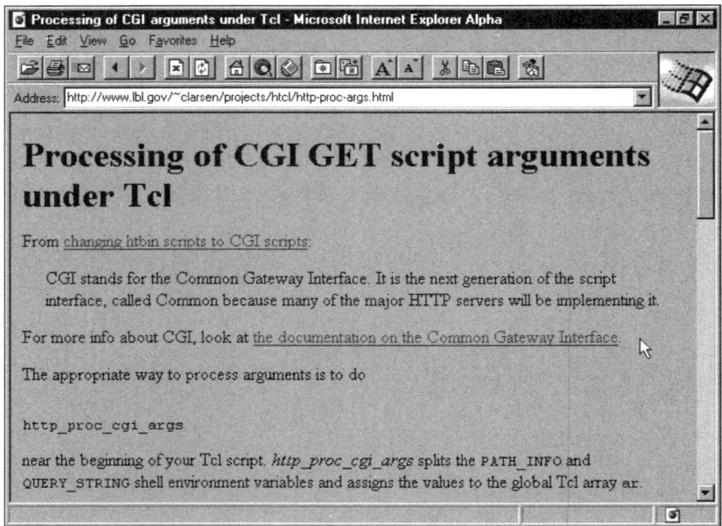

Figure 10-5: *Tcl CGI scripts are available at this site.*

Listing 10-4 shows the Tcl code for a CGI e-mail script. In other words, this code allows the sending of an e-mail message from inside a CGI script.

Listing 10-4: A Generic E-Mail Tcl CGI Script

```
#!/usr/local/bin/tclsh
##
## generic email the form input to the WWW_user
##
## J.M. Ivler (ivler@crl.com) - 5/8/95  V2.0
## Special thanks to Kevin Kenny @ G.E. Corporate R&D for his⮐
suggestions
##
##
## Changes from V1.0:
##  Runproc option is GONE. It was a *very* bad idea... :-)
##    [once implemented, we saw it as a *major* security hole⮐
for the server]
##  Added localonly option for the Webmaster to set
##  Added sendvar option for the Webmaster to set
##  Allowed the sendvar option to be reset by the user
##  Changed the temp file id from date-time to pid (KK
suggestion)
##  No longer using [exec env] to get the WWW_ list (KK⮐
suggestion)
```

```
##
##
## This code still requires uncgi. uncgi is a program➥
created/maintained by
## Steven Grimm <koreth@hyperion.com> . It is available➥
via FTP at:
## ftp.hyperion.com or ftp://ftp.crl.com/users/iv/ivler/➥
uncgi_13.tar.gz or
## http://www.crl.com/~ivler/uncgi_13.tar.gz . The version➥
this was tested
## with was V1.3, and that is what is maintained on *.crl.com.
##
## NOTE: Yeah it says 1.2, but it is 1.3... and don't even➥
look at the
##       version in the .c file
##
##
## INFOBAHN XPRESS GIVES NO WARRANTY, EXPRESSED OR
## IMPLIED, FOR THE SOFTWARE AND/OR DOCUMENTATION PROVIDED,
## INCLUDING, WITHOUT LIMITATION, WARRANTY OF MERCHANTABILITY
## AND WARRANTY OF FITNESS FOR A PARTICULAR PURPOSE.
##
## (c) Copyright 1995, Infobahn Xpress, Los Alamitos, CA.➥
All Rights Reserved.
##
## Permission is granted to redistribute freely and use for➥
any purpose,
## commercial or private, so long as this copyright notice is➥
retained
## and the source code is included free of charge with any➥
## binary distributions.
##
##
##---------------------------------------------------------------
##
## set the localonly option to allow or disallow users to use➥
internet
## mail specs in the mailto value. Setting to true will allow➥
mail to only
## be sent to valid users at the current host. Setting to➥
false will allow
## any form to be used as an anonymous internet remailer.➥
While the default
## has been set to false, we highly recommend setting it to➥
true.
##
```

(continued)

Listing 10-4 *(continued)*:

```
## localonly - false=allow internet specs
set localonly false
##
## sendvar defines a default output mode for the mailer. It⮐
states that the
## output will either output the varname/value pair, or the ⮐
value only.
## This has been set up to allow the Webmaster to establish a⮐
default method
## for a site. The user has the ability to override the default⮐
by setting
## the value "sendvar" inside their form to true or false.
##
## sendvar - true=output "varname=value" pairs   -   ⮐
false=output value only
set sendvar true
##
##
## start the processing
##
puts "Content-type: text/HTML\n"
puts "<title>E-mail Response Status</title>"
##
## Thanks to Kevin... this is a V2.0 enhancement for getting⮐
all the WWW_
## environment variables. The "foreach" and the "if" are *much*⮐
faster than
## the V1.0 method of [exec env].
##
foreach envvar [lsort [array names env] ] {
 if {[regexp {^WWW_} $envvar]} {
  set varname [join [lrange [split [lindex [split $envvar =] 0]⮐
_] 1 end ] _]
  if {$varname != ""} {
   set var($varname) $env(WWW_$varname)
  }
 }
}
## set some initial flags, and then check for known and expected⮐
WWW_ values
## that allow the user to reset some of the flags.
set knt 0
set msub false
set mailto false
```

```
## allow the user to change the value of sendvar from the
Webmasters default
## to their choice...
if {[info exists env(WWW_sendvar)]} {
 set sendvar $env(WWW_sendvar)
}
## User has used their own subject line for the mail message
if {[info exists env(WWW_msub)]} {
 set msub true
}
## User is sending mail, not echoing output to screen
if {[info exists env(WWW_mailto)]} {
 set mailto true
 set fname [pid].txt
 set f1 [open /tmp/$fname w]
}
##
## build the mail message / write the output to screen
##
foreach vname [array names var] {
 incr knt
 if {$sendvar} {
  set ostring($knt) "$vname = $var($vname)"
 } else {
  set ostring($knt) $var($vname)
 }
 if {$mailto} {
  puts $f1 "$ostring($knt)"
 } else {
  puts "$ostring($knt) <br>"
 }
}
##
## If mail, then send it
##
if {$mailto} {
 puts $f1 "\n\nThis was generated from a form at:
$env(PATH_TRANSLATED)"
 close $f1
##
## Local only processing... this is how we stop anonymous
e-mailers
##
```

(continued)

Listing 10-4 *(continued)*:

```
  if {$localonly} {
   if {[regexp "@|!|%" $env(WWW_mailto)]} {
    puts "<center><h1>An invalid form of e-mail notation from↵
this server has been used</h1>"
    puts "Please use the back key to exit.</center>"
    exit
   }
  }
   if {$msub} {
    exec mailx -s "$env(WWW_msub)" $env(WWW_mailto)↵
< /tmp/$fname
   } else {
    exec mailx -s "from the CGI automailer @ $env(SERVER_NAME)"↵
$env(WWW_mailto) < /tmp/$fname
   }
  }
  exec rm /tmp/$fname
 puts "<center><h1>Mail sent to $env(WWW_mailto)</h1>"↵
 puts "<h2>Thank you for your participation $var(name).</h2>↵
Your answers have been processed, please use the back key to↵
exit the survey.</center> <hr><P> <address>&#169; Copyright↵
1995, Infobahn Xpress, Los Alamitos, CA. All Rights Reserved.↵
</address>" }
```

The Tcl/Tk combination

- Is a powerful scripting interpreted language.
- Supports rapid application development.
- Executes interpreted scripts on the fly.
- Can combine parts and features of different programs into a single application.
- Is extremely easy to learn and understand.

You can find more information about Tcl/Tk at

```
http://www.sco.com/Technology/tcl/Tcl.html.
```

Using Visual Basic for CGI applications

Windows CGI opened up CGI programming for Visual Basic programmers. The Windows CGI is included with several of the Web server software applications that are based on Windows. Figure 10-6 shows an excellent place to look for information.

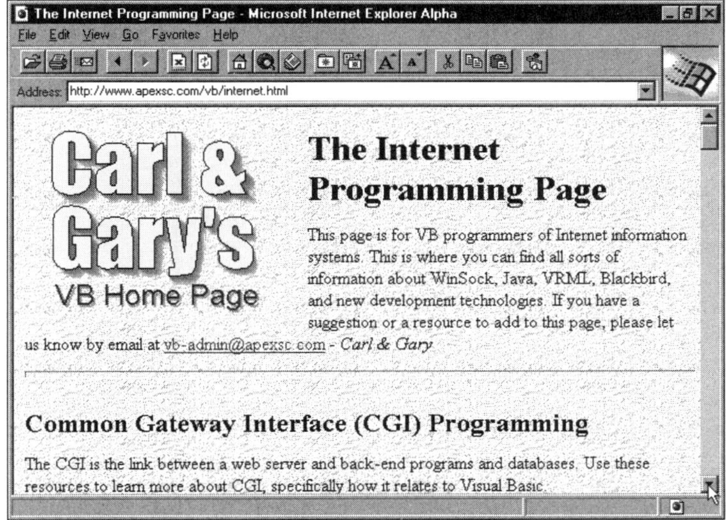

Figure 10-6: Visual Basic CGI scripts are available at this site.

Because Visual Basic does not require the overhead that is needed to start and maintain the DOS shell, scripts written for the Windows CGI using Visual Basic operate slightly faster than similar applications that are designed to operate from a DOS shell.

Recently, Microsoft announced the release of Visual Basic Script. Visual Basic Script is expected to provide scripting, automation, and customization capabilities to Web applications. Visual Basic Script is a subset of Visual Basic and is fully compatible with both Visual Basic and Visual Basic for Applications.

You can find more information about Visual Basic Script at

```
http://198.105.232.6/IntDev/vbs/vbscript.htm.
```

Building CGI Applications

Before we leave this chapter, we want to walk through the creation of a simple CGI application. The example uses Visual Basic 4.0 to create CGI scripts and applications.

We'll create a simple program using Visual Basic 4.0. This program uses the Visual Basic CGI interface. If you haven't upgraded to Visual Basic 4.0 and are still operating with Visual Basic 3.0, you can still build an application such as this.

This little VB application is what programmers like to call a "Hello World" application. It is simply to show you how an application can be built using Visual Basic and Win-CGI. It is not meant as a usable application (although it could be used as such).

Depending on which program you are using, you need either CGI.BAS or CGI32.BAS. CGI.BAS (the 16-bit version) is in the \CGI-SRC\WIN\ subdirectory of the QuarterDeck WebServer software. A 32-bit version, CGI32.BAS, is available on the Internet at `http://website.ora.com/software/`.

Add to your project the version (16-bit or 32-bit) of the .BAS file with which you'll be working. Now type Listing 10-5.

Listing 10-5: VRE_CGI.BAS

```
Sub CGI_Main()
     Send "Content-type:text/html"
     Send "<html>"
     Send "<head>"
     Send "<title>VREvolution VB Program</title>"
     Send "</head>"
     Send "<body>"
     Send "<h1><c><b>VREvolution<b><c></h1>"
     Send "<hr>"
     Send ""
    Send "<h2><i>Exloring the Quantum Dimensions of⮐
Cyberspace<i></h2>"
     Send ""
     Send "</body>"
     Send ""
     Send "</html>"
End Sub
```

As you can see, you place an HTML command in the output by simply using the `Send` function. This function is defined for you in either CGI.BAS or CGI32.BAS, depending on which one you decide to use. You need to compile this and create an executable before moving on to creating the HTML page that calls this CGI executable.

Now, create an HTML file such as Listing 10-6.

Listing 10-6: EXAMPLE.HTM

```
<HTML>
<!—Purpose: HTML file to hold our Visual Basic CGI⮐
application. -->
<!—Author:  76270.551@CompuServe.com -->
<!—Version: 1.0; 2 April 1996 -->
<HEAD>
<TITLE>VREvolution VB application Web Interface</TITLE>
</HEAD>
<BODY>
<P><A HREF="cgi-win/VRE_CGI.EXE">Click Here</A>
</BODY>
</HTML>
```

View this page with your Web browser and click on the hyperlink. The Visual Basic CGI script will place VREvolution and Exploring the Quantum Dimensions of Cyberspace on your screen. Keep in mind that this application is a very simple example, but it shows what you can do very quickly with Visual Basic as your CGI programming language.

VREvolution Site Diary: Installment 10

It's readily apparent that the future has great things in store for 32-bit Windows environments. As a result, we're moving away from programming and writing for the 16-bit platform and moving exclusively toward the 32-bit platforms.

This means that our programming has moved to the 32-bit version of Visual Basic 4.0 and to Visual C++ 4.0. The disadvantage of using these two languages in the creation of Interactive CGI applications is that their use on the Web is new and, therefore, there is a lack of available scripts and programs. The advantages of these languages lie in their capabilities.

Summary

In this chapter, you learned what CGI is.

You were exposed to various CGI programming languages.

You created a simple Visual Basic CGI application.

Your next step is to use various tools to set up search engines, databases, e-mail, and image maps.

Databases, Search Engines, E-Mail, and Image Maps

In This Chapter

Creating and using image maps at your Web site

Using Visual Basic to create a mail application for your Web site

Adding a database to your Web site

Adding a search engine for your Web site

Building a guestbook application for your Web site with Visual Basic

VREvolution Site Diary

In this chapter, you learn how to add and, in some cases, how to create a few of the kinds of applications that you can use to increase your Web site's interactivity. The applications that you will build are created in Microsoft Visual Basic 4.0 and Visual C++ 4.0.

Adding and Building Your Own Web Site Applications

In this chapter, we discuss adding or building five different types of applications to your Web site:

- A clickable image map that visitors can use to get from one location to another within your site
- A mail application that visitors can use to leave messages for other visitors
- A database for your site
- A search engine for your site
- A guestbook application

So get ready and begin creating your first interactive application.

Image maps

Image maps are an exciting form of interactivity that you can use on your Web site. They provide a way to make your site easier for visitors to navigate. This is particularly true if you have a number of graphics to use as menu selections.

We look at two methods for creating image maps. The first method involves the use of a program such as Thomas Boutell's MapEdit. This program is available on the Web at `http://sunsite.unc.edu/pub/packages/infosystems/WWW/tools/mapedit`. Another good free program for Windows is MapThis!

The second method for creating your image maps is through the use of a button bar.

MapEdit

Before we get into the details of using MapEdit, we want to suggest some rules of thumb for creating image maps. There are no hard and fast rules for the creation of image map graphics, but you'll probably want to set some standards for your own graphics to maintain a coherent feel to your pages.

Setting standards for your image maps

We try to follow these standards:

- Whichever software you choose for creating images, it must be able to save your graphics as either GIF files or as JPG files. Whether you're using PhotoShop, CorelDraw, PaintShop, or something else really doesn't matter.
- Keep in mind that graphics that have solid or nearly solid backgrounds compress better than those that have textured backgrounds. As a result, you should use a solid background whenever possible.
- Set a standard size for all of your graphics. The team at the University of Texas at Austin that is responsible for Web pages suggests making all of your graphics 6½ inches wide (468 pixels) and 3 inches tall (216 pixels). This size works well with the default width of windows in Netscape, and it does not require users who have 13-inch monitors to scroll in order to see the whole graphic.
- Another standard that you may want to follow is to set all of your graphics at 72 dpi (dots per inch), which is the resolution of most monitors.
- Keep your graphic size to no more than 35K. The larger the file size, the longer it will take your users to access the page that this graphic is located on.

Using MapEdit

The steps in using MapEdit are simple.

1. **Open the graphic that you plan to use for the image map or create a new image map by choosing File⇨Open/Create from the menu bar and then creating a graphic.**

   Next, you need to create a new hot spot on the graphic.

2. **Choose Tools⇨Rectangle.**

   You can choose any tool, but for this example, choose Rectangle.

   The hot spots are defined by numbered pairs of *x* and *y* coordinates. These coordinates are defined with 0,0 being the upper-left corner of the graphic.

   You can choose from a number of shapes for defining hotspots: circles, rectangles, and polygons. In the case of NSCA servers, you also can choose points. The coordinate pairs that are generated vary, based on the shape.

   The following three shapes are examples of what we are describing:

   - A circle is defined by the center point and any point along the circumference.
   - A rectangle is defined by the upper-left and lower-right corners of the rectangle.
   - An oval is defined by the upper-left and lower-right corners of the rectangle that would fit perfectly within the oval.

3. **Click the left mouse button in the center of the rectangular area that you want to use.**

4. **Drag to the outer edge of the area that you are using and then click the right mouse button.**

   A frustrating thing about using MapEdit is that the hot spots can't overlap. The only way to change the location of the hot spot after you've drawn it is to delete it and start over, so you need to place and size the rectangle correctly.

5. **After you define the region of the graphic to be used, define the hyperlink in the dialog box that is shown in Figure 11-1.**

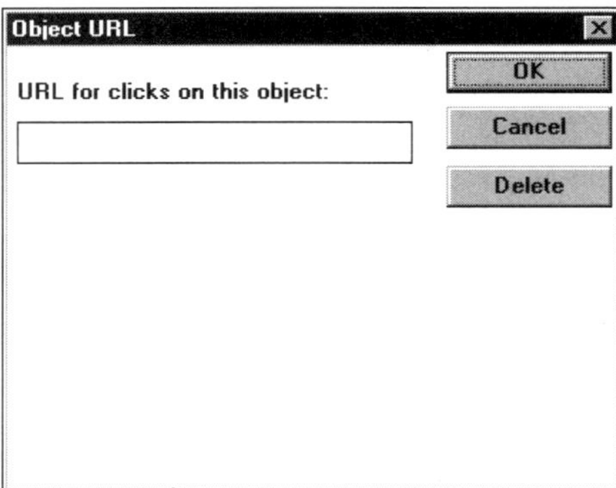

Figure 11-1: Define the URL for the area you've chosen.

Enter the URL for the document that you want to link to the selected region. You also can make this a URL for a graphic, an animation, a VRML world, a video clip, or an audio clip.

When entering these URLs, however, you need to make sure that you've taken into account where these files are located in relationship to the page where this image map is to be located. Your best bet is probably to use the absolute URLs for the files in question.

6. **Now, repeat the process outlined in Steps 2 through 5 until you've defined all of the remaining links for all of the remaining locations that you want on the graphic.**

7. **Choose File⇨Save As to save the map file.**

   Place the map file in the same folder as the graphic that owns it. You also need to select the correct file format (see Figure 11-2). You have two choices, NCSA or CERN. The format is determined by the server that you are using. The NCSA image map data file specifies the default URL, and then it specifies the coordinates of the area defined. The CERN image map data file is just as simple, but the order of the URL and coordinates is reversed. Keep in mind that the CERN file format is rarely used in the United States.

   The final step is to make sure that everything is working correctly.

8. **Choose Tools⇨Test+Edit.**

9. **Click within one of the active areas that you defined earlier.**

   Check to make sure that the links are what you want. You can edit the links if you need to.

One final note concerning MapEdit: This program is not freeware. It was created by Thomas Boutell and boutell.com, Inc. You have 30 days to evaluate the software. If you decide to continue using it after those 30 days, you are expected to license your copy or discontinue using the software.

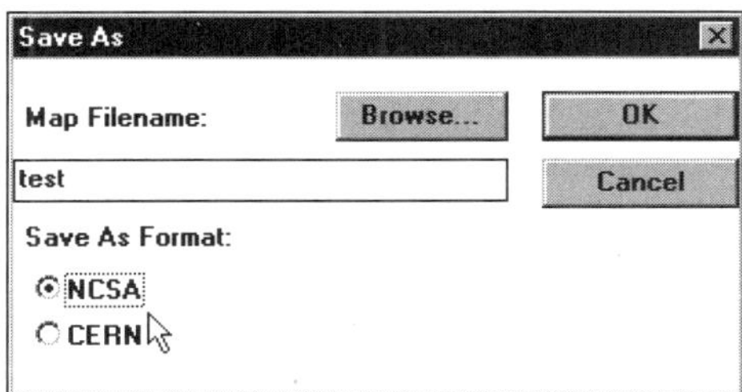

Figure 11-2: Choose either NCSA or CERN, depending on the server you are using.

Button bars

For those of you who decided to use space on someone else's server, chances are good that you aren't able to get into the \CGI-BIN\ subdirectory on your provider's server. Consequently, you don't have the option of creating image maps.

Or do you?

The use of the button bar gives the impression of an image map, but it is actually several different graphics with their own `<A HREF>` statements. This method is faster than the image map technique and works despite the lack of access to the \CGI-BIN\ subdirectory. Be sure to use the form `<img border=0 ...>` to get around the border tribute of the image tag.

Mail applications

"Mail applications?" you ask.

Even though e-mail may not offer some of the novelty that other applications provide on the Web, e-mail continues to be one of the most highly interactive features of the Web and the Internet. In the next few pages, you take a quick look at three uses of e-mail that, when used correctly, can increase the level of interactivity that's available to both you and visitors to your Web site. The first example is the use of e-mail to keep yourself informed about what people think of your Web site.

<A HREF="mailto: - ">

In at least one location on your Web pages, you should have a place where visitors can send e-mail to your e-mail address to tell you what they think of your Web site. This is especially important when you are adding CGI scripts and other interactive methods to your pages. "Why?" you ask. The main reason you need this feedback is because, more than likely, these forms of interactivity are not going to work right at first and you need to know this. Also, chaos theory suggests that the more complex something is, the more likely something is to go wrong. Interactivity is complex.

While we were getting the guestbook application ready for this chapter, our site locked up on some of our users. This situation was especially aggravating to them because during the first day of these problems, there was no place on any of our pages that listed an e-mail address or a mail link where users could contact us to notify us of the problem. By the second day of the site's operation, we had corrected this oversight by setting up a hyperlink. The hyperlink, as shown in Figure 11-3, is represented by the words *Contact us*. The HTML statement that achieves this is

```
<A HREF="mailto:76270.551@CompuServe.com">Contact us</A>
```

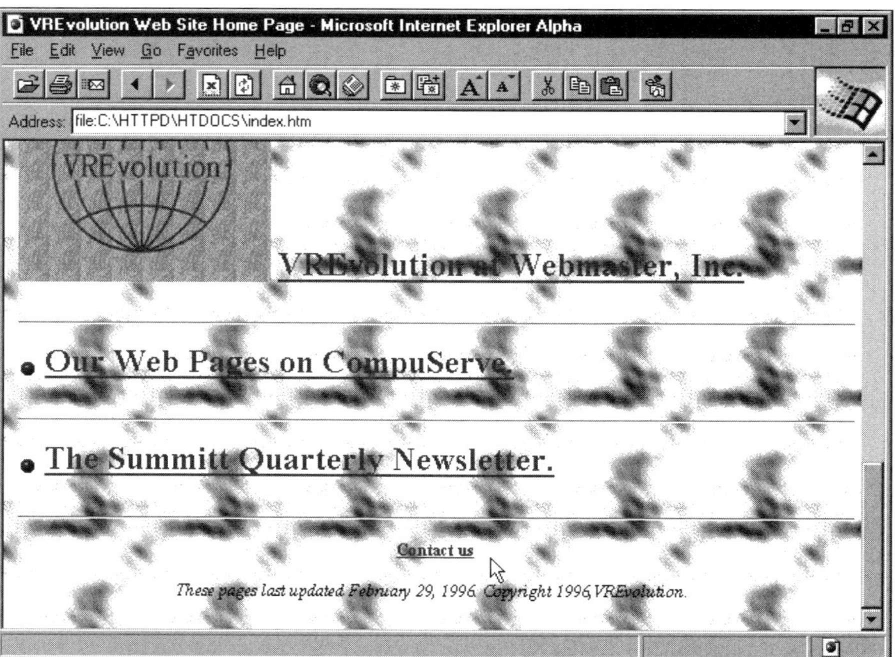

Figure 11-3: Users can use the Contact us hyperlink to send us e-mail about our Web pages.

SMTP

The next example of the use of e-mail covers the installation of an SMTP post office application on your server. You'll remember that your Web server is assigned a connection to port 80. SMTP dialogs are assigned connections to port 25.

SMTP is the most widely used e-mail exchange protocol on the Internet. This protocol is used for mail transfers from host to host. We use a program called WINSMTP on our system (see Figure 11-4).

Figure 11-4: WINSMTP is an easy-to-use post office application for your Web Site.

Adding a database

There are many ways you can add a database to your Web site. One of the easiest is to download WinWeb Base from `http://www.homepage.aus.net/timothy/#wws`. This shareware program was created by Finnish native Timo Autiokari using Visual Basic 3.0.

The program enables you to create a database, such as a phone and address book, stock-data information, price lists, or another simple listing, that your users can search for information they need. You can create the database file using just about any spreadsheet program because the database file is a simple comma-separated value file.

WinWeb Base allows an unlimited number of search definitions and an easily customizable response page. The search string can include up to five words and can search whole records or selectable columns only. A 1MB file can be processed in only a few seconds on a 486/33. Installation is as simple as copying WWBASE.EXE into your \CGI-WIN\ subdirectory and copying WWBASE.INI into your \WINDOWS\ subdirectory.

Adding a search engine

In addition to the search engine used with the database, you can add a search engine that will search your entire Web site for specific words. WinWeb Search, another shareware program by Autiokari, is a Visual Basic 3.0 program that adds advanced search capabilities to your server. This program returns the title text of the matched file as a hypertext link in a new HTML page.

Searches are based on plain English. Common words such as *a, the,* and *and* are ignored. You can also define other words that you want to be ignored in searches on your server. Your search string can be up to 20 words, and preceding a word with a plus sign forces an exact match, while preceding words with a minus sign rejects documents containing that word.

Installation is as simple as copying WWSEARCH.EXE into your \CGI-WIN\ subdirectory and copying WWSEARCH.INI into your \WINDOWS\ subdirectory.

Guestbook

WebServer allows for the use of Windows CGI (WinCGI), a system developed by Robert Denny. WinCGI uses INI files to pass information back and forth between the server software and the CGI applications. As a result, you can make any Windows application into a CGI application.

Denny developed WinCGI with Visual Basic in mind and has written several Visual Basic CGI examples and tutorials that are available on the Web. You can find many of these examples and tutorials at `http://website.ora.com`. Denny also is the developer of the WebSite server software for Windows NT and the Windows HTTPD server software for Windows 3.1, both of which we discuss in Chapter 3.

GUESTBK.EXE is a database program that we created using Denny's WinCGI. The program either displays an HTML form for visitors to fill out, or adds data to the database The information contained in the database will consist of the information supplied by people visiting your site. The guestbook, then, can be thought of as a list of people who have visited the site and have noted that visit by signing the guestbook.

GUESTBK.EXE is written in Visual Basic. For those of you who want to build this application yourself, GUESTBK.MAK, CGI.BAS, and GUESTBK.BAS are on the CD-ROM.

CGI.BAS, which was written by Denny, is in the \CGI-SRC\ subdirectory of both the demo and commercial versions of Quarterdeck WebServer. Several other server software applications also supply this file with their CGI applications.

Depending on whether your server software is 16-bit or 32-bit, you need to compile GUESTBK.BAS with the appropriate version of Visual Basic and include either CGI.BAS or CGI32.BAS. Listing 11-1 shows GUESTBK.BAS.

Listing 11-1: GUESTBK.BAS

```
modInfoForm - 1
#Option Explicit
Sub Inter_Main()
    MsgBox "This CGI program displays a data entry form and
      processes entries via "Windows CGI 1.1", 64, "Customer
      Info Script"
End Sub
Sub CGI_Main()
#
    Dim szRealName As String
    Dim szUserName As String
    Dim szURL As String
    Dim szCity As String
    Dim szState As String
    Dim szCountry As String
    Dim szComments As String
    Dim dbGuests As Database
    Dim szSQL As String
    Dim lRows As Long
    Dim szQuote As String

    szQuote = Chr$(34)

    Select Case CGI_RequestMethod
        Case "POST" '- A POST method was executed.

            '- Retrieve the user data
            szRealName = GetSmallField("RealName")
            szUserName = GetSmallField("UserName")
            szURL = GetSmallField("URL")
            szCity = GetSmallField("City")
```

(continued)

Listing 11-1 *(continued)*:

```
szState = GetSmallField("State")
szCountry = GetSmallField("Country")
szComments = GetSmallField("Comments")

'— Open the Access database
Set dbGuests = OpenDatabase(App.Path & "\Guests.MDB")

'— Create an append query to insert a record.
szSQL = "INSERT INTO GuestInfo (RealName, UserName,↵
     URL, "
szSQL = szSQL & "City, State, Country,"
szSQL = szSQL & "Comments) "
szSQL = szSQL & "VALUES (" & szQuote & szRealName &↵
     szQuote
szSQL = szSQL & ", " & szQuote & szUserName & szQuote
     & " , "
szSQL = szSQL & szQuote & szURL & szQuote & ", " &↵
     szQuote
szSQL = szSQL & szCity & szQuote & ", " & szQuote
szSQL = szSQL & szState & szQuote & ", " & szQuote↵
     & szCountry & szQuote
szSQL = szSQL & ", " & szQuote & szComments &↵
     szQuote & ")"
' MsgBox szSQL
'— Insert the data
On Error Resume Next
dbGuests.Execute szSQL, dbFailOnError
If Err = 0 Then
    '— The append query worked.
    Send "Content-type: text/html"
    Send ""
    Send "<TITLE>Thank You!</TITLE>"
    Send "<HEAD><CENTER><H1>Thank you for
      completing our form!</H1></CENTER>"
    Send "</HEAD><P><HR SIZE=7><P>"
    Send "The following information was saved in↵
      our guestbook:"
    Send "<P>"

modInfoForm - 2
```

```
            Send "<PRE>"
            Send "<B>              Name: </B>" & szRealName
            Send "<B>             Email: </B>" & szUserName
            Send "<B>               URL: </B>" & szURL
            Send "<B>          Location: </B>" & szCity &⮐
              ", " & szState & " " & szCountry
            Send "<P>"
            Send "<B>          Comments: </B>" & szComments
            Send "</PRE><P><P><HR SIZE=7><P>"
        Else
            '— The append query didn't work for some reason.
            Send "Status: 500 Internal Server Error"
            Send "Content-type: text/html"
            Send ""
            Send "<TITLE>Error saving data</TITLE>"
            Send "<HEAD><CENTER><H1>Error saving data</H1>⮐
              </CENTER>"
            Send "</HEAD><P>"
            Send "There was a problem saving your data to⮐
              the Guestbook database. "
            Send "Error Text: " & Error
            Send "Contact the system administrator at <A⮐
              HREF=" & "mailto:"
            Send CGI_ServerAdmin & ">" & CGI_ServerAdmin &⮐
              "</A><P>"
        End If
        '— Close the database.
        dbGuests.Close

    End Select
End Sub
```

If you want to learn CGI programming with Visual Basic, we suggest that you type the code yourself. Experience is the best teacher. If you don't want to type the listing, our version of GUESTBK.BAS is on the *Creating Cool Interactive Web Sites CD-ROM.*

Our version of GUESTBK.BAS, in addition to other programs and applications, is available for download at the VREvolution Web Site: `http://vrevolution.pitton.com`.

VREvolution Site Diary: Installment 11

Creating and installing the examples and CGI applications took a great deal of time. As we said earlier in the book, running a Web site requires a considerable amount of time.

And don't think that you can create the pages and leave them for visitors to look at. You need to be there on almost a daily basis to make changes and correct little mistakes.

One person we know (we won't tell who) misspelled the word *February* on that individual's Web pages. This person also misspelled our last name, but we can't complain too much about that. IDG Books, in the Web pages announcing our book, *Creating Cool 3D Web Worlds with VRML,* did the same thing.

The moral here is to check and recheck your pages. In the long run, you'll be glad you did.

Summary

In this chapter, you began to build your own CGI applications for your site by looking at a variety of possibilities.

You created an image map for your site.

You added e-mail capability to your site.

You created and added a guestbook application to your site.

The next chapter begins with a look at applications that help you keep track of the use of your Web site. The first application is a program that counts the number of visits to your Web site. We look also at several other applications for gathering Web site statistics.

Web Site Usage Statistics

In This Chapter

Examining the access logs for WebServer

Examining the error logs for WebServer

Building a counter program in C++

Examining the statistics of your specific Web site

VREvolution's Site Diary

As we have said previously in this book, maintaining a Web site is a time-consuming activity. You can make it more manageable, however, by obtaining, creating, and using specific types of applications that report statistics on the use and users of your Web site. In this chapter, we examine, discuss, and explore some of these applications.

In Chapter 5, we walk you through the installation and setup of the Quarterdeck WebServer software. In that installation process, you create two .LOG files that can be manipulated from the WebServer Setup dialog box (see Figure 12-1) under Administration and Logging.

These two files are the access log and the error log. You designate the location of these two files in the Administration and Logging dialog box (see Figure 12-2). If you accept the defaults during installation, these files are in the \HTTPD\LOGS\ subdirectory. We discuss the access log file first.

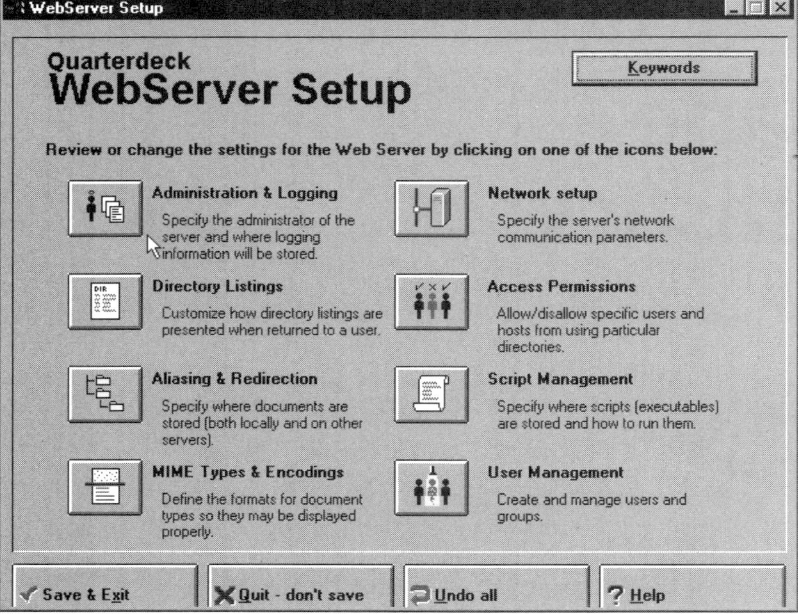

Figure 12-1: To manipulate the .LOG files, choose the Administration & Logging button in the WebServer Setup dialog box.

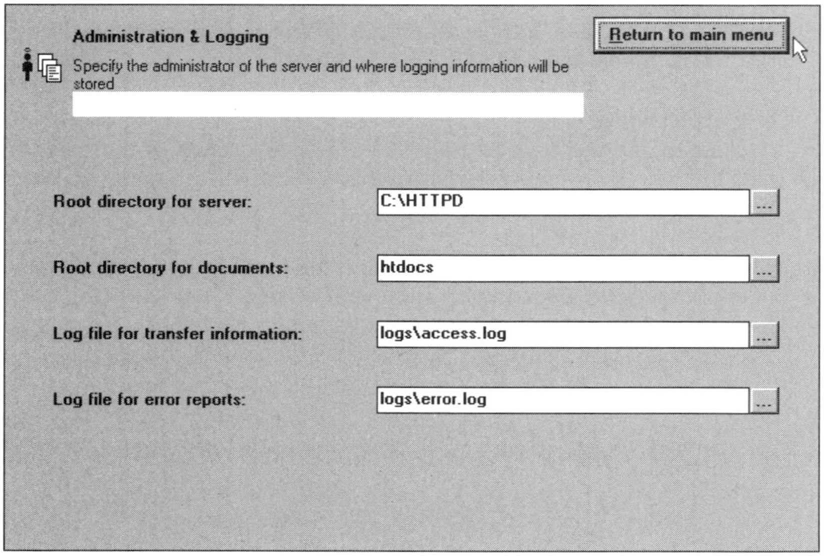

Figure 12-2: Designating the location of your Access and Error log files.

The WebServer Access Log

The ACCESS.LOG file stores information about successful file requests that are made to your Web site. In other words, when someone visits your site, their Web browser software contacts your Web server software and requests your server's home page. With WebServer, that home page is called INDEX.HTM.

If your server provides your home page to the visitor's Web browser, the file request is considered successful. Listing 12-1 shows an example from our ACCESS.LOG.

Listing 12-1: A Portion of Our ACCESS.LOG for March 5, 1996

```
grumpy.pitton.com - - [04/Mar/1996:12:39:15 +-600] "GET / HTTP/⮐
1.0" 200 1718
grumpy.pitton.com - - [04/Mar/1996:12:39:17 +-600] "GET /images/⮐
bkg14.gif HTTP/1.0" 200 5563
grumpy.pitton.com - - [04/Mar/1996:12:39:17 +-600] "GET /images/⮐
dotblue.gif HTTP/1.0" 200 153
grumpy.pitton.com - - [04/Mar/1996:12:39:18 +-600] "GET /images/⮐
vrml.gif HTTP/1.0" 200 5212
grumpy.pitton.com - - [04/Mar/1996:12:39:32 +-600] "GET /images/⮐
vre_logo.jpg HTTP/1.0" 200 41754
grumpy.pitton.com - - [04/Mar/1996:12:40:47 +-600] "GET /⮐
tblcont.htm HTTP/1.0" 200 1773
grumpy.pitton.com - - [04/Mar/1996:12:40:49 +-600] "GET /images/⮐
bkg19.gif HTTP/1.0" 200 4278
grumpy.pitton.com - - [04/Mar/1996:12:41:01 +-600] "GET /⮐
download.htm HTTP/1.0" 200 4365
grumpy.pitton.com - - [04/Mar/1996:12:41:04 +-600] "GET /images/⮐
bkg44.gif HTTP/1.0" 200 5596
searstower.ecn.purdue.edu - - [04/Mar/1996:13:04:43 +-600]⮐
"GET / HTTP/1.0" 200 1718
searstower.ecn.purdue.edu - - [04/Mar/1996:13:04:44 +-600]⮐
"GET /images/bkg14.gif HTTP/1.0" 200 5563
searstower.ecn.purdue.edu - - [04/Mar/1996:13:04:44 +-600]⮐
"GET /images/dotblue.gif HTTP/1.0" 200 153
searstower.ecn.purdue.edu - - [04/Mar/1996:13:04:46 +-600]⮐
"GET /images/vrml.gif HTTP/1.0" 200 5212
sneezy.pitton.com - - [04/Mar/1996:14:17:56 +-600] "GET / HTTP/⮐
1.0" 200 1718
sneezy.pitton.com - - [04/Mar/1996:14:18:09 +-600] "GET /images/⮐
dotblue.gif HTTP/1.0" 200 153
```

(continued)

Listing 12-1 ***(continued):***

```
sneezy.pitton.com - - [04/Mar/1996:14:18:09 +-600] "GET /images↩
bkg14.gif HTTP/1.0" 200 5563
sneezy.pitton.com - - [04/Mar/1996:14:18:27 +-600] "GET /images/↩
vrml.gif HTTP/1.0" 200 5212
sneezy.pitton.com - - [04/Mar/1996:14:19:02 +-600] "GET /images/↩
vre_logo.jpg HTTP/1.0" 200 41754
sneezy.pitton.com - - [04/Mar/1996:14:20:06 +-600] "GET /↩
tblcont.htm HTTP/1.0" 200 1773
sneezy.pitton.com - - [04/Mar/1996:14:20:28 +-600] "GET /images/↩
bkg19.gif HTTP/1.0" 200 4278
156.142.100.67 - - [04/Mar/1996:14:25:47 +-600] "GET / HTTP/1.0"↩
200 1718
156.142.100.67 - - [04/Mar/1996:14:25:54 +-600] "GET /images/↩
dotblue.gif HTTP/1.0" 200 153
156.142.100.67 - - [04/Mar/1996:14:25:54 +-600] "GET /images/↩
vrml.gif HTTP/1.0" 200 5212
156.142.100.67 - - [04/Mar/1996:14:25:54 +-600] "GET /images/↩
bkg14.gif HTTP/1.0" 200 5563
vrevolution.pitton.com - - [04/Mar/1996:18:43:11 +-600] "GET /↩
index.htm HTTP/1.0" 200 1659
vrevolution.pitton.com - - [04/Mar/1996:18:43:15 +-600] "GET↩
/images/bkg14.gif HTTP/1.0" 304 150
vrevolution.pitton.com - - [04/Mar/1996:18:43:16 +-600] "GET↩
/images/vre1.wav HTTP/1.0" 304 150
vrevolution.pitton.com - - [04/Mar/1996:18:43:19 +-600] "GET↩
/images/vre_logo.jpg HTTP/1.0" 304 150
vrevolution.pitton.com - - [04/Mar/1996:18:43:21 +-600] "GET↩
/images/dotblue.gif HTTP/1.0" 304 150
vrevolution.pitton.com - - [04/Mar/1996:18:43:22 +-600] "GET↩
/images/vrml.gif HTTP/1.0" 304 150
vrevolution.pitton.com - - [04/Mar/1996:18:43:49 +-600] "GET↩
/cgi-win/bmcount.exe?/count.dat HTTP/1.0" 0 0
toto.pitton.com - - [04/Mar/1996:19:18:38 +-600] "GET / HTTP/↩
1.0" 200 1659
toto.pitton.com - - [04/Mar/1996:19:20:18 +-600] "GET / HTTP/↩
1.0" 200 1659
toto.pitton.com - - [04/Mar/1996:19:21:02 +-600] "GET /↩
tblcont.htm HTTP/1.0" 200 1773
toto.pitton.com - - [04/Mar/1996:19:21:42 +-600] "GET / HTTP/↩
1.0" 200 1659
dd66-163.compuserve.com - - [04/Mar/1996:20:54:41 +-600] "GET /↩
HTTP/1.0" 200 1728
```

```
dd66-163.compuserve.com - - [04/Mar/1996:20:54:45 +-600] "GET↩
/images/bkg14.gif HTTP/1.0" 200 5563
dd66-163.compuserve.com - - [04/Mar/1996:20:54:45 +-600] "GET↩
/images/dotblue.gif HTTP/1.0" 200 153
dd66-163.compuserve.com - - [04/Mar/1996:20:54:46 +-600] "GET↩
/images/vrml.gif HTTP/1.0" 200 5212
dd66-163.compuserve.com - - [04/Mar/1996:20:55:03 +-600] "GET↩
/images/vre_logo.jpg HTTP/1.0" 200 41754
dd66-163.compuserve.com - - [04/Mar/1996:20:56:22 +-600] "GET↩
/tblcont.htm HTTP/1.0" 200 1773
dd66-163.compuserve.com - - [04/Mar/1996:20:56:25 +-600] "GET↩
/images/bkg19.gif HTTP/1.0" 200 4278
```

Look at Listing 12-1 carefully. Notice that each entry in this log file contains information about the IP's making the connection, the date and time, the type of access, and what was accessed.

To make this log's entries clearer, we'll examine the last entry in Listing 12-1 section by section.

```
dd66-163.compuserve.com - - [04/Mar/1996:20:56:25 +-600] "GET↩
/images/bkg19.gif HTTP/1.0" 200 4278
```

The first section of this entry contains information about who accessed the server. We know from the information `dd66-163.compuserve.com` that someone using CompuServe's Internet access servers made this access.

The second section designates the date and time of the access. Our friend on CompuServe accessed the server on March 4, 1996, at a little before 9 p.m. The `+-600` refers to our server's location in the central time zone.

The type of access was a "GET" action, and the material accessed was a background graphic located in the /images/ subdirectory.

Again, these types of entries in the Access log reflect successful access to the material on your server. Unsuccessful file requests are stored in the Error log.

The WebServer Error Log

The ERROR.LOG file stores information about unsuccessful file requests made to your Web site — in other words, when someone visits your site and doesn't get the files their Web browser software requests from your Web server software.

Whenever your server software fails to provide the file requested to the visitor's Web browser, the file request is considered unsuccessful. Listing 12-2 provides an example of our ERROR.LOG.

Listing 12-2: An Excerpt from Our Error Log in February 1996

```
[22/Feb/1996:14:38:10 +-600] Quarterdeck WebServer: access to⮐
htdocs/bkg14.gif failed for vrevolution.pitton.com, reason:⮐
File does not exist
[22/Feb/1996:14:38:12 +-600] Quarterdeck WebServer: access to⮐
htdocs/winword/internet/vre_logo.jpg failed for⮐
vrevolution.pitton.com, reason:
File does not exist
[22/Feb/1996:14:38:13 +-600] Quarterdeck WebServer: access to⮐
htdocs/constlin.gif failed for vrevolution.pitton.com, reason:⮐
File does not exist
[22/Feb/1996:14:38:13 +-600] Quarterdeck WebServer: access to⮐
htdocs/dotblue.gif failed for vrevolution.pitton.com, reason:⮐
File does not exist
[22/Feb/1996:15:24:18 +-600] Quarterdeck WebServer: access to⮐
htdocs/dotblue.gif failed for vrevolution.pitton.com, reason:⮐
File does not exist
[22/Feb/1996:15:24:19 +-600] Quarterdeck WebServer: access to⮐
htdocs/dotblue.gif failed for vrevolution.pitton.com, reason:⮐
File does not exist
[24/Feb/1996:22:22:47 +-600] Quarterdeck WebServer: access to⮐
htdocs/inet/webcomps/cgi-bin/win/comps/ed.exe failed for⮐
vrevolution.pitton.com, reason: File does not exist
[28/Feb/1996:08:08:06 +-600] Quarterdeck WebServer: access to⮐
htdocs/guestbook.html failed for⮐
vrevolution.pitton.com, reason: File does not exist
[28/Feb/1996:08:09:41 +-600] Quarterdeck WebServer: access to⮐
htdocs/guestbook.html failed for vrevolution.pitton.com,⮐
reason: File does not exist
[28/Feb/1996:08:14:52 +-600] Quarterdeck WebServer: access to⮐
htdocs/guestbook.html failed for vrevolution.pitton.com,⮐
reason: File does not exist
[28/Feb/1996:08:18:05 +-600] recv() on sock 66 Unexpected socket⮐
closure, code = 10054
[28/Feb/1996:08:18:30 +-600] send() on sock 73 Unexpected socket⮐
closure, code = 10054
```

```
[28/Feb/1996:11:28:33 +-600] Quarterdeck WebServer: access to
htdocs/cgi-bin/counter.exe docname=index.html failed for
vrevolution.pitton.com, reason: File does not exist
[28/Feb/1996:11:28:36 +-600] Quarterdeck WebServer: access to
htdocs/cgi-bin/counter.exe docname=index.html failed for
vrevolution.pitton.com, reason: File does not exist
[28/Feb/1996:15:47:52 +-600] Unexpected socket closure on sock
152 during script
[28/Feb/1996:16:02:48 +-600] Unexpected socket closure on sock 2
during script
[28/Feb/1996:16:05:34 +-600] Quarterdeck WebServer: access to
htdocs/htdocs/guestbk.htm failed for vrevolution.pitton.com,
reason: File does not exist
[28/Feb/1996:16:10:33 +-600] Unexpected socket closure on sock 9
during script
[28/Feb/1996:16:37:46 +-600] send() on sock 22 Unexpected socket
closure, code = 10054
[28/Feb/1996:18:17:48 +-600] send() on sock 36 timed out
[28/Feb/1996:21:57:53 +-600] Unexpected socket closure on sock
89 during script
[28/Feb/1996:22:20:00 +-600] Unexpected socket closure on sock
17 during script
[28/Feb/1996:22:36:51 +-600] Quarterdeck WebServer: access to
htdocs/BACK.GIF failed for vrevolution.pitton.com, reason: File
does not exist
[28/Feb/1996:22:36:52 +-600] Quarterdeck WebServer: access to
htdocs/DONT.GIF failed for vrevolution.pitton.com, reason: File
does not exist
[28/Feb/1996:22:36:52 +-600] Quarterdeck WebServer: access to
htdocs/BACK.GIF failed for vrevolution.pitton.com, reason: File
does not exist
[28/Feb/1996:22:36:53 +-600] Quarterdeck WebServer: access to
htdocs/DONT.GIF failed for vrevolution.pitton.com, reason: File
does not exist
[28/Feb/1996:22:36:53 +-600] Quarterdeck WebServer: access to
htdocs/BACK2.GIF failed for vrevolution.pitton.com, reason:
File does not exist
[28/Feb/1996:22:41:13 +-600] Unexpected socket closure on sock
21 during script
[29/Feb/1996:07:51:42 +-600] 500 Server Error
[29/Feb/1996:08:04:47 +-600] 500 Server Error
[29/Feb/1996:08:17:48 +-600] 500 Server Error
[29/Feb/1996:08:30:20 +-600] 500 Server Error
```

This listing contains many errors. We want to examine them to see whether we can determine their causes.

The majority, as in the following example, occurred simply because the requested files either did not exist in the specified directory or, possibly, didn't exist at all.

```
[28/Feb/1996:08:14:52 +-600] Quarterdeck WebServer: access to⮐
htdocs/guestbook.html failed for vrevolution.pitton.com, reason:⮐
File does not exist
```

This example shows that the file guestbook.html did not exist in the \HTDOCS\ subdirectory. This does not necessarily mean that the file doesn't exist, just that the hyperlink that called this file called for it in the wrong place. In other words, the file might exist in another subdirectory and the hyperlink didn't find it.

This type of error can be corrected without too much difficulty. Finding the causes of other errors and correcting them isn't quite so easy, as shown in the following examples:

```
 [28/Feb/1996:16:37:46 +-600] send() on sock 22 Unexpected⮐
socket closure, code = 10054
```

This error gives us enough information to start looking for what the error was. You'll notice that the error occurred from an unexpected socket closure on socket number 22 during a `send()`. An error code of `10054` was also generated. This information may not be as simple to decipher as the information in the previous examples, but it is more helpful than some of the other responses that we might get.

To drive this home, take a look at these examples:

```
[28/Feb/1996:15:47:52 +-600] Unexpected socket closure on sock⮐
152 during script
[28/Feb/1996:16:02:48 +-600] Unexpected socket closure on sock⮐
2 during script
[28/Feb/1996:16:10:33 +-600] Unexpected socket closure on sock⮐
9 during script
[28/Feb/1996:18:17:48 +-600] send() on sock 36 timed out
[28/Feb/1996:21:57:53 +-600] Unexpected socket closure on sock⮐
89 during script
[28/Feb/1996:22:20:00 +-600] Unexpected socket closure on sock⮐
17 during script
```

Notice that these examples provide some information but less information than the examples in the preceding listing. Here we know that most of the errors were caused by socket closures during a script. In the other example, the `send()` seems to have timed out.

In these examples, even less information was available to us for debugging our server software and applications. But still, as you can see in the preceding examples, there was at least something to work with. The following examples provide almost nothing to work from:

```
[29/Feb/1996:07:51:42 +-600] 500 Server Error
[29/Feb/1996:08:04:47 +-600] 500 Server Error
[29/Feb/1996:08:17:48 +-600] 500 Server Error
[29/Feb/1996:08:30:20 +-600] 500 Server Error
```

These examples show a code 500 server error. This code is a generic code for server errors, so it provides little information from which we can determine how to fix the problem.

When code 500 server errors occur, it is hoped that your visitors will send you a message explaining what page they were accessing and what was happening when the error occurred. We have created a Visual Basic CGI project that requests this type of information from visitors. Listing 12-3 shows an excerpt from the project.

Listing 12-3: Error Excerpt from GUESTBK.BAS
(full listing available in Chapter 11)

```
gCantOpen:
    Send ("HTTP/1.0 500 Server Error")
    Send ("Server: " & CGI_ServerSoftware)
    Send ("MIME-version: 1.0")
    Send ("Content type: text/html")
    Send ("")
    Send ("<HTML><HEAD>")
    Send ("<TITLE>Error in " & CGI_ExecutablePath + "</TITLE>")
    Send ("<H1>Error in " + CGI_ExecutablePath + "</H1>")
    Send ("</HEAD></BODY>")
    Send ("An error has occurred in " + CGI_ExecutablePath +⮐
 ".<P>")
    Send ("<PRE>Failed to open the guestbook file " & BOOK_FILE)
    Send ("It appears hopelessly locked. </PRE>")
```

(continued)

Listing 12-3 *(continued)*:

```
    Send ("<I>Please</I> note what you were doing when this↵
problem occurred,")
    Send ("so we can identify and correct it. Write down the Web↵
page you were using,")
    Send ("any data you might have entered into a form or search↵
box, and ")
   Send ("anything else that you think may help us duplicate↵
thisproblem. Then contact the")
    Send ("administrator of this service:")
    Send ("<A HREF=""mailto:" & CGI_ServerAdmin & """>")
    Send ("<ADDRESS>&lt;" + CGI_ServerAdmin + "&gt;</ADDRESS>")
    Send ("</A><BODY></HTML>")
End Sub
```

You should include routines such as this in your CGI applications so that you can get information that will help you track down errors and correct them.

Tracking down errors in CGI applications is one aspect of maintaining control over your Web site. Another is knowing how many people have visited your site.

Building Your Own Counter Program

There's really no easy and absolutely accurate way to know how many people have visited your Web site. An interesting essay titled "Why web usage statistics are (worse than) meaningless" can be found at `http://www.cranfield.ac.uk/stats/saltlick.html`. With that said, the counter that you build in this section is about as accurate as television rating services are.

The counter tells you how many times a given Web page on your site has been hit. This number can give you a general idea, if someone isn't just hitting your page to run up the counter, of how many times your server was accessed during a given period of time.

This code was written in Visual C/C++ 4.0 and was provided by Mark Owen of WebMaster, Inc. To create the counter, type the code that is shown in Listing 12-4 and compile it according to the instructions.

Listing 12-4: COUNTER.C

```
#include <stdio.h>

int increment (FILE *, char *);

void main ()
{
   FILE *fp;



        printf("There has been an error!");

   printf("Content-type:text/html\n\n");
   printf("This page has been accessed <b>%fp</b> times since
    March 10, 1996.");

return;
}


int increment (FILE *ptr, char *name)
{
   int i=0;

   ptr = fopen(name, "r");
   if (ptr) {
       fscanf(ptr, "%d", &i);
       fclose(ptr);
   }
   i++;
   ptr = fopen(name, "w");
   if (ptr) fprintf(ptr, "%d", i);
   else return 0;
   fclose(ptr);
   return 1;
}
```

Change the following line of code in the C code to reflect the date you want listed:

```
printf("This page has been accessed <b>%fp</b> times since↵
 March 10, 1996.");
```

Compile this code after you've set the project as an MS-DOS executable. Place the binary executable in your \CGI-BIN\DOS\ subdirectory.

Make sure you have a file named .count.total in the same subdirectory as the executable. This file can be created using a simple text editor. Create the file and save it but don't put anything in it. The C executable will take care of that. In the HTML file, add the following line in the location where you want the counter to show:

```
<!-#exec cgi="/cgi-dos/counter"-->
```

This CGI script in C provides you with a place on your page that tells you how many times this page has been accessed. This particular CGI is executed as a server side include (SSI). An SSI makes use of special extensions to the HTML protocol and, therefore, looks a lot like HTML. Basically, SSIs are scripts that echo data back to the client as HTML.

Many Web experts consider SSIs to be dangerous. For example, a user could embed an SSI command in data that is then sent to the server when the script echoes the data back to the client. When the SSI command is executed, the results could be inappropriate and in some cases dangerous to the server. In the final analysis, however, SSIs, although they introduce some insecurity into the system, are probably no more dangerous than any other CGI scripts that allow the execution of external commands.

This counter program could also be written in Visual Basic.

Looking at Your Web Site, Statistically Speaking

One of the last things that we look at in this chapter is getting statistics from your Web site. The number of applications that are available to you for getting statistics depends on what server software you are using.

For example, the WebSite server software contains a rather useful statistical analysis tool called WebView. WebView is installed when you install the

WebSite server software. A statistical analysis application called QuickStats, which is on WebView's Tools menu, gives you a brief synopsis of the information concerning your site.

Other statistical analysis tools come with some server packages. For example, Quarterdeck's WebSTAR software includes statistical analysis tools as part of the package's control center.

There are also several packages available for download from the Web. Table 12-1 provides a list of these applications and the locations where you can find them.

Table 12-1 Web Site Statistical Analysis Tools

Tool	Location
analog	`http://www.statslab.cam.ac.uk/~sret1/analog/`
bert	`http://onyx.slu.edu/dylan/bert.html`
Combined Log Handling System	`http://www.hensa.ac.uk/tools/www/logtools/`
DStats	`http://super.sonic.net/brooke/`
ErrorChk	`http://coney.gsfc.nasa.gov/Syeds/software/errorchk.html`
getstats	`http://www.eit.com/software/getstats/getstats.html`
MK-Stats	`http://web.sau.edu/~mkruse/mkstats/index.html`
Quickstats	`http://spwww.mcit.med.umich.edu/~jauderho/scripts/quickstats.html`
SingleStat	`http://www.usacomputers.net/tech/snglstat.htm`
Snowhare's Log Analysis Tools	`http://www.netimages.com/~snowhare/utilities/`
VBStats	`http://website.ora.com/software/VBStat31A.ZIP`
WebStat	`http://www.pegasus.esprit.ec.org/people/sijben/statistics/advertisement.html`
WebStat Explorer	`http://www.huntana.com/webstat/`
WebTrends	`http://www.cgsoftware.com/webtrend.htm`
WOA	`http://www.lbl.gov/~sls/woa/woa.html`
Wusage	`http://siva.cshl.org/wusage.html`
wwwstat	`http://www.ics.uci.edu/WebSoft/wwwstat/`

QuickStats (see Figure 12-3) gives you information such as the following:

- The total number of requests since the server has gone into operation
- The number of new users
- The number of HTML files served on a specific day
- The number of non-HTML files served on a specific day
- The number of CGI applications served on a specific day
- The number of errors or files that didn't work the way they were supposed to on a specific day
- The total number of requests on a specific day
- The average number of requests per hour on that day
- The average number of requests per day
- The number of unique hosts, or other servers, that visited your site that day

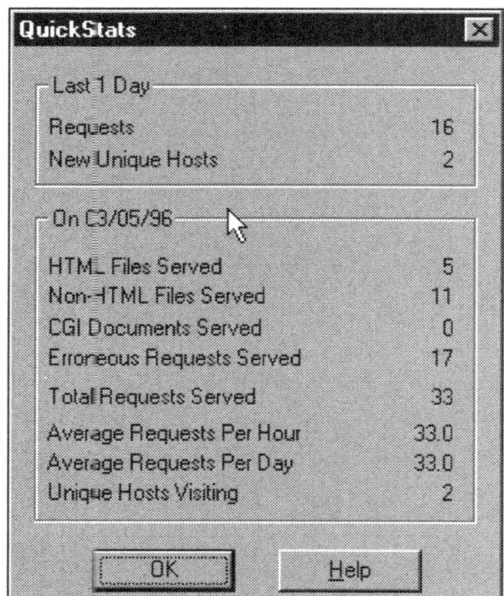

Figure 12-3: QuickStats provides a large amount of information concerning your WebSite software.

WebView, which comes with the WebSite server software, is just one site statistics program that can be used. A variety of other commercial programs that can provide you with site statistics are also available.

VREvolution Site Diary: Installment 12

The counter program was a difficult program to install for VREvolution. WebServer software does not allow for SSIs. WinWeb Homepage, from Timo Autiokari, enabled us to add the counter, a time and date display, and much more. Using some of the statistics programs discussed in the preceding pages, we are able to keep track of the usage of our site.

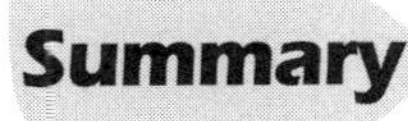

Summary

In this chapter, you looked at access and error logs for WebServer.

You constructed your own CGI counter program to keep track of the visitors to your Web site.

You looked at the QuickStats program that is available in the server program WebSite.

Chapter 13 is the last chapter in this book. It covers some of the ways that you can promote your site. You also find out how your site can pay for itself.

Promoting and Advertising Your Web Site

In This Chapter

Determining the purpose of your Web site

Letting people know where your site is

Making money from your site

Looking at the VREvolution Site Diary

In the preceding chapters, we've looked briefly at Web server software, HTML, VRML, Java, audio and video clips, and CGI. We also have described how we've used those components to create an interactive Web site for VREvolution. Just having a site doesn't do VREvolution much good, however. We need to tell people what the purpose of our site is so that they will visit it.

Why Have We Gone to All This Trouble?

We have gone to considerable trouble and expense to create an interactive Web site.

The purposes of VREvolution's Web site

Our reasons for creating this Web site have revolved around a threefold purpose. We described those reasons in the introduction to this book, but we want to look at them again.

VREvolution's educational purpose

VREvolution's primary purpose is to educate people concerning virtual reality and 3-D graphics. The Web site enables VREvolution to effectively make educational materials available through the World Wide Web.

VREvolution's practical purpose

Another of VREvolution's purposes is a more practical one. As authors, we are continually being asked what company we are with. VREvolution gives us an answer to that question. Another concern has been to effectively distribute information and practice the programming skills that we write about. The Web site gives us the ability to distribute this type of information.

VREvolution's financial purpose

Finally, a side effect of the first two purposes is that we can use the skills that we've developed with virtual reality, 3-D graphics, and the Web to earn money by creating Web sites for others. We also can earn money by renting space on our server to others.

What happens when you don't know the purpose of your Web site?

You need to determine what the purpose of your site is. Not knowing what the purpose of your Web site is may lead to higher costs and more work.

Higher costs

If you don't know the purpose of your site, you may end up spending more of your hard-earned funds than necessary. For example, you may purchase software and hardware that you don't need.

What hardware and software do you need? How do you know what hardware and software you need until you have a purpose?

More work

Creating interactive Web pages for your site takes time. Although creating pages can be fun, long pages can be tedious and, well, work. To create these pages only to find that they aren't what you wanted can be rather frustrating.

Know the purpose of your site

When you know what your purpose is, you spend less of your valuable resources on dead ends. Before you market your Web site, and products and services if you have them, you need to ask yourself two questions:

- What benefit do your clients obtain from you?
- What is special or unique about what you offer?

How Do You Let People Know Where Your Site Is?

The purpose of your site determines how you need to go about letting people know where your site is. Marketing your organizational site is quite different from telling people about your hobby site.

Self-marketing is a combination of four marketing methods:

- Direct marketing
- Inventive advertising
- Word of mouth
- Public relations

Four of the ways that you can promote your site are similar to these four marketing techniques:

- Internet directories (direct marketing)
- Internet marketing organizations (inventive advertising)
- Internet newsgroups (word of mouth)
- Link trading (public relations)

Internet directories

If you've had any exposure at all to the World Wide Web, you've probably used one of the Internet directories that are available. In setting up your site, you probably took advantage of these directories in searching for information about HTML, VRML, Java, CGI, and the other components.

Two types of directories are available. The first type is represented by a directory such as Yahoo, which gets its information from people who are just like you and us. Registration with this type of directory service is almost always free. Table 13-1 lists some of these kinds of directories. The second type of directory sends out search robots to gather its information. Some directories do a mixture of the two methods.

Table 13-1 Internet Directory Indexes

Type	Directory Name	URL
Business	Apollo Advertising	http://apollo.co.uk/
Business	BizWeb	http://www.bizweb.com/InfoForm/infoform.html
Business	Commercial Sites Index	http://www.directory.net/dir/submit.cgi
Business	Global Online Directory	http://www.cityscape.co.uk/gold/indexdir.html
Business	Internet Mall	http://www.mecklerweb.com/imall/howto.html
Business	Internet YellowPages	http://www.yellow.com/cgi-bin/online
Business	Open Market's Commercial Site Index	http://www.directory.net/
Business	Product.Com	http://www.product.com/
Business	WWW Business Yellow Pages	http://www.cba.uh.edu/ylowpges/ypform.html
Computer	World Wide Web Virtual Library	http://www.w3.org/hypertext/DataSources/bySubject/Overview.html
General	ALIWEB	http://web.nexor.co.uk/public/aliweb/aliweb.html
General	City.Net	http://www.city.net
General	EINet Galaxy	http://www.einet.net/cgi-bin/annotate
General	Harvest Gatherers	http:/rd.cs.colorado.edu/Harvest/brokers/register-with-CU-gatherers.html
General	Inter-Links	http://alpha.acast.nova.edu/start.html
General	InterNIC Directory of Directories	http://ds.internic.net/ds/dsdirofdirs.html
General	The Living City	http:/www.cadvision.com/top.html
General	Lycos	http://fuzine.mt.cs.cmu.edu/mlm/lycos-register.html

Table 13-1: Internet Directory Indexes

Type	Directory Name	URL
General	Mother-Of-All-BBS	http://www.cs.colorado.edu/homes/mcbryan/public_html/bb/summary.html
General	NCSA's What's-New Page	http://www.ncsa.uiuc.edu/SDG/Software/Mosaic/Docs/submit-to-whats-new.html
General	Netscape's What's New Page	http://home.mcom.com/home/whats-new.html
General	Nikos	http://www.rns.com/www_index/new_site.html
General	Online Whole Internet Catalog	http://nearnet.gnn.com/wic/about.rescat.html
General	Otis	http://www.interlog.com/~gordo/ottis_index.html
General	Special Internet Connections	http://www.uwm.edu/Mirror/inet.services.html
General	WebCrawler	http://webcrawler.cs.washington.edu/WebCrawler/SubmitURLS.html
General	Web of Wonder	http://www.digimark.net/wow
General	White NetPages	http://www.aldea.com/whitepages/addform.html
General	Yahoo	http://www.yahoo.com/
Special*	Submit It!	http://www.cen.uiuc.edu/~banister/submit-it/

* Submit It! is a service that you can use to register with a number of different directories that are included in this list.

Using some of these Internet Directories is a form of direct marketing in that many of them require you to submit the information about your site to the directory yourself. You can use this form of direct marketing to get the word out about your site.

Internet marketing organizations

Some individuals and companies will, for a price, promote your Web site for you. These individuals and organizations offer services ranging from finding other Web servers, directories, and indexes to list your Web site with to providing "advertising space" on their own servers and offering advice or advertising campaigns. Prices for these services vary considerably, so be sure to compare costs if you are considering one of them.

One service of this type is called the *electronic mall.* This kind of service charges a fee for a simulated storefront in an electronic mall. The format for these electronic malls varies, but basically they are lists of hyperlinks. Table 13-2 lists several electronic mall services.

Table 13-2 Electronic Malls

Name of the Electronic Mall	URL
The Branch Mall	`http://florist.com:1080/`
Commerce Net	`http://www.commerce.net/`
The Internet Mall	`http://www.mecklerweb.com/imall/imall.htm`
The Internet Plaza	`http://plaza.xor.com/`
NetMall	`http://www.ais.net:80/netmall/`

Electronic malls are a form of inventive advertising, but what you can do yourself by way of other methods that we discuss in this chapter can far exceed these efforts.

Internet newsgroups

Word of mouth has almost always been one of the best methods of advertising and self-promotion. Posting a message concerning your site to relevant Internet newsgroups is an easy way to advertise your site. Keep in mind, however, that these kinds of advertising announcements are, in general, not wanted by newsgroups. The consequences of posting unwanted materials can range from flaming and other forms of hate mail to permanent expulsion from the newsgroup.

Where to post your message

Some newsgroups, however, were created specifically for the purpose of making advertising announcements. Table 13-3 provides a list of some newsgroups that are appropriate for posting messages announcing your Web site. Keep in mind that these announcements will only be carried for a limited amount of time.

Table 13-3 Internet Newsgroups

Newsgroup URL	Announcement Type
`comp.infosystems.www.announce`	Publicizes new Web offerings
`what's-new@ncsa.uiuc.edu`	Mosaic's What's New page
`www-announce@W30.cern.ch`	CERN Mailing list
`www-request@info.cern.ch`	CERN WWW new servers list

Make sure that you read the FAQ at `http://www.halcyon.com/grant/charter.html` before you post your message. Also check the FAQ at each location before you post. These FAQs will tell you whether you can post your message to this particular newsgroup. They also explain how to format your message.

Niche and industry newsgroups, publications, and online services

Look for newsgroups that have an interest in the kind of information that your site caters to. Make sure that you locate and read the newsgroup's FAQ.

Check the specialty and industry magazines and journals that you receive. If you're reading them, chances are that people who may be interested in your site read them also. Find a fax number and send a copy of your announcement to the magazines and journals.

Find out about local bulletin board systems (BBSs). Use your communication software to call the BBS and post a copy of your announcement in the BBS's general message area.

Finally, you may want to find out whether you can post a copy of your announcement to your favorite discussion groups on one of the online services, such as America Online, CompuServe, or Prodigy.

What should be in your message?

In general, your message should not be what some might consider "ad copy," and keeping your message to 10 or 15 lines is probably best. You also need to remember that you are pointing the way to your Web site and not selling a product.

Another idea is to make your message look similar to a press release. No matter which way you decide to go with your message, you need to remember to include the following basic information:

- Who owns the Web site. Whether the owner is an individual, an organization, or a corporation, you need to provide this information in your announcement.
- How someone can contact you about either the information or your site. You should include both a phone number and an e-mail address.
- What's at your site. Make sure that you stress what value a visitor will obtain by visiting your site.
- Your URL.

Here's an example of an announcement:

> VREvolution Information Release
>
> February 27, 1996
>
> Pittsburg, KS. VREvolution is pleased to announce the establishment of an experimental World Wide Web site in conjunction with Paul and Mary Summitt's soon-to-be released IDG book, *Creating Cool Interactive Web Sites*. To reach VREvolution's experimental Web site, please point your Web browser at the following URL:
>
> http://206.53.99.200/
>
> Here's what you can expect to find on the Web pages:
>
> - Virtual reality and VRML worlds, discussions, and Web hyperlinks
> - Discussions about 3D graphics
> - Interactive Web tools and hyperlinks
>
> Paul and Mary Summitt are also the authors of IDG's *Creating Cool 3D Web Worlds with VRML* and five chapters in SAMS' *CYBERLIFE!* They also are the principle authors of the user manual for Waite's *VRBASIC*.

For more information about VREvolution, its experimental Web site, or any of VREvolution's offerings or products, please contact Mary J. Summitt at VREvolution. She can be reached by e-mail at 76270.551@compuserve.com. Please visit our Web site soon!

Other places you should notify

One of the first places that you should send your announcement is to your local newspapers, radio stations, and television stations. Fax or mail your announcement to the business editor or news director of the papers and stations.

If there is a local computer club that publishes a magazine or newsletter, send a copy of your announcement to its technology reporter. While you're at it, let all of the local computer clubs and computer stores in your area know about your site by sending them copies of your announcements.

You also can send your announcement to computer magazines. Many times, some magazines will announce new Web sites. Table 13-4 lists some of the e-mail addresses for some of the magazines that occasionally announce Web sites.

Table 13-4 Computer Magazines

Magazine	E-Mail Address	Phone #
Computer Life	`ceditors.notes@mail.zd.ziff.com`	415-357-5355
Internet World	`info@mecklermedia.com`	603-924-7271
IWAY	`editors@iway.mv.com`	603-924-9334
NetGuide	`netmail@netguide.cmp.com`	526-562-5000
Wired	`editor@wired.com`	415-222-6249

Link trading

Good public relations will get you plenty of free publication. One form of free publication is exchanging hyperlinks with others.

We say "exchanging hyperlinks" because you should ask permission before you place hyperlinks on your page, and the person whose page you are establishing a hyperlink to, of course, will place a hyperlink to your page in return. This way, both of you get free advertising.

Making Money from Your Site

You can make money from and with your Web site in a variety of ways. Before you go any further, however, we want you to understand that you don't just hang up a sign, open a bank account, and wait for the money to roll in. Each of the possibilities that we discuss for making money requires a great deal of effort and much more professional responsibility than we can cover here. These are just possibilities that you may want to look into.

Consulting

Businesses and companies are looking for people to help them get online. Such consultants recommend everything from hardware to software.

Offering Web page design services

You've learned a great deal about Web page design in setting up your site. There are people who don't have the time to learn what you know. These people will pay for your skills.

Renting out space on your server

If you have installed your own server, you are now in the position of being able to rent out space to others. You can rent 1MB or 2MB subdirectories for other people to use for their own Web pages.

Setting up an Internet mall

You can rent single Web pages to local and area businesses that want to list their own products and services.

VREvolution Site Diary: Installment 13

We've now come to the close of our last chapter of this book. This book has been an experiment and an exploration. The Site Diary has been the place where we have discussed how we were using the information we've covered in the chapters.

Because we experiment with a variety of Web technologies at our site, we have done little marketing other than by word of mouth and link exchanging. This book will introduce many users to our site. We've discussed our site in some of the newsgroups and forums that we participate in. We've also exchanged links with other individuals whose interests are similar to ours.

Summary

In this chapter we've discussed:

Deciding what the purpose of your Web site is. Remember, not knowing your purpose can lead to higher costs and more work than necessary in building your site.

Letting people know where your Web site is. The four basic methods of letting people know where your site is are: Internet directories, Internet marketing organizations, Internet newsgroups, and link trading.

Making money with your Web site. Remember, any method of making money that we discuss in this chapter will require much effort in order to bring it to fruition.

The only thing left for us to do is let you close the book so that you can get to work establishing and maintaining your Web site.

Good luck. See you in cyberspace.

PART V APPENDIX

The Accompanying CD-ROM

The Accompanying CD-ROM

This appendix is designed to help you install the software that is on the *Creating Cool Interactive Web Sites CD-ROM.* This list is alphabetical by the company that distributes the software. Each software application is described and the instructions for installing it on your computer are given.

In addition to the software described in the following pages, the CD-ROM contains a FILES folder with examples we use in the book. One program in the FILES folder is GUESTBK.EXE. For GUESTBK.EXE to run on your system, copy VB40016.DLL and VB40032.DLL into your Windows system subdirectory (both .DLL files are in the FILES folder). If you have Visual Basic 3.0, you can compile the program yourself, and it will run with your VBRUN300.DLL.

The UTILS folder contains the WINZIP compressing/uncompressing utility.

Caligari's Fountain

Fountain is a VRML world-authoring program and VRML viewer created by Caligari Corporation. We discuss Fountain in Chapter 7.

The minimum hardware and software requirements for this product are

- A 486 CPU
- At least 8MB of RAM
- A SLIP/PPP connection
- A minimum 14.4K modem

Installing Fountain is easy. We discuss these instructions briefly in Chapter 7 but go into a little more detail here. Follow these instructions:

1. **Go to the subdirectory on the *Creating Cool Interactive Web Sites CD-ROM.***

2. **Double-click on the SETUP.EXE file.**

   After a moment, you see Figure A-1 on your monitor.

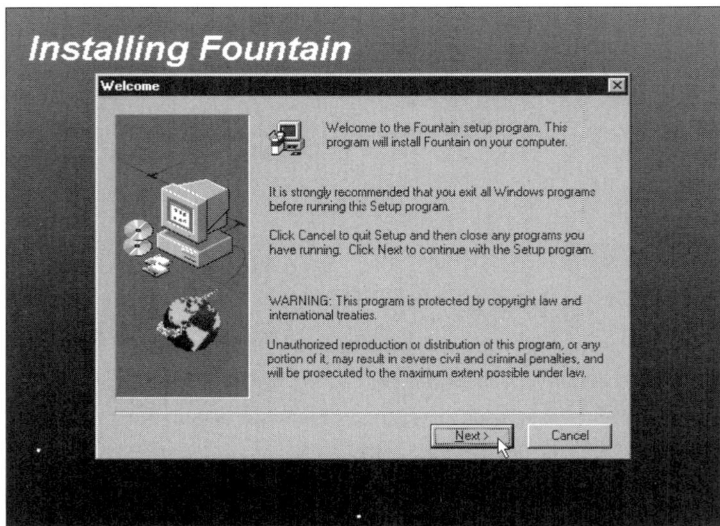

Figure A-1: Fountain's setup program is easy to use.

3. **Click the Next button.**

   You see the Fountain software license agreement.

4. **In order to continue, click the Yes button.**

5. **Figure A-2 appears on your screen.**

   You can change the default destination directory if you want to.

6. **Click the Next button.**

   The software begins installing onto the destination drive and build a program group. When it's completed, you see a screen that is similar to Figure A-3.

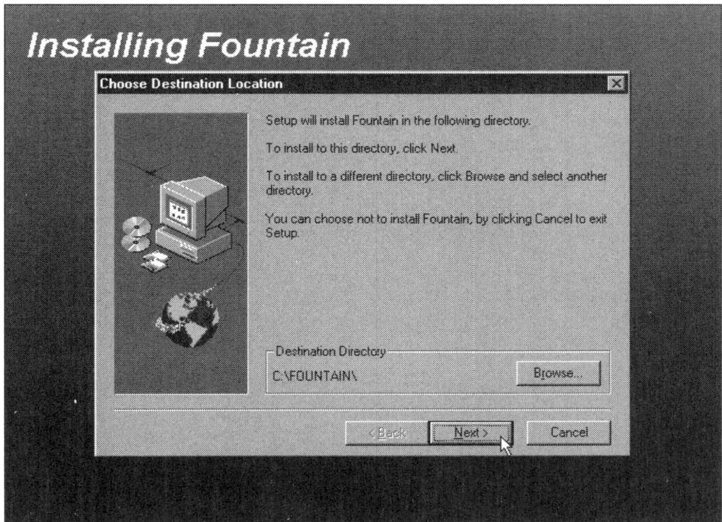

Figure A-2: Determine the drive and subdirectory in which you want to install Fountain.

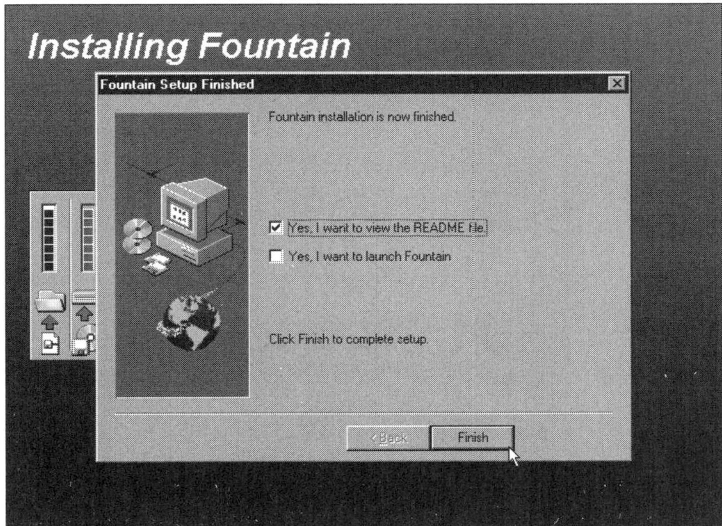

Figure A-3: Choose whether you want to view the README file or run Fountain.

7. **Choose either to view the README file or to run Fountain and then click the Finish button.**

The Fountain Software is now ready to use.

Catalyst's SocketWrench/VB

SocketWrench/VB is part of Catalyst Software's larger TCP/IP programming package. It requires Windows 3.1 or higher, Visual Basic 3.0 or higher, and the Windows Sockets 1.1 library. Windows 95 includes TCP/IP as part of the base operating system. The Catalyst TCP/IP package includes an easy-to-understand tutorial called "An Introduction to TCP/IP Programming with SocketWrench/VB."

Installation of this software product is relatively simple. Follow these instructions:

1. **Change to the \CATALYST\ subdirectory on the *Creating Cool Interactive Web Sites CD-ROM.***
2. **Run the SETUP.EXE program.**

   You see a screen that is similar to the one in Figure A-4.

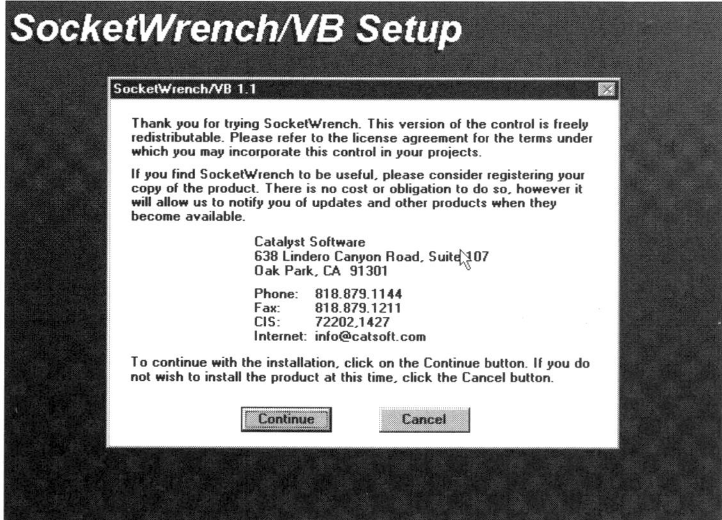

Figure A-4: SocketWrench/VB opening screen.

3. **Click on the Continue button.**

   At this point, you can change the drive and subdirectory for the SocketWrench/VB files if you want to (see Figure A-5).

   If the directory where you've slated the software to be installed does not exist, you are asked whether you want to create this directory.

4. **Click on Yes.**

The software is installed. When the installation is nearly complete, the setup program asks whether you want to create a program group for this installation.

5. **Click on Yes.**

   The program group is created.

6. **Click on OK when you see the window telling you that the product has been installed successfully.**

7. **View the README.WRI file and any other documentation that has been included.**

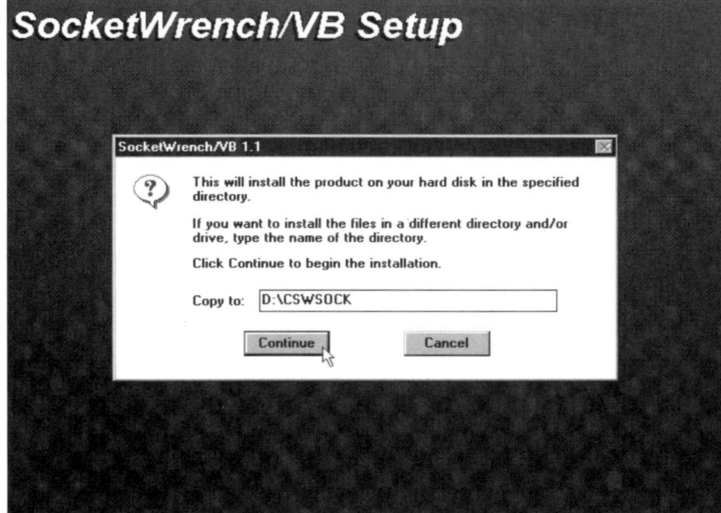

Figure A-5: Tell the Setup program where you want to install SocketWrench/VB.

The SocketWrench/VB software is now completely installed and ready to use.

CompuServe's Home Page Wizard and Publishing Wizard

CompuServe's Home Page Wizard and Publishing Wizard enable you to create and publish your Web pages on CompuServe's server. We discuss these two applications in Chapter 2.

Installation of this software is simple:

1. **Change to the \CIS\HPWIZ\ subdirectory on the *Creating Cool Interactive Web Sites CD-ROM.***

2. **Double-click on the SETUP.EXE program to launch and install the installation wizard program.**

   You see something similar to Figure A-6 on your screen.

Figure A-6: Home Page Wizard's installation is simple.

3. **Click on Next.**

   Your screen changes, and something resembling Figure A-7 appears.

4. **Choose the type of installation you want and where you want the software installed.**

   We recommend that you install the software on the same drive and in the same subdirectory as your other CompuServe software. If you aren't sure how to do this, just accept the defaults.

5. **After you select the type of installation and where you want it installed, click on Next.**

   The next screen asks what folder you want the icons from this software to be located in. We recommend that you accept the defaults.

6. **Click on Next.**

   The software is installed.

   When the software installation is competed, a dialog box appears, asking whether you want to view the Readme file. If you leave the Readme file checked, that file is displayed on the screen when you click on Finish.

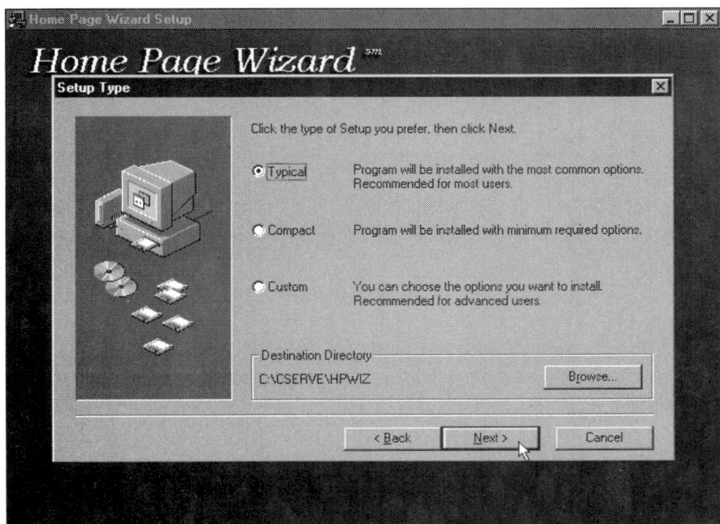

Figure A-7: Choose the kind of installation you want.

CompuServe's Home Page and Publishing Wizards are now ready for you to use.

CompuServe's WinCIM 2.0

CompuServe's WinCIM 2.0 was first introduced and discussed in Chapter 1. Installing this software is direct and straightforward. Follow these simple instructions:

1. **Change to the \CIS\WINCIM\ subdirectory on the *Creating Cool Interactive Web Sites CD-ROM.***
2. **Double-click on the SETUP.EXE program to launch and install the installation wizard program.**

   Soon you see something similar to Figure A-8 on your screen.
3. **Click on Next.**

   Your screen changes, and something resembling Figure A-9 appears.
4. **Choose whether you want to use CompuServe's Winsock or use another version of Winsock.**

   If you already have a CompuServe Winsock, as in an upgrade as represented in Figure A-9, decide whether to use the old Winsock or the new one.

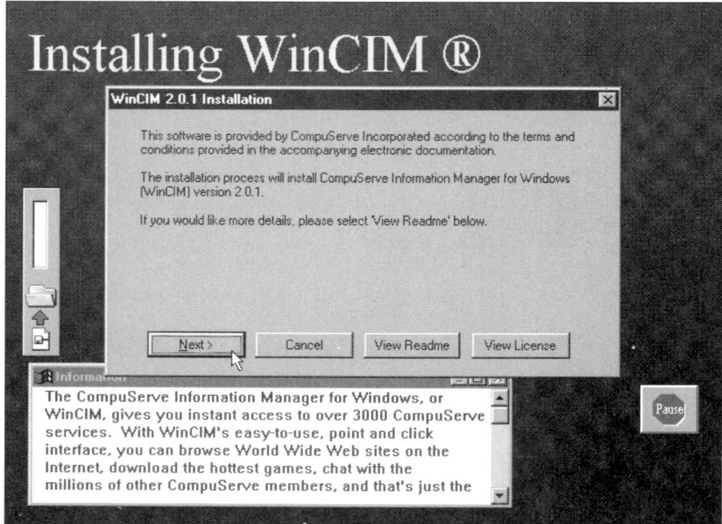

Figure A-8: *As with Home Page Wizard, WinCIM's installation is simple.*

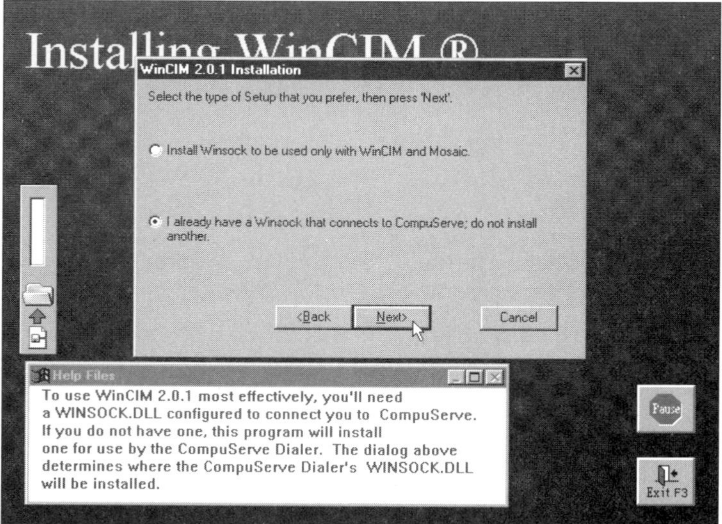

Figure A-9: *Choose which Winsock you want to use.*

5. **After you select the Winsock installation, click on Next.**

   You see a screen that asks whether you want to include the CompuServe sign-up software.

6. **If this is your first time using CompuServe, make sure that this option is checked; otherwise, make sure that it is unchecked.**
7. **In the same dialog box, determine the drive and subdirectory where you want the CompuServe WinCIM software installed.**
8. **Click on Next.**

   The software is installed.

   After the software installation is competed, a dialog box appears, asking whether you want to view the Readme file. When you click on Finish, the Readme file is displayed on your screen.

CompuServe's WinCIM is on your hard drive and ready to use.

Dart's PowerTCP

PowerTCP, from Dart Communications, is a set of TCP/IP communications libraries that enable you to built TCP/IP applications using Visual Basic. Installation is easy. Follow these steps:

1. **Change to the \DART\ subdirectory on the *Creating Cool Interactive Web Sites CD-ROM.***
2. **Double-click on the PT16-109.EXE program.**

   You see something similar to Figure A-10 on your screen.

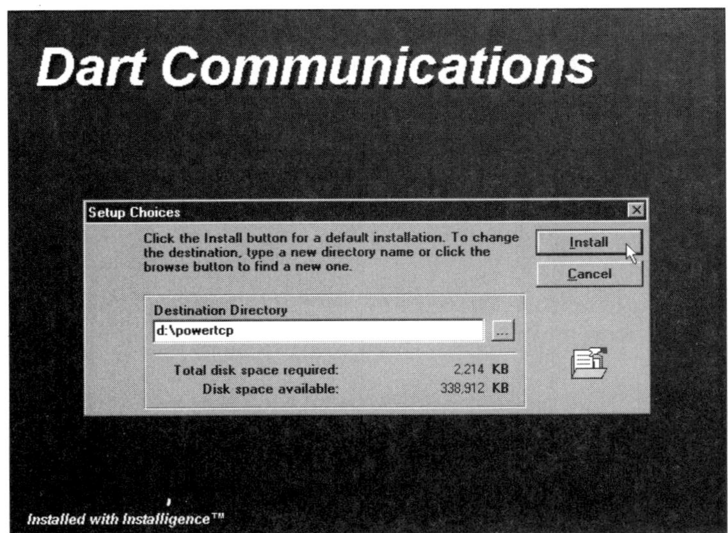

Figure A-10: Choose where you want to install PowerTCP.

3. **Click on Install.**

   Your screen changes, and something resembling Figure A-11 appears.

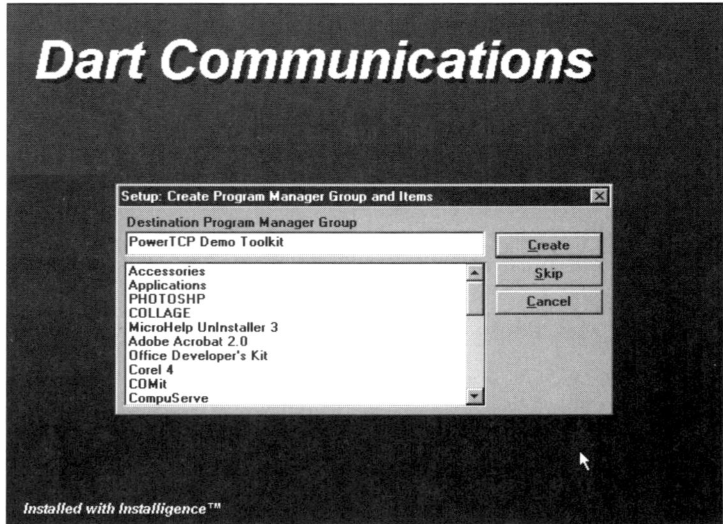

Figure A-11: Choose the name of the group that you want PowerTCP installed to.

4. **After you select the group that you want PowerTCP installed in, click on Create.**

   The software is installed to the selected hard drive. When the software installation is competed, a window appears, thanking you for selecting this software.

Dart Communications' PowerTCP software is now ready for your use.

IDS's VRealm

Integrated Data Systems and Portable Graphics are the distributors of VRealm, which we discuss in Chapter 7.

Installation is simple:

1. **Change to the \VREALM\ subdirectory on the *Creating Cool Interactive Web Sites CD-ROM.***

2. **Double-click on the SETUP.EXE program.**

   Soon something similar to Figure A-12 appears on the screen.

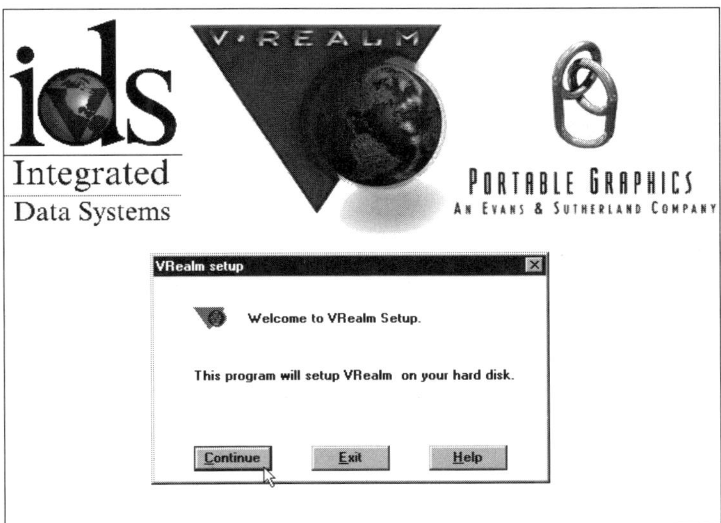

Figure A-12: *It's easy to install VRealm.*

3. **Click on Continue.**

   Your screen changes, and you have the option of choosing Windows 95 or Windows NT, as shown in Figure A-13.

4. **Choose the operating system that you use.**
5. **Click on Continue to see something resembling Figure A-14 on your screen.**
6. **Click on Continue.**

   The software is installed, and you see a screen telling you that the setup is complete.

7. **Click on OK.**

IDS's VRealm software is ready to use.

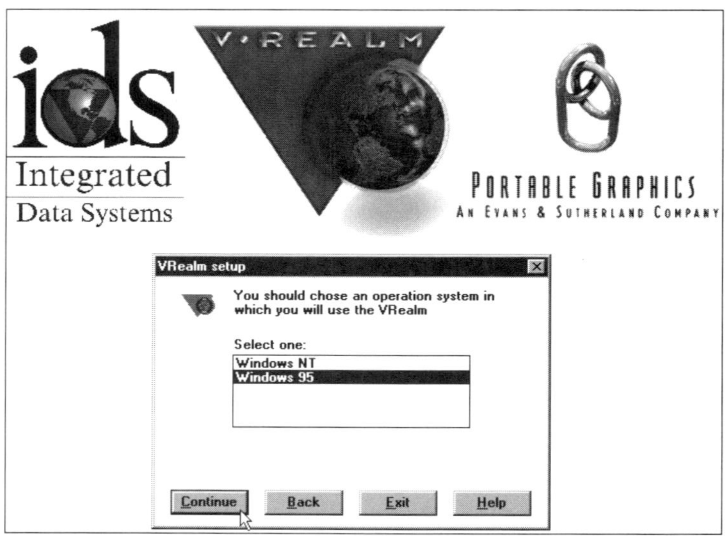

Figure A-13: Pick which operating system you are using.

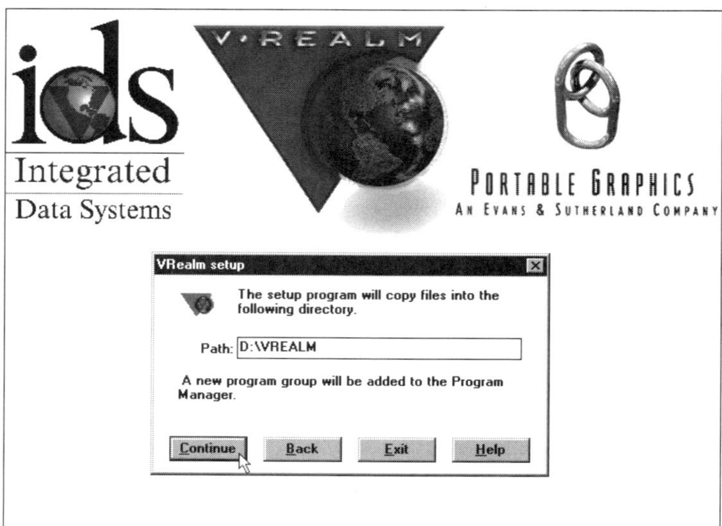

Figure A-14: Select the drive and directory where you want VRealm installed.

Intervista's WorldView

Intervista's WorldView software is discussed in Chapter 7. The installation of this software is easy:

1. **Change to the \WRLDVIEW\ subdirectory on the *Creating Cool Interactive Web Sites CD-ROM.***
2. **Double-click on the INSTALL.EXE program.**

   Soon you see something similar to Figure A-15.

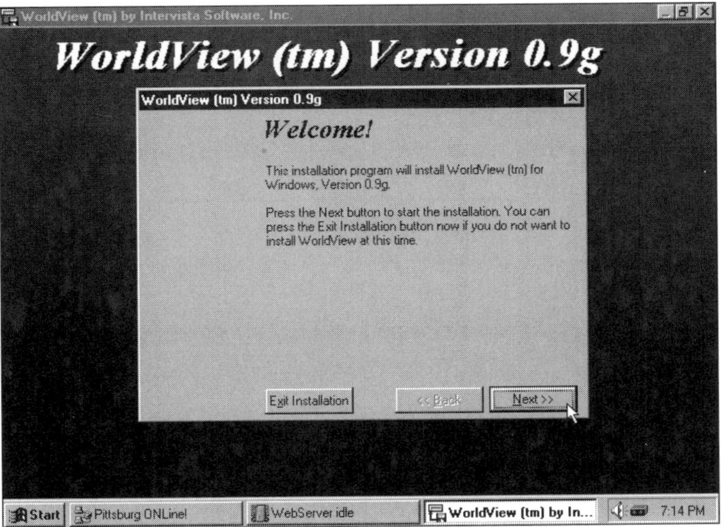

Figure A-15: WorldView's Welcome screen.

3. **Click on Next.**

   Your screen changes slightly, and you are given the opportunity to change the installation drive and directory, as in Figure A-16.
4. **Click on Next.**

   The program gives you the opportunity to determine whether any files that will be replaced in this installation should be backed up first.
5. **Make your selection and then click on Next.**
6. **Choose the directory that you want the backed up files to be placed in and click on Next again.**

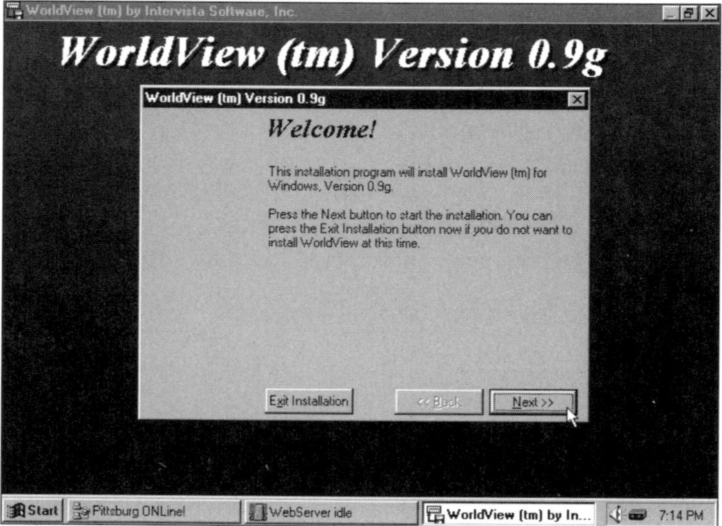

Figure A-16: Choose where you want to install WorldView.

The installation program gives you the opportunity of deciding whether you want WorldView in the Start menu.

7. **Make your choice and click on Next again.**

   Everything is ready to begin the installation.

8. **Click on Start Install.**

   WorldView is installed according to the options you've chosen in this process. During this process, the installation software also asks to install Reality Lab's software so that WorldView will run properly.

9. **Click on OK.**

   After Reality Lab has been installed properly, a dialog box appears.

10. **Click on OK.**

Intervista's WorldView is ready to use.

Microsoft Internet Assistant for Word

Microsoft's Internet Assistant for Word is discussed in Chapter 6. You need Microsoft Word in order to use this software. The installation process is easy:

1. **Change to the \MSIA95\ subdirectory on the *Creating Cool Interactive Web Sites CD-ROM.***

2. **Double-click on the WORDIA2B.EXE program.**

   The installation process begins at this point.

3. **Make sure that you answer all of the questions that the installation software asks.**

   Otherwise, just sit back and wait. When the installation process is complete, you are given the choice of launching Word or exiting.

Microsoft's Internet Assistant for Word is now installed on your hard drive.

Microsoft Internet Explorer 2.0

Microsoft Internet Explorer 2.0 is discussed in Chapter 6 and Chapter 7. Installing Internet Explorer is simple:

1. **Change to the \MSIE95\ subdirectory on the *Creating Cool Interactive Web Sites CD-ROM.***
2. **Double-click on the MSIE20.EXE program.**

   The installation process begins.

3. **Make sure that you answer all of the questions that the installation software asks.**

   Otherwise, just sit back and wait. When the installation is complete, a dialog box appears telling you so.

4. **Click on OK.**

Microsoft's Internet Explorer is now installed on your hard drive.

Microsoft VRML Add-In for Internet Explorer

Microsoft VRML Add-In for Internet Explorer is discussed in Chapter 7. Adding the VRML capabilities is easy. Follow these steps:

1. **Change to the \MSIEVRML\ subdirectory on the *Creating Cool Interactive Web Sites CD-ROM.***
2. **Double-click on the VRML20.EXE program.**

   The installation process begins at this point.

3. **Make sure that you answer all of the questions that the installation software asks; otherwise, just sit back and wait.**

When the installation process is complete, click on the OK button.

The VRML Add-In for Microsoft's Internet Explorer is now installed on your hard drive.

NETCOM NetCruiser

NETCOM's NetCruiser is another service connection package that we discuss in Chapter 1. Installing the NETCOM NetCruiser package is simple. Follow these instructions:

1. **Change to the \NETCOM\ subdirectory on the *Creating Cool Interactive Web Sites CD-ROM.***
2. **Double-click on the SETUP.EXE program.**
3. **In the Welcome dialog box, choose the drive and directory that you want to install the software in.**

   The default designation is C:\NETCOM.

   You are asked to tell the installation software your modem type, speed, and COM port in various dialog boxes during the installation.
4. **Answer all questions to complete the installation, and when the installation process is complete, click on OK.**
5. **Double-click on the NetCruiser registration icon.**

   You need to have a credit card handy to complete your registration and open your Internet account.

NETCOM NetCruiser is ready to use.

PSI's Pipeline USA

Pipeline USA is from Performance Systems International (PSI). PSI's Pipeline USA is another service connection package that we discuss in Chapter 1. Installation of the Pipeline USA package is simple. Follow these instructions.

1. **Change to the \PSINET\ subdirectory on the *Creating Cool Interactive Web Sites CD-ROM.***
2. **Double-click on the SETUP.EXE program.**
3. **You see an initial dialog box, shown in Figure A-17, where you need to choose the drive and directory in which you want to install the software.**

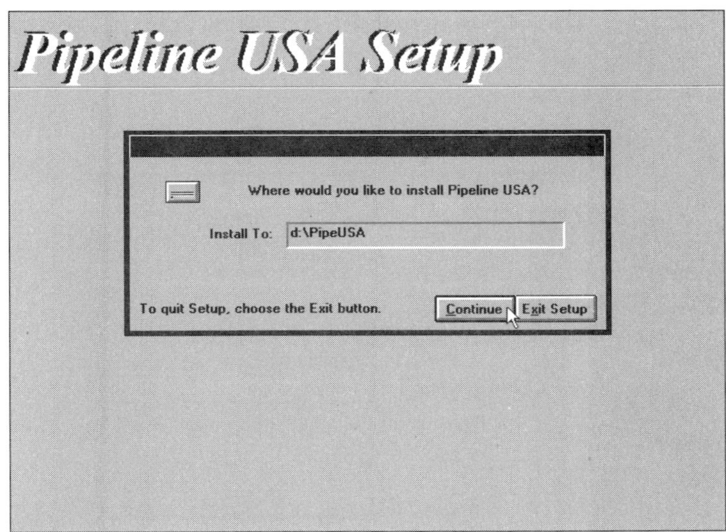

Figure A-17: Choose where you want to install Pipeline USA.

The default designation is C:\PIPELINE.

4. **Click on Continue to have the software begin installing.**
5. **When the installation is complete, a dialog box informs you.**
6. **Click on OK.**
7. **Double-click on the Pipeline icon.**

   You soon see a dialog box such as the one shown in Figure A-18.

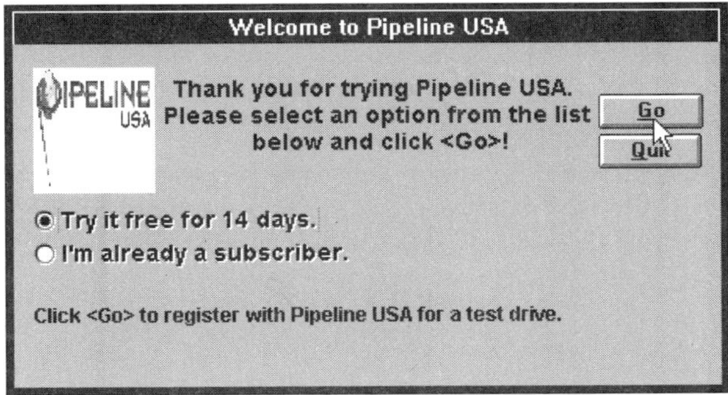

Figure A-18: Pipeline USA has a 14-day free trial.

8. **Click Go to establish your 14-day free trial account.**

   The Connect to Pipeline USA! screen, as shown in Figure A-19, appears.

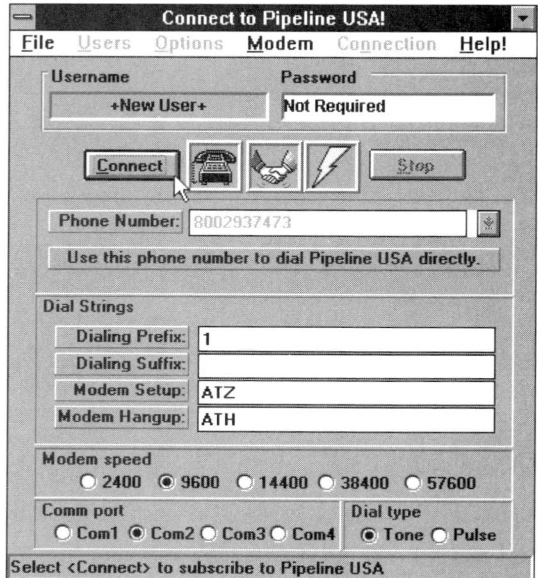

Figure A-19: *Be sure to set the Modem speed, Comm port, and Dial type in this window.*

   The defaults are 9600 baud, Comm port 2, and Dial type Tone.

9. **Make any necessary adaptations to these settings and click on Connect.**

   After you are connected, a menu appears that provides you with a list of access numbers.

Follow the onscreen directions, and your registration will soon be complete. Pipeline USA is now ready for you to use (see Figure A-20).

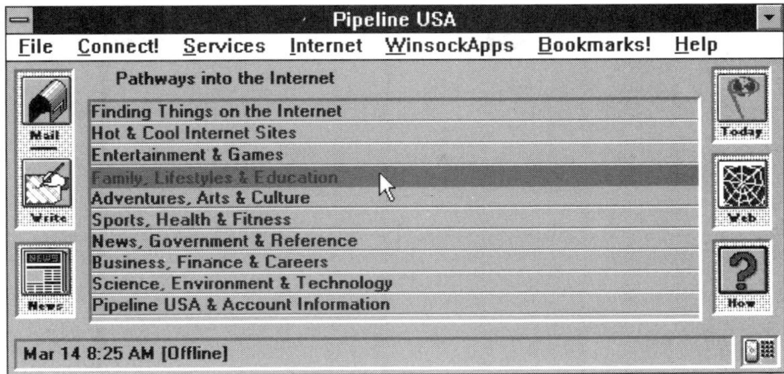

Figure A-20: Pipeline USA provides an integrated user interface for your use.

Quarterdeck's Mosaic and WebServer

Quarterdeck's Mosaic is discussed in Chapter 1. Quarterdeck's WebServer (also known as WebStar), is covered in Chapter 3 and Chapter 5.

The CD-ROM contains full working versions (rather trial versions) of this software, plus Clean Sweep uninstaller software and WebAuthor. They are encrypted, which means you need to register and pay Quarterdeck for the software before accessing it from the CD-ROM.

To access the Quarterdeck software, follow these instructions:

1. **Go to the \QDECK\ subdirectory on the *Creating Cool Interactive Web Sites CD-ROM.***
2. **Double-click on the SETUP.EXE file.**
3. **You will be led through screens on registering and paying for the software.**

If you wish to try trialware versions of Quarterdeck software, visit its Web site at `www.quarterdeck.com`. to see what is available for downloading. Because Web pages change frequently, you may wish to check the site on a regular basis. Quarterdeck's trialware runs for 30 days after you download it.

SoftQuad's HoTMetaL

SoftQuad's HoTMetaL is discussed in Chapter 6. Follow these easy directions:

1. **Change to the \HOTMETAL\ subdirectory on the *Creating Cool Interactive Web Sites CD-ROM.***
2. **Double-click on the SETUP.EXE program.**

   The installation process begins. Make sure that you answer all of the questions that the installation software asks. A dialog box informs you when the installation is complete.

HoTMetaL is now installed on your hard drive.

Virtus WalkThrough VRML

Virtus WalkThrough VRML is a VRML-authoring software package from Virtus Corporation. We discussed this authoring tool package in Chapter 7. Installing this VRML-authoring tool is simple. Follow these instructions.

1. **Change to the \VWTVRML\ subdirectory on the *Creating Cool Interactive Web Sites CD-ROM.***
2. **Double-click on the SETUP.EXE program.**

   You see an initial dialog box, as in Figure A-21.
3. **Click on Continue.**

   You see a dialog box that is similar to Figure A-22.
4. **Choose the type of installation you want.**

   The default is a full installation.
5. **Click on Continue.**

   You see a dialog box, which is shown in Figure A-23, where you can change the location where you want to install this software. The default location is C:\VWTVRML\.

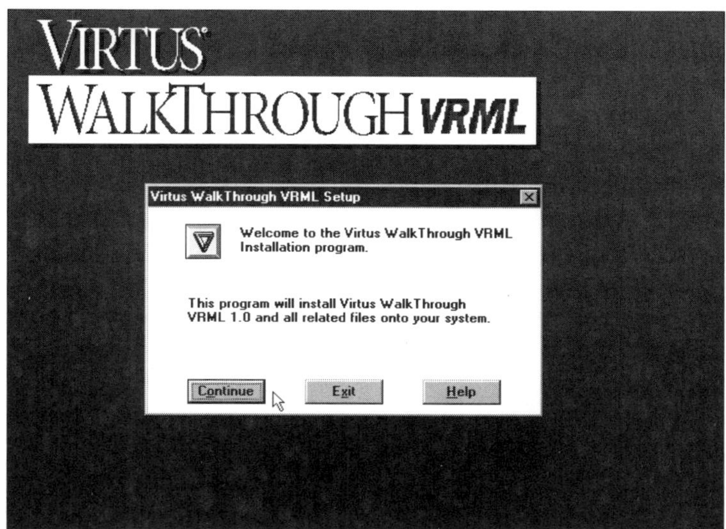

Figure A-21: Welcome to the Virtus WalkThrough VRML Installation program.

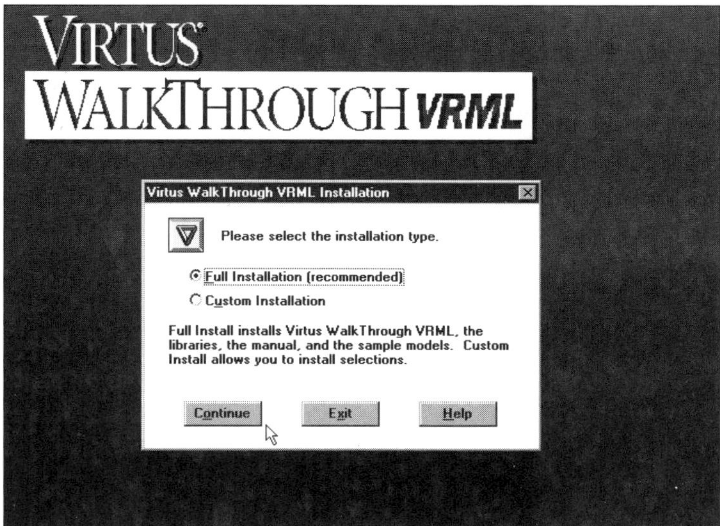

Figure A-22: Choose Full Installation or Custom Installation.

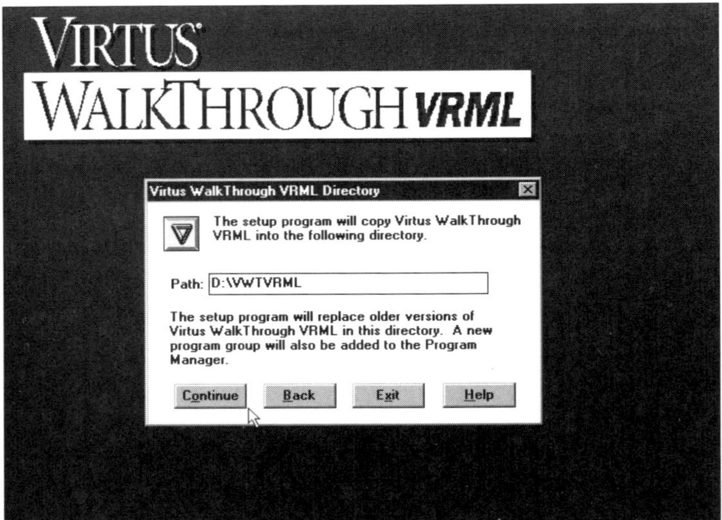

Figure A-23: You can change where Virtus WalkThrough VRML will be installed.

6. **Change the location where you want to install the software or accept the default and then click on Continue.**

   The software is installed to your hard drive.

7. **When the installation is complete, click on the OK button.**

Virtus WalkThrough VRML is now installed and ready for you to use.

WebMania!

WebMania! is an HTML authoring package. We discuss this package in Chapter 6. Installation of the WebMania! package is simple. Follow these instructions.

1. **Change to the \WEBMANIA\ subdirectory on the *Creating Cool Interactive Web Sites CD-ROM.***

2. **Double-click on the SETUP.EXE program.**

   You see an initial dialog box.

3. **Choose the location where you want the software to be installed and click on OK.**
4. **The software is installed to your hard drive.**

   When the installation is complete, click on OK.

WebMania! is now installed and ready for you to use.

Symbols & Numbers

(continued)

Q

Y

10/31/95

"A lot easier to use than the book Excel gives you!"

Lisa Schmeckpeper, New Berlin, WI, on PC World Excel 5 For Windows Handbook

Official Hayes Modem Communications Companion
by Caroline M. Halliday

ISBN: 1-56884-072-1
$29.95 USA/$39.95 Canada
Includes software.

1,001 Komputer Answers from Kim Komando
by Kim Komando

ISBN: 1-56884-460-3
$29.99 USA/$39.99 Canada
Includes software.

BESTSELLER!

PC World DOS 6 Handbook, 2nd Edition
by John Socha, Clint Hicks, & Devra Hall

ISBN: 1-878058-79-7
$34.95 USA/$44.95 Canada
Includes software.

PC World Word For Windows® 6 Handbook
by Brent Heslop & David Angell

ISBN: 1-56884-054-3
$34.95 USA/$44.95 Canada
Includes software.

BESTSELLER!

PC World Microsoft® Access 2 Bible, 2nd Edition
by Cary N. Prague & Michael R. Irwin

ISBN: 1-56884-086-1
$39.95 USA/$52.95 Canada
Includes software.

PC World Excel 5 For Windows® Handbook, 2nd Edition
by John Walkenbach & Dave Maguiness

ISBN: 1-56884-056-X
$34.95 USA/$44.95 Canada
Includes software.

PC World WordPerfect® 6 Handbook
by Greg Harvey

ISBN: 1-878058-80-0
$34.95 USA/$44.95 Canada
Includes software.

QuarkXPress For Windows® Designer Handbook
by Barbara Assadi & Galen Gruman

ISBN: 1-878058-45-2
$29.95 USA/$39.95 Canada

NATIONAL BESTSELLER!

Official XTree Companion, 3rd Edition
by Beth Slick

ISBN: 1-878058-57-6
$19.95 USA/$26.95 Canada

NATIONAL BESTSELLER!

PC World DOS 6 Command Reference and Problem Solver
by John Socha & Devra Hall

ISBN: 1-56884-055-1
$24.95 USA/$32.95 Canada

SUPER STAR

Client/Server Strategies™: A Survival Guide for Corporate Reengineers
by David Vaskevitch

ISBN: 1-56884-064-0
$29.95 USA/$39.95 Canada

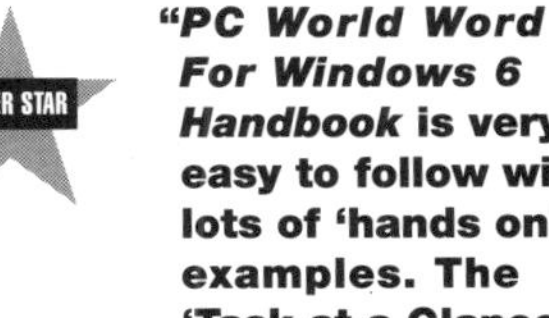

"*PC World Word For Windows 6 Handbook* is very easy to follow with lots of 'hands on' examples. The 'Task at a Glance' is very helpful!"

Jacqueline Martens, Tacoma, WA

"Thanks for publishing this book! It's the best money I've spent this year!"

Robert D. Templeton, Ft. Worth, TX, on MORE Windows 3.1 SECRETS

For scholastic requests & educational orders please call Educational Sales, at 1. 800. 434. 2086

FOR MORE INFO OR TO ORDER, PLEASE CALL ▶ 800. 762. 2974

For volume discounts & special orders please call Tony Real, Special Sales, at 415. 655. 3048

10/31/95

"*Macworld Complete Mac Handbook Plus CD* covered everything I could think of and more!"

Peter Tsakiris, New York, NY

"Very useful for PageMaker beginners and veterans alike—contains a wealth of tips and tricks to make you a faster, more powerful PageMaker user."

Paul Brainerd, President and founder, Aldus Corporation

"Thanks for the best computer book I've ever read—*Photoshop 2.5 Bible*. Best $30 I ever spent. I *love* the detailed index....Yours blows them all out of the water. This is a great book. We must enlighten the masses!"

Kevin Lisankie, Chicago, Illinois

"*Macworld Guide to ClarisWorks 2* is the easiest computer book to read that I have ever found!"

Steven Hanson, Lutz, FL

"...thanks to the *Macworld Excel 5 Companion*, 2nd Edition occupying a permanent position next to my computer, I'll be able to tap more of Excel's power."

Lauren Black, Lab Director, Macworld Magazine

Macworld® QuarkXPress 3.2/3.3 Bible
by Barbara Assadi & Galen Gruman

ISBN: 1-878058-85-1
$39.95 USA/$52.95 Canada

Includes disk with QuarkXPress XTensions and scripts.

Macworld® PageMaker 5 Bible
by Craig Danuloff

ISBN: 1-878058-84-3
$39.95 USA/$52.95 Canada

Includes 2 disks with PageMaker utilities, clip art, and more.

Macworld® FileMaker Pro 2.0/2.1 Bible
by Steven A. Schwartz

ISBN: 1-56884-201-5
$34.95 USA/$46.95 Canada

Includes disk with ready-to-run data bases.

Macworld® Word 6 Companion, 2nd Edition
by Jim Heid

ISBN: 1-56884-082-9
$24.95 USA/$34.95 Canada

Macworld® Guide To Microsoft® Word 5/5.1
by Jim Heid

ISBN: 1-878058-39-8
$22.95 USA/$29.95 Canada

Macworld® ClarisWorks 2.0/2.1 Companion, 2nd Edition
by Steven A. Schwartz

ISBN: 1-56884-180-9
$24.95 USA/$34.95 Canada

Macworld® Guide To Microsoft® Works 3
by Barrie Sosinsky

ISBN: 1-878058-42-8
$22.95 USA/$29.95 Canada

Macworld® Excel 5 Companion, 2nd Edition
by Chris Van Buren & David Maguiness

ISBN: 1-56884-081-0
$24.95 USA/$34.95 Canada

Macworld® Guide To Microsoft® Excel 4
by David Maguiness

ISBN: 1-878058-40-1
$22.95 USA/$29.95 Canada

ORDER FORM

3/26/96

Order Center: **(800) 762-2974** *(8 a.m.–6 p.m., EST, weekdays)*

Quantity	ISBN	Title	Price	Total

Shipping & Handling Charges

	Description	First book	Each additional book	Total
Domestic	Normal	$4.50	$1.50	$
	Two Day Air	$8.50	$2.50	$
	Overnight	$18.00	$3.00	$
International	Surface	$8.00	$8.00	$
	Airmail	$16.00	$16.00	$
	DHL Air	$17.00	$17.00	$

*For large quantities call for shipping & handling charges.
**Prices are subject to change without notice.

Ship to:

Name ______________________

Company ______________________

Address ______________________

City/State/Zip ______________________

Daytime Phone ______________________

Payment: ☐ Check to IDG Books Worldwide (US Funds Only)
☐ VISA ☐ MasterCard ☐ American Express

Card # ______________________ Expires ____________

Signature ______________________

Subtotal ____________

CA residents add applicable sales tax ____________

IN, MA, and MD residents add 5% sales tax ____________

IL residents add 6.25% sales tax ____________

RI residents add 7% sales tax ____________

TX residents add 8.25% sales tax ____________

Shipping ____________

Total ____________

Please send this order form to:

IDG Books Worldwide, Inc.
Attn: Order Entry Dept.
7260 Shadeland Station, Suite 100
Indianapolis, IN 46256

Allow up to 3 weeks for delivery.
Thank you!

IDG BOOKS WORLDWIDE, INC. END-USER LICENSE AGREEMENT

Read This. You should carefully read these terms and conditions before opening the software packet(s) included with this book ("Book"). This is a license agreement ("Agreement") between you and IDG Books Worldwide, Inc. ("IDGB"). By opening the accompanying software packet(s), you acknowledge that you have read and accept the following terms and conditions. If you do not agree and do not want to be bound by such terms and conditions, promptly return the Book and the unopened software packet(s) to the place you obtained them for a full refund.

1. License Grant. IDGB grants to you (either an individual or entity) a nonexclusive license to use one copy of the enclosed software program(s) (collectively, the "Software") solely for your own personal or business purposes on a single computer (whether a standard computer or a workstation component of a multiuser network). The Software is in use on a computer when it is loaded into temporary memory (i.e., RAM) or installed into permanent memory (e.g., hard disk, CD-ROM, or other storage device). IDGB reserves all rights not expressly granted herein.

2. Ownership. IDGB is the owner of all right, title, and interest, including copyright, in and to the compilation of the Software recorded on the disk(s)/CD-ROM. Copyright to the individual programs on the disk(s)/CD-ROM is owned by the author or other authorized copyright owner of each program. Ownership of the Software and all proprietary rights relating thereto remain with IDGB and its licensors.

3. Restrictions on Use and Transfer.

   (a) You may only (i) make one copy of the Software for backup or archival purposes, or (ii) transfer the Software to a single hard disk, provided that you keep the original for backup or archival purposes. You may not (i) rent or lease the Software, (ii) copy or reproduce the Software through a LAN or other network system or through any computer subscriber system or bulletin-board system, or (iii) modify, adapt, or create derivative works based on the Software.

   (b) You may not reverse engineer, decompile, or disassemble the Software. You may transfer the Software and user documentation on a permanent basis, provided that the transferee agrees to accept the terms and conditions of this Agreement and you retain no copies. If the Software is an update or has been updated, any transfer must include the most recent update and all prior versions.

4. **<u>Restrictions on Use of Individual Programs</u>.** You must follow the individual requirements and restrictions detailed for each individual program in the appendix of this Book. These limitations are contained in the individual license agreements recorded on the disk(s)/CD-ROM. These restrictions may include a requirement that after using the program for the period of time specified in its text, the user must pay a registration fee or discontinue use. By opening the Software packet(s), you will be agreeing to abide by the licenses and restrictions for these individual programs. None of the material on this disk(s) or listed in this Book may ever be distributed, in original or modified form, for commercial purposes.

5. **<u>Limited Warranty</u>.**

   (a) IDGB warrants that the Software and disk(s)/CD-ROM are free from defects in materials and workmanship under normal use for a period of sixty (60) days from the date of purchase of this Book. If IDGB receives notification within the warranty period of defects in materials or workmanship, IDGB will replace the defective disk(s)/CD-ROM.

   (b) **IDGB AND THE AUTHORS OF THE BOOK DISCLAIM ALL OTHER WARRANTIES, EXPRESS OR IMPLIED, INCLUDING WITHOUT LIMITATION IMPLIED WARRANTIES OF MERCHANTABILITY AND FITNESS FOR A PARTICULAR PURPOSE, WITH RESPECT TO THE SOFTWARE, THE PROGRAMS, THE SOURCE CODE CONTAINED THEREIN, AND/OR THE TECHNIQUES DESCRIBED IN THIS BOOK. IDGB DOES NOT WARRANT THAT THE FUNCTIONS CONTAINED IN THE SOFTWARE WILL MEET YOUR REQUIREMENTS OR THAT THE OPERATION OF THE SOFTWARE WILL BE ERROR FREE.**

   (c) This limited warranty gives you specific legal rights, and you may have other rights which vary from jurisdiction to jurisdiction.

6. **<u>Remedies</u>.**

   (a) IDGB's entire liability and your exclusive remedy for defects in materials and workmanship shall be limited to replacement of the Software, which may be returned to IDGB with a copy of your receipt at the following address: Disk Fulfillment Department, Attn: Creating Cool Interactive Web Sites, IDG Books Worldwide, Inc., 7260 Shadeland Station, Ste. 100, Indianapolis, IN 46256, or call 1-800-762-2974. Please allow 3-4 weeks for delivery. This Limited Warranty is void if failure of the Software has resulted from accident, abuse, or misapplication. Any replacement Software will be warranted for the remainder of the original warranty period or thirty (30) days, whichever is longer.

(b) In no event shall IDGB or the author be liable for any damages whatsoever (including without limitation damages for loss of business profits, business interruption, loss of business information, or any other pecuniary loss) arising from the use of or inability to use the Book or the Software, even if IDGB has been advised of the possibility of such damages.

(c) Because some jurisdictions do not allow the exclusion or limitation of liability for consequential or incidental damages, the above limitation or exclusion may not apply to you.

7. **U.S. Government Restricted Rights.** Use, duplication, or disclosure of the Software by the U.S. Government is subject to restrictions stated in paragraph (c) (1) (ii) of the Rights in Technical Data and Computer Software clause of DFARS 252.227-7013, and in subparagraphs (a) through (d) of the Commercial Computer—Restricted Rights clause at FAR 52.227-19, and in similar clauses in the NASA FAR supplement, when applicable.

8. **General.** This Agreement constitutes the entire understanding of the parties and revokes and supersedes all prior agreements, oral or written, between them and may not be modified or amended except in a writing signed by both parties hereto which specifically refers to this Agreement. This Agreement shall take precedence over any other documents that may be in conflict herewith. If any one or more provisions contained in this Agreement are held by any court or tribunal to be invalid, illegal, or otherwise unenforceable, each and every other provision shall remain in full force and effect.

CD-ROM Installation Instructions

Insert the accompanying CD-ROM into your CD-ROM drive. From the Explorer, open the desired program folder and double-click on INSTALL.EXE or SETUP.EXE. If you do not see INSTALL.EXE or SETUP.EXE for the program you want to install, refer to the appendix for further instructions.

See the appendix for more details on the useful programs included on the *Creating Cool Interactive Web Sites CD-ROM.*